## Payment Type

MasterCard      XXXXXXXXXXXX2738

15-Aug-2018

| | |
|---|---|
| **Total Payments** | **$84.75** |
| Order Total | $84.75 |
| Outstanding | $0.00 |

D1252046

## 3 Backordered and Pending

| Item | Description | Price | QTY | Total |
|---|---|---|---|---|
| 1 | EVIDENCE-FED RULES...2017-2018 SUPPL., | $16.00 | 1 | $16.00 |
| | | | Sub-total | **$16.00** |
| | | | + Shipping | $0.00 |
| | | | + Tax | $0.96 |
| | | Total | 1 Item(s) | **$16.96** |

# Customer Copy

Box No **3918-1-F18-SHP**

Order No   87435620-1
Placed On  17-Jul-2018
Invoice    15-Aug-2018

87435620-1

## Sold To

**Joy Matthews**
6085 Majors Ln Apt 10
Columbia, MD - 21045, US
Phone:   (240)380-7928
E-Mail:  joyalexandra@umaryland.

## Ship To

**Joy Dodge**
8713 Hummingbird Court
Laurel, MD - 20723, US
Phone: (240)380-7928
Tracking   1Z274695039772 1482

**Standard Shipping $7.50**

## Ship from

**University of Maryland Baltimore Bookstore**

621 West Lombard St.
Baltimore City, MD - 21201, US
E-Mail:sm639@bncollege.com
Website
http://umb.bncollege.com
Phone:   **(410)706-7788**

## 1 Your Order

| Item | Description | Price | QTY | Discount | Total |
|------|-------------|-------|-----|----------|-------|
| 1 | MODEL WITNESS EXAMINATIONS, New | $79.95 | 1 | $0.00 | $79.95 |

|  |  |
|---|---|
| Sub-total | $79.95 |
| + Shipping | $0.00 |
| + Tax | $4.80 |
| **Total Amount** 1 Item(s) | **$84.75** |

## 2 Processed Payments

| Account No | Date | Amount |
|------------|------|--------|

# MODEL WITNESS EXAMINATIONS

## Fourth Edition

.

# MODEL WITNESS EXAMINATIONS

## Fourth Edition

Paul Mark Sandler
James K. Archibald

Cover design by Tamara Kowalski/ABA Design

Printed in the United States of America.

20 19 18 17 16  5 4 3 2 1

**Library of Congress Cataloging-in-Publication Data**
Names: Sandler, Paul Mark, author. | Archibald, James K. (James Kenway), 1949- author.
Title: Model witness examinations / Paul Mark Sandler and James K. Archibald.
Description: Fourth edition. | Chicago : American Bar Association, 2016.
Identifiers: LCCN 2016001421 (print) | LCCN 2016001833 (ebook) | ISBN 9781634253468 (alk. paper) | ISBN 9781634253475 ()
Subjects: LCSH: Examination of witnesses--United States.
Classification: LCC KF8950 .S236 2016 (print) | LCC KF8950 (ebook) | DDC
347.73/75--dc23
LC record available at http://lccn.loc.gov/2016001421

# Contents

## Part 2: Cross-Examination and Redirect . . . . . . . . . . . . . . . . . 269

Chapter 10

## Cross-Examination . . . . . . . . . . . . . . . . . . . . . . . . . . . . . . . . . . . . 271

Chapter 11

## Redirect . . . . . . . . . . . . . . . . . . . . . . . . . . . . . . . . . . . . . . . . . . . . . . 307

# Foreword

Some trial lawyers look for every advantage over their competitors. These lawyers keep close to the vest their techniques for handling witnesses and offering and objecting to evidence. They do not share the jewels that they have garnered over many years of experience.

Other trial lawyers love the concept of trials, admire their comrades in the trenches, understand that their own skills and talents benefited from the guidance they received from their predecessors at the bar, and want to give something back to the profession in which they take pride. Paul Mark Sandler and James K. Archibald of Baltimore, Maryland, are two of the best examples of such trial veterans. They are confident, experienced, talented lawyers who take time from busy trial schedules and demanding practices to offer young lawyers the wisdom they have learned from years of trying cases.

*Model Witness Examinations* is a gift to young lawyers and to older lawyers who are called in mid- or late career to try cases. The book demonstrates how to offer testimony on direct examination, how to cross-examine and impeach various types of witnesses, and how to use discovery in the examination of witnesses. Sandler and Archibald not only illustrate model examinations, they also offer citations to rules and cases that can be relied upon by an advocate preparing an examination on an important point.

The illustrations are authentic. Sandler and Archibald know what issues arise at real trials, and their experience enables them to offer examples that are genuinely useful. They also know the danger in lawyers trying to use the exact same words and phrases over and over and advise their readers that the model examinations are starting, not ending, points. They are not a substitute for strategic thinking and are not meant to be the last word on effective advocacy.

In short, *Model Witness Examinations* is a wonderful gift from two lawyers who love the trial process to all those who will follow them.

Stephen A. Saltzburg
Washington, D.C.

# Introduction to the Fourth Edition

It is still true. What we wrote in the introduction to the first edition in 1997 was that one of the hardest tasks of a trial lawyer is to ask the right question. Asking it well can sometimes be an even greater challenge. Whether focusing on direct examination or cross-examination, there are many ways to accomplish the goal of eliciting facts. We continue to hope that the material in this Fourth Edition of our book will enable the advocate to grasp the fundamental requirements in selected types of examinations of witnesses, and thereby freeing the advocate to focus on the refinement of courtroom style and strategic approaches to posing the questions.

The examinations consist of both model examinations—a series of questions utilized to solicit facts and opinions from the witnesses in situations that recur sometimes specifically and other times generally, and must be reasonably adhered to in order for counsel to obtain the needed evidence. Each model examination is preceded by contextual outline, followed by a comment annotated to the cases, statutes, the Federal Rules of Evidence, and valuable secondary sources.

This Fourth Edition includes new model questions and commentary on direct examination, its purpose, form and structure; the introduction of social media evidence, and numerous models for cross-examination. Commentary is updated as are case citations and secondary sources.

We issue a word of caution as we have in prior Editions: The model examinations cannot be simply lifted from the page and applied during the course of a trial. The models are only suggested organizational structures, which contain the basic questions designed to elicit an answer necessary to obtain a desired result. The trial and lawsuit is more art than science. Differing approaches can be used to the same end. The model examinations in this work are the threads from which the trial lawyer can weave his or her own cloth.

Although comments following the model examinations include tactics, and practice points on the conduct of examination, as well as a presentation of evidentiary discussions, we do not attempt to teach trial tactics. For example, consider the cross-examination of a witness utilizing a transcript to impeach. One approach consists of soliciting facts from the witness to contradict the deposition. Then counsel reminds the witness that she or he was deposed; elicits that the witness was deposed in the lawyer's office; that the witness took an oath; that the witness's recollection of events was fresher in her mind at the time of the deposition than at trial; and finally, a reminder that when counsel took the deposition the witness testified one way in the deposition and another way at trial.

Another approach to impeachment using a transcript is to only remind the witness that she just testified that the accident occurred at 10:00 p.m., but in the deposition at a certain page and line the witness swore that the accident occurred at 6:00 p.m. For consideration of trial tactics, *see Anatomy of A Trial – A Handbook for Young Lawyers, Second Edition* (Paul Mark Sandler, Esq. with contributions from members of the Bench, ABA Publishing 2014.)

We express our gratitude to Cynthia Hines, paralegal in the law firm of Shapiro Sher Guinot and Sandler for her assistance, and Michael Berman, Esquire, for his valuable assistance relating to the chapters on authentication of social media evidence.

Paul Mark Sandler, Esquire
James K. Archibald, Esquire
January 2016

# About the Authors

**Paul Mark Sandler** is a partner in the law firm of Shapiro Sher Guinot & Sandler, P.A., and is an active trial lawyer representing many notable clients in a wide variety of cases in state and federal courts. He is the author of *Anatomy of a Trial: A Handbook for Young Lawyers, Second Edition;* and *Raising the Bar: Practice Tips and Trial Technique for Young Lawyers.* He is co-author of *The 12 Secrets of Persuasive Argument, Discovery Problems and Their Solutions, Maryland Discovery Problems and Solutions, Pleading Causes of Action in Maryland, Pattern Examinations of Witnesses for the Maryland Lawyer,* and co-editor of *Appellate Practice for the Maryland Lawyer: State and Federal.* Mr. Sandler is a frequent lecturer on trial and appellate practice, and contributor to legal publications on the topics of trial practice and persuasion. He is founder and former chair of the Litigation Section of the Maryland State Bar Association, and past secretary of the Litigation Section of the American Bar Association. Mr. Sandler is also a Fellow of the American College of Trial Lawyers, and Chairs the Committee on Teaching Trial and Appellate Advocacy for 2015-2016. He received his undergraduate degree from Hobart College, his law degree from Georgetown University Law Center, and was admitted to the Maryland Bar in 1972.

**James K. Archibald** is Of-Counsel to the Baltimore law firm of Wright Constable & Skeen. He has maintained a varied litigation practice for many years. Mr. Archibald is a former president of the Maryland Association of Defense Trial Counsel and has been active in the Litigation Section of the ABA, the Defense Research Institute, and the International Association of Defense Counsel. He is a fellow of the American College of Trial Lawyers. He is also the co-author of *Pleading Causes of Action in Maryland.* He has written numerous articles on litigation issues and has lectured widely on litigation topics and techniques. He received his law degree from the University of Maryland in 1975, after completing his undergraduate education at Johns Hopkins University.

# Part 1

# Direct Examination

# Direct Examination | 1

## A. PURPOSE, FORM, AND STRUCTURE

The government in a 1930s criminal case calls a witness, Matthew Esworthy, to identify an individual whom the government contends fled the scene of a crime in an automobile with one of the defendants as a passenger.

### Prosecutor:

Q. Please introduce yourself to the Jury.

A. My name is Matthew Esworthy, and I live in Baltimore, Maryland.

Q. How old are you, sir?

A. 38 years old.

Q. Why are you here today?

A. I was subpoenaed to be here.

Q. Do you have a family?

A. Yes. I am married and have four children—two girls and twin boys.

Q. What are their names and ages?

A. Linda is 8; Susan is 7; and the twins Jack and Jimmy are 5.

Q. What is your wife's name?

A. Margaret.

Q. How would you describe your health today?

A. Excellent.

Q. Was it excellent on April 15, 1930, the date of the murder in Baltimore?

A. Yes.

Q. How is your eye sight today?

A. Excellent.

Q. How was your eye sight last April 15, 1930?

A. Excellent.

Q. Do you need to wear glasses today?

A. No.

Q. Did you need to wear glasses last year?

A. No.

Q. How is your ability to see distances today?

A. Excellent.

Q. What about last year? How was your ability to see distances?

A. Excellent.

Q. How is your hearing today?

A. Excellent.

Q. How was it last year?

A. Excellent.

Q. Do you work for a living?

A. Yes.

Q. What do you do?

A. I am a railroad crossing guard for B&O Railroad.

Q. On April 15, 1930, what, if any, work were you doing?

A. I was working as a railroad crossing guard for B&O Railroad.

Q. Where were you posted last year?

A. Shawan Crossing in Hunt Valley, Maryland.

Q. What were your duties in that job?

A. To stop cars from crossing the tracks when trains were approaching.

Q. How would you do this?

A. I was given a schedule of when trains were to arrive at Shawan crossing; just prior to the scheduled arrival, or if the train were late, just as the train was approaching, I go to Shawan Road from my shanty and with a stop sign bring approaching cars to a halt.

Q. Let me show you the Commonwealth's exhibit and ask, do you recognize this?

A. Yes.

Q. What is it?

A. It is the stop sign I use, but without the handle.

**Prosecutor:** Now let's talk about what you saw that day, April 15, 1930.

Q. Where were you on that afternoon around 4 p.m.?

A. At my job at the crossing.

Q. What day of the week was April 15, 1930?

A. It was a Thursday.

Q. How do you recall that day?

A. It was the day of the murder in Baltimore, and the day I encountered Herman Bissel in a speeding car.

Q. How did you encounter Mr. Bissel on April 15, 1930?

A. Around 4:15 in the afternoon I was sitting by the window in my shanty which is at the crossing on Shawan Road; the 4:10 p.m. train coming from the south was late; and as I was looking at the clock at 4:15, I heard the train approaching.

Q. What did you do when you heard the train approaching?

A. I walked quickly outside to see if there were any cars coming.

Q. Did you see any cars approaching?

A. I sure did. I saw a car approaching.

Q. From what direction?

A. It was coming east from Falls Road and very fast.

Q. Why do you say it was coming very fast?

A. I could see the car, and also the dust it kicked up.

Q. As you saw the car approaching very fast, did you take any action?

A. Yes; I stood on the east side of the track, the same side as my shanty, and held up my sign.

Q. Could you see the speeding car approaching?

A. Yes.

Q. Did the driver appear to heed your sign?

A. No.

Q. What did you do?

A. I walked across the track to the west side, and stretched out my arm holding the sign in the air.

Q. Can you show us?

(Witness takes the sign and raises it.)

Q. Did the car appear to be slowing down and stopping?

A. No.

Q. Did you have any concerns?

A. Yes.

Q. What were those concerns?

A. Well it looked as if the car was not going to stop, but it did not have time to get across the tracks ahead of the train.

Q. What did you do?

A. I started jumping with the sign in my right hand, and waving my left hand.

Q. Please demonstrate.

(Witness does so from the witness stand.)

Q. Did the car slow down?

A. Yes, and it stopped about 3 feet ahead of me.

Q. What occurred after the car stopped 3 feet ahead of you?

A. A man stuck his head out of the passenger seat window and shouted at me.

Q. What did he say?

A. He shouted: "What the hell are you holding me up for?"

Q. Did you observe this person?

A. Yes.

Q. Could you get a good look at him from 3 feet away?

A. Yes.

Q. Did he say or do anything else at that time when the car was about 3 feet away?

A. Yes.

Q. What?

A. He pointed his finger at me.

Q. Obviously someone was driving the car?

A. Yes

Q. Could you see the driver at the time?

A. No.

Q. Then how could you see the person who spoke to you?

A. He put his head out the window and pointed at me.

Q. And at the time the man spoke to you when the car was 3 feet away, where were you standing?

A. On the west side of the tracks.

Q. Did you have any trouble hearing the man at 3 feet away?

A. Absolutely not.

Q. Did you have any trouble seeing the man at 3 feet away?

A. No Sir, I did not.

Q. After the man yelled at you, and shook his finger at you, what did you do?

A. I stepped back on the side of the tracks where my shanty was located.

Q. Did you say anything to the man?

A. No.

Q. Why not?

A. I was startled—my tongue was tied—the situation was very odd; a speeding car and this man yelling at me while all I was trying to do was my job telling them to stop 'cause a train was coming.

Q. Did the fact that you were startled impair in any way your ability to see this man?

A. No, absolutely not.

Q. Could you see inside the car?

A. Yes.

Q. Tell us whether you saw any passengers?

A. I saw one passenger in the back seat.

Q. Did you get a good look at the passenger?

A. No, not really.

Q. Did you get a good look at the man who shouted and waved his finger at you?

A. Absolutely.

Q. Mr. Esworthy, let me show you a photograph which has been previously marked as Exhibit 119. Can you identify this photograph?

A. This is a photograph of Mr. Herman Bissel.

Q. Is this the man who shouted and pointed his finger at you on April 15, 1930?

A. I am positive it is.

Q. Let me move on to a different topic . . .

### Comment

The purpose of direct examination is to argue or prove your case through questions to and answers from the witness. Arguably, direct examination is the most important part of the trial. In most cases direct examination is the stage of the trial when the judge or jury has the best opportunity to assess the proof or defense of the claims. During direct examination, unlike on cross-examination, the witness does most of the speaking, not the lawyer. Certainly direct examination is the most difficult part of the trial, because the required form of the questions, non-leading, deprives counsel of control.

Asking non-leading questions sometimes poses challenges in controlling the testimony and the witness. When you ask leading questions as permitted on cross-examination, you control the testimony by almost testifying for the witness: "It snowed last night?" "You came home after dinner?" But when you must ask non-leading questions ("Can you tell us what the weather was last night?") you could get more explanation than you anticipated ("Well, I can't recall, but I do remember that the roads were slick, and cars were skidding."). Many lawyers have been surprised by a witness's response to an open-ended question on direct examination. Frequently even the most careful preparation of a witness is no safeguard against the witness's desultory response to your questions.

The reason leading questions are prohibited on direct examination, with limited exceptions, is that the judge or jury must hear evidence from the witness and not from counsel. (*See* Chapter 10, *infra,* on Cross-Examination). The distinction between leading and non-leading questions is that the leading question suggests the answer. The non-leading question does not. "It snowed yesterday?" is a leading question. Some non-leading alternatives include: "Did it snow last night?" or "Tell us whether or not it snowed last night?" Some examples of permissible use of leading questions include confronting a hostile witness, reviewing uncontroversial matters, questioning children or senior citizens, or introducing new topics in your examination with a topical oral sentence.

As you ask questions during direct, beware of the distinction between prohibited leading questions, and leading questions that may be tolerated. These include questions that are used to save time, and do not relate to important facts or refer to facts that are generally in evidence. "You saw the man who shouted at you from a distance of three feet?" is leading. It may be more efficient than "What was the distance between you and the man you saw at the RR crossing?" If the record is saturated with testimony that the witness was three feet from the man who shouted and waived his finger, the shorter, leading question might well be acceptable to opposing counsel and the court. In the hypothetical examination above, the following questions and answers reflect the use of a leading question on direct:

Q. Did he say or do anything else at that time when the car was about 3 feet away?

A. Yes.

Q. What?

A. He pointed his finger at me.

Q. Obviously someone was driving the car? (no objection; if there were it could be overruled with perhaps a statement from the judge. "Let's move on with the next question, and please avoid leading questions.")

A. Yes.

Generally, however, leading questions should be avoided on direct, and saved for cross-examination. Sometimes in the heat of trial you may have trouble asking a non-leading question after an objection is sustained. This predicament is not unusual. Don't panic. Try rephrasing the question using the word "whether." For example, "You then went to the bar after the reception?" could be rephrased as "Can you tell us whether you went to the bar after the reception?"

The best form of question on direct is non-leading, short, and clear. Avoid compound questions. Questions such as "Did you see Mr. Brown enter the bar and assault the plaintiff?" should be avoided. They are confusing. If the answer is yes, to which part of the question does the answer refer? Most judges will sustain an objection to compound questions. Consider FRE 611, which gives the judge discretion to control the mode and order of examining witnesses.

While the best form of questions in examining witnesses are short and clear, sometimes using the answer in a prior question as part of the next question can be effective. The repetition helps make salient points memorable. The techniques of repeating the answer to a previous question in the next question are known as looping and incorporation. These techniques help make the examination memorable. For example consider the questions in the above hypothetical examination as illustrating the technique of looping:

Q. Why do you say it (the car) was *approaching very fast*?
A. I could see the car, and also the dust it kicked up.
Q. As you saw the car *approaching very fast, kicking up dust*, did you take any action?

Incorporation is similar to looping. The previous answer is incorporated in to the next question without making it obvious. For example:

Q. Did you have any trouble hearing *the man at 3 feet away*?
A. Absolutely not.
Q. Did you have any trouble seeing *the man at 3 feet away*?
A. No Sir, I did not.

A direct examination should have a beginning, middle, and an end. Honoring the concept of primacy and recency, begin strong and end strong. Most of us remember best what we hear first and last. Repetition helps, and using looping and incorporation aid the memory.

Consider structuring the examination as follows:

1. The introduction, where you establish the credibility of the witness and try to predispose the judge, jury, or arbitrator to believe her or him. In the above hypothetical, humanizing Mr. Esworthy as a family man, and bringing out that he was subpoened, may have given the impression that the witness was not biased.

2. The context of the witness's testimony. Here you demonstrate that the witness is qualified to present credible testimony on the subjects on which the witness is called to testify. In the above

hypothetical, the witness testifies that he had good health, including excellent sight and hearing at the time of the incident. Thus, counsel sets the stage for his subsequent testimony of identification.

3. The main substance of the testimony. Here you advance the facts you wish to assert. In our hypothetical the witness in detail describes the incident.

4. Immunization is where you pose questions that opposing counsel might ask on cross-examination. Doing so can enhance the credibility of the witness, and can take the wind out of the sails of opposing counsel. For example, asking Mr. Esworthy the question about whether he could see the man shouting at him although Esworthy was startled, prepares the jury for potential challenges to Esworthy's ability to properly identify the individual:

Q. Did you say anything to the man?

A. No.

Q. Why not?

A. I was startled—my tongue was tied—the situation was very odd; a speeding car and this man yelling at me while all I was trying to do was my job telling them to stop 'cause a train was coming.

Q. Did the fact that you were startled impair in any way your ability to see this man?

A. No, absolutely not.

5. The conclusion, where you drive home your most important points:

Q. Mr. Esworthy, let me show you a photograph which has been previously marked as Exhibit 119. Can you identify this photograph?

A. This is a photograph of Mr. Herman Bissel.

Q. Is this the man who shouted and pointed his finger at you on April 15, 1930?

A. I am positive it is.

Finally, to effectively conduct direct examination and also cross-examination consideration of how to authenticate documents and visuals is essential. *See, infra*, Chapter 3.

For more suggestions on Direct Examination, *see Anatomy of a Trial, a Handbook for Young Lawyers,* Second Edition, Paul Mark Sandler, ABA Litigation Section (2014).

# *Recollection* 2

## A. PRESENT RECOLLECTION REVIVED

During the course of a criminal trial, a police officer is on the witness stand. The officer has no present recollection of the description of the alleged assailant, which was related to him by an eyewitness. Another police officer, however, now deceased, recorded the eyewitness's description in a police offense report. Defense counsel desires to use that offense report to refresh the recollection of the witness on the stand. The defense rests on the discrepancy between the eyewitness's description of the height of the assailant and the height of the defendant, which is 5 feet 4 inches.

### Defense Counsel:

Q. Officer, what time did you arrive at the scene on the day of the incident?

A. Around 10:30 a.m., five minutes after the robbery.

Q. What did you do upon arriving at the scene?

A. I conducted a routine investigation.

Q. What did your investigation consist of?

A. Interviewing witnesses, inspecting the crime scene to see if there was any evidence left by the robber, and calling for the crime lab.

Q. Did any of the witnesses furnish you a description of the assailant?

A. Yes, one witness did.

Q. Tell us, please, what description did that witness give of the robber?

A. I don't remember.

Q. Is there anything that could refresh your recollection as to the description given?

A. Officer Smith, who is now deceased, accompanied me to the scene and recorded the statements of all witnesses. His report might help me remember.

Q. Did Officer Smith also record in his offense report the description of the one witness you referred to?

A. I believe he did, yes.

Q. Let me show you what has been marked for identification purposes as Exhibit 26. Do you recognize it?

A. This is Officer Smith's report.

Q. Please read the report to yourself, officer. (Officer reads the report.)

Q. Is your recollection refreshed?

A. Yes, it is.

Q. Now, sir, tell us what description was given of the robber by the one witness who offered a description.

A. John Peabody described the robber as a tall, thin man approximately 6 feet in height with a mustache and long curly hair.

## *Comment*

Although not absolute prerequisites in every jurisdiction, the key circumstances enabling a witness to refer to his or her notes for purposes of refreshing recollection are (1) that the witness cannot recall particular facts, and (2) that a particular document or memory aid, prepared by either the witness or someone else, might help the witness recall the particular facts. *See Rush v. Illinois Central Railroad Company*, 399 F.3d 705, 716 (6th Cir. 2005) ("Proper foundation requires that the witness's recollection . . . be exhausted, and that the time, place and person to whom the statement was given be identified. When the court is satisfied that the memorandum on its face reflects the witness's statement or one the witness acknowledges, and in [its] discretion the court is further satisfied that it may be of help in refreshing the person's memory, the witness should be allowed to refer to the document.") (quoting *Goings v. United States*, 377 F.3d 753, 760 (8th Cir. 1967), *cert. denied*, 393 U.S. 883 (1968)); *See United States v. Morlang*, 531 F.2d 183, 191 (4th Cir. 1975); *Wilcox v. State*, 143 So.3d 359, 378 (Fla. 2014) (when a writing is used only to revive present recollection of a fact, it is not required that the writing be written by the witness).

In *United States v. Mkhsian*, 5 F.3d 1306, 1313 (9th Cir. 1993), *rev'd on other grounds, United States v. Keys*, 133 F.3d 1282 (9th Cir. 1998), however, the Ninth Circuit Court of Appeals held that "it is not essential that the prosecutor first establish that the witness has exhausted his present recollection before [the prosecutor] can refresh his memory." The court further observed that "[t]he trial court has 'wide limits of discretion' in its decisions to permit the prosecution to refresh the memory of a witness." *Id.* at 1312 (citation omitted). *But see United States v. Balthazard*, 360 F.3d 309, 318 (1st Cir. 2004) (holding that a document could not be introduced to refresh the witness's testimony when the witness refused to acknowledge that his memory was impaired). Examples of when the foundational requirement of showing exhausted memory is relaxed include efforts to expedite or better organize the thoughts of a witness, and efforts to refresh the recollection of a witness who does not realize that he or she has forgotten important details. *See Doty v. Elias*, 733 F.2d 720, 725 (10th Cir. 1984); *United States v. Thompson*, 708 F.2d 1294, 1300–01 (8th Cir. 1983).

If a review of the document or memory aid refreshes the witness's memory, the witness may testify to the matters that he or she has recalled. *See United States v. Humphrey*, 279 F.3d 372 (6th Cir. 2002); *United States v. Frederick*, 78 F.3d 1370, 1376–77 (9th Cir. 1996). The witness may be permitted to consult the memory aid while he or she is testifying, if permitted to do so by the court. But a witness may not "testify at trial from prepared notes under the guise of refreshing recollection." *Hall v. American Bakeries Co.*, 873 F.2d 1133, 1136 (8th Cir. 1989); *see United States v. Rydland*, 461 Fed. Appx. 208 (4th Cir. 2012) (per curiam) (unpublished) (no abuse of discretion in not permitting defendant to use her notes while testifying on direct); *United States v. Rinke*, 778 F.2d 581, 587–88 (10th Cir. 1985); *United States v. Scott*, 701 F.2d 1340, 1446 (11th Cir. 1983).

The witness in this case is not required to state that he prepared the report, knew of the report at the time it was prepared, or even that the report was or is correct. However, from a tactical point of view, the more detailed facts the witness can offer to demonstrate the trustworthiness of the document or memory aid he utilizes to refresh his recollection, the greater the impact will be upon the trier of fact.

It is the testimony of the witness that is admitted into evidence. The memory aid used to refresh recollection is merely the stimulus for triggering recollection and is not evidence itself. Moreover, a document may be used to refresh a witness's recollection and elicit testimony, notwithstanding the fact that the document is itself inadmissible. *United States v. Scott*, 701 F.2d 1340, 1346 (11th Cir.), *cert. denied*, 464 U.S. 856 (1983).

In addition, the memory aid need not be a document or a writing. It may be anything that triggers the memory, *e.g.,* "[t]he creaking of a hinge, the whistling of a tune, the smell of seaweed . . . ." *Fanelli v. United States Gypsum Co.*, 141 F.2d 216, 217 (2d Cir. 1944); *see United States v. Rappy*, 157 F.2d 964, 967–68 (2d Cir.), *cert. denied*, 329 U.S. 806 (1946) ("anything may in fact revive a memory: a song, a scent, a photograph, an allusion, even a past statement known to be false"); *United States v. Shinderman*, 515 F.3d 5, 18 (1st Cir. 2008) (the writing used to refresh a recollection need not be independently admissible evidence).

Opposing counsel may examine the memory aid, show it to the jury and attempt by questioning the witness to show that the memory aid did not refresh recollection or that refreshed recollection is unreliable. "When a witness declares that [something] has evoked a memory, the opposite party may show either that it has not evoked what appears to the witness as a memory or that, although it may so appear to him, the memory is a phantom and not a reliable record of its content." *United States v. Riccardi*, 174 F.2d 883, 888 (3d Cir.), *cert. denied*, 337 U.S. 941 (1949). *Accord, 20th Century Wear, Inc. v. Sanmark-Stardust Inc.*, 747 F.2d 81, 93 (2d Cir. 1984), *cert. denied*, 470 U.S. 1052 (1985); *United States v. Wright*, 489 F.2d 1181, 1188–89 (D.C. Cir. 1973); *United States v. DiMauro*, 614 F. Supp. 461, 466 (D. Me. 1985); *Kater v. Maloney*, 459 F.3d 56, 67 (1st Cir.), *cert. denied*, 549 U.S. 1344 (2007) (allowing the testimony of a witness whose memory had been refreshed prior to trial by hypnosis because the facts the witness testified to had been documented prior to the hypnosis). Opposing counsel may use the memory aid to impeach the witness. Since the memory aid is not evidence, use of the memory aid or cross-examination relating to the memory aid is for the purpose of testing whether the witness's memory has been refreshed. *See also* 1 McCormick on Evidence § 9 at 50 (Kenneth S. Broun ed., 7th ed. 2013).

Under FRE 612, if a witness uses a writing to refresh memory, the adverse party is entitled to examine the writing, cross-examine the witness on it, and to introduce it for impeachment purposes. *See Borel v. Fibreboard Paper Prods. Corp.*, 493 F.2d 1076 (5th Cir. 1973); *Las Vegas Sands v. Eighth Jud. Dist. Ct.*, 130 Nev. Adv. Op. 13, 319 P.3d 618 (2014).

Whether the police officer in this pattern can testify to a hearsay declaration by an absent witness might present a problem. *See, e.g., United States v. Smith*, 521 F.2d 957 (D.C. Cir. 1975); 2 McCormick on Evidence § 296 (Kenneth S. Broun ed., 7th ed. 2013). However, assume that an appropriate hearsay exception such as "excited utterance," or res gestae in state court proceedings, would be recognized, or that the out-of-court description of the witness is not offered to prove the truth of the matter asserted but for the purpose of impeaching the previous trial testimony of the eyewitness. *See infra* p. 17 for discussion of hearsay contained within past recollection recorded and *infra* Chapter 3.B., 3.I., and 3.J. for discussions of hearsay contained within business records, police accident reports, and public records, respectively.

For a discussion concerning the difference between present recollection revived and past recollection recorded, *see United States v. Riccardi*, 174 F.2d 883, 886 (3d Cir.), *cert. denied*, 337 U.S. 941 (1949). *Accord*, *United States v. Rinke*, 778 F.2d 581, 588 (10th Cir. 1985). *See also* 1 McCORMICK ON EVIDENCE § 9 (Kenneth S. Broun ed., 7th ed. 2013).

## B. PAST RECOLLECTION RECORDED

During a criminal trial, a police officer is on the witness stand. She has some recollection of the description of the assailant given to her by an eyewitness to a murder. She does not, however, recall the details of the eyewitness's description. Defense counsel wants to introduce the police officer's personal notes, which contain the statement given by the eyewitness, to demonstrate that his client was not the assailant, since the assailant was 6 feet tall and the defendant's height is 5 feet 4 inches.

### Defense Counsel:

Q. What time did you arrive at the scene on the day of the incident?

A. Around 10:30 a.m., five minutes after the robbery.

Q. What did you do upon arriving at the scene?

A. I conducted a routine investigation.

Q. What did your investigation consist of?

A. Interviewing witnesses, inspecting the crime scene to see if there was any physical evidence left by the robber, and calling for the crime lab.

Q. Did any of the witnesses furnish descriptions of the assailants?

A. Yes.

Q. How many witnesses furnished descriptions?

A. I cannot remember. I believe one.

Q. Tell us what description that witness gave of the robber.

A. I can't remember the details of the description, although I remember generally that the witness described the robber as being rather tall.

Q. Did you take any notes while you interviewed the witnesses to the incident?

A. Yes.

Q. Did you record in those notes the one eyewitness description of the assailant to which you previously referred?

A. Yes.

Q. Do you have your notes with you?

A. Yes.

Q. May I see them?

A. Yes.

Q. If the court please, I would ask that the police officer's notes be marked as the next exhibit for identification.[1] In whose handwriting are these notes?

A. Mine.

Q. When were the notes prepared?

A. About five minutes after the incident occurred.

Q. Where were the notes prepared?

A. At Hansen's Grocery, the scene of the incident.

Q. Were the facts recorded in your report when they were fresh in your mind?

A. Yes.

Q. Did these notes accurately reflect the facts as you obtained them and recorded them?

A. Yes.

Q. Are you satisfied now that the notes are accurate?

A. Yes.

Q. Do you have sufficient recollection about the matters contained in your notes to testify fully and accurately concerning those matters?

A. No.

Q. Would your notes refresh your recollection?

A. Not fully, no.

**Defense Counsel:** We offer the notes in evidence.

**U.S. Attorney:** Objection. The witness indicated that he had some recollection of the description he obtained from the witness. Since the witness has some recollection of what occurred with regard to his interviews, the notes are inadmissible in evidence under the doctrine of past recollection recorded. The witness's memory is not exhausted.

---

1. The practice from marking and introducing exhibits varies from court to court. Consult the local rules.

**The Court:** Rule 803(5) provides that it is not necessary that the witness lack all recollection of the event. The Federal Rules provide that the witness need only testify that he has insufficient recollection to enable him to testify fully and accurately. However, I shall sustain your objection in part on the grounds that Rule 803(5) of the Federal Rules of Evidence does not allow defense counsel to introduce this writing in evidence unless the government requests that it be introduced. The federal rule, however, does permit the witness to read the document in evidence. Therefore, I shall allow the officer to read portions of her report in evidence. (Officer reads eyewitness description reflecting that assailant was described as 6 feet in height.)

### Comment

The foundation necessary in federal court to introduce a document or other record considered to be a prior hearsay statement pursuant to the doctrine of past recollection recorded requires the following testimony: (1) that the writing was made by, or adopted by, the witness at a time when the witness had a clear recollection of the event; (2) that the document was accurate at the time of the writing or at the time the witness adopted the writing; (3) that the witness presently vouches for the accuracy of the writing; and (4) that the witness lacks sufficient recollection to testify fully and accurately about the events contained in the document. *See* Fed. R. Evid. 803(5); *United States v. Orm Hieng*, 679 F.3d 1131 (9th Cir. 2012); (proper foundation was laid); *Equal Employment Opportunity Commission v. Staffmark Investment, LLC*, 67 F. Supp.3d 885, 30 A.D. Cases 1016 (E.D. Ill. 2014); *United States v. Rommy*, 506 F.3d 108, 138 (2d Cir. 2007); *United States v. Cash*, 394 F.3d 560, 564 (7th Cir. 2005); *United States v. Porter*, 986 F.2d 1014, 1016–17 (6th Cir.) (citation omitted), *cert. denied*, 510 U.S. 933 (1993); *United States v. Ray*, 768 F.2d 991, 994–95 (8th Cir.) (citation omitted), *appeal decided by* 777 F.2d 423 (8th Cir. 1985), *overruling recognized by United States v. Anderson*, 570 F.3d 1025 (8th Cir. 2009); *United States v. Patterson*, 678 F.2d 774, 778 (9th Cir.), *cert. denied*, 459 U.S. 911 (1982). *See also Alicea v. Ralston*, 279 Fed. Appx. 179, 181–82 (3d Cir. 2008); *In re Messenger*, 32 F. Supp. 490 (E.D. Pa. 1940); *United States v. Giovanelli*, 747 F. Supp. 915 (S.D.N.Y. 1989); 7 MICHAEL H. GRAHAM, HANDBOOK OF FEDERAL EVIDENCE § 803(5) (7th ed. 2012); *United States v. Porter*, 986 F.2d 1014, 1017 (6th Cir. 1993) (holding that "Rule 803(5) does not specify any particular method of establishing the knowledge of the declarant nor the accuracy of the statement"); *Parker v. Reda*, 327 F.3d 211 (2d Cir. 2003) (same).

The most important consideration involving the doctrine of past recollection recorded is the requisite degree of impaired memory to establish a proper foundation to have the document admitted in evidence. Federal Rule of Evidence 803(5) requires that the witness demonstrate insufficient recollection to enable him to testify fully and accurately. This standard offers a compromise approach between two schools of thought: (1) the traditional approach, which requires that total failure of memory be established before invoking the doctrine; and (2) the minority approach, which recognizes the doctrine of past recollection recorded on the basis of the trustworthiness of the writing rather than the state of mind of the witness at the time of his testimony.

The federal rule's compromise is that a somewhat faded memory will suffice. *See generally* 2 McCORMICK ON EVIDENCE § 282 at 421-423 (Kenneth S. Broun ed., 7th ed. 2013); Fed. R. Evid. 803(5) advisory committee's note and practice comment for cases construing the rule. Nonetheless, where a witness "retained some independent memory of what was said," and does not testify he or she is unable to recall any particular aspect of the past events, courts "have held that it is error for the district court to admit evidence under Rule 803(5) without a showing that the witness lacks sufficient memory to testify fully." *United States v. Dazey*, 403 F.3d 1147, 1166–67 (10th Cir. 2005).

The advisory committee on the proposed rules deemed the compromise approach desirable, because a total absence of the requirement of memory impairment "would encourage the use of statements carefully prepared for purposes of litigation under the supervision of attorneys, investigators, or claim adjusters." *See United States v. Judon*, 567 F.2d 1289, 1294 (5th Cir.) (quotation omitted), *appeal after remand*, 581 F.2d 553 (5th Cir. 1978).

The proponent of the past recollection recorded cannot introduce the document in evidence without a proper basis, but the witness is permitted to read from the document. *United States v. Shinderman*, 515 F.3d 5, 18 (1st Cir. 2008). On the other hand, the adverse party may offer the document as an exhibit. Even if the adverse party does not offer the document into evidence, the document should be marked for identification and made part of the record. *See Judon, supra*, 567 F.2d at 1294.

The witness testifying under the doctrine of past recollection recorded must have personal knowledge of the underlying events. Where the testifying witness cannot recall reviewing the statement when it was recorded and cannot attest to its accuracy while testifying, the statement is not admissible. *United States v. Mornan*, 413 F.3d 372, 377 (3d Cir. 2005). But where the statement was recorded by someone other than the declarant, "accuracy may be established through the testimony of the person who recorded the statement." *Id.* at 378.

If the writing contains information which itself is hearsay, that hearsay can only be admitted over objection pursuant to a hearsay exception. *See, e.g.*, *United States v. Smith*, 521 F.2d 957 (D.C. Cir. 1975); 2 McCORMICK ON EVIDENCE § 296 (Kenneth S. Broun ed., 7th ed. 2013). For example, in the present pattern, "excited utterance" might qualify as an exception, depending on the factual circumstances. If no exception to the hearsay rule is applicable, the witness who offered the description of the assailant to the police officer must testify. The police report would then be admissible through the officer as the past recollection of the observer, not of the police officer. *See Swart v. United States*, 394 F.2d 5, 6 (9th Cir. 1968).

Moreover, the examination of the police officer to elicit testimony concerning the witness's description of the assailant can be construed as non-hearsay if the examination is designed for impeachment purposes rather than for the truth of the matter asserted. *See supra* Chapter 2.A. for discussion of hearsay problem with present recollection revived and *infra* Chapters 3.B., 3.I., and 3.J. for discussion of hearsay contained within business records, police accident reports, and public records.

Finally, the trial judge has discretion to determine whether the witness actually satisfies the requirements of the rule. For example, if a witness was intoxicated when he recorded a statement, he may not have accurately understood the facts at the time of the recording. *See United States v. Edwards*, 539 F.2d 689, 692 (9th Cir.), *cert. denied*, 429 U.S. 984 (1976); *United States v. Riccardi*, 174 F.2d 883 (3d Cir.), *cert. denied*, 337 U.S. 941 (1949). *But see United States v. Porter*, 986 F.2d 1014, 1017 (6th Cir.), *cert. denied*, 510 U.S. 933 (1993), where the witness stated that because of drug use she could not be sure that her past statement was truthful, and the court permitted the doctrine to be invoked based on the trustworthiness of the document.

## C. IDENTIFICATIONS, JUDICIAL AND EXTRAJUDICIAL

Joan Tisdale is the victim of rape. As a witness for the prosecution, she is asked to identify the defendant as her assailant.

**Prosecutor:**

Q. Ms. Tisdale, what opportunity, if any, did you have to observe your assailant?

A. During the entire rape his face was only inches away from mine.

Q. Did you have an opportunity to closely observe his face?

A. Yes.

Q. How long a period of time did you observe his face?

A. For at least five minutes.

Q. What were the lighting conditions at the time of the incident?

A. Although there were no lights in the car, it was stopped about 15 feet from a street light, and the car light went on when he opened the car and pushed me out.

Q. Did you observe anything unusual about your assailant's appearance?

A. He was missing both front teeth and had a two-inch scar over his left eye.

Q. Would you please indicate the location of the scar? (Witness indicates.) Let the record reflect that Ms. Tisdale indicated a scar at approximately a 45-degree angle starting approximately one-half inch above the left eyebrow on the forehead.

Q. Can you identify the person who raped you?

A. Yes.

Q. Is he in this courtroom today?

A. Yes.

Q. Would you point to him, please?

A. (Witness points to the defendant.)

Q. How is the defendant dressed today?

A. He is wearing brown pants and a gray sweatshirt.

Q. Do you observe any marks on his face?

A. Yes, I see a scar over his left eye.

**Prosecutor:** Let the record reflect that the witness has identified the defendant.

Q. Ms. Tisdale, after the incident, did you have occasion to identify your assailant?

A. Yes.

Q. When?

A. Two days later. Officer Johnson brought me twelve photographs to examine.

Q. Ms. Tisdale, I show you State's Exhibit 31, (A) through (L), and ask if you can identify the exhibit for us.

A. Yes, this is the group of photographs that Officer Johnson brought to me. (These photographs were previously introduced through Officer Johnson, the officer conducting the photo identification. The officer also identified Exhibit 31(B) as a photograph of the defendant and the photograph identified by the witness.)

Q. What instructions, if any, did you receive from the police officer who showed you the photographs?

A. I was told to look at the photographs and to state whether I could identify the individual who raped me.

Q. Were you able to identify the individual?

A. Yes.

Q. Who did you identify from the photographs?

A. The same man I just identified in this court.

Q. Would you please identify that picture for us.

A. (Witness points to the photograph she had identified before Officer Johnson.)

**Prosecutor:** Let the record reflect that Ms. Tisdale has identified Exhibit 31(B) as the photograph she had identified as that of her assailant when Officer Johnson brought the twelve photographs to her to examine.

Q. Ms. Tisdale, have you had any other occasions to see the defendant?

A. Yes.

Q. Can you tell us when and under what circumstances?

A. Yes.

Q. Please do so.

A. I came to the police station about two weeks after the rape and was asked to look at five men.

Q. Where were these men?

A. They were standing in a lineup in a room, through which I could see, and I understand that they could not see me.

Q. Did you have any trouble in observing the individuals in the lineup?

A. No.

Q. How far away from the individuals in the lineup were you?

A. Less than 12 feet.

Q. How much time did you spend at this lineup?

A. I spent about 5 minutes, but I identified my assailant within 1 minute of looking at the individuals in the lineup.

Q. Describe what the men in the lineup were doing while you were looking at them.

A. They were standing in a line facing forward.

Q. What instructions, if any, did you receive from the police who conducted the lineup?

A. I was told to look at the people and to state whether I could identify the individual who raped me.

Q. Were you able to identify the individual who raped you?

A. Yes.

Q. Ms. Tisdale, I show you Exhibit 34 for identification and ask if you can identify it.

A. Yes, this is a photograph of the group of men I viewed at the police station and from which I identified my assailant. (This photograph of the lineup was previously introduced through the police officer conducting the lineup.)

Q. Can you identify in Exhibit 34 the individual whom you identified at the lineup?

A. Yes.

Q. Would you please take this pencil and mark with a check mark above the individual you identified?

A. Yes.

Q. Do you see the person in this courtroom whom you identified at the lineup?

A. Yes.

Q. Would you point to him, please?

A. (Witness points to the defendant.)

### Comment

The identification of a defendant in the courtroom is referred to as a judicial or in-court identification. An identification made prior to trial, either by photograph or lineup, is known as an extrajudicial or out-of-court identification. Principles governing the admissibility of photographic identifications and lineup identifications are the same. *See United States v. DeCologero*, 530 F.3d 36, 62 (1st Cir. 2008) ("When considering whether a pretrial identification procedure raises a very substantial likelihood of irreparable misidentification, a court first determines whether the identification procedure was impermissibly suggestive, and if it was, the court then looks to the totality of the circumstances to decide whether the identification was still reliable." (citations omitted)); *Perry v. New Hampshire*, 132 S. Ct. 716 (2012) (out-of-court identification will be excluded only if the circumstances under it was made, which were arranged by law enforcement, so suggest its unreliability that its admission would be unfair and a violation of due process); *see also Clark v. Hoffner*, 2014 WL 806393 (E.D. Mich. 2014) (Due Process Clause does not require a preliminary inquiry into the reliability of an eye witness identification when the identification was not procured under unnecessarily suggestive circumstances arranged by law enforcement, citing *Perry v. New Hampshire*, 132 S.Ct. 716, 730 (81 L. Ed.2d 694 (2012)); *United States v. Marchand*, 564 F.2d 983 (2d Cir. 1977), *cert. denied*, 434 U.S. 1015 (1978) (photographic identification); *United States v. Fabio*, 394 F.2d 132 (4th Cir. 1968) (pre-indictment lineup). The federal rule generally considers the testimony of identification as non-hearsay. *See* Fed. R. Evid. 801(d)(1)(C).

There are three elements composing the proper foundation for a judicial or in-court identification: (1) the witness must be present at trial and testify about the event in question; (2) the witness must have the ability to reconstruct the occurrence and identify the defendant from the witness's observation of him at the time of the event; and (3) the defendant must be present in the courtroom to enable the witness to observe him and compare his appearance to that of the perpetrator. *United States v. Crews*, 445 U.S. 463, 471 (1980); *United States v. Thompson*, 524 F.3d 1126, 1135 (10th Cir. 2008) (when the initial identification is in court, "there are different considerations, the jury can observe the witness during the identification process and is able to evaluate the reliability of the initial identification") (quoting *United States v. Robertson*, 19 F.3d 1318 (10th Cir. 1994); *United States v. Foppe*, 993 F.2d 1444, 1450 (9th Cir.), *cert. denied*, 510 U.S. 1017 (1993).

There is "no requirement, either in the Constitution or in the usual rules that apply to the admission of evidence, that a witness who makes an extrajudicial identification must repeat the identification in the courtroom." *Foxworth v. St. Amand*, 570 F.3d 414, 427 (1st Cir. 2009). Nevertheless, evidence of an extrajudicial or out-of-court identification is admissible to corroborate a judicial or in-court identification. A proper foundation requires (1) a showing of circumstances precluding unfairness, (2) testimony demonstrating the reliability of the identification, and (3) an in-court identification serving as a predicate for the corroboration. *See Manson v. Brathwaite*, 432 U.S. 98 (1977); *Neil v. Biggers*, 409 U.S. 188 (1972);

*United States v. Hilario-Hilario*, 529 F.3d 65 (1st. Cir. 2008); *Amador v. Quarterman*, 458 F.3d 397, 413 (5th Cir.), *cert. denied*, 550 U.S. 920 (2007); *Kennaugh v. Miller*, 289 F.3d 36 (2d Cir.), *cert. denied*, 537 U.S. 909 (2002); *United States v. Donaldson*, 978 F.2d 381 (7th Cir. 1992). *But see United States v. Saunders*, 501 F.3d 384, 391–92 (4th Cir. 2007), *cert. denied*, 128 S.Ct. 1107 (2008) (There are five factors to consider when deciding if an out-of-court identification is admissible: "(1) the witness's opportunity to view the suspect at the time of the crime; (2) the witness's degree of attention at the time; (3) the accuracy of the witness's initial description of the suspect; (4) the witness's level of certainty in making the identification; and (5) the length of time between the crime and the identification.") (quoting *United States v. Johnson*, 114 F.3d 435, 441 (4th Cir. 1997)).

In the federal courts, evidence of an extrajudicial identification may be offered as independent substantive evidence of identity, even if the witness is unable to make an in-court identification. The rationale for this rule rests upon the notion that the earlier identification has greater probative value than the subsequent in-court identification with the pressures and suggestions surrounding the trial. *See Gilbert v. California*, 388 U.S. 263, 272 n.3 (1967); *Samuels v. Mann*, 13 F.3d 522, 527 (2d Cir. 1993), *cert. denied*, 513 U.S. 849 (1994); *Jamison v. Grier*, No. 01 CIV 6678, 2002 U.S. Dist. LEXIS 1160, at *38 (S.D.N.Y. Jan. 25, 2002)[2].

However, the federal rules specifically require the presence of the declarant and that he or she be subject to cross-examination as a prerequisite to admissibility of extrajudicial identifications.

A witness's in-court identification may be upheld even if it was based on an unduly suggestive extrajudicial identification. In *Haliym v. Mitchell*, 492 F.3d 680 (6th Cir. 2007), the court upheld an in-court identification by a young child, even though it was based on a prior photo-array identification that was clearly excessively suggestive. *Id.* at 704, 707. The court concluded: "Since the procedure by which [the witness] identified Petitioner was unnecessarily suggestive, we must ask 'whether, under all the circumstances, that suggestive procedure gave rise to a substantial likelihood of irreparable misidentification.'" *Id.* at 704 (quoting *Manson v. Brathwaite*,

---

2. Throughout this book, we have included citations to unpublished decisions. Some jurisdictions allow unpublished decisions to be cited in court papers; other jurisdictions do not. *See* Fed. R. Evid. 801(d)(1)(C).

432 U.S. 98, 107 (1977)). In *Manson*, the Supreme Court identified five factors to consider when determining whether an unnecessarily suggestive lineup or display was nevertheless reliable: "(1) the witness' opportunity to view the suspect; (2) the witness' degree of attention; (3) the accuracy of the witness' prior description of the criminal; (4) the level of certainty demonstrated by the witness at the time of the identification; and (5) the time between the crime and the identification." *Manson*, 432 U.S. at 114. The *Haliym* court considered the above five factors, as well as other factors particular to the case: "Although these factors were not identified in *Manson* (and indeed were not present on *Manson*'s facts), we conclude that they are nevertheless relevant to whether a 'suggestive procedure gave rise to a substantial likelihood of irreparable misidentification.'" *Haliym*, 492 F.3d at 705.

The federal rules do not limit testimony establishing the statement of identification solely to the identifying witness. The rationale for the rule remains fully applicable when the person who testifies to the statement of identification is not the person who uttered it, as long as the latter also testifies and is available for cross-examination. *See United States v. Lopez*, 271 F.3d 472, 485 (3d Cir. 2001), *cert. denied*, 535 U.S. 908 (2002); *United States v. O'Malley*, 796 F.2d 891, 899 (7th Cir. 1986); *United States v. Elemy*, 656 F.2d 507, 508–09 (9th Cir. 1981); *United States v. Irby*, 517 F.2d 506 (4th Cir. 1975), *cert. denied sub nom. Smith v. United States*, 424 U.S. 973 (1976).

This pattern illustrates an in-court identification and an extrajudicial identification that corroborates the in-court identification. Notice the way the witness linked the photograph identification to "the same man I just identified in this court." This out-of-court identification can also be used as substantive evidence. If, for example, the witness is unable to identify the defendant at trial, and the prior extrajudicial identifications are the only evidence linking the defendant to the commission of the crime, those identifications would be treated as substantive evidence in the case.

Constitutional considerations play a significant role in the admissibility of extrajudicial identifications in criminal cases. These considerations are discussed in such cases as *Perry v. New Hampshire*, 132 S. Ct. 716 (2012); *Manson v. Brathwaite*, 432 U.S. 98 (1977), *Kirby v. Illinois*, 406 U.S. 682 (1972), and *Webster v. State*, 474 A.2d 1305 (Md. 1984). *See also United States v. Moody*, 206 F.3d 609 (6th Cir.), *cert. denied*, 531 U.S. 925 (2000); *Hanks v. Jackson*, 123 F. Supp. 2d 1061 (E.D. Mich. 2000);

*United States v. Douglas*, 525 F.3d 225, 242 (2d Cir. 2008) (Defendant's due process rights include the right not to be the "object of suggestive police identification procedures that make identification unreliable."); *United States v. Saunders*, 501 F.3d 384, 381–90 (4th Cir.), *cert. denied*, 128 S. Ct. 1107 (2008) ("Due process principles prohibit the admission at trial of an out-of-court identification obtained through procedures 'so impermissibly suggestive as to give rise to a very substantial likelihood of irreparable misidentification.' The Due Process Clause is not implicated, however, if the 'identification was sufficiently reliable to preclude the substantial likelihood of misidentification.'") (quoting *Simmons, supra*, 390 U.S. 377, 384 (1968), and *United States v. Johnson*, 114 F.3d 435, 442 (4th Cir. 1997)). *See also, United States v. Rogers*, 126 F.3d 655, 657 (5th Cir. 1997). Under federal law, a defendant wishing to challenge the legality of an identification in a criminal case must exercise his rights by filing a motion to suppress. *See* Fed. R. Crim. P. 12.2.

# Documents and Electronically Stored Information

# 3

## A. PRIVATE WRITINGS

Plaintiff Boady, claiming to be the owner of 3245 Walnut Hill Road, institutes suit against Defendant Butterball claiming damages for failure to pay rent. Defendant claims that the property is not owned by Plaintiff, but by Plaintiff's mother. Plaintiff's counsel seeks to introduce in evidence the deed to the property and a lease.

### Plaintiff's Counsel:

Q. Mr. Boady, who is the owner of the premises known as 3245 Walnut Hill Road?

A. I am, sir.

Q. And when did you acquire ownership of the property?

A. Ten years ago, in 2005.

Q. From whom did you purchase the property?

A. Ronald Hall.

**Plaintiff's Counsel:** Your Honor, we would like to mark this document as Exhibit No. 1 for identification. (The exhibit is marked.)

Q. Can you identify Exhibit No. 1 for identification?

A. Yes, this is the deed to 3245 Walnut Hill Road, which I acquired ten years ago.

Q. Did you subsequently have this deed recorded?

A. Yes.

Q. When?

A. Immediately after the settlement for the property.

Q. Where was the deed recorded?

A. In the Circuit Court for Baltimore County.

Q. Directing your attention to the last page, can you identify the signature appearing above the word grantor?

A. Yes.

Q. Whose signature is it?

A. It is the signature of the person who sold me the house, Mr. Ronald Hall.

Q. Let the record reflect that the witness is pointing to the signature written in the space above the name Ronald Hall.

Q. Did Mr. Hall execute this deed in your presence?

A. Yes, he did.

**Plaintiff's Counsel:** Exhibit No. 1 for identification is offered in evidence. The deed bears liber and folio number BLW 2601/131.

Q. Mr. Boady, what use, if any, do you make of the premises 3245 Walnut Avenue?

A. I rented it to Henry Butterball.

Q. Do you have a lease with Mr. Butterball?

A. Yes.

**Plaintiff's Counsel:** Please mark this document as Plaintiff's Exhibit No. 2 for identification. (The exhibit is marked.)

Q. Mr. Boady, I show you Plaintiff's Exhibit No. 2 for identification. Can you identify this document?

A. This is the lease agreement which Mr. Butterball and I entered into.

Q. Directing your attention to page 3, can you identify any of the signatures as your own?

A. Yes.

Q. Do you see the signature of Mr. Butterball on that page?

A. I do.

Q. Did Mr. Butterball sign this lease in your presence?

A. Yes, he did.

Q. When and where?

A. On October 1, 2005, in my office in downtown Baltimore.

Q. What were the rental terms under the lease?

A. The lease is a year-to-year lease with the monthly rental of $450.

**Plaintiff's Counsel:** I offer Plaintiff's Exhibit No. 2 for identification in evidence.

## Comment

Authentication "is satisfied by evidence sufficient to support a finding that the matter in question is what the proponent claims." Fed. R. Evid. 901(a). Authenticity "is in the category of relevancy dependent upon fulfillment of a condition of fact and is governed by the procedure set forth in Rule 104(b)." advisory committee note, Fed. R. Evid. 901(a). Rule 104(b) provides that "when relevancy depends upon fulfillment of a condition of fact, the court shall admit it upon, or subject to, the introduction of evidence sufficient to support a finding of the fulfillment of the condition."

*In re James E. Long Constr. Co.*, 557 F.2d 1039, 1041 (4th Cir. 1977). *See United States v. Landy*, 676 F.3d 444, 454 (5th Cir. 2012) (authentication rules set a "low bar"). In *Lorraine v. Markel Am. Ins. Co.*, 241 F.R.D. 535 (D. Md. 2007), Judge Grimm described ways in which electronically stored information (ESI), such as screenshots of internet sites, e-mails, and text messages can be authenticated, "including testimony by a person with first-hand knowledge, circumstantial evidence, and computer forensic experts." 6A LYNN MCCLAIN, MARYLAND EVIDENCE, STATE AND FEDERAL, § 901:12 at 876-877 (3d ed. 2013).

There are various requirements and techniques for authenticating documents that constitute private writings. *See United States v. Young*, 753 F.3d 757, 774 (8th Cir. 2014) ("a proponent may use circumstantial evidence to satisfy" the standard for authentication under Fed. R. Evid. 901(a)); *United States v. McMahon*, 938 F.2d 1501, 1508–09 (1st Cir. 1991) (authenticity of unsigned note was based on circumstantial indicia of ownership). A document may be authenticated with circumstantial evidence, "including the document's own distinctive characteristics and the circumstances surrounding its discovery." *In re McLain,* 516 F.3d 301, 308 (5th Cir. 2008) (citations omitted); *see United States v. Sutton*, 426 F.2d 1202, 1207 (D.C. Cir. 1969) (while 'mere contents' are ordinarily insufficient evidence of genuineness, contents may be considered in conjunction with other circumstances).

Thus, for example, the First Circuit in *Yongo v. INS*, 355 F.3d 27 (1st Cir. 2004) held that German immigration records could be authenticated through an INS officer's testimony regarding their source and their appearance. *Id.* at 31. *See Vatyan v. Mukasey*, 508 F.3d 1179 (9th Cir. 2007) ("Vatyan provided evidence that arguably could have supported authentication. A longtime resident of Armenia, Vatyan testified that he recognized the official stamps on the documents as stamps of the Armenian government. Moreover, he attempted to establish a chain of custody by explaining how the documents came into his possession."). *But see Gas Technology Institute v. Rehmat*, 524 F. Supp. 2d 1058 (N.D. Ill. 2007) ("It is undisputed that the documents were gathered from Rehmat's home. Beyond that, however, there is no indication that they are what they purport to be—not even so much as handwriting identification. There is, as just one example, a dispute as to whether Serge actually received Plaintiff's Exhibit 25, an unsigned and undated letter to him, signed 'Amir.'"). *See also United States v. Bello-Perez,* 977 F.2d 664, 671–72 (1st Cir. 1992) ("Anonymous correspondence" may be sufficiently distinctive in its "appearance, contents, substance, internal patterns or other distinctive characteristics" to meet the authentication requirement); *United States v. Natale*, 526 F.2d 1160, 1173 (2d Cir. 1975), *cert. denied*, 425 U.S. 950 (1976) (holding that the prosecution established "a rational basis from which the jury may conclude that the exhibit [a notebook] did, in fact, belong to the appellants" based on the contents of the notebook, the presence of the appellants at the office where the notebook was discovered, and one appellant's admission that the office belonged to him); *United States v. Brown*, 688 F.2d 1112, 1116 (7th Cir. 1982); *John Paul Mitchell Sys. v. Quality King Distributors, Inc.*, 106 F. Supp. 2d 462, 471–72 (S.D.N.Y. 2000), *summary judgment granted, summary judgment denied*, 2001 U.S. Dist. LEXIS 11587 (S.D.N.Y. Aug. 10, 2001). *See Wells v. Liddy*, 37 Fed. Appx. 53, 63 (4th Cir. 2002) ("[T]he mere announcement of identity *by a person who has placed a telephone call* does not suffice to make it admissible against the person so identified . . . the content of the conversation combined with the caller's self-identification can sufficiently support a finding that the caller is who she says she is.").

The point of a Rule 901(b)(8) inquiry is to determine whether the documents in question are, in fact, what they appear to be. "Although the rule requires that the document be free of suspicion, that suspicion does not go to the content of the document but rather to whether the document is what it purports to be. . . ." *Kalamazoo River Study Group v. Menasha Corp.*, 228 F.3d 648, 661 (6th Cir. 2000), *appeal after remand*, 274 F.3d 1043 (6th Cir. 2001). Questions as to the documents' content and completeness bear upon the weight to be accorded the evidence and do not affect the threshold question of authenticity. *Id. United States v. Skipper*, 74 F.3d 608, 612 (5th Cir. 1996); *United States v. Manning*, 56 F.3d 1188, 1199 (9th Cir. 1995); *United States v. Holmquist*, 36 F.3d 154, 167 (1st Cir. 1994), *cert. denied*, 514 U.S. 1064 (1995); *Downes v. Volkswagen of America, Inc.*, 41 F.3d 1132, 1143 (7th Cir. 1994); *United States v. Coohey*, 11 F.3d 97, 99 (8th Cir. 1993); *United States v. Thorne*, 997 F.2d 1504, 1508 (D.C. Cir.), *cert. denied*, 510 U.S. 999 (1993); *United States v. Branch*, 970 F.2d 1368, 1370 (4th Cir. 1992); *United States v. Ruggiero*, 928 F.2d 1289, 1303 (2d Cir.), *cert. denied*, 502 U.S. 938 (1991); *Threadgill v. Armstrong World Indus., Inc.*, 928 F.2d 1366, 1375 (3d Cir. 1991); *In re Grey*, 902 F.2d 1479, 1482 (10th Cir. 1990); *Stuckey v. N. Propane Gas Co.*, 874 F.2d 1563, 1574 (11th Cir. 1989); *United States v. Carriger*, 592 F.2d 312, 315–16 (6th Cir. 1979); *Ragan v. Jeffboat LLC*, 149 F. Supp. 2d 1053, 1062 (S.D. Ind. 2001); *United States v. Ziesman*, 409 F.3d 941, 953 (8th Cir. 2005); *United States v. Pang*,

362 F.3d 1187, 1192 (9th Cir.), *cert. denied*, 543 U.S. 943 (2004) (in order to authenticate invoices, the government had to "come forward with evidence sufficient to support a finding that the invoices were what they purported to be"); *Menlo Logistics, Inc. v. Western Expo, Inc.*, 269 Fed. Appx. 715, 717 (9th Cir. 2008) ("a document can be authenticated 'by a witness who wrote it, signed it, used it, or saw others do so'"); *Ferguson v. United States*, 484 F.3d 1068, 1075 (8th Cir. 2007); *Thanongsinh v. Board of Education*, 462 F.3d 762, 779 (7th Cir. 2006). Compare with self-authentication requirements and techniques associated with certain documents, such as public records. *See infra* Chapter 3.J.; Fed. R. Evid. 902(3).

The introduction of deeds, leases, letters, and related documents follows a similar pattern. This pattern illustrates the method of authentication through testimony based on direct observation that establishes the following facts: (1) time and place the witness observed the execution of the document; (2) the circumstances under which the document was executed; and (3) that the witness recognizes the document that is being offered in evidence. *See United States v. Scurlock*, 52 F.3d 531, 538–39 (5th Cir. 1995); *United States v. Reilly*, 33 F.3d 1396, 1404 (3d Cir. 1994); *United States v. Chu Kong Yin*, 935 F.2d 990, 995 (9th Cir. 1991), *cert. denied*, 511 U.S. 1035 (1994); *Denison v. Swaco Geolograph Co.*, 941 F.2d 1416 (10th Cir. 1991); *NLRB v. General Wood Preserving Co.*, 905 F.2d 803, 811 (4th Cir.), *cert. denied*, 498 U.S. 1016 (1990); *United States v. Durham*, 868 F.2d 1010 (8th Cir.), *cert. denied*, 493 U.S. 954 (1989); *United States v. Drougas*, 748 F.2d 8, 26 (1st Cir. 1984); *United States v. Sliker*, 751 F.2d 477, 488 (2d Cir. 1984), *cert. denied*, 470 U.S. 1058 (1985); *United States v. Brown*, 688 F.2d 1112, 1116 (7th Cir. 1982); *Bury v. Marietta Dodge*, 692 F.2d 1335, 1338 (11th Cir. 1982); *United States v. Bruner*, 657 F.2d 1278, 1284 (D.C. Cir. 1981); *Bridger v. Union Railway*, 355 F.2d 382, 391–92 (6th Cir. 1966).

When appropriate, proof of recording of the document is helpful. *See* 28 U.S.C. § 1739 (1994); *Amoco Prod. Co. v. United States*, 852 F.2d 1574, 1580 (10th Cir. 1988); *Compton v. Davis Oil Co.*, 607 F. Supp. 1221 (D. Wyo. 1985).

In some cases it is possible to satisfy the Federal Rule of Evidence 901(a) requirement of sufficiency of evidence for authentication by drawing an inference from the lack of evidence. *See, e.g., In re James E. Long Construction Co.*, 557 F.2d 1039, 1041 (4th Cir. 1977). In that case, the court held that there existed a permissible inference, from silence and other evidence, that a signature was genuine in light of Federal Rule of Evidence 901(a).

Under Federal Rule of Evidence 803(14), evidence of the recording of a document that purports to establish or affect an interest in property is sufficient proof of the content of the original recorded document, and of its execution and delivery by each person by whom it purports to have been executed. The rule provides, however, that the evidence of the recording must be a record from a public office authorized by statute to record documents of that kind in that office. The rule specifically exempts such records from the hearsay doctrine. *See Connecticut Light & Power Co. v. Federal Power Comm'n*, 557 F.2d 349 (2d Cir. 1977); *Amoco Prod. Co. v. United States*, 455 F. Supp. 46 (D. Utah 1977), *rev'd on other grounds*, 852 F.2d 1574 (10th Cir. 1988); *Compton v. Davis Oil Co.*, 607 F. Supp. 1221 (D. Wyo. 1985). *See generally Greycas, Inc. v. Proud*, 826 F.2d 1560, 1567 (7th Cir. 1987), *cert. denied*, 484 U.S. 1043 (1988); *United States v. Ruffin*, 575 F.2d 346, 357 (2d Cir. 1978); *United States v. Weinstock*, 863 F. Supp. 1529, 1534 (D. Utah 1994); *United States v. Boulware*, 384 F.3d 794, 806 (9th Cir. 2004).

Some of the other methods used to authenticate private writings include: (1) testimony of a non-expert witness as to the genuineness of handwriting, based upon the witness's familiarity with that handwriting. *See infra* Chapter 6.D. for an illustration of this technique; *see also* Fed. R. Evid. 901(b)(2); (2) the expert opinion of a document examiner. *See infra* Chapter 7.I. for an illustration of this technique; *see also* Fed. R. Evid. 901(b)(3); (3) comparison by the trier of fact or expert with exemplars, which have been authenticated. *See* Fed. R. Evid. 901(c)(3); (4) the distinctive characteristic method, which allows a witness to authenticate a document by its contents when, for example, a letter is shown to contain information that persons other than the purported sender are unlikely to possess. *See* Fed. R. Evid. 901(b)(4); and (5) the so-called "reply doctrine," which allows a private writing to be authenticated when it has been mailed and shown by its contents to be in reply.

Authentication requirements are similar in civil and criminal cases. Nevertheless, criminal cases place on the prosecution the additional burden of establishing chain of custody, the procedures of which are, in many instances, governed by statutes. *See* Fed. R. Evid. 901(b)(10).

## B. BUSINESS RECORDS

John Smith, defendant in a criminal case, claims that at the time of the murder he was purchasing stereophonic equipment at Sears. Defense counsel wants to introduce the sales slip and then call the salesman as a witness. Counsel subpoenas the area credit manager, requesting all credit records pertaining to John Smith during the summer of 2008.

### Defense Counsel:

Q. Would you state your name, please?

A. Margaret Jefferson.

Q. Where do you live?

A. 214 Gough Street in Baltimore City.

Q. What is your present occupation?

A. Area Credit Manager for Sears.

Q. What are your responsibilities in that position?

A. I am responsible for maintaining all records pertaining to charge accounts with Sears stores in the Baltimore metropolitan area.

Q. Did you receive a subpoena to come to court today?

A. Yes.

Q. And what did that subpoena request you to bring with you?

A. All sales slips and records pertaining to John Smith for the summer of 2008.

Q. Did you bring those records with you?

A. Yes.

Q. May I please have those records? (Witness hands documents to counsel.)

**Defense Counsel:** Your Honor, may we have these records marked as Defendant's Exhibits Nos. 1(a) through (c) for identification?

Q. Were these documents that you handed to me, which have been marked as Defendant's Exhibits Nos. 1(a) through (c) for identification, maintained by you?

A. Yes.

Q. Please identify the documents.

A. They consist of three sales slips made out by our salesperson, all pertaining to the account of John Smith.

Q. Were these documents prepared in the regular course of business? (Alternatively: "Were these records kept in the regular course of a regularly conducted business activity?")

A. Yes.

Q. Was it the regular course of business for Sears to have records such as these prepared?

A. Yes.

Q. Do you know the circumstances of their being prepared?

A. Yes.

Q. Please explain.

A. On the day of sale, the salesperson would fill out these slips, the purchaser would sign in the presence of a salesperson, and the salesperson would hold the original sales slip to be forwarded to my office at the end of the day.

Q. How do you know this?

A. From years of working at Sears—it is standard operating procedure.

**Defense Counsel:** We offer Exhibits Nos. 1(a) through (c) for identification in evidence.

## *Comment*

The business records exception to the hearsay rule applies in both civil and criminal cases when (1) the records were made and kept in the regular course of business activity; (2) it was a regular practice of the business to make and keep such written records; (3) the records were made at or near the time of the act, event, or diagnosis; and (4) they were made by a person with knowledge, or from information transmitted by a person with knowledge. Fed. R. Evid. 803(6); *see Kasper Global Collection & Brokers, Inc. v. Global Cabinets & Furniture Mfrs., Inc.*, 952 F. Supp.2d 542 (S.D.N.Y. 2013) (invoices and billing records would be admissible under the business records exception to the hearsay rule only if sponsoring witness established that the invoices were made at or near the time of the transactions at issue, that they were kept in the course of regularly-conducted business activity, and that it was the regular practice of that business activity to make records); *Hansen v. Fincantieri Marine Group, LLC*, 763 F.3d 832 (7th Cir. 2014) (health care provider's medical certification that employee had a chronic serious health condition was admissible); *United States v. Ary*, 518 F.3d 775, 786 (10th Cir. 2008). The "principal precondition to admission of documents as business records pursuant to Fed. R. Evid. 803(6) is that the records have sufficient indicia of trustworthiness to be considered reliable." *Health Alliance Network, Inc. v. Continental Cas. Co.*, 245 F.R.D. 121, 130 (S.D.N.Y. 2007), *aff'd*, 294 Fed. Appx. 680 (2008) (unreported decision). *See United States v. Salgado*, 250 F.3d 438, 451 (6th Cir.), *cert. denied*, 534

U.S. 936 (2001); *United States v. Williams*, 205 F.3d 23, 32–33 (2d Cir.), *cert. denied*, 531 U.S. 885 (2000); *United States v. Sutton*, 2000 U.S. App. LEXIS 31929, at *4 (7th Cir. Dec. 6, 2000); *United States v. Reyes*, 157 F.3d 949, 951 (2d Cir. 1998); *Phoenix Assoc. III v. Stone*, 60 F.3d 95, 100 (2d Cir. 1995); *Firemen's Fund Ins. Co. v. Thien*, 63 F.3d 754, 757 (8th Cir. 1995); *United States v. Warren*, 42 F.3d 647, 656 (D.C. Cir. 1994); *United States v. Console*, 13 F.3d 641, 656 (3d Cir. 1993), *cert. denied*, 511 U.S. 1076, *cert. denied*, 513 U.S. 812 (1994); *United States v. Emenogha*, 1 F.3d 473, 483 (7th Cir. 1993), *cert. denied*, 510 U.S. 1080 (1994); *United States v. Bland*, 961 F.2d 123, 127 (9th Cir.), *cert. denied*, 506 U.S. 858 (1992); *United States v. Arboleda*, 929 F.2d 858, 869 (1st Cir. 1991); *In re Custodian of Records of Variety Distrib., Inc.*, 927 F.2d 244, 246 (6th Cir. 1991); *United States v. Saunders*, 886 F.2d 56, 58 (4th Cir. 1989); *United States v. Veytia-Bravo*, 603 F.2d 1187, 1191–92 (5th Cir. 1979), *cert. denied*, 444 U.S. 1024 (1980); *United States v. Snyder*, 787 F.2d 1429, 1434 (10th Cir.), *cert. denied*, 479 U.S. 836 (1986); *United States v. Dreer*, 740 F.2d 18, 19 (11th Cir. 1984); *United States v. Ortiz*, 182 F. Supp. 2d 443, 451 (E.D. Pa. 2000); *United States v. Gurr*, 471 F.3d 144 (D.C. Cir.), *cert. denied*, 127 S. Ct. 2146 (2007); *United States v. Baker*, 458 F.3d 513, 519 (6th Cir. 2006); *United States v. Fujii*, 301 F.3d 535, 539 (7th Cir. 2002); *Thanongsinh v. Board of Educ.*, 462 F.3d 762, 775–76 (7th Cir. 2006).

Hospital records, police reports, computer printouts, and even summaries or compilations made from business records can be included within this business record doctrine. Federal Rule of Evidence 803(6) defines "business" to include "institution, association, profession, occupation and calling of every kind, whether or not conducted for profit." *See United States v. Cameron*, 699 F.3d 621 (1st Cir. 2012) (Google and Yahoo records admitted as business records). As discussed ahead, federal court practice does not require the custodian or person who has possession of the record to have been the maker of the record. *See also NRRM, LLC v. Mepco Fin. Corp.*, 2015 WL 1501897 (N.D. Ill. 2015)

"The essential component of the business records exception is that each actor in the chain of information is under a business duty or compulsion to provide accurate information." *United States v. McIntyre*, 997 F.2d 687, 699 (1993). *See* 2 McCormick on Evidence § 290 at 445-446 (Kenneth S. Broun ed., 7th ed. 2013).

Although a proper foundation is required for introduction of evidence under the business record doctrine, it is not always necessary that the foundation consist of direct testimony that the document was prepared in the regular course of business. For example, one of the sales slips in this pattern examination could have been introduced by the defendant, claiming that it was the sales slip he received when he made the purchase. The court could conclude from the circumstances and the nature of the document that it was made in the regular course of business. *See United States v. Penninger*, 456 Fed. Appx. 214 (4th Cir. 2011, *cert. denied* 132 S. Ct. 2115 (2012) (per curiam) (commodity futures trading logs properly admitted where foundation for admissibility was based on judicial notice of the nature of the business and there are sufficient circumstances demonstrating the trustworthiness of the documents); *Fed. Deposit Ins. Corp. v. Staudinger*, 797 F.2d 908 (10th Cir. 1986); *Bank of New York v. Calloway*, 157 So. 3d 1064 (Fla. Dist. Ct. App. 2015), *reh'g denied* (Mar. 3, 2015), *review denied*, No. SC15-545, 2015 WL 4886204 (Fla. Aug. 17, 2015); *United States v. Salgado*, 250 F.3d 438, 451 (6th Cir.), *cert. denied*, 534 U.S. 936 (2001); *Arbuckle v. Dorsey*, 1999 U.S. App. LEXIS 20687, at *12 (10th Cir. Aug. 30, 1999) (person supplying information must be under a legal duty of accuracy); *City of Tuscaloosa v. Harcros Chems.*, 159 F.3d 548, 559 (11th Cir. 1998), *cert. denied*, 528 U.S. 812 (1999); *United States v. Johnson*, 971 F.2d 562, 570–72 (10th Cir. 1992); *Itel Capital Corp. v. Cups Coal Co.*, 707 F.2d 1253, 1259 (11th Cir. 1983); *United States v. Hing Shair Chan*, 680 F. Supp. 521 (E.D.N.Y. 1988); *Zenith Radio Corp. v. Matsushita Elec. Indus. Co.*, 505 F. Supp. 1190, 1236 (E.D. Pa. 1980), *aff'd in part, rev'd in part*, 723 F.2d 238 (3d Cir. 1983), *rev'd on other grounds*, 475 U.S. 574 (1986); *see United States v. McIntyre*, 997 F.2d 687, 699–700 (10th Cir. 1993).

However, the more prudent practice is to authenticate the document by formal foundation. Alternatively, the Federal Rules of Evidence do provide for self-authentication of business records. *See* Rule 902(11). Self-authentication involves providing a written declaration from the custodian of the records that sets out the elements of a business record under Rule 803(6) sufficiently in advance of trial to allow adverse parties to inspect and challenge the admissibility of the documents. Many local rules establish a procedure for the introduction of all documents, including business records. Hence, the authenticity of business records can be stipulated prior to trial.

In this pattern, counsel questioned: "Were these documents prepared in the regular course of business?" and "Was it the regular course of business for Sears to have records such as these prepared?" An alternative form of the question is, "Were these records kept in the regular course of a regularly conducted business activity?" *See* Fed. R. Evid. 803(6). This alternative is suggested by at least one commentator. *See* 4 MICHAEL H. GRAHAM, HANDBOOK OF FEDERAL EVIDENCE, § 803.6 (7th ed. 2012).

Federal Rule of Evidence 803(6) requires testimony for establishing foundation by either the custodian of the records or other qualified witnesses. *See Butler v. IMA Regiomontana S.A. de C.V.*, 2000 U.S. App. LEXIS 1607, at *11 (9th Cir. Feb. 3, 2000); *Hoselton v. Metz Baking Co.*, 48 F.3d 1056 (8th Cir. 1995); *United States v. Chatman*, 994 F.2d 1510 (10th Cir.), *cert. denied*, 510 U.S. 883 (1993); *Elgabri v. Lekas*, 964 F.2d 1255 (1st Cir. 1992); *Raphaely Int'l, Inc. v. Waterman S.S. Corp.*, 972 F.2d 498 (2d Cir. 1992), *cert. denied*, 507 U.S. 916 (1993); *United States v. Pelullo*, 964 F.2d 193, 201 (3d Cir. 1992), *appeal after remand*, 14 F.3d 881 (3d Cir. 1994), *on remand to* 895 F. Supp. 718 (E.D. Pa. 1995); *United States v. Jacoby*, 955 F.2d 1527 (11th Cir. 1992), *cert. denied*, 507 U.S. 920 (1993); *United States v. Muhammad*, 928 F.2d 1461 (7th Cir. 1991); *United States v. Ray*, 930 F.2d 1368, 1370 (9th Cir. 1990), *cert. denied*, 498 U.S. 1124 (1991) ("[t]he phrase 'other qualified witness' is broadly interpreted to require only that the witness understand the record-keeping system"); *Ledbetter v. Commissioner*, 837 F.2d 708 (5th Cir.), *cert. denied*, 488 U.S. 856 (1988); *United States v. Mahar*, 801 F.2d 1477 (6th Cir. 1986); *United States v. Ortiz*, 182 F. Supp. 2d 442, 451 (E.D. Pa. 2000); *In re Denslow*, 104 B.R. 761, 765 (E.D. Va. 1989); *United States v. Gwathney*, 465 F.3d 1133, 1140–41 (10th Cir.), *cert. denied*, 550 U.S. 927 (2007); *United States v. Christ*, 513 F.3d 762, 769 (7th Cir. 2008) (witness laying the foundation does not have to have personal knowledge of the actual records, only of the procedures used to create the records); *United States v. Baker*, 458 F.3d 513, 519 (6th Cir. 2006).

Federal procedures require all those transmitting and recording to do so in the "regular practice of that activity." Fed. R. Evid. 803(6); *see United States v. Kelly*, 349 F.2d 720, 772 (2d Cir. 1965), *cert. denied*, 384 U.S. 947 (1966); *United States v. Ary*, 518 F.3d 775, 787 (10th Cir. 2008). For example, a letter recording a settlement demand in the regular course of an insurance company's business is a business record. *See Twin City Fire Ins. Co. v. Country Mut. Ins. Co.*, 23 F.3d 1175, 1182 (7th Cir. 1994). However, the contents of the letter are double hearsay and must meet an exception to be admitted. In Twin City Fire Ins. Co., the settlement demand referred to in the letter was a verbal act and thus non-hearsay. *Id.* at 1183. Therefore, both the letter and its contents were admissible. *See Chadwell v. Koch Ref. Co.*, 251 F.3d 727, 731–32 (8th Cir. 2001); *Schering Corp. v. Pfizer Inc.*, 189 F.3d 218, 239 (2d Cir. 1999), amended in part, 2000 U.S. Dist. LEXIS 9446 (S.D.N.Y. July 7, 2000). *See also United States v. Nicholson*, 924 F.2d 1053 (4th Cir.), *cert. denied*, 501 U.S. 1211 (1991), where the Court held that although a sales receipt constituted a business record, the hearsay exception could not be extended to the name of the purchaser; and *United States v. Cone*, 714 F.3d 197 (4th Cir. 2013) ("customers' e-mails complaining that goods they received from business addressee were counterfeit were admissible as non-hearsay, to show that defendant-recipients were on notice, but court committed error-albeit harmless-in declining to give limiting instruction; e-mails were not admissible as business records simply because business retained them") (6A LYNN MCCLAIN, MARYLAND EVIDENCE, STATE AND FEDERAL § 803(6):2 at 566 (3d ed. 2013)).

Use of the business records exception at the second level of hearsay is analyzed in two interesting cases: *United States v. Bortnovsky*, 879 F.2d 30, 34 (2d Cir. 1989), and *United States v. Snyder*, 787 F.2d 1429, 1434 (10th Cir.), *cert. denied*, 479 U.S. 836 (1986). These cases held that in order for second- and third-level hearsay to be admissible under the business records exception to the hearsay rule, each level of hearsay must satisfy one of the exceptions. *See also United States v. Walker*, 272 F.3d 407 (7th Cir. 2001), *cert. denied*, 122 S. Ct. 1456 (2002); *United States v. Pena-Gutierrez*, 222 F.3d 1080 (9th Cir.), *cert. denied*, 531 U.S. 1057 (2000); *United States v. Vigneau*, 187 F.3d 70 (1st Cir. 1999), *cert. denied*, 528 U.S. 1172 (2000); *Sana v. Hawaiian Cruises, Ltd.*, 181 F.3d 1041 (9th Cir. 1999); *Twin City Fire Ins. Co. v. Country Mut. Ins. Co.*, 23 F.3d 1175 (7th Cir. 1994); *United States v. Franks*, 939 F.2d 600 (8th Cir. 1991); *United States v. Cruz*, 894 F.2d 41 (2d Cir. 1990), *cert. denied*, 498 U.S. 837 (1990); *United States v. Furst*, 886 F.2d 558 (3d Cir. 1989), *cert. denied*, 493 U.S. 1062 (1990), *appeal after remand*, 918 F.2d 400 (3d Cir. 1990); *Rassoulpour v. Washington Metro. Area Transit Auth.*, 826 F.2d 98, 100–01 (D.C. Cir. 1987); *Ricciardi v. Children's Hosp. Med. Ctr.*, 811 F.2d 18, 22 (1st Cir. 1987); *Clark v. City of Los Angeles*, 650 F.2d 1033, 1037 (9th Cir. 1981), *cert. denied*, 456 U.S. 927 (1982); *United States v. Yates*, 553 F.2d 518, 521 (6th Cir. 1977); *Florida*

*Canal Indus., Inc., v. Rambo*, 537 F.2d 200 (5th Cir. 1976); *United States v. Burruss*, 418 F.2d 677, 678 (4th Cir. 1969); *Boca Investerings P'shp v. United States*, 128 F. Supp. 2d 16, 20–21 (D.D.C. 2000), *judgment entered*, 167 F. Supp. 2d 298 (D.D.C. 2001); 2 McCORMICK ON EVI-DENCE § 324.1 (Kenneth S. Broun ed., 7th ed. 2013); *United States v. Gurr*, 471 F.3d 144, 151 (D.C. Cir. 2006).

Under the federal rules, the same hearsay, offered in a civil case or offered against the government in a criminal case, might be viewed differently if the 803(6) business record is also admissible as a public record pursuant to Federal Rule of Evidence 803(8).

Rule 803(8) exempts certain types of investigative reports from the hearsay rule—for example, factual findings in investigative reports in civil cases. However, whether an inadmissible hearsay declaration in a business record will be admitted via the public record and report doctrine will depend on whether the trial judge deems the statement and full report reliable. *See* generally *Wilson v. Zapata Off-Shore Co.*, 939 F.2d 260 (5th Cir. 1991) ("If both the source and the recorder of the information, as well as every other participant in the chain producing the record, are acting in the regular course of business, the multiple hearsay is excused by Rule 803(6). However, if the source of the information is an outsider, as in the facts before us, Rule 803(6) does not, by itself, permit the admission of the business record. The outsider's statement must fall within another hearsay exception to be admissible because it does not have the presumption of accuracy that statements made during the regular course of business have."). *United States v. Gray*, 852 F.2d 136 (4th Cir. 1988); *United States v. Nixon*, 779 F.2d 126 (2d Cir. 1985); *Wilson v. Attaway*, 757 F.2d 1227 (11th Cir. 1985); *Washington Cent. R.R. Co. v. Nat'l Mediation Bd.*, 830 F. Supp. 1343 (E.D. Wash. 1993).

The term "factual findings" can be construed to include opinions. *See Beech Aircraft Corp. v. Rainey*, 488 U.S. 153 (1988); *United States v. Midwest Fireworks Mfg. Co.*, 248 F.3d 563, 566 (6th Cir. 2001); *Bank of Lexington & Trust Co. v. Vining-Sparks Sec., Inc.*, 959 F.2d 606 (6th Cir. 1992); *Ellis v. Int'l Playtex, Inc.*, 745 F.2d 292 (4th Cir. 1984). The justification for allowing opinions and conclusions into evidence when they are contained within a public record is the assumption that a public official will perform his duty properly and not remember details independently of the record. Factors used to determine admissibility of such opinions and conclusions include timeliness of the investigation, special skills of the official, and possible motivation problems. *See* 5 Jack B. Weinstein & Margaret A. Berger, Weinstein's Federal Evidence § 803.10 (Joseph M. McLaughlin ed., Matthew Bender 2d ed. 2014). *See also infra* Chapter 3.I., relating to police accident reports; *infra* Chapter 3.J.i., relating to certified public records; *infra* Chapter 3.D. G., relating to ESI; and *supra* Chapters 2.A. and 2.B., for discussions of hearsay problems and firsthand knowledge problems with present recollection revived and past recollection recorded.

## C. COPIES OF BUSINESS RECORDS

A defendant in a criminal case claims he was elsewhere at the time of the murder, purchasing stereophonic equipment at Sears. Defense counsel wishes to introduce a scanned copy of the sales slip consummating the sale. Defense counsel subpoenas the area credit manager, requesting all credit records pertaining to the defendant, John Smith, during the summer of 2014.

### Defense Counsel

Q. Would you state your name, please?

A. Margaret Jefferson.

Q. Where do you live?

A. 214 Gough Street in Baltimore City.

Q. Mrs. Jefferson, what is your present occupation?

A. Area Credit Manager for Sears.

Q. What are your responsibilities in that position?

A. I am responsible for maintaining all records pertaining to charge accounts with Sears stores in the Baltimore Metropolitan area.

Q. Did you receive a subpoena to come to court today?

A. Yes.

Q. And what did that subpoena request you to bring with you?

A. All sales slips and records pertaining to John Smith for the summer of 2014.

Q. Did you bring those records with you?

A. Yes, but they are scanned copies.

Q. Where are the originals?

A. After my office receives the originals and they are scanned, we destroy the originals.

Q. Is that what occurred in this case?

A. Yes.

Q. May I please have those records? (Witness hands documents to counsel.)

**Defense Counsel:** Your Honor, may we have these records marked as Defendant's Exhibits Nos. 1(a) through (c) for identification?

Q. Were these documents that you handed to me, which have now been marked as Defendant's Exhibits Nos. 1(a) through (c) for identification, maintained by you?

A. Yes.

Q. Can you identify them?

A. Yes. They consist of three sales slips pertaining to the account of John Smith.

Q. Were these documents prepared in the regular course of business?

A. Yes.

Q. Was it the regular course of business for Sears to have records such as these prepared?

A. Yes.

Q. And was it in the regular course of business to scan the original sales slips?

A. Yes.

Q. Do you know the circumstances and procedure of the scanned copies being prepared?

A. Yes.

Q. Please explain.

A. Well, on the day of sale, the salesperson would fill out sales slips, the purchaser would sign in the presence of a salesperson, and the salesperson would hold the original sales slip to be forwarded to my office at the end of the day. Then the slips are reproduced by a scanning process on a weekly basis. The records are scanned on an Eastman Kodak machine, under the direction of the custodian of records. The scanned copies are saved and the original sales slip discarded.

Q. Do the scanned copies accurately reflect the original?

A. Yes, it does.

Q. How do you know this?

A. From years of working at Sears—it is standard operating procedure, and from personal observations.

**Defense Counsel:** Now, Your Honor, we offer Defendant's Exhibits Nos. 1(a) through (c) for identification in evidence.

## *Comment*

Under the Uniform Photographic Copies of Business and Public Records as Evidence Act, photographic copies, microfilm, microcard, or miniature photographic copies of documents that qualify as business records or records maintained in the regular course of business activity may be introduced in evidence regardless of whether the original documents are in existence and available. 28 U.S.C. § 1732 (2009). Duplicates or other evidence of the contents of documents that do not fall within the business record doctrine are not governed by the Uniform Photographic Copies of Business and Public Records as Evidence Act. However, Federal Rule 1003 provides for the admissibility of duplicates in federal proceedings, and Federal Rule 1004 provides for admissibility of other evidence of contents upon the loss or destruction of the original. *See Montoya v. Romero*, 956 F. Supp.2d 1268 (D.N.M. 2013) (defendant village police officer made diligent efforts to locate his original belt recording of encounter with arrestee, as element for admission of secondary evidence under exception to best evidence rule when all originals are lost or destroyed and the loss or destruction is not by the proponent acting in bad faith, in arrestee's action asserting tort and civil rights claims; officer asserted that, despite efforts to find an original, the recording could not be found on his old computer drive, the court in which arrestee had been prosecuted had not retained a copy, and the district attorney's office did not have a copy).

## D. ESI: RECORDS STORED

The government, in a criminal case involving credit card fraud, seeks to introduce electronic records maintained by Second National Bank of Maryland. These records reflect the occasions when a merchant used a credit card terminal to process a charge on the credit card allegedly used by the defendant.

### Prosecutor:

Q. Would you state your name, please?
A. Margaret Jefferson.
Q. Where do you live?
A. 214 Gough Street in Baltimore City.
Q. What is your present occupation?

A. I am the information technology supervisor of the credit card authorization department of the Second National Bank of Maryland.

Q. What are your responsibilities in that position?

A. I maintain the automated system that communicates with merchants' credit card terminals. When a customer swipes his or her card at a merchant's terminal, that terminal automatically verifies the validity of the card and that the customer has sufficient credit or funds to make his or her purchase.

Q. Did you receive a subpoena to come to court today?

A. Yes.

Q. And what did that subpoena request you to bring with you?

A. Printouts of ESI reflecting verifications of Visa card number 0006167 during the months of January, February, and March 2014.

Q. Did you bring those records with you?

A. Yes.

Q. May I please have those records? (Witness hands documents to counsel.)

**Prosecutor:** May we have these records marked as Government's Exhibits No. 1(a) through (c) for identification?

Q. Were these documents that you handed to me, which have now been marked as Government's Exhibits No. 1(a) through (c) for identification, maintained by you?

A. Yes.

Q. Can you identify these for us?

A. Yes. They are the computer printouts of our records showing requests for verification of Visa card number 0006167 received by our system in January, February, and March 2014.

Q. Were these documents prepared in the regular course of business?

A. Yes.

Q. Was it the regular course of business for the bank to generate records such as these?

A. Yes.

Q. Do you know the circumstances of their being prepared?

A. Yes.

Q. Please explain.

A. When a customer swipes his credit card using a credit card terminal, the terminal uses a phone line to connect to our computer system. Our system verifies that the customer's account is valid and that sufficient funds are available to cover the transaction's cost. The system also holds the funds—deducts them from the customer's credit limit—to cover the amount of the transaction. These actions, the verification and the hold, are noted in a computer database file on our system. Each card we process has its own database file. Using a computer program, we can access the database and print out records for any card we process.

Q. Are the computer and software program that were used to communicate with merchant terminals standard equipment?

A. Yes.

Q. What type of computer and software were used?

A. A Dell server computer and a Sun Microsystems database software program.

Q. Are those reliable equipment for executing and recording credit authorizations?

A. Yes.

Q. Have you been trained to use and maintain this equipment?

A. Yes.

Q. Does the database software accurately record when a merchant requests authorization for a credit card processed by your company?

A. Yes.

Q. Are there measures to prevent individuals from altering the database file to show authorizations that never took place, or to delete or change authorizations that did take place?

A. Yes. The system is password-protected and backed up every day in a read-only format. Only specified personnel have access to modify data. We run biweekly checks to make sure that the database files have not been altered improperly. The database files are backed up daily, which means the data is copied to tape and stored in a safe place solely as a means of security.

Q. Is this printout an accurate representation of the data stored in the computer?

A. Yes, most definitely. It is a routine process, and all our records are stored on the computer.

**Prosecutor:** We offer Exhibits No. 1(a) through (c) for identification in evidence.

### Comment

There are basically two types of electronic evidence: (1) evidence that derives from electronically-stored declarations of individuals, such as electronically generated bills, accounting records, charges and summaries, and e-mail; and (2) electronic evidence that includes output generated automatically by a programmed process without input from individuals, such as automated telephone call records, simulations, or enhanced photographic images. GREGORY P. JOSEPH, MODERN VISUAL EVIDENCE § 7.01[2][a] (2014).

With respect to the first category, a computer printout "is admissible under Rule 803(6) as a business record if the offeror establishes a sufficient foundation in the record for its introduction." *United States v. Salgado*, 250 F.3d 438, 451 (6th Cir.), *cert. denied*, 534 U.S. 936 (2001); *see Dutch v. U.S.*, 997 A.2d 685, 689–90 (D.C. 2010) (computer printouts properly admitted as business records under Fed. R. Evid. 803(6) where testimony showed that the data used to create the printouts were data stored in a company's system created and used by its merchants in the regular course of the check-cashing business); *United States v. Bonomolo*, 556 Fed. Appx. 71 (2nd Cir. 2014) (computer generated spreadsheets came within business records exception to hearsay rule); *Dyno Construction Co. v. McWane, Inc.*, 198 F.3d 567, 575–76 (6th Cir. 1999) (computer printout of business records held admissible); *United States v. Briscoe*, 896 F.2d 1476, 1494 (7th Cir. 1990) ("It is well established that computer data compilations are admissible as business records under Fed. R. Evid. 803(6) if a proper foundation as to the reliability of the records is established.") *Accord, United States v. Salgado*, 250 F.3d 438, 451 (6th Cir.), *cert. denied*, 534 U.S. 936 (2001); *United States v. De Georgia*, 420 F.2d 889 (9th Cir. 1969); *United States v. Fusero*, 106 F. Supp. 2d 921, 924–25 (E.D. Mich. 2000). Other hearsay exceptions—for example, public records—may be applicable to computer printouts. *See* Fed. R. Evid. 902(4); *United States v. Ryan*, 969 F.2d 238 (7th Cir. 1992). Electronic evidence that is not derived from business records requires proper authentication as well—for example, evidence derived from scientific experiments, or visual animations. *See, e.g., infra* Chapter 5.C.

With regard to the second category of electronic evidence, evidence created automatically, courts have held that such evidence does not qualify as hearsay because "[o]nly a person may be a declarant and make a statement." *See United States v. Washington*, 498 F.3d 225, 231 (4th Cir. 2007). For example, in *United States v. Hamilton*, 413 F.3d 1138 (10th Cir. 2005), the Tenth Circuit concluded that the computer-generated header information that accompanied a pornographic image on the internet was not a hearsay statement. "Of primary importance to this ruling . . . [wa]s the uncontroverted fact that the header information was automatically generated by the computer . . . without the assistance or input of a person." *Id*. at 1142. Similarly, in *United States v. Khorozian*, 333 F.3d 498 (3d Cir. 2003), the Third Circuit determined that the transmission information on a faxed document was not a hearsay statement because it was automatically generated by the fax machine. *But see United States v. Salgado*, 250 F.3d 438 (6th Cir. 2001) (stating that telephone numbers recorded and stored by computer were hearsay statements that were admissible under the business records exception).

The authentication of computer-based evidence in federal courts is generally deemed sufficient when counsel adheres to Federal Rule of Evidence 901(b)(9). This rule provides that authentication requirements for introducing a process or system are satisfied when there is a showing that the process or system produces an accurate result. The proponent of computerized evidence must satisfy the burden of establishing the following: (1) the accuracy of the computer printout; (2) that the process was properly operated; (3) that the computer data were secure; and (4) that the information printed out was accurate. *See also United States v. Salcido*, 506 F.3d 729, 733 (9th Cir. 2007) ("In this case, the government properly authenticated the videos and images under Rule 901 by presenting detailed evidence as to the chain of custody, specifically how the images were retrieved from the defendant's computers."), *cert. denied*, 128 S. Ct. 1918 (2008); *United States v. Hardrick*, 766 F.3d 1051 (9th Cir. 2014) *cert. denied*, (U.S. Oct. 5, 2015); *United States v. Jackson*, 208 F.3d 633, 638 (7th Cir), *cert. denied*, 531 U.S. 973 (2000); *United States v. Hutson*, 821 F.2d 1015 (5th Cir. 1987); *United States v. Glasser*, 773 F.2d 1553 (11th Cir. 1985); *United States v. Croft*, 750 F.2d 1354 (7th Cir. 1984); *In re Dow Corning Corp.*, 250 B.R. 298, 317–18 (E.D. Mich. 2000), *judgment entered*, 2001 U.S. Dist. LEXIS 10660 (E.D. Mich. July 27, 2001), *dismissed without prejudice*, 2002 U.S. Dist. LEXIS 6484 (E.D. Mich. Mar. 29, 2002), for additional discussions on establishing foundations of computer evidence.

Authentication problems with computer evidence can be minimized by pretrial cooperation between counsel. The MANUAL FOR COMPLEX LITIGATION recommends that discovery of computerized evidence should be undertaken to avoid unnecessary delay of trial. MANUAL FOR COMPLEX LITIGATION § 11.423 (4th ed. 2004).

## E. ESI: E-MAIL CHAINS/STRINGS

Sherilynn Rogers, a former professor, sues Chase College for wrongful termination based on her gender. The university's defense is that students had repeatedly complained of the professor's in-class demeanor and conduct. It produces e-mails from Lionel Ellison, the dean of student affairs, to Frederick Keyes, the dean of faculty. In these e-mails, Dean Ellison forwarded e-mails that he had purportedly received from several students complaining about Professor Rogers.

### Defendant's Attorney:

Q. Please introduce yourself to the jury.

A. My name is Frederick Keyes.

Q. And who is your current employer?

A. Chase College.

Q. What is your position at the college?

A. I am the Dean of Faculty.

Q. What are your responsibilities?

A. I have the final word on all hiring and firing decisions for the college faculty, professors, and lecturers.

Q. Do you have an e-mail address at work?

A. Yes, I do.

Q. And do you receive e-mails in the course of the day from faculty and administrators at the college?

A. Yes, several dozen a day.

Q. Dean Keyes, please review exhibit 1 for identification. Can you identify it?

A. Yes.

Q. What is it?

A. This is a document I received containing a string of e-mails.

Q. Can you identify the domain name in the sender field?

A. Yes, "@chase.edu" is our school. In fact, I use the same domain, as do all of my colleagues and employees. We have used it for many years.

Q. Do you recognize "LEllison?"

A. Yes.

Q. How do you recognize LEllison?

A. I have worked with Dean Ellison and we have communicated by e-mail in the course of academic affairs for many years. As such, and based on university protocol of using a first initial and last name in faculty e-mail, I recognize it as my colleague Dean Ellison.

Q. Could you describe what you see in the subject field for this e-mail?

A. Yes. It has the term "FD" followed by a colon, which indicates that Dean Ellison was sending me an e-mail he had received from someone else. The subject of that e-mail was "Professor Rogers's ancient studies class."

Q. Please describe the contents of the e-mail itself.

A. Dean Ellison wrote a note to me: "This is the third complaint about Professor Rogers's inappropriate touching of students." Below that is a copy of the e-mail, showing his e-mail address as the recipient. That e-mail contains the complaint of improper conduct.

Q. And what address is shown for the sender of that e-mail addressed to Dean Ellison?

A. In the "sender" field for that e-mail, there's an address: KWein001@ Chase.edu.

Q. What if any significance does that e-mail address have for you?

A. I recognize it as the e-mail account of a Chase College student. You see, faculty, staff, and administrator e-mail addresses have our first initial followed by our entire last name. Student e-mail addresses have the first letter of the student's first name, followed by the first four letters of the student's last name, followed by a three-digit number.

## *Comment*

An e-mail or e-mail string must be properly authenticated in order to be admitted into evidence. Courts have struggled with e-mail authentication because of the possibility of unauthorized users obtaining entry to e-mail accounts: "[a]n unauthorized person may be able to obtain access to an unattended computer. Moreover, a document or database located on a networked-computer system can be viewed by persons on the network who may modify it." *Lorraine v. Markel American Insurance Co.*, 241 F.R.D. 534, 548 (D. Md. 2007) (quoting 5 JACK B. WEINSTEIN & MARGARET A. BERGER, WEINSTEIN'S FEDERAL EVIDENCE § 900.01[4][a] (Joseph M. McLaughlin ed., Matthew Bender 2d ed. 2014). *See ATS International Services, Inc. v. Kousa International, LLC*, 2014 WL 1745004 (D. Md. 2014) (business e-mails containing information showing the origin of the transmission and identifying the employer-company may be sufficient to authenticate an e-mail under Fed. R. Evid. 902(7)). E-mail can be authenticated in several different ways; the recipient's address, the sender's address, and the contents of an e-mail are all useful authentication techniques. In *Lorraine*, the district court for the District of Maryland discussed e-mail authentication options extensively: "An e-mail message's distinctive characteristics, including its 'contents, substance, internal patterns, or other distinctive characteristics, taken in conjunction with circumstances' may be sufficient for authentication. . . . E-mails may even be self-authenticating. Under Rule 902(7) labels or tags affixed in the course of business require no authentication." *Lorraine*, 241 F.R.D. at 554. However, the *Lorraine* court cautioned that "[t]he sending address in an e-mail message is not conclusive, since e-mail messages can be sent by persons other than the named sender." *Id.*[1]

Because of the possibility of e-mails being sent fraudulently, it is best to have a witness with personal knowledge authenticate the e-mail or e-mail chain: "authentication requires testimony from a person with personal knowledge of the transmission or receipt to ensure its trustworthiness." *Id.* (quoting WEINSTEIN at § 900.07[3][c]; *but see United States v. Safavian*, 435 F. Supp. 2d 36, 40 (D.D.C. 2006) (allowing e-mails to be authenticated by circumstantial evidence alone).

Chain e-mails can present hearsay difficulties as well. Often chain e-mails will be admitted under the hearsay exception for business records. *See* Fed. R. Evid. 803(6). However, some courts are reluctant to allow e-mails and chain e-mails to be considered under that exception. Several courts have discussed e-mail chains in the context of the business records exception. *See, e.g., Lorraine v. Markel American Ins. Co.*, 241 F.R.D. 534, 572 (D. Md. 2007). In analyzing the ruling in another case, *State of New York v. Microsoft*, No. Civ. A. 98-1233, 2002 WL 649951 (D.D.C. April 12, 2002), the *Lorraine* court neatly summed up the difficulty with chain e-mails and the business records exception:

The court was particularly careful in analyzing the hearsay issues associated with e-mail chains involving multiple employees of the same employer. It held that to establish a proper foundation, the proponent would have to show that when the source of the information related in the e-mail is someone other than the maker of the e-mail, that the source, the maker, "as well as every other participant in the chain producing the record are, acting in the regular course of [the] business. . . . [I]f the source of the information is an outsider, Rule 803(6) does not, by itself, permit the admission of the business record." *Lorraine*, 241 F.R.D. at 572 (quoting *New York v. Microsoft*, 2002 WL 649951, at *14).

If the source of the information is an outsider, then the outsider's statements would have to fall within some other exception for the document

---

1. Under some circumstances, the production of a document, such as an e-mail, may serve as sufficient authentication at trial. *See, e.g.,* Grimm, Hon. Paul W.; Ziccardi, Michael V. Esq.; and Major, Alexander W. Esq. (2009) "Back to the Future: Lorraine v. Markel American Insurance Co. and New Findings on the Admissibility of Electronically Stored Information," Akron Law Review: Vol. 42: Iss. 2, Article 2.

to be admissible. Similarly, in *Rambus Inc. v. Infineon Tech.*, AG, 348 F. Supp. 2d 698 (E.D. Va. 2004), the court noted that "[t]o satisfy Rule 803 (6) each participant in the chain which created the record—from the initial observer-reporter to the final entrant—must generally be acting in the course of the regularly conducted business.

> . . . If some participant is not so engaged, some other hearsay exception must apply to that link of the chain." *Id.* at 706–07. Other courts are notably more lenient with regard to the admissibility of chain e-mails: "While the defendant is correct that earlier e-mails that are included in a chain—either as ones that have been forwarded or to which another has replied—may be altered, this trait is not specific to e-mail evidence. It can be true of any piece of documentary evidence. . . . The possibility of alteration does not and cannot be the basis for excluding e-mails as unidentified or unauthenticated as a matter of course." *United States v. Safavian*, 435 F. Supp. 2d 36, 40–41 (D.D.C. 2006). The *Lorraine* court ultimately concluded that "some courts will require the proponent of electronic business records or e-mail evidence to make an enhanced showing in addition to meeting each element of the business records exception . . . others will be content to view electronic business records in the same light as traditional 'hard copy' records."

*Lorraine*, 241 F.R.D. at 574.

For the purposes of a privilege log, most courts require that each separate e-mail communication in a string e-mail be identified, and only the parts of the e-mail string that are actually privileged can be withheld. *Muro v. Target Corp.*, 243 F.R.D. 301 (N.D. Ill. 2007), *aff'd in part, rev'd in part*, 250 F.R.D. 350, 7th Cir. *aff'd on other grounds*, 580 F.3d 485 (2009). *In re Universal Service Fund Telephone Billing Practices Litig.*, 232 F.R.D. 669 (D. Kan. 2005) (Rule 26(b) (5) requires that each communication be identified in a privilege log; therefore, chain e-mails cannot merely be listed as one single communication); *Barton v. Zimmer, Inc.*, No. 1:06-CV-208, 2008 WL 80647 (N.D. Ind. Jan. 7, 2008).

In *Universal*, the court rejected the defendants' argument that e-mail chains were similar in nature to conversations and thus should be treated as one communication: "[T]he obvious and unavoidable byproduct of the rule advanced by [the defendants] would be stealth claims of privilege which, by their very nature, could *never* be the subject of a meaningful challenge by opposing counsel or actual scrutiny by a judge; this, in turn, would render Fed. R. Civ. P. 26(b)(5) a nullity." 232 F.R.D. at 673. The *Universal* court, like other courts that have tackled this issue, was concerned with the likelihood that e-mail chains that parties claim are privileged actually contain both privileged and unprivileged e-mails; allowing parties to list the e-mail chains as one communication without first identifying each individual e-mail would prevent the other party from being able to view information it was entitled to. *Id.* The *Universal* court, therefore, quickly distinguished e-mail chains from other types of conversations:

[E]-mail strands may span several days, which in and of itself makes them quite different from a meeting or a conversation. . . . [T]he individuals receiving or being copied on the e-mails within a strand may and usually do vary; . . . e-mail may be sent or copied to an individual or group of individuals who are not part of the attorney-client relationship, thus waiving the privilege . . . [O]ne e-mail within a strand in which counsel are senders, recipients, or being copied may contain entirely factual and thus non-privileged information, while another e-mail within the same strand may quite clearly seek or render legal advice. *Id.*

The *Muro* court voiced a similar concern to that of the *Universal* court, explaining that the privilege log needed to contain enough information so the court could determine which parts of the e-mail strand were privileged and could be withheld and which were not: "Without more information, the plaintiff and the court cannot determine whether each individual who participated in the communication is sufficiently identified with the corporation such that his or her participating in the communication did not compromise its confidentiality." *Muro*, 243 F.R.D. at 308.

Counsel should be aware that e-mail chains also present a higher than usual risk of inadvertent disclosure because of the ease with which many different e-mails can "piggyback" onto others. A simple click of the mouse and an e-mail string with privileged communications can be forwarded to non-privileged parties, resulting in a waiver of privilege. *See* PAUL W. GRIMM, CHARLES S. FAX & PAUL MARK SANDLER, DISCOVERY PROBLEMS AND THEIR SOLUTIONS 95-104 (2d ed. 2009).

## F. ESI: Social Media

In a murder case the defendant denies being in the State of Maryland at the time of a murder that was committed in Baltimore. The police print out on their office computer a page from the Facebook account of the defendant's girlfriend, Ms. Janice George. The Facebook page reflects a message ostensibly from the defendant to the girlfriend stating that he enjoyed being with the girlfriend at her Baltimore home on the same day that the murder was committed. The girlfriend is not available to testify.

To prove that the defendant was lying about being out of town, prosecutors wish to introduce Ms. George's Facebook page.

### Prosecutor:

Q. Please introduce yourself to the jury.

A. My name is James Stewart.

Q. Who is your current employer?

A. The Baltimore City Police Department.

Q. What is your position with the police department?

A. I am a homicide detective.

Q. Detective Stewart, please review Exhibit 1 for identification. Can you identify it?

A. Yes.

Q. What is it?

A. This is a printout of the page from the Facebook account of Ms. Janice George, the girlfriend of the defendant in this case.

Q. How do you know that this is a page from Ms. George's Facebook account?

A. The Facebook account contains detailed biographical information concerning Ms. George, includes her photograph, describes her relationship with the defendant, and has a detailed account of her activities over the past several years.

Q. Do you see a message dated November 1, 2013, purporting to be a message from the defendant to Ms. George?

A. Yes.

Q. Do not read the content of the message at this time. However I invite your attention to the sender's identification as Bear.

Q. What significance does the use of the nickname "Bear" have for you?

A. "Bear" is the nickname that the defendant uses with his friends and associates. In addition, the word "Bear" is followed by a drawing of a bear cub. I recognize this drawing as identical to the drawing of a bear cub that the defendant uses in his e-mail correspondence that I have previously examined. In addition, I have personally seen the same bear cub design that the defendant has tattooed on his right arm.

Q. How did you come to obtain the Defendant's e-mails?

A. The defendant previously voluntarily provided me with printouts of several dozen of his e-mails, all of which he signed with the nickname "Bear" and which included the drawing of the bear cub.

**Prosecutor:** I move into evidence the Facebook page of Ms. Janice George.

**Defense Counsel:** Objection. How do we know that that Mr. Ryan, the defendant, really did author the e-mail? Someone else could have written and sent it. The document has not been properly authenticated.

**Court:** Overruled. I am satisfied that the Government has met its burden of authentication. It is within the province of the jury to assess and weigh the evidence presented by the Government to determine whether it was the defendant, rather than another who created the Facebook page in question. Although there is a line of cases requiring the Government to eliminate the likelihood that another user could have created the message at issue, my view is that the Government has satisfied its burden of proof, and the jury can make its own determination.

**Prosecutor:** Please read the message.

A. "Mary, I had a great time being with you earlier today and really enjoyed seeing the great job you have done redecorating your apartment here in Baltimore. Love, Bear."

## *Comment*

The requirement of authentication is a condition precedent to admitting evidence, including social media evidence like the girlfriend's Facebook page in the example. Rule 901 of the Federal Rules of Evidence governs the authentication of evidence and provides, in pertinent part: "To satisfy the requirement of authenticating or identifying an item of evidence, the proponent must produce evidence sufficient to support a finding that the item is what the proponent claims it is." FRE 901(a). Rule 901 "does not definitively establish the nature or quantum of proof that is required preliminarily to authenticate an item of evidence." *United States v. Vayner*, 769 F.3d 125 (2d Cir. 2014), quoting *United States v. Sliker*, 751 F.2d 477, 499 (2d Cir. 1984). The "proof of authentication may be direct or circumstantial." *United States v. Al-Moayad*, 545 F.3d 139, 172 (2d Cir. 2008). A document can be authenticated by "distinctive characteristics of the document itself, such as its appearance, contents, substance, internal patterns, or other distinctive characteristics, taken in conjunction with the circumstances." *Id.* at * 3, quoting, *United States v. Maldonado-River*a, 922 F.2d 934, 957 (2d Cir. 1990).

Social media has been defined as "forms of electronic communications. . . through which users create online communities to share information, ideas, personal messages, and other content (as videos)." Honorable

Paul W. Grimm, et al., Authentication of Social Media Evidence, 36 Am. J. Trial Advoc., 433, 434 (2013). "Through these sites, users can create a personal profile, which usually includes the user's name, location, and often a picture of the user." *Parker v. State*, 85 A. 3d 682, 685 (Del. 2014). The task of authenticating social media evidence arises from the fact that "many users also create fake user profiles." *Id.*, n.17, citing Katharina Krumbholz et al., Fake Identities in Social Media: A Case Study on the Sustainability of the Facebook Business Model, 4 J. Service Sci. Res. 175, 177 (2012) (noting that 5 percent to 6 percent of registered Facebook accounts are fake accounts). As the Supreme Court of Delaware recently noted in *Parker*, 85 A. 3d at 685–86:

> On many sites such as Facebook or Twitter, a user will post content—which can include text, pictures, or videos—to that user's profile page delivering it to the author's subscribers. Often these posts will include relevant evidence for trial, including party admissions, inculpatory or exculpatory photos, or online communication between users. But there is a genuine concern that such evidence could be faked or forged, leading some courts to impose a high bar for the admissibility of such social media evidence. Other courts have applied a more traditional standard, "determining the admissibility of social media evidence based on whether there was sufficient evidence of authenticity for a reasonable jury to conclude that the evidence was authentic." This approach recognizes that the risk of forgery exists with any evidence and the rules provide for the jury to ultimately resolve issues of fact.

(Quoting Grimm, et al., *supra*, at 441 (collecting cases)).

In his seminal, 100 page opinion in *Lorraine v. Markel America Ins. Co.*, 241 F.R.D. 534, 73 Fed. R. Evid. Serv. 446 (D. Md. 2007), Judge Grimm stated that in order for ESI, including social media evidence, to be admissible, it must be: (1) relevant, (2) authentic, (3) not hearsay or admissible under an exception to the rule barring hearsay evidence, (4) an original or duplicate, or admissible as secondary evidence to prove its contents, and (5) its probative value must outweigh its prejudicial effect. *See also State v. Gibson*, 2015 WL 1962850 (Ohio, 2015).

With respect to authentication of social media and other ESI, Judge Grimm and his co-authors state in their article, Authentication of

Social Media Evidence, 36 Am. J. Trial Advoc., 433, 458, that "[a] trial judge should admit the evidence if there is plausible evidence of authenticity produced by the proponent of the evidence and only speculation or conjecture—not facts—by the opponent of the evidence about how, or by whom, it 'might' have been created. Too many courts that considered authenticity of social media evidence completely overlooked this important distinction and, in doing so, made questionable rulings excluding evidence that should be admitted."

Judge Grimm points out that "[a] litigant may authenticate social media evidence ... by use of Rules 901 and 902" of the Federal Rules of Evidence." *Id.* at 461. As Judge Grimm and his co-authors explain, the most helpful methods of authentication of social media evidence under Rules 901 and 902 include the following: (1) under Rule 901(b)(1), calling a witness, including but not limited to a custodian for the social media site, with personal knowledge that a social media "screen shot" was created by the witness, who would testify that the social media posting was indeed that of the witness; (2) under Rule 901(b)(3), calling a computer forensic expert to authenticate the social media evidence; (3) under Rule 901(b)(3), having the fact finder "authenticate social media evidence when shown an example of a posting that is known to have been made by the person that you contend authored the posting by comparing it to a posting of unknown authenticity" (*id.* at 468); (4) under Rule 901(b)(4), showing that the "distinctive circumstances or characteristics" of the social media posting, including "any distinguishing language, abbreviations, slang, punctuation, use of emoticons, nick names, content that was uniquely known by the person you claim is the author, internet address, date, and any other factors that are unique to the person that you claim authored it" (*id.* at 469–70); (5) calling a witness with personal knowledge "to explain how the social media evidence was created or, alternatively, is an expert qualified" to opine that the social media posting is authentic; (6) in the case of official, government websites, using Rule 902(5) to show that the website information constitutes a self-authenticating "official publication" (*id.* at 472); and using Rule 902(6), under which social media sites that are online versions of "newspapers and periodicals" may be self-authenticating (*id.* at 472).

As noted, courts have diverged in establishing standards for authenticating social media evidence, with some courts applying a higher standard than others. The higher standard for social media authentication is best exemplified by the Maryland Court of Appeals' decision in *Griffin v. State*, 419 Md. 343, 19 A.3d, 415 (2011). There, the State sought to introduce a post from the MySpace profile of Jessica Barber, the defendant's girlfriend, stating, "snitches get stitches." *Id.*, 19 A.3d at 418, 423. In order to prove that the post was written by Barber, the State sought to authenticate the evidence using the picture of Barber, coupled with her birth date and location, which were displayed on her MySpace profile. The State did not ask Barber to authenticate the page on the witness stand or introduce electronic records definitively showing that Barber had authored the post.

The Maryland Court of Appeals held that the State failed to properly authenticate Barber's post and thus did not adequately link both the profile and the "snitches get stitches" posting to Barber. The Court explained that the trial court "failed to acknowledge the possibility or likelihood that another user could have created the profile in issue or authored the 'snitches get stitches' posting." *Id.* at 423. Thus, to properly authenticate social media posts, the Court held that the admitting party should either (1) ask the purported creator if she created the profile and the post, (2) search the internet history and hard drive of the purported creator's computer "to determine whether that computer was used to originate the social networking profile and posting in question," or (3) obtain information directly from the social networking site to establish the appropriate creator and link the posting in question to the person who initiated it. *Id.* at 427–28. "Several courts have followed the reasoning of *Griffin* out of the concern that social media evidence could be a fake, a digital alteration of an alleged creator's profile, or a posting by another using the alleged creator's profile." *Parker*, 85 A.3d at 686. *See, e.g., St. Clair v. Johnny's Oyster & Shrimp, Inc.*, 76 F.Supp. 2d, 773, 773–74 (S.D. Tex. 1999); *People v. Beckley*, 85 Cal. App. 4th 509, 110 Cal. Rptr. 3d 362, 367 (2010); *State v. Eleck*, 130 Conn. App. 632, 23 A.3d 818, 825 (2011); *Commonwealth v. Williams*, 456 Mass. 857, 926 N.E. 2d 1162, 1172–73 (2010). *See also Sublet v. State*, 442 Md. 632, 113 A.3d 695 (2015), where the Court of Appeals of Maryland adopted a standard for determining authentication of social media evidence. The standard for authentication is one that depends on "a context-specific determination": whether there is sufficient proof for a reasonable juror to conclude that the proof of authenticity is satisfied. *See also United States v. Vayner*, 769 F.3d 125 (2d Cir. 2014).

"The alternative line of cases is best represented by a Court of Criminal Appeals of Texas case, *Tienda v. State* [358 S.W. 3d 633 (Tex. Crim. App. 2012)]." *Parker*, 85 A.3d at 686. In *Tienda*, the State introduced into evidence the names and account information associated with three MySpace profiles that tended to indicate the defendant's knowledge of or responsibility for a murder. Several of the posts complained about the author's electronic monitor, which the defendant wore prior to trial. On appeal, the defendant argued that the State did not properly authenticate the MySpace profile or the individual posts to attribute them to the defendant. The Court explained that "the best or most appropriate method for authenticating electronic evidence will depend upon the nature of the evidence and the circumstances of the particular case." *Tienda*, 358 S.W. 3d at 639. This could include "direct evidence from a witness with personal knowledge, . . . comparison with other authenticated evidence, or . . . circumstantial evidence." *Id.* at 638. Rather than imposing a requirement that the proponent prove that the social media evidence was not fraudulent, the Texas Court explained that the standard for determining admissibility is whether "a jury could reasonably find [the] proffered evidence authentic." *Id.*

> Ultimately, the Texas Court found that the State had sufficiently authenticated the defendant's MySpace posts and pictures. The Court explained that the combination of facts—including photos, contextual references to the defendant's life, and the posts about his ankle monitor—was circumstantial evidence "sufficient to support a finding by a rational jury that the MySpace pages that the State offered into evidence were created by the [defendant]." Further, the Court explained that it was the province of the jury to assess and weigh the evidence presented by the State to determine whether it was the defendant, rather than some unidentified conspirators or fraudsters, who created and maintained the MySpace pages. Courts in Arizona and New York have followed the rationale of *Tienda v. State.* The premise of the Texas approach is that the jury—and not the trial judge—ultimately resolves any factual issue on the authentication of social media evidence.

*Parker*, 85 A.3d at 687, citing, *State v. Assi*, 212 WL 3580488, at *3 (Ariz. Ct. App. Aug. 21, 2012); *People v. Valdez*, 201 Cal. App. 4th 1429, 135 Cal. Rptr. 3d 628, 633 (2011); *People v. Clevenstine*, 68 A.D. 3d 1448, 891 N.Y.S. 2d 511, 514 (2009). In adopting the *Tienda* standard for admissibility of social media evidence, the *Parker* court stated: "Notably, this approach has been praised by Judge Paul Grimm, District Court Judge for the District of Maryland, and his colleagues in their recent article, *Authentication of Social Media Evidence.*"

Accordingly, the *Parker* court concluded that social media evidence should be subject to the same authentication requirements as any other evidence. "The requirement of authentication or identification as a condition precedent to admissibility is satisfied by evidence sufficient to support a finding that the matter in question is what its proponent claims" under Delaware Rule of Evidence 901(a), which tracks Fed. R. Evid. 901(a). While noting the concern that social media evidence could be falsified, the *Parker* court concluded that the existing evidence rules provide appropriate framework for determining its admissibility. The court held that a proponent of social media evidence may use any form of authentication available, including witness testimony, corroborative circumstances, distinctive characteristics, or descriptions and explanations of the technical process or system that generated the evidence in question, in order to authenticate a social media post. Applying this standard, *Parker* held that the social media post was sufficiently authenticated. The court noted that the substance of the Facebook post referenced the fight that occurred between the defendant and the victim. Although the post did not mention the victim by name, it was created on the same day after the altercation and referenced a fight with another woman. The victim's testimony provided further authenticating evidence. She testified that she viewed the defendant's post through a mutual friend. Thereafter, the victim "shared" the post and published it on her own Facebook page. "Collectively, this evidence was sufficient for the trial court to find that a reasonable juror could determine that the proffered evidence was authentic. The trial court did not abuse its discretion in admitting Parker's Facebook post." 85 A.3d at 688.

In *United States v. Castillo*, 409 F. App'x 250 (11th Cir. 2010), the district court admitted a MySpace photograph at trial, concluding that the website was probative of the defendant's possession of the gun charged in the indictment, namely an AR-15, which was depicted in the MySpace photograph. The Eleventh Circuit affirmed the trial court's decision to admit the evidence.

In *Commonwealth v. Amaral*, 941 N.E. 2s 1143 (Mass. Ct. App. 2011), the prosecutor introduced e-mails between the defendant's account and that of an undercover officer posing as a 15-year-old girl. The e-mails included plans to meet at a specific time and place, the defendant's telephone number, and defendant's photograph. The Court of Appeals affirmed the trial court's decision to admit the evidence, stating that while "[m]ere identity of name is not sufficient to indicate an identity of [a] person," other confirming facts such as the defendant's picture and phone number were sufficient to authenticate the e-mails.

In *Purdy v. Massachusetts*, 945 N.E. 2d 442 (Mass. 2011), the defendant tried to exclude e-mails that were sent from an account that resembled the defendant's name. Friends of the defendant knew that the defendant had used this account, and e-mails from the account were later discovered by police on a hard drive belonging to the defendant. Despite the defendant's claim that other persons used the account, the court found that the circumstances substantially corroborated the defendant as the author of the e-mails.

An e-mail address alone that resembles that a person's name will be insufficient for authentication, in and of itself, but it may be a factor to be weighed by the court. Other factors such as detailed signature blocks or unique speech patterns may lead a court to find that e-mails were properly authenticated. For example, in *United States v. Hassan*, 742 F.3d 104 (4th Cir. 2014), the two defendants were convicted of terrorism-related crimes. The prosecutors presented Facebook pages, YouTube videos, and other online videos that were posted by the defendants. The defendants' Facebook pages were presented in the form of "screenshots" taken at various times, which provided information relating to the defendants including their biographical information, photographs, and links to the relevant YouTube videos.

In *Dickens v. State*, 927 A.2d 32 (Md. 2007), the Maryland Court of Appeals upheld the trial court's admission of text messages, offered for the purpose of showing that the sender had threatened his estranged wife over a period of time before murdering her. Applying Maryland's authentication of evidence rule, the court held that the messages were sufficiently authenticated by circumstantial evidence: two of the messages were sent contemporaneously with defendant's criminal activities, and referred to defendant's wife, son, and their wedding vows, which indicated that the defendant sent the text messages. *See also Carpenter v. State*, 196 Md. App. 212, 9 A.2d 99 (2010).

In contrast, in cases where the communications do not contain distinctive characteristics, the courts may require expert testimony or additional corroborating evidence for authentication. For example, in *Commonwealth v. Williams*, 926 N.E. 2d 1162 (Mass 2010), the Massachusetts Supreme Judicial Court held that the proponent of evidence from a MySpace account had shown only that the evidence came from a particular profile page, but not from a specific person.

Once the trial judge makes a preliminary determination that evidence is authentic, the evidence is presented to the jury, and the jury decides how to weigh any further concerns about the authenticity and veracity of the evidence, including matters raised on cross-examination. For example, in *People v. Clevenstine*, 891 N.Y.S. 2d 511 (N.Y. App. Div. 2009), the court said that the possibility that a third party had accessed the defendant's social network account was a question appropriately left for the jury. That is, the court recognized that a person could take an image from an unrelated website, copy it, and then post it on another person's social media profile page. Under *Clevenstine*, the possibility that a social media page could have been "hacked" goes to the weight of the evidence, not its admissibility.

A lawyer attempting to authenticate Facebook or other social media evidence should consider taking measures to address the possibility that a third party hacked the account. In *Connecticut v. Eleck*, 23 A.3d 818 (Conn. App. Ct. 2011), the court determined that the prosecutor did not properly authenticate the Facebook messages at issue, where the defendant agreed that the messages originated from his account, but provided evidence that his account might have been hacked. *Eleck* emphasized that the proponent needs to negate the defendant's contention that someone hacked his account in order to authenticate the content. *See also Sublet v. State*, 442 Md. 632, 113 A.3d 695 (2015); *Boyd v. State*, 2015 WL 1955570 (Miss. Apr. 30, 2015).

Consider hiring a "digital notary" to authenticate social media evidence and internet-based content. A digital notary attests to the authenticity of a digital item as it is reflected at a particular date and time. In simple terms, digital notaries "seal" a digital item with specialized software in order to preserve the integrity of the item and digitally date and time-stamp the item. Digital notaries perform a wide variety of services, including the authentication of social media content; internet postings; digital photographs; and text messages or instant messages. *See, e.g.,* United States District Court for the District of Maryland's "Suggested Protocol for Discovery of Electronically Stored Information (ESI)" at p. 21 http://www.mdd.uscourts.gov/news/news/esiprotocol.pdf (The Court's Protocol recommends the use of a digital notary for the production of native electronic files.). The uses of digital notaries are only limited by the creativity of the attorney involved.

Finally, the use of social media evidence can create ethical dilemmas and pitfalls for lawyers. In 2012, the ABA House of Delegates issued proposals that addressed the ethical duties of lawyers who use social media.

For example, social media profiles and posts could constitute advertising and could violate restrictions applicable to traditional forms of lawyer advertising. Lawyers may not list themselves as "experts" or "specialists" unless the lawyer is appropriately certified as a specialist. Lawyers should not assume that they can "friend" judges or jurors. They should avoid social media communications with represented parties, and lawyers should not provide specific legal advice on a social media network, because the lawyer's communications could create an attorney-client relationship with readers, or impermissibly disclose privileged information.

A lawyer may not create a false social media profile in order to mask his or her identity and use the false identity to review another person's website or profile. A lawyer reviewing social media to perform juror research must be aware that an automated notice may be sent to the juror identifying the name of the person viewing the juror's social media account. A lawyer may view or monitor the social media profile of a juror, provided that there is no communication with a juror. Viewing the public portion of a social media profile is permitted as long as there is no automatic message sent to the account owner of such viewing . But this is a murky area. Many public social media profiles register the identification of the viewer. It is recommended that before counsel view the public portion of a juror's web page that counsel seek permission from the judge, and even ask the judge to advise the jury that the lawyers may be looking at their web page and that it is proper for them to do so. Counsel should also consider familiarizing themselves with applicable ethical guidelines. In the event the lawyer learns from a social media site of possible juror misconduct, the lawyer must promptly bring the matter to the court's attention.

## G. ESI: SOCIAL MEDIA—FORENSIC EXAMINER

In a murder case, Defendant James Ryan, denies being in the State of Maryland at the time of a murder that was committed in Baltimore. The police retain a forensic examiner to authenticate a public Facebook page that purportedly belongs to Defendant's girlfriend, Ms. Janice George. The public Facebook page reflects a message ostensibly from Defendant Ryan to the girlfriend stating that he enjoyed being with the girlfriend at her Baltimore home on the same day that the murder was committed. The girlfriend is not available to testify.

To prove that Defendant Ryan was lying about being out of town, prosecutors wish to introduce Ms. George's Facebook page.

Out of the presence of the jury, the prosecutor calls to the stand a certified computer forensic examiner, Steve Stern. After the witness is qualified as an expert (*see* Chapter 7.A. *infra*), counsel questions the witness as follows:

### Prosecutor:

Q.  As a qualified computer forensic examiner, do you have any particular expertise in examining computers to determine whether particular pages such as those on Facebook are authentic?

A.  Yes.

Q.  Let me show you Exhibit 1 marked for identification, and ask if you can identify it for us?

A.  Yes, this is a "screen shot" that I forensically collected that purports to be the public Facebook web page of Ms. Janice George.

Q.  Does the screen shot contain a true and accurate representation of what purports to be Ms. George's Facebook web page?

A.  Yes it does. Exhibit 1 accurately represents what was available on the Internet at the Facebook web site in November 2013.

Q.  How can you be sure that you are correctly identifying what purports to be Ms. George's public Facebook web page in your screen shot?

A.  I used an automated forensic collection tool to gather the screen shot or copy of the Facebook web page identified as belonging to Ms. George. Importantly, the tool also captured the metadata for the Facebook web page, which provides information that helps verify its authenticity. I then independently verified the Facebook page content and confirmed that the page contained several years of photographs that appear to be Ms. George. The "About" section of the web page contains information that correctly matches Ms. George's birthday, cell phone, work history, and school history.

Q.  Mr. Stern please explain the chain of custody you maintained between the capture of the Facebook web page.

A.  My forensic tool establishes a defensible chain of custody through several functions. First, the software calculates and stores a unique MD5 hash value for each individual social media item and it is maintained from capture to export. Automated logging and reports are generated. Key metadata are captured through deeply integrated APIs written by Facebook. Unlike self collection which stores the information without HASH values in HTML files that can be easily modified, my forensic tool stores the data in an encrypted database and maintains the original time stamps which protects the integrity of the chain of custody from collection through analysis.

Q. Has this forensic tool been used in other litigation matters, and accepted as forensically sound by other courts?

A. Yes, I have used this forensic tool in other matters and it has been accepted by Federal and State courts throughout the United States.

Q. Does the Facebook web page purported to belong to Ms. George contain a post dated November 1, 2013 between a person identified as "Bear" and Ms. George?

A. Yes.

Q. Please do not read the content of the November Facebook post at this time. What significance does the use of the name "Bear" have for you?

A. It is my understanding that "Bear" is an alias used by Defendant Ryan. It is also my understanding that Ms. George is Defendant Ryan's girlfriend. I have reviewed e-mail messages both sent to and received by Defendant Ryan. In communications addressed to Defendant Ryan at his personal e-mail address, friends and family members routinely refer to the Defendant as "Bear." E-mail messages sent by Defendant Ryan contain a signature block including the Defendant's first name, followed by the nickname "Bear" in quotes and the Defendant's last name. His signature block also contains a GIF image of a bear cub, which is identical to the bear cub tattoo that can be seen on the Defendant's right forearm in the profile picture on the Facebook page, which has the same user ID and user name found in the metadata of the post, and also contains a picture of Defendant Ryan.

Q. How did you come to obtain the Defendant's e-mails?

A. Using forensically-sound tools and techniques, I collected e-mail from the cellular phone taken by police from Defendant Ryan's pocket at the time of his arrest. The electronic serial number (ESN) and phone number of the phone matched the ESN and phone number assigned to Defendant Ryan's cellular telephone account by his carrier.

Q. Did you find any information regarding a Facebook account loaded on the phone?

A. Yes, I found a Facebook application that was configured to log in using Defendant Ryan's e-mail address. I was also able to determine that his Facebook user ID and username matched the Facebook profile used to create the November 1, 2013 post in question.

Q.  Mr. Stern, please walk us through how you came to the conclusion that Defendant Ryan did in fact make the post on November 1, 2013.

A.  After gathering the data in the method I described before, I examined metadata for the creation time and determined that the post was created at 9:00 p.m. GMT which converts to 4:00 p.m. EST and 5:00 p.m. EDT. I also examined the modified time to see that the post was not modified or changed in anyway after the creation date. I then examined the application field of the post which determines whether the post was made from an iPhone, Android, or other social media application. The metadata field shows that the post was made from an iPhone application which means that the Facebook app was installed on an iPhone. Next, I determined that the user id and name matches over 100 other posts from the same user name and id. This means that the person that made this post had to have done so using the exact same account id that was discovered on the iPhone that is owned and controlled by Defendant Ryan. Based on the combination of these various fields and consistency with other posts made before and after the post in question, absent any viable evidence or explanation otherwise, I conclude that there is substantial and consistent evidence to conclude that Defendant Ryan likely made these posts from Mr. Ryan's iPhone, on November 1, 2013 at 4:00 p.m. EST.

Q.  How can you be sure that you are correctly identifying what purports to be Defendant's Ryan's post on Ms. George's public Facebook web page?

A.  I examined the post in question and the underlying data supplied by Facebook. Facebook creates a unique ID for each post. First, I determined the unique ID of the poster/author of a Facebook item known as the user_ID as well as the user_name for the post. I also gathered the created_time and updated_time of the post. For comparison, I gathered these same fields from other posts before and after the post at question in this case. In each case, the Facebook user ID and name matched.

**Prosecutor**:  I offer Exhibit 1 for identification into evidence as the Government's Exhibit 1.

**Defense Counsel**: Objection on the basis of the failure of the Government to produce sufficient evidence of authenticity of the Facebook web page and the November post on the web page. How do we know that Mr. Ryan, the Defendant, really did author the Facebook post and that this is really Ms. George's Facebook page? Someone else could have created a Facebook page claiming to be Ms. George, or posted claiming to be "Bear." The images in the report purporting to be Ms. George's Facebook web page have not been properly authenticated.

**Court:** Overruled. I am satisfied that the Government has met its burden of authentication. It is within the province of the jury to assess and weigh the evidence presented by the Government to determine whether it was Ms. George who created the Facebook web page, and whether Defendant Ryan, rather than another, created the Facebook post in question. Although there is a line of cases requiring the Government to eliminate the likelihood that another user could have created the message at issue, my view is that the Government has satisfied its burden of proof, and the jury can make its own determination.

Q. Mr. Stern, please read the Facebook post, dated November 1, 2013, between Ms. George and Defendant Ryan.

A. "Mary, I had a great time being with you earlier today and really enjoyed seeing the great job you have done redecorating your apartment here in Baltimore. Love, Bear."

## Comment

As discussed in the comment to Section F, *supra,* the requirement of authentication is a condition precedent to admitting evidence, including social media evidence like Ms. George's public Facebook page in the example above. Rule 901 of the Federal Rules of Evidence governs the authentication of evidence and provides, in pertinent part: "To satisfy the requirement of authenticating or identifying an item of evidence, the proponent must produce evidence sufficient to support a finding that the item is what the proponent claims it is." FRE 901(a). "[E]vidence may be authenticated in many ways. . . [and] the type and quantum of evidence necessary to authenticate a web page will always depend on the context." *United States v. Vayner*, 769 F.3d 125, 133 (2d Cir. 2014). *Vayner*, and the cases that will likely follow, remind us that "evidence derived from the Internet required 'greater scrutiny' than authentication of any other record." *United States v. Ulbricht*, 79 F. Supp. 3d 466, 488 (S.D.N.Y.

2015), quoting *Vayner,* 769 F.3d at 131 n.5). *See also Sublet v. State,* 442 Md. 632, 113 A.3d 695 (2015).

Note in this example that the Government's expert witness provided ample direct and circumstantial evidence that: (i) the Facebook web page actually existed on the Internet on November 1, 2013, (ii) that the Facebook page appeared to belong to Ms. George, and (iii) that the post was linked to the Defendant. If one wishes to link a specific person to the creation of a web page, under *Vayner,* there must be sufficient direct or circumstantial evidence that indeed that person actually created the page or was responsible for its contents. *Vayner,* 769 F.3d at 130. The Court of Appeals for the Second Circuit, in *Vayner,* explained "[h]ad the government sought to introduce, for instance, a flyer found of the street that contained [the Defendant's] Skype address and was purportedly written or authorized by him, the district court surely would have required some evidence that the flyer did, in fact, emanate from [the Defendant]. Otherwise, how could the statements in the flyer be attributed to him?" *Id.,* quoting *United States v. Dhinsa,* 243 F.3d 635, 658–59 (2d Cir. 2001) ("[A] mere assertion of identity by a person talking on the telephone is not in itself sufficient to authenticate the person's identity. . .").

## H. LAW ENFORCEMENT REPORTS

A defendant is charged with felony murder on a federal reservation. The crucial evidence against the defendant was the decedent's wife's identification of defendant as the assailant. Defense counsel wishes to introduce the police report to develop inconsistencies between the wife's description of the assailant moments after the incident and her testimony in court. The wife initially indicated to the police that the robbery occurred at 7:00 p.m., although she testified in court that the robbery occurred at 6:00 p.m. The wife also reported to the police that the assailant was approximately 5 feet 8 inches tall. The defendant is 5 feet 3 inches. She testified in court that she had observed the defendant in the neighborhood prior to the incident, although she reported the opposite to the police at the time of the incident.

### Defense Counsel:

Q. Officer, would you state your name please?
A. James Stone.

Q. And where are you now employed?

A. Federal Bureau of Investigation.

Q. How long have you been employed by the FBI?

A. Twenty years.

Q. Directing your attention to August 5, 2014, did you have occasion to report to the scene of a homicide?

A. Yes, I did.

Q. Where?

A. 1413 Highlander Road.

Q. Can you explain to us the circumstances of your being called to that location?

A. I received a radio dispatch that a shooting and robbery had occurred. I immediately drove to that location from a point approximately two and a half miles away.

Q. What did you do upon arriving at the scene?

A. I conducted a routine investigation.

Q. What did your investigation consist of?

A. Interviewing witnesses, inspecting the crime scene to see if there was any physical evidence left by the assailant or assailants, and I called for the crime lab.

Q. When you arrived at the scene, who, if anyone, was present?

A. When I entered the bar I saw three people. One woman stated that she was the wife of the decedent, and two other individuals approached and indicated that they had been entering the bar when two people ran out.

Q. Did you obtain any statements from these individuals?

A. Yes.

Q. Did you record these statements as part of your report?

A. Yes.

Q. Do you have a copy of your report with you?

A. Yes.

**Defense Counsel:** We would like to have the agent's report marked as Defense Exhibit No. 1 for identification.

Q. Was this report prepared in the regular course of business?

A. Yes.

Q. Was it in the regular course of business for police officers to prepare records such as these?

A. Yes.

Q. When did you prepare this report?

A. Within minutes after I arrived at the scene.

Q. And when was that?

A. 7:30 p.m.

Q. And when did the incident occur?

A. At approximately 7:15 p.m.

Q. We offer Defense Exhibit No. 1 for identification in evidence.

Q. Referring to your report, did Mrs. Smith, the wife of the decedent, give you a description of the assailant?

A. Yes, she did.

Q. What description did she give?

A. The assailant was approximately 5 feet 8 inches or 5 feet 9 inches with long stringy hair and a mustache.

Q. Did Mrs. Smith indicate that the robbery occurred at a particular time?

A. Yes, she did.

Q. What did she tell you?

A. She said the robbery occurred at 6:00 p.m.

Q. Did Mrs. Smith indicate to you whether she had ever seen the assailant prior to the incident?

A. She indicated and I noted in the report that she had never seen the assailant before the incident.

## Comment

Considered as business records, police offense reports, law enforcement agency reports, and similar records are admissible in a criminal case when offered by a defendant to support a defense. *See United States v. Angulo-Hernandez*, 565 F. 3d 2 (1st Cir. 2009) (State Department's certificate proving it complied with Maritime Drug Law Enforcement Act by obtaining consent from flag nation to enforce laws of the United States against those aboard ship was admissible; certificate was relevant to the jurisdictional issue before the court, was admissible under the hearsay exception for public records, and was self-authenticating); *Endsley v. Luna*, 750 F. Supp.2d 1074 (C.D. Cal. 2010), affirmed 473 F. App'x.745 (9th Cir. 2012) (exception to prohibition on hearsay for reports of public offices or agencies applied to facts contained in document created by Department of Justice in anticipation of potential litigation with State of California to seek remedies for pattern and practice of conduct that violated constitutional and federal statutory rights of persons with mental illness who were served in public institutions, and thus facts were admissible in civil rights action brought by civilly committed person alleging that implementation of model violated his rights under due process clause, although its legal conclusions were not admissible); *United States v. Versaint*, 849 F.2d 827, 830–32 (3d Cir. 1988); *United States v. Smith*, 521 F.2d 957 (D.C. Cir. 1975); *Virgin Islands v. Peterson*, 131 F. Supp. 2d 707, 712 (D.V.I.), *aff'd*, 281 F.3d 220 (3d Cir. 2001).

The prosecution is usually prohibited from introducing police offense reports in evidence because of the right of the defendant under the confrontation clause to insist on having witnesses against him appear in court and testify. *Palmer v. Hoffman*, 318 U.S. 109 (1943). *See Crawford v. Washington*, 541 U.S. 36, 68 (2004) ("Whatever else the term [testimonial] covers, it applies at a minimum to prior testimony at a preliminary hearing, before a grand jury, or at a former trial; and to police interrogations."); *United States v. Smith*, 521 F.2d 957 (D.C. Cir. 1975); *United States v. Burruss*, 418 F.2d 677 (4th Cir. 1969); *United States v. Felix*, 467 F.3d 227, 236 (2d Cir. 2006) (autopsy reports are "reports kept in the course of a regularly conducted business activity"); *United States v. Weiland*, 420 F.3d 1062, 1075 (9th Cir.), *cert. denied*, 547 U.S. 1114 (2006). *See also* Fed. R. Evid. 803(8)(C), which recognizes that offense reports can also be treated as public records but are not admissible against a defendant in a criminal case.

The issue that has sparked some disagreement among the circuits is whether the prosecution can introduce "matters observed by police officers and other law enforcement personnel," proscribed by Federal Rule 803(8)(B), into evidence through another hearsay exception. *See United States v. DiSantis*, 565 F.3d 354 (7th Cir. 2009) ("DiSantis's prior inconsistent statements in his police report qualified as party admissions, and the district court committed no error in instructing the jury that they could consider those statements for their truth."); *United States v. Yakobov*, 712 F.2d 20, 25 (2d Cir. 1983) (permitting the introduction of hearsay through Rule 803(10)); *United States v. Sawyer*, 607 F.2d 1190, 1193 (7th Cir. 1979), *cert. denied*, 445 U.S. 943 (1980); *United States v. Oates*, 560 F.2d 45 (2d Cir. 1977), *remanded to* 445 F. Supp. 351 (E.D.N.Y.), *aff'd*, 591 F.2d 1332 (2d Cir. 1978). *See also United States v. Ybarra*, 2000 U.S. App. LEXIS 26000, at *2 (9th Cir. Aug. 7, 2000);

*United States v. Pena-Gutierrez*, 222 F.3d 1080, 1087 (9th Cir.), *cert. denied*, 531 U.S. 1057 (2000); *United States v. Brown*, 9 F.3d 907 (11th Cir. 1993), *cert. denied*, 513 U.S. 852 (1994); *United States v. Smith*, 973 F.2d 603 (8th Cir. 1992); *United States v. Dancy*, 861 F.2d 77, 79 (5th Cir. 1988); *United States v. Hayes*, 861 F.2d 1225 (10th Cir. 1988); *United States v. Chavez*, 481 F.3d 1274, 1275 (10th Cir. 2007) (officer's testimony as to his observations and radio report violated the confrontation clause, but nevertheless was harmless error); *United States v. Coleman*, 631 F.2d 908, 912 (D.C. Cir. 1980); *United States v. Orozco*, 590 F.2d 789 (9th Cir.), *cert. denied*, 442 U.S. 920 (1979). *See discussion infra* Chapter 3.I. on police accident reports.

As with all business records or evidentiary writings that are admissible, items recorded in offense reports based upon hearsay are inadmissible unless covered by an appropriate hearsay exception. *See United Technologies Corp. v. Mazer*, 556 F.3d 1260 (11th Cir. 2009) ("It is well established that entries in a police report which result from the officer's own observations and knowledge may be admitted but that statements made by third persons under no business duty to report may not."). However, in this particular pattern, even if a hearsay exception were not applicable to the witness's statements, hearsay is admissible to impeach a testifying witness by a prior inconsistent statement. In this pattern, since Mrs. Smith's in-court testimony was inconsistent with the report, the defense attorney could introduce the report regardless of its hearsay contents. Prior inconsistent statements are admissible in federal court proceedings to impeach a testifying witness. *See* Fed. R. Evid. 613. Under Federal Rule of Evidence 801(d)(1), the prior inconsistent statement could even be admissible as substantive evidence. The federal rule limits the admissibility as substantive evidence of the prior statement made "under penalty of perjury at a trial, hearing, or other proceeding or in a deposition", at a "proceeding," and views the prior inconsistent statement as non-hearsay.

## I.   POLICE ACCIDENT REPORTS

A plaintiff institutes suit for negligence against a defendant, claiming damages for injuries sustained during an automobile collision. One of the issues at trial is whether the street where the collision occurred had two or three northbound lanes. Counsel for the plaintiff calls the police officer who reported to the accident scene to demonstrate that the defendant was incorrect when he testified that there were three northbound lanes.

## Plaintiff's Counsel:

Q. Officer, what time did you arrive at the scene of the incident?

A. Around 10:30 a.m., ten minutes after the collision.

Q. How did you learn of the collision?

A. Radio report.

Q. What did you do upon arriving at the scene?

A. I conducted a routine investigation.

Q. What did your investigation consist of?

A. I interviewed the drivers of both automobiles, inquired as to whether there were any witnesses and there were none, and prepared a report of the incident.

Q. Does your report contain a diagram of the location of the accident, as well as the positions of the automobiles after the impact?

A. Yes, it does.

Q. Who prepared that diagram?

A. I did, in my report.

Q. What was the diagram based upon?

A. Things that I personally observed.

Q. Do you have a copy of that report with you?

A. Yes.

Q. May I see it please? (Witness hands document to counsel.)

**Plaintiff's Counsel:** Please mark this police report as Plaintiff's Exhibit No. 1 for identification.

Q. With regard to this police report, Plaintiff's Exhibit No. 1 for identification, was this document prepared in the regular course of business?

A. Yes, it was.

Q. Was it in the regular course of business for police officers to prepare records such as these?

A. Yes.

Q. When did you prepare this report?

A. At the accident scene, approximately ten minutes after the accident had occurred.

**Plaintiff's Counsel:** We offer Plaintiff's Exhibit No. 1 for identification in evidence. The officer may then be questioned on the basis of the police report as follows:

Q. Officer, where did this accident occur?

A. At the intersection of Old Court Road and Reisterstown Road in Pikesville, Maryland. The accident occurred in the northbound lane of Reisterstown Road near the parking lot of Foods Corp.

Q. How many northbound lanes were there on Reisterstown Road on the day of the accident?

A. Two.

Q. Does your diagram indicate the number of northbound lanes?

A. Yes.

Q. What does your diagram show?

A. Two northbound lanes.

Q. Is your diagram accurate?

A. I drew the diagram accurately reflecting the number of lanes on the road. There were only two lanes.

Q. Would you step down and come to the blackboard and please draw for us roughly how your diagram appears on the police report?

A. On my diagram, this is just roughly how it was. (Officer sketches diagram showing only two lanes.)

## *Comment*

Police accident reports and items appearing in them that are within the personal observation of the investigating officer are admissible pursuant to Federal Rule of Evidence 803(6) (Records of Regularly Conducted Activity). *See, e.g., Ramrattan v. Burger King Corp.*, 656 F. Supp. 522 (D. Md. 1987) (police report is a business record, but portions of report containing statements of third party witnesses who were not acting "in the regular course of police business" is not admissible under FRE 803(6)); *Fogal v. Coastal Restaurant Management, Inc.*, 452 F. Supp. 2d 1286, 1298, n.10 (S.D. Ga. 2004); *Juaire v. Nardin*, 395 F.2d 373, 379 (2d Cir.), *cert. denied*, 393 U.S. 938 (1968). *See generally United States v. Warren*, 42 F.3d 647, 656 (D.C. Cir. 1994); *United States v. Snyder*, 787 F.2d 1429, 1434 (10th Cir. 1986), *cert. denied*, 479 U.S. 836 (1986); *United States v. Pazsint*, 703 F.2d 420 (9th Cir. 1983), *appeal after remand*, 728 F.2d 411 (9th Cir. 1984); *United States v. Halperin*, 441 F.2d 612 (5th Cir. 1971); *United States v. Martin*, 434 F.2d 275 (5th Cir. 1970); *United States v. Graham*,

391 F.2d 439 (6th Cir.), *cert. denied*, 390 U.S. 1035, *cert. denied*, 393 U.S. 941 (1968); *Bowman v. Kaufman*, 387 F.2d 582 (2d Cir. 1967); *Coyle v. Kristjan Palusalu Maritime Co.*, 83 F. Supp. 2d 535, 544 (E.D. Pa. 2000), *aff'd without op.*, 254 F.3d 1077 (3d Cir. 2001). As is true of all business records, items based on hearsay and conclusions of the officer are not admissible through accident reports unless by way of some independent exception to the hearsay rule. An officer's notations of the length of skid marks and the dimensions of the road would be admissible within the police report. However, the officer's notation as to who is responsible would not be admissible, unless the officer saw the accident or unless a statement placing responsibility upon one driver or the other satisfied a hearsay exception. *See Rassoulpour v. Washington Metro. Area Transit Auth.*, 826 F.2d 98 (D.C. Cir. 1987); *United States v. Smith*, 521 F.2d 957 (D.C. Cir. 1975); *Moore v. Indehar*, 514 F.3d 756, 761 (8th Cir. 2008); *United States v. Vigneau*, 187 F.3d 70 (1st Cir. 1999). *See also* Fed. R. Evid. 805, which governs the admissibility of hearsay within hearsay.

Diagrams contained within police reports are also admissible if they reflect items within the personal observation of the investigating officer.

Federal Rule of Evidence 803(8) exempts from the hearsay rule factual findings in investigative reports when offered in civil cases or against the government in criminal cases. However, to what extent an inadmissible hearsay declaration or conclusion presented without first-hand knowledge in a police accident report will be admitted under the public records and report doctrine will depend on the extent to which the trial judge deems the statement and full report reliable. *See United States v. Versaint*, 849 F.2d 827 (3d Cir. 1988); *United States v. Hardin*, 710 F.2d 1231, 1237 (7th Cir.), *cert. denied*, 464 U.S. 918 (1983); *Thibodeaux v. Wellmade*, 2014 WL 1329802 (E.D. La. 2014); *Ellis v. Int'l Playtex, Inc.*, 745 F.2d 292 (4th Cir. 1984); *United States v. Stone*, 604 F.2d 922, 925 (5th Cir. 1979); *United States v. Orozco*, 590 F.2d 789, 793–94 (9th Cir.), *cert. denied*, 442 U.S. 920 (1979); *Baker v. Elcona Homes Corp.*, 588 F.2d 551 (6th Cir. 1978), *cert. denied*, 441 U.S. 933 (1979). *See also* 5 JACK B. WEINSTEIN ET AL., WEINSTEIN'S FEDERAL EVIDENCE § 803.10 (2d ed. 2014).

Consider the following situation: In a police offense report, the officer recorded that, based upon his investigation determining skid marks measuring 100 feet, the operator of one motor vehicle was traveling at an excessive speed. This conclusion would be inadmissible under the business records

exception of Federal Rule of Evidence 803(6). However, this report is arguably admissible pursuant to Federal Rule of Evidence 803(8).

## J.  PUBLIC RECORDS

### i.  *Certified*

The government prosecutes a rape case. The victim testifies that after
she was raped, her assailant asked her not to be angry and stated that he
had been convicted of assault with intent to rape in 2000 and had been
paroled in 2004. The defendant sought to establish that he was not the
assailant, since he had not been paroled in 2004. The government, on rebuttal, desires to introduce in evidence a certified copy of the records of
the Department of Parole and Probation of Baltimore City, which reflect
that the defendant was on parole in 2004 from a conviction of assault
with intent to rape. The records are to be offered for the limited purpose
of establishing the identity of the accused by proving he had been paroled in 2004.

> **Prosecutor:** Your Honor, before we call our next witness, the State
> would like to introduce in evidence a certified copy of the records of
> the Department of Parole and Probation of Baltimore City for the year
> 2004 insofar as they pertain to the defendant, Ron Smothers.
> **Defense Counsel:** I would object to the introduction of this document
> unless a proper foundation is established. Certainly, an officer from
> the department should be present to authenticate this record.
> **The Court:** Is this document a copy of a public record certified as a
> true copy by the custodian of the records?
> **Prosecutor:** Yes, Your Honor.
> **The Court:** Federal Rule of Evidence 803(8). The objection is over-
> ruled.

### *Comment*

Federal Rule of Evidence 803(8) provides the hearsay exception for public
records in federal court. *See Beech Aircraft Corp. v. Rainey*, 488 U.S. 153
(1988); *Ellis v. Int'l Playtex, Inc.*, 745 F.2d 292 (4th Cir. 1984); *Harlamert
v. World Finer Foods, Inc.*, 489 F.3d 767, 773 (6th Cir. 2007). The rule does
not distinguish between federal and non-federal offices, and exempts three

types of public records from the hearsay rule: (a) records of the performance of official duties; (b) reports of observations made pursuant to law as to which there was a duty to report; and (c) factual findings in investigative reports in civil cases, or, if offered against the government, in criminal cases. If a public record meets the conditions of Rule 902(4) and the requirement for contemporaneousness imposed by Rule 803(6) (Records of Regularly Conducted Activity), Rule 803(8) eliminates foundation requirements. *See* 5-803 WEINSTEIN'S FEDERAL EVIDENCE § 803.10 (2014). *See also supra* Chapter 3.I. (Police Accident Reports) and 3.B. (Business Records). Another advantage of Rule 803(8) is that it might allow in evidence hearsay statements and statements based on other than the firsthand knowledge of the recorder. *See* 5 JACK B. WEINSTEIN ET AL., WEINSTEIN'S FEDERAL EVIDENCE § 803.10 (2d ed. 2014).

The term "factual findings" is broadly construed. *See Beech Aircraft Corp. v. Rainey*, 488 U.S. 153 (1988). The rule established in *Beech* is that factual findings can include factually based conclusions or opinions. *See also Clark v. Clabaugh*, 20 F.3d 1290 (3d Cir. 1994); *Bank of Lexington & Trust Co. v. Vining-Sparks Sec. Inc.*, 959 F.2d 606 (6th Cir. 1992); *Lubanski v. Coleco Indus.*, 929 F.2d 42 (1st Cir. 1991); *Hines v. Brandon Steel Decks, Inc.*, 886 F.2d 299 (11th Cir. 1989), *on remand to* 754 F. Supp. 199 (M.D. Ga. 1991), *aff'd*, 948 F.2d 1297 (11th Cir. 1991), *cert. denied*, 503 U.S. 971 (1992); *Koonce v. Quaker Safety Prods. & Mfg. Co.*, 798 F.2d 700, 720 (5th Cir. 1986); *Ellis v. Int'l Playtex, Inc.*, 745 F.2d 292 (4th Cir. 1984); *Jenkins v. Whittaker Corp.*, 785 F.2d 720, 726 (9th Cir.), *cert. denied*, 479 U.S. 918 (1986); *In re Air Crash Disaster at Stapleton Int'l Airport*, 720 F. Supp. 1493 (D. Colo. 1989), *rev'd on other grounds*, 964 F.2d 1059 (10th Cir. 1992).

The justification for allowing opinions and conclusions into evidence when they are contained within a public record is the dual assumption that a public official will perform his or her duty properly and would not remember details independently of the record. Factors used to determine the admissibility of such opinions and conclusions include timeliness of the investigation, special skills of the official and potential motivational problems. *See supra* Chapter 3.I., relating to police accident reports; Chapter 3.D., relating to computer print-outs; and Chapters 2.A. and 2.B., for discussions of hearsay problems and firsthand knowledge problems with present recollection revived and past recollection recorded.

Federal Rule of Evidence 902(4) provides that copies of public records, books, papers, or proceedings of any agency of the government or any of its political subdivisions shall be received in evidence in any court if certified as true copies by the custodian of the record, book, paper, or proceeding, and if otherwise admissible. Public records are self-authenticating when certified by the appropriate custodian. Federal Rule of Evidence 1005 provides that if a copy that complies with Rule 902(4) cannot be obtained by exercise of reasonable diligence, then other evidence of the contents may be given.

### ii. *Uncertified*

Same facts as stated in previous pattern, except the government calls the custodian of records of the Department of Parole and Probation of Baltimore City for purposes of demonstrating that the defendant's record corresponds to that of the assailant.

### Prosecutor:

Q. Would you state your name?

A. Henry Jones.

Q. Where are you employed?

A. The Baltimore City Department of Parole and Probation.

Q. For how long have you been employed in that department?

A. For 16 years.

Q. What position do you hold within the department?

A. Custodian of Records.

Q. How long have you occupied that position?

A. For the past six months.

Q. Did you receive a subpoena to come to court today?

A. Yes.

Q. What, if anything, did the subpoena direct you to bring to court?

A. The records of Ron Smothers for the year 2004.

Q. Do you have those records, sir?

A. Yes, I do.

Q. May I please see them? (The witness hands the records to counsel.)

**Prosecutor:** May we have this document marked as Government's Exhibit No. 1 for identification?

Q. Are the records that you brought today recorded or filed in the office of the Department of Parole and Probation for Baltimore City?

A. Yes.

Q. Why does the Department of Parole and Probation of Baltimore City maintain such records?

A. Department policy requires that our office maintain complete and accurate records of each individual who has been paroled and whether or not he has complied with the conditions of parole.

Q. How do you know that these records were recorded or filed within the department?

A. As the custodian of the records, I have access to all reports and documents, and when I received your subpoena, I went to our office files and located the particular document required.

Q. Do you know who prepared the record pertaining to the defendant?

A. Yes. It has the initials A.Q. at the bottom.

Q. And what do those initials stand for?

A. Adam Quarles; he was my predecessor.

Q. Was this document prepared within the course of law, regulation, or public duty?

A. Yes, it was.

**Prosecutor:** We offer State's Exhibit No. 1 in evidence.

## *Comment*

Introduction of an uncertified public record is similar to the introduction of business records, except that in authenticating uncertified public records, counsel must establish that the record was authorized or required to be recorded or filed pursuant to law, regulation, or public duty, and that the document was in fact recorded or filed in a public office and is from the public office where items of such nature are kept. Fed. R. Evid. 901(b)(7); *United States v. Ingram*, 613 F. Supp.2d 1069 (N.D. Iowa 2009), *aff'd* 594 F.3d 972 (8th Cir. 2010); *United States v. Lock*, 425 F.2d 313 (5th Cir. 1970). Rule 901(b)(7) extends the authentication principle to include data stored electronically. *See United States v. Estrada-Eliverio*, 583 F.3d 669, 672–73 (9th Cir. 2009), *cert. denied*, 131 S. Ct. 579, 178 L.Ed 2d 423 (2010) ("FRE 901(b)(1) provides that a witness with knowledge of a document can authenticate it by testifying that it is what it is claimed to be, and FRE 901(b)(7) provides for the authentication of a public record with evidence that [a purported public record] . . . is from the public office where items of this nature are kept. A party need only make a prima facie showing of authenticity so that a reasonable juror could find in favor of authenticity or identification"), quoting *United States v. Workinger*, 90

F.3d 1409, 1415 (9th Cir. 1996). *United States v. Meienberg*, 263 F.3d 1177, 1181 (10th Cir. 2001); *United States v. Hernandez-Herrera*, 952 F.2d 342, 343 (10th Cir. 1991). *See also* 7 JOHN HENRY WIGMORE, WIGMORE ON EVIDENCE § 2158 (Chadbourn rev. ed. 1978 & Supp. 2014).

However, in light of Federal Rule of Evidence 902 providing for self-authentication of certified public documents, counsel should think twice before requiring clerks of public offices to appear in court to authenticate public records.

## K.  HOSPITAL RECORDS

The plaintiff sues Aetna Trucking Company for personal injuries suffered as a result of an automobile collision. The defendant wishes to introduce hospital records relating to a previous injury sustained by the plaintiff in an automobile accident in which she injured her lower back. The hospital records contain a statement by an orthopedic surgeon describing plaintiff's back injury resulting from the previous automobile accident. Defense counsel subpoenas the custodian of records of the hospital.

### Defense Counsel:

Q.  Please state your occupation and tell us where you work.

A.  I am the medical records custodian of Exeter Hospital in Philadelphia.

Q.  What are your duties as custodian of records?

A.  I am in charge of the keeping and filing of medical records made in the hospital.

Q.  Were you served with a subpoena to produce the hospital records of Bernice Feldapple, plaintiff in this case, who was a patient at Exeter Hospital in November of 2013?

A.  Yes.

Q.  Did you bring those records with you today?

A.  Yes.

**Defense Counsel**: Please mark these hospital records as Defendant's Exhibit No. 1 for identification.

Q.  Where did you obtain these medical records of Bernice Feldapple?

A.  In the medical records file in our hospital.

Q.  How do you know that these are the medical records of the plaintiff, Bernice Feldapple?

A. The file reflects the full name of the patient, her home address, the date she was admitted to the hospital, and the date she was discharged, and I matched this information with that contained on your subpoena.

Q. Were these records prepared in the regular course of business?

A. Yes.

Q. Was it the regular course of business for Exeter Hospital to prepare and maintain records such as these?

A. Yes.

Q. Is it the regular course of business of the hospital for the entries in these records to be made at or near the time that the matters recorded are observed?

A. Yes.

Q. Was it the regular course of business for a history of the patient's complaint to be included in the medical records?

A. Yes.

Q. Who records this history?

A. The doctor on duty when the patient comes into the receiving room.

Q. From whom does the doctor obtain the history he or she records?

A. From the patient, or if the patient is unable to communicate, from anyone else who is able to give it.

Q. Is a statement of the patient's condition on discharge ordinarily included as a part of the medical records of the hospital?

A. Yes.

Q. How is this statement prepared?

A. The physician takes notes while giving the patient a final examination, reviews the chart to the extent necessary and, as promptly as possible, dictates a statement of the patient's condition, and this statement is typed by the secretary.

Q. When is this report made?

A. Either right after the examination or at the end of the day.

**Defense Counsel:** We offer Exhibit No. 1 for identification in evidence. (Subsequently, during the course of direct examination of the plaintiff's doctor, the following questions are asked.)

Q. Doctor, please refer to the discharge report. Does the report describe Bernice Feldapple's condition at the time of her discharge?

A. There is a statement that she was in poor condition.

Q.  What is the date of that discharge summary?

A.  June 15, 2014.

Q.  Does the discharge summary indicate why Mrs. Feldapple was admitted to the hospital?

A.  No.

Q.  Does the history contained in the hospital records indicate the reason Mrs. Feldapple was admitted to the hospital?

A.  The history reflects that she was admitted to the hospital following a motor vehicle accident.

Q.  What treatment, if any, is described in the records?

A.  A disc operation, among other things.

Q.  Who noted in the discharge summary that Mrs. Feldapple underwent surgery for her disc?

A.  The operating surgeon made this statement in his operative report, and this was transferred to the discharge summary by Dr. Smock.

### *Comment*

The introduction of hospital records follows basically the same form as the introduction of business records pursuant to Federal Rule of Evidence 803(6). *See Petrocelli v. Gallison*, 679 F.2d 286 (1st Cir. 1982); *Rivers v. Union Carbide Corp.*, 426 F.2d 633 (3d Cir. 1970); *Harris v. Smith*, 372 F.2d 806 (8th Cir. 1967); *Thomas v. Hogan*, 308 F.2d 355 (4th Cir. 1962); *Turner v. Inland Tugs Co.*, 689 F. Supp. 612 (E.D. La. 1988). Hospital records clearly fall within the business record doctrine.

*See Wilson v. Zapata Off-Shore Co.*, 939 F.2d 260 (5th Cir. 1991); *Bondie v. Bic Corp.*, 947 F.2d 1531 (6th Cir. 1991); *Stull v. Fuqua Indus. Inc.*, 906 F.2d 1271 (8th Cir. 1990); *United States v. Hershenow*, 680 F.2d 847 (1st Cir. 1982); *United States v. Sackett*, 598 F.2d 739 (2d Cir. 1979); *Ascher v. Gutierrez*, 533 F.2d 1235 (D.C. Cir. 1976); *Rivers v. Union Carbide Corp.*, 426 F.2d 633 (3d Cir. 1970); *Picker X-Ray Corp. v. Frerker*, 405 F.2d 916 (8th Cir. 1969); *Thomas v. Hogan*, 308 F.2d 355 (4th Cir. 1962); *United States v. Grant*, 2002 CAAF LEXIS 370, at *9 (C.A.A.F. Apr. 18, 2002).

However, the complete hospital record is not always admissible. Federal Rule of Evidence 803(4) and case law require for admissibility that statements in hospital records be pathologically germane to the physical condition that caused the patient to be hospitalized. *Stull v. Fuqua Indus., Inc.*, 906 F.2d 1271, 1273 (8th Cir. 1990) (holding that the explanation that the accident occurred when the plaintiff "jumped off the mower" was inadmissible); *Forbis v. McGinty*, 292 F. Supp. 160, 162 (D. Me. 2003). A statement is pathologically germane if it has a significant bearing upon or relation to the disease or injury that one suffers. Thus, in the pattern examination, the surgeon's statement appearing in the hospital record about plaintiff's previous disc operation would be admissible. *See Cook v. Hoppin*, 783 F.2d 684, 690 (7th Cir. 1986).

Counsel appearing in federal court are not required to adhere to the distinction made in some state courts between the treating and non-treating physician. Federal Rule of Evidence 803(4) eliminated the distinction made by case law between the treating physician and the so-called examining physician. *See* 7 MICHAEL H. GRAHAM, HANDBOOK OF FEDERAL EVIDENCE § 803.4 (7th ed. 2012). *See also O'Gee v. Dobbs Houses, Inc.*, 570 F.2d 1084 (2d Cir. 1978); *Conte v. AGF Assoc.*, 1999 U.S. Dist. LEXIS 21482, at *6 (D. Conn. Sept. 3, 1999).

If statements as to how an accident occurred appear within the hospital records, they are inadmissible unless they are part of the history taken by hospital personnel and are necessary information to aid in treatment or diagnosis. History includes physical and mental background as well as present condition. Thus, for example, that part of the hospital record is admissible which reveals that the patient was in an automobile accident, but the particulars of how the accident occurred are not admissible unless the details of the occurrence are themselves pathologically germane. *See McCollum v. McDaniel*, 2002 U.S. App. LEXIS 4825, at *12 (4th Cir. Mar. 25, 2002); *Bucci v. Essex Ins. Co.*, 393 F.3d 285, 298 (1st Cir. 2005); *Rock v. Huffco Gas & Oil Co.*, 922 F.2d 272 (5th Cir. 1991); *United States v. Pollard*, 790 F.2d 1309 (7th Cir. 1986), *overruled on other grounds, United States v. Sblendorio*, 830 F.2d 1382 (7th Cir. 1987); *United States v. Nick*, 604 F.2d 1199 (9th Cir. 1979); *Walker v. West Coast Fast Freight, Inc.*, 233 F.2d 939 (9th Cir. 1956); *Lewis v. Velez*, 149 F.R.D. 474 (S.D.N.Y. 1993); *Virgin Islands v. Morris*, 191 F.R.D. 82, 85–87 (D.V.I. 1999). Statements identifying the perpetrator of sexual abuse are admissible as statements made for diagnosis and treatment under Federal Rule of Evidence 803(4). *See, e.g., United States v. Yazzie*, 2002 U.S. App. LEXIS 4504, at *9 (9th Cir. Mar. 12, 2002); *United States v. Gabe*, 237 F.3d 954, 957–58 (8th Cir. 2001); *United States v. King*, 2000 U.S. App. LEXIS 18108, at *21 (10th Cir. July 26, 2000), *cert. denied*, 531 U.S. 1028 (2000); *United States v. Tome*, 61 F.3d 1446 (10th Cir. 1995); *United States v. Yazzie*, 59 F.3d 807 (9th Cir. 1995); *United States v. Yellow*, 18 F.3d 1438 (8th Cir. 1994); *United States v. Joe*,

8 F.3d 1488 (10th Cir. 1993), *cert. denied*, 510 U.S. 1184 (1994); *United States v. Cherry*, 938 F.2d 748 (7th Cir. 1991); *United States v. Kappell*, 418 F.3d 550, 556 (6th Cir.) (extending the principle to include statements made to psycho-therapists and social workers), *cert. denied*, 547 U.S. 1056 (2006); *United States v. Peneaux*, 432 F.3d 882, 893–94 (8th Cir.), *cert. denied*, 127 S. Ct. 42 (2006); *Willingham v. Crooke*, 412 F.3d 553, 562 (2005).

The foundation for hospital records need not always consist of testimonial evidence. In some instances the court may properly conclude from the circumstances and the nature of the documents involved that they were made in the regular course of business. *See generally United States v. Johnson*, 971 F.2d 562, 570–72 (10th Cir. 1992); *Itel Capital Corp. v. Cups Coal Co.*, 707 F.2d 1253, 1259 (11th Cir. 1983); *United States v. Hing Shair Chan*, 680 F. Supp. 521 (E.D.N.Y. 1988); *Zenith Radio Corp. v. Matsushita Elec. Indus. Co.*, 505 F. Supp. 1190, 1236 (E.D. Pa. 1980), *aff'd in part, rev'd in part*, 723 F.2d 238, *rev'd on other grounds*, 475 U.S. 574 (1986).

## L.  MEDICAL AND REPAIR BILLS, PAID AND UNPAID

A plaintiff institutes suit against a defendant for personal injuries sustained as a result of slipping on a banana peel in the defendant's supermarket. Plaintiff's special damages included a $1,500 medical bill from Dr. Willard Applejack, an orthopedic surgeon. The plaintiff's attorney introduces the orthopedic surgeon's medical bill as an exhibit for identification during the plaintiff's testimony and follows up with the orthopedic surgeon to establish the document's competency to be admitted in evidence.

### Plaintiff's Counsel Examining Plaintiff:

Q.  You testified that from September 1, 2013 to October 14, 2014, you visited Dr. Willard Applejack on sixteen occasions for purposes of medical examinations and treatment?

A.  Yes, that's right.

Q.  How many bills did you receive?

A.  Sixteen bills.

Q.  What were these bills for?

A.  For the examinations, tests, and treatment that I received.

Q.  Does this treatment rendered by Dr. Applejack include the physical therapy about which you testified?

A.  No, that was separate. I received separate bills from the therapist for those.

**Plaintiff's Counsel**: Please mark these documents as Plaintiff's Exhibit No. 13(a) through (p) for identification.

Q. Mrs. Smith, I show you Plaintiff's Exhibit No. 13(a) through (p) for identification and ask you if you recognize these documents?

A. Yes, they are the medical bills I received from Dr. Applejack.

Q. What was the total amount of those medical bills?

A. $1,500.

### Plaintiff's Counsel:

Q. Dr. Applejack, I show you Plaintiff's Exhibit No. 13(a) through (p) for identification and ask you if you recognize these documents, sir?

A. Yes, these documents represent medical bills that I sent to Mrs. Smith after each of her numerous visits to my office and after rendering various treatments to her.

Q. Can you tell us whether these bills are fair and reasonable?

A. Yes, they are, in my opinion, fair and reasonable.

Q. Were the services that you rendered to Mrs. Smith necessary?

A. Yes. Because of the serious injury that she sustained, the services that I rendered were necessary.

**Plaintiff's Counsel**: If the Court please, we offer Plaintiff's Exhibit No. 13(a) through (p) in evidence.

### *Comment*

In federal court, sufficient foundation exists for admissibility of medical bills and repair bills if there is testimony that the service was necessary, provided there is no evidence to show that the charges were unreasonable. *Collins v. Kibort*, 143 F.3d 331, 337 (7th Cir. 1998). *See generally DePonte v. Kamada*, 42 F.3d 1399 (9th Cir. 1994); *United States v. Lebovitz*, 669 F.2d 894, 901 (3d Cir. 1982), *cert. denied*, 456 U.S. 929 (1982); *In re 222 Liberty Assoc. v. Eesco Elec., Inc.*, 101 B.R. 856, 864 (E.D. Pa. 1989).

The practice for marking and introducing exhibits varies from court to court. Consult local rules. For example, Local Rule 106.2(h) of the Rules of the U.S. District Court for the District of Maryland requires the listing of all documents and records, other than impeachment documents, to be offered in evidence by each side. The rule also requires the parties to agree on which documents may be offered in evidence without the usual authentication. This requirement may be satisfied by attaching an exhibit list to the pretrial order. Though documents may be stipulated as authentic, they may be inadmissible on other grounds. The stipulation as to authenticity does not preclude objections for any other reason. Authentication stipulations avoid the time-consuming process of identification.

Local Rule 106.7(a) requires counsel, prior to trial, to attach tags to all exhibits. These tags may be obtained from the clerk. At least one business day before trial, counsel are required to file and serve upon each other two copies of an exhibit list. Prior to trial, in accordance with Local Rule 106.7(b), counsel are required to meet, review each other's proposed exhibits, and make the same available for copying.

Local Rule 107.5(b) provides that, unless counsel requests that an exhibit be marked for identification only, whenever an exhibit number is first mentioned by counsel during examination of a witness at trial, the exhibit will be considered admitted into evidence unless opposing counsel asserts an objection.

Federal Rule of Civil Procedure 26(a)(3) provides that the parties shall disclose, at least 30 days before trial, an identification of all trial exhibits. Within 14 days, a party may serve objections. Failure to object timely may result in a waiver.

Each judge uses his or her own format for pre-numbering exhibits. Generally, pre-numbering means that prior to trial, counsel tags with a number each document intended to be used during the course of the litigation. Pre-numbering does not mean that the exhibits have been marked for identification. This could require the clerk to retain the documents, even if they were never used during the trial by counsel.

# *Best Evidence or Original Document Problems*

# 4

## A. DUPLICATES—PHOTOGRAPHIC COPIES

Henry Witherspoon instituted suit against Ti-Con Pool Company for breach of contract resulting from the alleged failure of the pool company to properly install a swimming pool. The contract price was $15,000, and after full payment was made and the pool installed, cracks appeared in it. The pool company denies receiving notice that the pool was cracked until six weeks before the suit was filed, two and a half years after the appearance of the cracks.

Witherspoon's attorney intends to introduce a copy of a letter Witherspoon received from the president of the pool company. The original letter was sent to a subcontractor, requesting the subcontractor to investigate the plaintiff's claim that cracks appeared in the lining of the pool. The copy received by Witherspoon was dated three months after the alleged cracking appeared and would disprove the pool company's claim that it had no knowledge of the cracking.

### Plaintiff's Counsel:

Q. When did you first observe cracks appearing in the pool?

A. Approximately two or three weeks after we filled the pool with water.

Q. When did you first advise the pool company of this problem?

A. The day after I saw the first cracks appear, I telephoned the main office and told the secretary to have Mr. Winston, the president of the company, call me immediately.

Q. Did you ever attempt to contact him through other means than telephone?

A.  Yes, I wrote to him.

Q. Do you remember when you wrote?

A. No, I don't remember the exact date, but I do remember it was sometime during the month of June 2014.

Q. What response, if any, did you receive?

A. I received a copy of a letter that the president of the pool company wrote to one of his subcontractors, requesting that he drop by my house to investigate the report of cracks.

Q. Do you have with you now the copy of the letter?

A. Yes, I do.

Q. May I see it, please? (Witness hands the documents to counsel.)

**Plaintiff's Counsel:** Please mark this document as Plaintiff's Exhibit No. 4 for identification.

Q. Can you identify what is marked as Plaintiff's Exhibit No. 4 for identification?

A. Yes, I can. It is the copy of the letter I received from the president of the pool company.

Q. Do you know where the original of that letter is?

A. I presume the original document is in the possession of the sub-contractor.

**Plaintiff's Counsel**: We offer Plaintiff's Exhibit No. 4 for identification in evidence.

## Comment

The "Best Evidence Rule" stands for the principle that requires the production of the original of a document to prove the contents of that document. However, in practice, because of all the exceptions accorded by the federal rules of evidence, the rule manifests itself as a mere "preference" for the original.

Certain types of copies, such as printouts from computers, carbon copies of contracts, and prints from photographic negatives, are considered to be originals in and of themselves. Fed. R. Evid. 1001(3). Other types of copies, which are produced by methods that virtually eliminate the possibility of error, are considered duplicates. A photocopy is an example. Federal Rule of Evidence 1001(4) provides:

> A "duplicate" is a counterpart produced by the same impression as the original, or from the same matrix, or by means of photography, including enlargements and miniatures, or by mechanical or electronic recording, or by chemical reproduction, or by other equivalent technique which accurately reproduces the original.

Federal Rule of Evidence 1003 permits the admissibility of duplicates, unless a genuine question is raised about the authenticity of the document or it would be unfair to admit the duplicate in place of the original. *See United States v. Ramentol*, 410 F. App'x 236, 242 (11th Cir. 2011 (per curiam)) (duplicate was properly admitted where no genuine issue of admissibility was raised); *United States v. Milkiewicz*, 470 F.3d 390, 396 (1st

Cir. 2006); *Railroad Management Co., LLC v. CFS Lousiana Midstream Co.*, 428 F.3d 214, 220 n.3 (5th Cir. 2005); *United States v. Stewart*, 420 F.3d 1007 (9th Cir. 2005); *United States v. Bennett*, 363 F.3d 947, 953 (9th Cir.), *cert. denied*, 543 U.S. 950 (2004); *Peat, Inc. v. Vanguard Research, Inc.*, 378 F.3d 1154, 1160 (11th Cir. 2004); *United States v. Grimmer*, 1999 U.S. App. LEXIS 26218, at *4 (2d Cir. Oct. 14, 1999); *United States v. Moore*, 30 F.3d 135 (6th Cir. 1994); *United States v. Harris*, 898 F.2d 148 (4th Cir.), *cert. denied*, 497 U.S. 1030 (1990); *United States v. Patten*, 826 F.2d 198 (2d Cir.), *cert. denied*, 484 U.S. 968 (1987); *United States v. Garmany*, 762 F.2d 929 (11th Cir. 1985), *cert. denied*, 474 U.S. 1062 (1986); *United States v. Balzano*, 687 F.2d 6 (1st Cir. 1982).

Furthermore, Federal Rule of Evidence 1004 provides that other evidence of the contents of original documents is admissible when the originals have been lost or destroyed through no bad faith of the proponent, when the originals are unobtainable, when the originals are under control of the opponent and not produced after notice, or when the documents pertain to collateral matters. *E.g., Southern Union Co. v. Liberty Mut. Ins. Co.*, 581 F. Supp. 2d 120, 129 (D. Mass. 2008). Essentially, these rules restate the common law, but without recognizing "degrees" of secondary evidence. Thus, if the original document is unavailable, the proponent need not introduce the most reliable copy, and once the conditions of the rules are satisfied, the proponent may prove the contents of the writing by any secondary evidence properly admitted. *See, e.g., Nicholas v. Wal-Mart Stores, Inc.*, 2002 U.S. App. LEXIS 6206, at *13 (4th Cir. Apr. 4, 2002) (relying on transcript of missing recording); *United States v. Jimenez*, 256 F.3d 330, 348 (5th Cir. 2001) (relying on evidence of custom and regular business practice to establish existence and contents of missing business documents); *Sicherman v. Diamoncut*, 2000 U.S. App. LEXIS 3357, at *11 (6th Cir. Feb. 29, 2000) (relying on handwritten ledger sheet, computer printouts, and photocopies of adding machine tapes in place of missing inventory cards and computer records); *CP Interests, Inc. v. California Pools, Inc.*, 238 F.3d 690, 699 (5th Cir. 2001); *Dugan v. R.J. Corman Co.*, 344 F.3d 662 (7th Cir. 2003); *Telecom Technical Services, Inc. v. Rolm Co.*, 388 F.3d 820, 830 (11th Cir. 2004).

Consider also that photocopies of business records and public records are admissible under certain circumstances. *See supra* Chapter 3.B., 3.J.

## B. USE OF SECONDARY EVIDENCE

The same facts apply as stated in previous pattern, except Witherspoon's attorney intends to introduce a manually prepared duplicate of the original letter Witherspoon received from the president of the pool company disputing that cracks appeared. The letter negates the defense. The original letter was destroyed by fire.

### Plaintiff's Counsel:

Q. When did you first observe cracks appearing in the pool?

A. Approximately two to three weeks after we filled the pool with water.

Q. When did you first advise the pool company of this problem?

A. The day after I saw the first cracks appear, I telephoned the main office and told the secretary to have Mr. Winston, the president of the company, call me immediately.

Q. Did you ever attempt to contact him through other means than telephone?

A. Yes, I wrote to him.

Q. Do you remember when you wrote?

A. No, I don't remember the exact date, but I do remember it was sometime during the month of June 2014.

Q. Did you receive a reply?

A. Yes, I did. I received a letter from Mr. Winston.

Q. Do you have that letter with you in court today?

A. No, sir, I do not.

Q. Can you tell us where that letter is now?

A. It was destroyed in a fire.

Q. What kind of fire?

A. There was a fire in my office and some of my records were destroyed. This letter was among those documents destroyed.

Q. Did you ever have occasion to make any copies of the original letter?

A. Yes, I did.

Q. When and for what reason?

A. After I received the letter at the office, I requested that my secretary retype the document. I wanted to bring a duplicate home to my wife, keep the original in my office files, and our Xerox machine was broken.

Q. Do you have that duplicate with you in court now?

A. Yes, I do.

**Plaintiff's Counsel:** Please mark this typed copy as Plaintiff's Exhibit No. 4 for identification.

Q. Is this copy of the letter now marked as Plaintiff's Exhibit No. 4 for identification an exact copy of the letter that you initially received?

A. Yes, it is.

**Plaintiff's Counsel:** We offer this typed copy in evidence as Plaintiff's Exhibit No. 4.

### Comment

Since the federal rules have abandoned the hierarchy of "degrees" of secondary evidence, if Mr. Witherspoon testified that the original letter he received from the pool company was destroyed by fire, he could establish the contents of the original letter by oral testimony rather than by introducing the duplicate, even if he had the copy available. *See infra* Chapter 4.C. Also, if Witherspoon knew of the existence of the copy of the destroyed letter, which the defendant maintained in his files, the federal rules would not require him to attempt to obtain it by summons or notice to produce. *See* Fed. R. Evid. 1004; *Banks v. Mitsubishi Motors Credit of America, Inc.*, 435 F.3d 538, 540 (5th Cir. 2005); *United States v. Stewart*, 420 F.3d 1007, 1022 (9th Cir. 2005); *Chester v. DirecTV, L.L.C.*, 607 F. App'x 362 (5th Cir. 2015); *Burt Rigid Box Inc. v. Travelers Prop. Cas. Corp.*, 126 F. Supp. 2d 596, 609 (W.D.N.Y. 2001), *aff'd in part, rev'd in part*, 302 F.3d 83 (2d Cir. 2002); *United States v. Dudley*, 941 F.2d 260 (4th Cir. 1991), *cert. denied*, 502 U.S. 1046 (1992); *United States v. Gerhart*, 538 F.2d 807 (8th Cir. 1976); *Davis v. Baron's Creditors Serv. Corp.*, 2001 U.S. Dist. LEXIS 19008, at *6 (N.D. Ill. Nov. 20, 2001); *Takeall v. Pepsico, Inc.*, 809 F. Supp. 19 (D. Md. 1992), *aff'd*, 14 F.3d 596 (4th Cir. 1993), *cert. denied*, 512 U.S. 1236 (1994); *Seiler v. Lucasfilm, Ltd.*, 613 F. Supp. 1253 (N.D. Cal. 1984), *aff'd*, 797 F.2d 1504 (9th Cir.), *opinion superseded by* 808 F.2d 1316 (9th Cir. 1986), *cert. denied*, 484 U.S. 826 (1987).

## C. USE OF SECONDARY EVIDENCE ESTABLISHING THE CONTENTS OF A DOCUMENT BY ORAL EVIDENCE

The same facts apply as stated in the previous pattern except counsel seeks to establish the content of the destroyed document by oral testimony.

### Plaintiff's Counsel:

Q. When did you first observe cracks appearing in the pool?

A. Approximately two to three weeks after we filled the pool with water.

Q. When did you first advise the pool company of this problem?

A. The day after I saw the first cracks appear, I telephoned the main office and told the secretary to have Mr. Winston, the president of the company, call me immediately.

Q. Did you ever attempt to contact him through other means than telephone?

A. Yes, I wrote to him.

Q. Do you remember when you wrote?

A. No, I don't remember the exact date, but I do remember it was sometime during the month of June 2014.

Q. Did you receive a reply?

A. Yes, I did. I received a letter from Mr. Winston.

Q. Do you have that letter with you in court today?

A. No, sir, I do not.

Q. Can you tell us where that letter is now?

A. It was destroyed in a fire.

Q. What kind of fire?

A. There was a fire in my home and some of my records were destroyed. This letter was among those documents.

Q. Do you recall the contents of that letter?

A. Yes, I do.

Q. What were the contents of the letter?


**Defense Attorney:** Objection.

**The Court:** What's the basis of the objection?

**Defense Attorney:** Before Mr. Witherspoon testifies as to the contents of the original letter, a proper foundation should be established to demonstrate that no copies of that letter are available.

**The Court:** Not under Rule 1004 of the Federal Rules of Evidence. Under this rule, there is no demarcation between degrees of secondary evidence. Even if a photographic copy does exist, the rules do not require that the copy be introduced in evidence as long as the original is lost or destroyed or not obtainable. Objection overruled. You may answer the question.

The letter was from Mr. Winston, president of the pool company. He wrote that he would send one of his subcontractors to my home to investigate my complaints that cracks had appeared in the swimming pool that he installed two months ago.

## Comment

Under the federal rules, when the original is unavailable, any form of secondary evidence is admissible as long as it meets other evidentiary requirements. Fed. R. Evid. 1004. *See, e.g., United States v. O'Connor*, 650 F.3d 839, 862 (2d Cir. 2011) (testimony as to contents of a handwritten note properly admitted where original of a writing has been lost or destroyed, other than as a result of bad faith on the part of the proponent of the evidence); *Simas v. First Citizens' Fed. Credit Union*, 170 F.3d 37, 51 (1st Cir. 1999) ("There is no general rule that proof of a fact will be excluded unless its proponent furnishes the best evidence in his power."); *United States v. Beltre*, 1999 U.S. App. LEXIS 20056, at *5 (4th Cir. Aug. 23, 1999); *Burt Rigid Box Inc. v. Travelers Prop. Cas. Corp.*, 126 F. Supp. 2d 596, 609 (W.D.N.Y. 2001), *aff'd in part, rev'd in part*, 302 F.3d 83 (2d Cir. 2002); *Paul Revere Annuity Ins. Co. v. Zang*, 81 F. Supp. 2d 227, 230 (D. Mass), *aff'd*, 226 F.3d 15 (1st Cir. 2000), *aff'd*, 248 F.3d 1 (1st Cir. 2001).

# Visuals—Demonstrative and Real Evidence

# 5

## A. PHOTOGRAPHS

Plaintiffs instituted a wrongful death action against defendant swimming club, which owned and operated a quarry used by the general public, upon payment of an admission fee, for swimming and sunbathing. The plaintiffs' decedent allegedly dived from a pier into the water, which was extremely shallow, and suffered a fatal skull fracture. The defendant claims that the plaintiffs' decedent dived off the side of the pier, which was blocked by a guardrail, instead of diving off the proper side, which had no guardrail. Defense counsel seeks to introduce a black and white photograph of the pier depicting the two sides and the end of the pier. On the side of the pier with the guardrail, the photograph shows a sign stating: "Caution, shallow water." A lifeguard has testified on the witness stand that she was on duty, in the lifeguard chair on Pier No. 4, at the time of the accident:

### Defense Counsel:

Q. Can you describe Pier 4 for us, Miss Smith?

A. Pier 4 was the farthest pier away from the first pier that you would see when you came onto the beach after you would pay your admission fee.

Q. Were there any railings on Pier 4?

A. There were railings on only one side of the pier, the left side facing the beach.

Q. Why were there railings on that side but not on the other?

A. On the side where the railing was located, the water was approximately three to four feet in depth, but on the other side the water was very deep.

Q. Were there any notices or signs that indicated the depth of the water?

A. Yes, on the railing side there was a sign every five feet that said, "Caution, shallow water."

**Defense Counsel:** Please mark this photograph as Defendant's Exhibit No. 12 for identification.

Q. I show you Defendant's Exhibit No. 12 for identification and ask you whether or not you can identify what is portrayed in this picture.

A. Yes, sir, I can.

Q. Please tell us what it is.

A. This is the pier that I described as Pier 4, where I sat as a lifeguard last summer.

Q. Does the photograph fairly and accurately represent Pier 4 in June, when the accident occurred?

A. Yes, it does.

**Defense Counsel:** We offer Defendant's Exhibit No. 12 for identification in evidence.

**The Court:** It will be received.

Q. May I show the photograph to the jury at this time, Your Honor?

**The Court:** You may hand it to the foreman, Counsel, and he will pass the photograph to the other jury members. (Proceedings suspended while jury examines photograph.)

### *Comment*

Photographs include still photographs, X ray films, videotapes, and motion pictures. Fed. R. Evid. 1001(2). The foundation for introducing photographs is the same in state and federal court. Photographs are admissible in the discretion of the court when the picture is shown to be a correct representation of the site, person, or object depicted. *See Zerega Ave. Realty Corp. v. Hornbeck Offshore Transp., LLC*, 571 F.3d 206 (2d Cir. 2009) (holding that trial judge properly sustained objection to admission of photograph because, while the witness identified the matter depicted, "counsel failed to follow up with the customary question as to whether the photographs fairly and accurately portrayed the area shown"); *United States v. Lawson*, 494 F.3d 1046, 1052 (D.C. Cir. 2007) (finding that "[a] photograph may be authenticated if a witness with knowledge of the scene testifies that it accurately depicts the scene it purports to represent"); *United States v. Hyles*, 479 F.3d 958, 969 (8th Cir. 2007); *Rush v. Illinois Cent. R. Co.*, 399 F.3d 705, 722 (5th Cir. 2005) (quoting Fed. R. Evid. 901(a): "authentication or identification as a condition precedent to admissibility is satisfied by evidence sufficient to support a finding that the matter in question is what its proponent claims."); *accord, United States v. Greatwalker*, 356 F.3d 908, 912 (8th Cir. 2004); *United States v. Smith*, 27 Fed. Appx. 577 (6th Cir. 2001) (unreported), *cert. denied sub nom. Hicks v. United States*, 535 U.S. 1059 (2002); *United States v. Joe*, 8 F.3d 1488, 1499 (10th Cir. 1993), *cert. denied*, 510 U.S. 1184 (1994); *Hurt v. Coyne*

*Cylinder Co.*, 956 F.2d 1319 (6th Cir. 1992); *Lubanski v. Coleco Indus., Inc.*, 929 F.2d 42, 47 (1st Cir. 1991); *Radford v. Seaboard Sys. R.R., Inc.*, 828 F.2d 1552 (11th Cir. 1987); *McEachron v. Glans*, 1999 U.S. Dist. LEXIS 21926, at *9 (N.D.N.Y. Aug. 23, 1999), *amended*, 1999 U.S. Dist. LEXIS 21928 (N.D.N.Y. Aug. 25, 1999). *Shushereba v. R.B. Indus., Inc.*, 104 F.R.D. 524, 531 (W.D. Pa. 1985). *But see American Wrecking Corp. v. Sec'y of Labor*, 351 F.3d 1254, 1262 (D.C. Cir. 2003); *United States v. Rodriguez-Pacheco*, 475 F.3d 434, 439 (1st Cir. 2007) (in child pornography cases, the prosecution must prove that the image in the photograph submitted at trial is of an actual child); *Sprynczynatyk v. General Motors Corp.*, 771 F.2d 1112, 117–18 (8th Cir. 1985), *cert. denied*, 475 U.S. 1046 (1986) (abuse of discretion to introduce a videotape of a hypnosis session because of its prejudicial effect). Often the requisite foundation is stated in these terms: that the photograph is fair and accurate, or that the photograph depicts a correct likeness of the scene it purports to represent. *Gilliam v. Foster*, 75 F.3d 881, 897 (4th Cir.), *cert. denied*, 517 U.S. 1220 (1996); *Bibbins v. Dalsheim*, 21 F.3d 13, 15 (2d Cir.), *cert. denied*, 513 U.S. 901 (1994); *United States v. Van Wyhe*, 965 F.2d 528, 532 (7th Cir. 1992); *Lubanski v. Coleco Indus., Inc.*, 929 F.2d 42 (1st Cir. 1991); *United States v. Rembert*, 863 F.2d 1023, 1027 (D.C. Cir. 1988); *Bannister v. Town of Noble*, 812 F.2d 1265, 1269–70 (10th Cir. 1987); *Saturn Mfg., Inc. v. Williams Patent Crusher & Pulverizer Co.*, 713 F.2d 1347, 1356 (8th Cir. 1983); *United States v. Stearns*, 550 F.2d 1167, 1168–69 (9th Cir. 1977); *United States v. Taylor*, 530 F.2d 639, 641 (5th Cir.), *cert. denied*, 429 U.S. 845 (1976); Gregory P. Joseph, Modern Visual Evidence § 4.02 (2014).

A witness or party can verify photographs, and it is not necessary to verify the photograph through the person who took the picture. *United States v. Rembert*, 863 F.2d 1023, 1026 (D.C. Cir. 1988); *United States v. Abayomi*, 820 F.2d 902, 908 (7th Cir. 1987), *cert. denied*, 484 U.S. 866 (1987); *United States v. Wilson*, 719 F.2d 1491, 1495 (10th Cir. 1983); *United States v. Rochan*, 563 F.2d 1246, 1251 (5th Cir. 1977). The witness must have familiarity with the subject of the photograph and so testify. *United States v. Wilder*, 526 F.3d 1, 15–16 (1st Cir. 2008) (a picture was not sufficiently authenticated by testimony from a doctor when that doctor had not taken the picture, and the only basis the doctor had for testifying that the picture was of an actual child was that it contained a high degree of anatomical correctness); *United States v. Henderson*, 68 F.3d 323, 324 (9th Cir. 1995); *United States v. Jackman*, 48 F.3d 1, 4 (1st Cir. 1995);

*United States v. Stormer*, 938 F.2d 759, 762 (7th Cir. 1991); *United States v. Wright*, 904 F.2d 403, 404 (8th Cir. 1990); *United States v. Rembert*, 863 F.2d 1023, 1026 (D.C. Cir. 1988); *United States v. Calhoun*, 544 F.2d 291, 295 (6th Cir. 1976); *United States v. Wilson*, 719 F.2d 1491, 1495 (10th Cir. 1983); *United States v. McNair*, 439 F. Supp. 103, 105 (E.D. Pa. 1977), *aff'd*, 571 F.2d 573 (3d Cir.), *cert. denied*, 435 U.S. 976 (1978).

Frequently, photographs that are taken subsequent to an occurrence will reflect changes that would cause the witness not to be able to testify that the object depicted is "correct" in its representation of the scene at the relevant time. Under these circumstances, counsel should qualify his or her question, *e.g.*, "With the exception of the telephone pole in the left-hand corner of this photograph, is this photograph, Defendant's Exhibit No. 12 for identification, a fair and accurate representation of the northwest corner of 42d Street and Taylor Avenue at the time of the accident?" If the changed condition depicted in the photograph substantially alters the identity of the original subject, the photograph might not be admissible. *See United States v. Stearns*, 550 F.2d 1167, 1170 (9th Cir. 1977); *United States v. White*, 454 F.2d 435, 438 (7th Cir. 1971), *cert. denied*, 406 U.S. 962 (1972); *Sears, Roebuck & Co. v. Penn Cent. Co.*, 420 F.2d 560, 563 (1st Cir. 1970); *Blum v. Cottrell*, 276 F.2d 689, 694 (4th Cir. 1960). However, once the court determines that a photograph is a correct likeness of what it purports to represent, differences between the actual portrayal and the photograph relate to the weight rather than the admissibility of the evidence. *Bridges v. Equitable Life Assur. Soc'y of the United States*, 1999 U.S. App. LEXIS 16282, at *4 (6th Cir. July 14, 1999); *Lubanski v. Coleco Indus., Inc.*, 929 F.2d 42, 47 (1st Cir. 1991); *Reed v. Tiffin Motor Homes, Inc.*, 697 F.2d 1192 (4th Cir. 1982); *Pritchard v. Downie*, 326 F.2d 323 (8th Cir. 1964).

Digital or electronically-generated or enhanced images may be improperly altered. Therefore, a proper foundation must be laid when offering digital evidence. In *Connecticut v. Swinton*, 847 A.2d 921 (Conn. 2004), the court held that there must be testimony by a person with some degree of computer expertise and familiarity with the imaging software. *Swinton* involved a computer-enhanced digital photographs of a bite mark on the victim's breast, and electronically-generated bite mark "overlays." The court affirmed the defendant's conviction of first degree murder, holding that a proper foundation for authentication of computer-generated or enhanced evidence involved: 1) the computer equipment is accepted in the field as standard and competent and was in good working order;

2) qualified computer operators were employed; 3) proper procedures were followed in connection with the input and output of information; 4) a reliable software program was utilized; 5) the equipment was programmed and operated correctly; and 6) the exhibit was properly identified as the output in question. The court ruled that the computer-enhanced photographs were properly admitted because they were sponsored by an expert with knowledge of the technology involved, but that the "overlay" images were improperly admitted because they were not sponsored by a person familiar with how they were made. Nevertheless, in light of the defendant's confession and other incriminating physical evidence, the court concluded that the improper admission of the Adobe Photo Shop overlays was harmless error.

It is not always appropriate to request that the jury view the photograph during the course of the trial, but counsel should consider this approach at appropriate times.

## B. VIDEO EVIDENCE

A plaintiff instituted suit against a defendant trucking company for damages allegedly sustained when the defendant's tractor-trailer collided with the plaintiff's vehicle. The plaintiff sustained lower-back injuries and testified that as a result of these injuries he was unable to participate in any athletics or household chores. The defendant engaged a professional photographer to video the plaintiff playing tennis six months after the accident. Counsel for the defendant attempts to introduce the motion pictures in evidence. He calls the photographer to the witness stand.

### Defense Counsel:

Q. What is your full name?
A. Harry Pentaquod.
Q. And with whom are you employed?
A. I am self-employed.
Q. What is your occupation?
A. I am a professional photographer.
Q. Do you take video recordings?
A. I do.
Q. Did you have occasion to take video recordings of the plaintiff, Bernard Howell?

A. Yes.

Q. Describe the circumstances.

A. You engaged me to take video recordings of Mr. Howell participating in any types of sports activities or doing any type of work outside of his home.

Q. And did you take such video recordings?

A. Yes, I did.

Q. Tell us when and the circumstances of your taking those pictures.

A. On August 18, 2014, I accompanied Mr. Dan Thoerosa, a private investigator, to the home of Mr. Howell. We arrived at 9:30 in the morning. Approximately 15 minutes after we arrived, Mr. Howell left the house, entered a 2004 Chevrolet, and proceeded to drive one mile north to the Sweetwater Tennis Courts. We followed his automobile to those tennis courts. I took my camera and equipment and positioned myself in a place where I could view the tennis courts and proceeded to take video recordings of Mr. Howell playing tennis.

Q. What type of camera did you use?

A. I used a Sony Handycam camcorder.

Q. Can you tell us what type of lens was used?

A. I used a 60X optical zoom lens.

Q. What storage medium did you use in the camcorder?

A. The camcorder stores the video recordings on a DVD disc.

Q. Was your camera in good working order that day?

A. Yes, it was.

Q. What did you do with the camera as you started taking pictures?

A. I focused the camera for the position, taking into consideration the distance and the appropriate lighting conditions.

Q. What pictures did you take that day?

A. I took pictures of Mr. Howell serving and playing tennis.

Q. How long did Mr. Howell play tennis?

A. Thirty minutes.

Q. Did you photograph all of his activity during the entire 30 minutes?

A. No, I photographed about 20 of the 30 minutes Mr. Howell was on the court.

Q. Was there anything that Mr. Howell did during the 30 minutes he was on the tennis court that you did not photograph?

A. Yes.

Q. What actions of Mr. Howell did you not photograph?

A. I stopped shooting when they changed sides of the court or had conversations with each other.

Q. After you made the recording, what did you do?

A. I removed the DVD from the camcorder and have had it in my possession since that time.

Q. And did you use a DVD player and television to view it after that?

A. Yes.

Q. And was the recording a true and accurate representation of the actions of Mr. Howell that you have testified to and that you witnessed while you were making the recording?

A. Absolutely.

Q. Did you edit in any way or cut this recording?

A. It has not been tampered with in any way.

Q. Do you have the DVD recording with you today?

A. Yes, I do.

**Defendant's Attorney**: I would like to have this film marked as Defendant's Exhibit A for identification.

Q. Sir, I show you Defendant's Exhibit A for identification and ask if this is the film that you took and have described in your testimony?

A. Yes.

**Defendant's Attorney**: I offer the film in evidence and ask that the movies be shown to the jury.

**The Court:** The ruling will be reserved subject to cross-examination by plaintiff's counsel.

## Comment

The foundation required to introduce video recordings is similar to the foundation for the introduction of still photographs. Photographs include still photographs, X ray films, videotapes, and video recordings. Fed. R. Evid. 1001(2). The foundation for introducing photographs is the same in state and federal courts. The basic testimony essential to authenticate motion pictures includes the identification of the person or place pictured, proof that the film is accurately representative of the person or place depicted, and testimony or evidence as to the circumstances of taking, developing, and projection. *See United States v. Morris*, 406 Fed. Appx. 758

(4th Cir. 2011), *cert. denied* 131 S. Ct. 3048 (2011) (affirming trial court's admission of subtitled video recordings of under cover drug sales); *Baker v. Canadian Nat'l/Illinois Central R.R.*, 536 F.3d 357, 368–69 (5th Cir. 2008) (affirming admission of surveillance videos of personal injury plaintiff); *Bannister v. Town of Noble*, 812 F.2d 1265, 1269–70 (10th Cir. 1987); *Louis Vuitton S.A. v. Spencer Handbags Corp.*, 765 F.2d 966, 973 (2d Cir. 1985); *Saturn Mfg., Inc. v. Williams Patent Crusher & Pulverizer Co.*, 713 F.2d 1347, 1356 (8th Cir. 1983); *United States v. Brannon*, 616 F.2d 413, 416–17 (9th Cir. 1980), *cert. denied sub nom. Cox v. United States*, 447 U.S. 908 (1980); *United States v. Bynum*, 567 F.2d 1167, 1171 (1st Cir. 1978); *United States v. Richardson*, 562 F.2d 476, 478–79 (7th Cir. 1977), *cert. denied*, 434 U.S. 1072 (1978); *Grimes v. Employers Mut. Liab. Ins. Co.*, 73 F.R.D. 607 (D. Alaska 1977). *See generally United States v. Patterson*, 277 F.3d 709, 713 (4th Cir. 2002); *Gilliam v. Foster*, 75 F.3d 881, 897 (4th Cir. 1996), *cert. denied*, 517 U.S. 1220 (1996); *United States v. Rembert*, 863 F.2d 1023, 1027 (D.C. Cir. 1988); *United States v. Taylor*, 530 F.2d 639, 641 (5th Cir.), *cert. denied*, 429 U.S. 845 (1976).

It is desirable, but not required, to establish the photographer's experience and qualifications and to elicit testimony as to the speed of the exposed frames per second, the type of lens used, and the distances. If the photographer is unavailable, an eyewitness can testify that the motion pictures were taken and were representative of the scene or individual depicted. *See Kortz v. Guardian Life Ins. Co.*, 144 F.2d 676 (10th Cir.), *cert. denied*, 323 U.S. 728 (1944). *See generally United States v. Rembert*, 863 F.2d 1023, 1026 (D.C. Cir. 1988); *United States v. Abayomi*, 820 F.2d 902, 908 (7th Cir.), *cert. denied*, 484 U.S. 866 (1987); *United States v. Wilson*, 719 F.2d 1491, 1495 (10th Cir. 1983); *United States v. Rochan*, 563 F.2d 1246, 1251 (5th Cir. 1977).

Opposing counsel is furnished the opportunity to voir dire the photographer or qualifying witness and to oppose the showing of motion pictures. In this pattern, plaintiff 's counsel could cross-examine the photographer to prove that while the movies were taken, the plaintiff stopped frequently to rest and constantly rubbed the lower part of his back, as if suffering discomfort. Counsel could attempt to establish that the photographer was guilty of selective photography and that the film does not fairly portray all of the relevant activity. Before the court determines that the pictures can be shown to the jury, the movies should be viewed out of the presence of the jury. In most instances, counsel is aware that his or her adversary will use movies, and the filing of a motion in limine (prior to trial) can often be a vehicle for determining whether a sufficient foundation has been established for the movies to be shown to the jury. After the movies are shown to the jury, opposing counsel has the further opportunity for re-cross-examination of the witness.

The introduction of videotape recordings is similar to the introduction of motion pictures and photographs. *See Hendricks v. Swenson*, 456 F.2d 503 (8th Cir. 1972); GREGORY P. JOSEPH, MODERN VISUAL EVIDENCE § 4.02[2] (2014). There is little difference in authentication. Videotape recordings are motion pictures made by recording both sight and sound electronically on magnetic tapes, whereas motion pictures and photographs rely on light to convey invisible images, which are then exposed or revealed through chemical processes. *See Kucharek v. Hanaway*, 714 F. Supp. 1499, 1511–14 (E.D. Wis. 1989), *rev'd on other grounds*, 902 F.2d 513 (7th Cir. 1990), *cert. denied*, 498 U.S. 1041 (1991); *United States v. Salcido*, 506 F.3d 729, 733 (9th Cir. 2007); *United States v. Zepeda-Lopez*, 478 F.3d 1213, 1222 (10th Cir. 2007); *United States v. Perez-Gonzalez*, 445 F.3d 39, 47 (1st Cir. 2006).

Videotape evidence often contains sound. Objections to narration on the basis of hearsay will usually be granted. If the narrator is available to testify and adopts the narration, the hearsay objection should be overruled. *See* Fed. R. Evid. 801 (d)(1) advisory committee's note; *United States v. McKneely*, 69 F.3d 1067, 1074 (10th Cir. 1995); *United States v. Weisz*, 718 F.2d 413, 430 n.104 (D.C. Cir. 1983), *cert. denied*, 465 U.S. 1027, *cert. denied sub nom. Ciuzio v. United States*, 465 U.S. 1034 (1984); GREGORY P. JOSEPH, MODERN VISUAL EVIDENCE § 4.02[4][a] (2014).

Videotape evidence can be offered to depict damages, demonstrations, or experiments. Consider the admissibility of a videotaped test, the results of which are offered as a predicate to the opinion of an expert, even though the test results are not offered as substantive evidence. *See Eagle-Picher Indus., Inc. v. Balbos*, 578 A.2d 228 (Md. App. 1990), *aff'd in part, rev'd in part*, 604 A.2d 445 (Md. 1992), where the court admitted a videotape of the decedent, who was comatose at the time; *United States v. Norris*, 217 F.3d 262, 270 (5th Cir. 2000), *cert. denied*, 122 S. Ct. 161 (2001); *Green v. Ford Motor Co.*, 2001 U.S. Dist. LEXIS 19883, at *3 (W.D. Va. Nov. 26, 2001); *Misener v. General Motors*, 165 F.R.D. 105, 108 (D. Utah 1996); *Datskow v. Teledyne Cont'l Motors Aircraft Prods.*, 826 F. Supp. 677, 685 (W.D.N.Y. 1993); *Culpepper v. Volkswagen of Am., Inc.*, 109 Cal. Rptr.

110, 117–18 (1973). *But see Finchum v. Ford Motor Co.*, 57 F.3d 526, 530 (7th Cir. 1995) (barring test because similarity of test to actual occurrence would lead to prejudice and confusion of the jury). *See also* GREGORY P. JOSEPH, MODERN VISUAL EVIDENCE § 4.02[4][b] (2014). It is helpful for appellate review to include a transcript of the video. *See Howe v. Varity Corp.*, 36 F.3d 746, 749 (8th Cir. 1994), *aff'd*, 516 U.S. 489 (1996); *United States v. Betancur*, 24 F.3d 73, 75 (10th Cir. 1994). *See generally Cox v. Louisiana*, 379 U.S. 536, 547 (1965); 5 LYNN MCLAIN, MARYLAND EVIDENCE: STATE AND FEDERAL § 403.5 (2d ed. 2001 & Supp. 2009). Enhanced videos can also be offered as evidence, provided there is a proper foundation. In *United States v. Seifert*, 445 F.3d 1043 (8th Cir. 2006), the court upheld the admission of a video that had been digitally enhanced by a computer program overseen by an electronic surveillance specialist. *Id.* at 1045. In upholding the introduction of the video the court explained: "The Government laid a proper foundation for the enhanced video. Although Hunter did not keep copies of the images at each stage of enhancement, he described in detail each step of that process. He explained that he did not brighten only the image of the suspect. Rather, he simultaneously brightened the image of the suspect and the surrounding area, which preserved their relative brightness." *Id.*

## C. COMPUTER ANIMATION

Plaintiff instituted suit against Health Forever, Inc. for negligent manufacturing of a heart valve. Counsel for the plaintiff seeks to introduce computer animation showing how defective heart valves can malfunction over time. The witness, Dr. Peter Hornride, is an expert in the field of cardiac transplants.

### Plaintiff's Counsel:

Q. Doctor Hornride, are you familiar with the heart valve manufactured by Health Forever, Inc., model number 401?

A. Yes, I am.

Q. What is the basis of your familiarity?

A. I have used this product in the course of treating many of my patients in need of a heart valve replacement.

Q. How many patients have you treated with this particular product?

A. Probably a total of 500 patients a year for the last four years.

Q. How was the valve used in the treatment that you gave these patients?

A. During open-heart surgery, I removed the defective heart valve from the patient and inserted and attached the artificial valve.

Q. Did you ever notice a problem with the defendant's product?

A. Yes. Early last year, I had several complaints from patients who had received the valve two to three years earlier. They complained of numbness in certain areas of their bodies, shortness of breath, tiring easily, and occasional chest pains. Upon further diagnosis, I determined that in nearly all of these cases, the component of the artificial valve designed to allow blood to flow in one direction, but not back in the other direction, was wedged in one position instead of moving freely as originally designed. In some patients, this resulted in the impediment of blood flow to certain parts of the body. In other patients, the result was an undertow of blood being pumped away from the heart in the wrong direction.

Q. Do you have a computer animation along with you today depicting the wedged valve and the end results, to help explain them to the jury?

A. Yes.

**Plaintiff's Attorney:** I ask that the computer animation contained on this diskette be marked as Plaintiff's Exhibit 24 for identification.

Q. Dr. Hornride, are you familiar with the computer animation introduced as Exhibit 24?

A. Yes.

Q. What is the basis of your familiarity?

A. I created the animation.

Q. How did you design it?

A. I used a preexisting medical program depicting a three-dimensional cross-section of the heart. The artificial valve image was scanned into the computer and scaled to the same size as the heart. I attached the valve image to the heart image and programmed in the ability to control the flow of blood through the artificial valve. Using the actual data gathered from my patients, the computer image can show how the blood flows through the artificial valve as originally designed and installed, versus how the blood flows through after the component inside the artificial valve becomes wedged in different positions.

Q. Is the computer image a true and accurate representation of a heart with an artificial valve?

A. Yes.

Q. Is the underlying data regarding the flow of blood through the artificial valve accurate, and was it accurately entered in the computer?

A. Yes.

**Plaintiff's Attorney:** Your Honor, I offer the computer animation into evidence and ask that the jury be allowed to see it.

**The Court:** The ruling will be reserved subject to cross-examination by defendant's counsel.

### Comment

Computer animations are often used to help an expert witness explain his or her testimony. *See supra* Chapter 3.D. for discussion of electronic evidence. These animations are admissible with the proper foundation. In the case of those animations that seek to illustrate, counsel must show sufficient similarity. *See State v. Thompson*, 788 N.W.2d 485 (Minn. 2010) (computer-generated animation depicting bloody shoeprints admissible where relevant and accurate); *Harris v. Poppell*, 411 F.3d 1189, 1197–98 (10th Cir. 2005); *Robinson v. Missouri P. R.R.*, 16 F.3d 1083, 1088–89 (10th Cir. 1994) (no abuse of discretion in admitting animation; court cautioned that "[b]ecause of its dramatic power, trial judges should carefully and meticulously examine proposed animation evidence for proper foundation, relevancy and the potential for undue prejudice."); *Green v. Ford Motor Co.*, 2001 U.S. Dist. LEXIS 19883, at 3–4 (W.D. Va. Nov. 26, 2001); *Datskow v. Teledyne Cont'l Motors Aircraft Prods.*, 826 F. Supp. 677, 685 (W.D.N.Y. 1993); *Harris v. State*, 2000 Okla. Crim. App. LEXIS 20, at *10 and n.4 (Okla. Crim. App. Oct. 23, 2000), *cert. denied*, 532 U.S. 1025 (2001). 1 Michael H. Graham, Handbook of Federal Evidence § 401.7 (7th ed. 2012). In the case of animations that go beyond illustration and present experimental elements, the issue of reliability comes into play. The admission of expert testimony in federal court is governed by Fed. R. Evid. 702. Rule 702 provides that if "scientific, technical, or other specialized knowledge will assist the trier of fact to understand the evidence or to determine a fact in issue," a witness who is "qualified as an expert by knowledge, skill, experience, training or education" may offer expert testimony, in the form of an opinion or otherwise, if three conditions are met: "(1) the testimony is based upon sufficient facts or data, (2) the testimony is the product of reliable principles and methods, and (3) the witness has applied the principles and methods reliably to the facts of the case."

Rule 702 places a "gatekeeping" obligation on a trial court. In performing this obligation, the trial court considers first "whether proffered scientific evidence is valid and reliable," and second "whether it will help the trier of fact, which is generally a question of relevance, or 'fit': assuming the evidence is reliable, does it apply to the facts in the individual case under consideration." *Newman v. Motorola, Inc.*, 218 F. Supp. 2d 769, 772 (D. Md. 2002), *superseded by statute on other grounds* as stated in *United States v. Hensley*, 91 F.3d 274 (1st Cir. 1996); *see Kumho Tire Co. v. Carmichael*, 526 U.S. 137, 141 (1999); *United States v. Mooney*, 315 F.3d 54, 62 (1st Cir. 2002). This "gatekeeping" obligation "applies not only to testimony based on 'scientific' knowledge, but also to testimony based on 'technical' and 'other specialized' knowledge." *Kumho*, 526 U.S. at 142. The purpose of the gatekeeping obligation is "to make certain that an expert, whether basing testimony upon professional studies or personal experience, employs in the courtroom the same level of intellectual rigor that characterizes the practice of an expert in the relevant field." *Id.* at 152.

Reliability determinations must be tied to the facts of the particular case. *Id.* at 150. The test of reliability is flexible, and the court may use the factors set forth by the Supreme Court in *Daubert v. Merrell Dow Pharm.*, 509 U.S. 579 (1993): (1) whether the proffered technique can be and has been tested; (2) whether the technique or theory has been subject to peer review; (3) the known or potential rate of error; and (4) the general acceptance of a technique in the relevant community. *See Kumho*, 526 U.S. at 149; *United States v. Forrest*, 429 F.3d 73, 80 (4th Cir. 2005). This list of factors "neither necessarily nor exclusively applies to all experts or in every case." *Id.* at 141.

In assessing the reliability of a proffered expert's testimony, "the court's inquiry under *Daubert* focuses not on the substance of the expert's conclusions, but on the principles and methodology used to generate the conclusions." *Clarke v. LR Systems*, 219 F. Supp. 2d 323, 332 (E.D.N.Y. 2002). "It is for the jury, not the Court, to determine whether an expert's opinions are suspect because facts upon which he relied were shown to be inaccurate or unproven." *S.E.C. v. Johnson*, 525 F. Supp. 2d 70, 76 (D.D.C. 2007).

An expert's qualifications are relevant to the reliability inquiry. *See United States v. Lopez-Medina*, 461 F.3d 724, 743 (6th Cir. 2006). But disputes about the strength of an expert's credentials, faults in an expert's decision to use a particular methodology, or the lack of textual authority for an expert's opinion "go to the weight, not the admissibility, of his testimony." *Clarke*, 219 F. Supp. 2d at 333. Acceptance of the methodology by the other party's expert may give additional credence to the reliability of the proffered testimony. *Correa v. Cruisers, a Div. of KCS Int'l, Inc.*, 298 F.3d 13, 26 (1st Cir. 2002).

Rule 702 was amended in the year 2000 in response to the Supreme Court's decision in *Daubert v. Merrell Dow Pharm.*, 509 U.S. 579 (1993). Advisory Committee Notes, 2000 Amendments, Fed. R. Evid. 702. The amended Rule 702 "reflects an attempt to liberalize the rules governing the admission of expert testimony. The rule clearly is one of admissibility rather than exclusion." *Sappington v. Skyjack, Inc.*, 512 F.3d 440, 448 (8th Cir. 2008) (citations omitted). As the Advisory Committee Notes state: "A review of the case law after *Daubert* shows that the rejection of expert testimony is the exception rather than the rule."

Many animations generated by computers present analyses of data to predict future events. In *Strock v. Southern Farm Bureau Cas. Ins. Co.*, 998 F.2d 1010 (4th Cir. 1993), the court admitted an animation re-creating hurricane damage. *See* HOTCHKESS & THOMAS, THE USE OF COMPUTER-IZED INFORMATION AT TRIAL, ABA Section of Litigation (1995), where the authors point out that:

> When animations are generated by computer, counsel should consider establishing that the data is accurate and was accurately entered; [should] present opinion testimony about the validity of the method used to present the animation; [and should establish] that the expert is familiar with the demonstrative exhibit; and that the exhibit will aid the judge or jury in understanding the expert's testimony.

## D. COMPUTER SIMULATION

Plaintiff John Smith sues Modern Ambulance, Inc. (MAT). The complaint alleges that one of MAT's drivers negligently caused an automobile collision resulting in substantial injury to the plaintiff. At trial, the plaintiff calls Dr. Julius Faerspanner as an expert witness. Plaintiff qualifies Dr. Faerspanner as an expert in vehicle analysis.

### Plaintiff's Counsel:

Q. Dr. Faerspanner, are you familiar with the vehicle collision that took place September 28, 2014, at the intersection of North Avenue and Howard Street, involving the plaintiff?

A. Yes I am.

Q. What is the basis of your familiarity?

A. I reviewed the police accident report, depositions of plaintiff, the ambulance driver, and the two police officers who reported to the accident scene, and several dozen photographs taken of the scene after the accident.

Q. Are you able to explain how the collision occurred?

A. Yes.

Q. Did you prepare a computer simulation that might aid you in your explanation?

A. Yes, I did.

Q. Could you describe for us how you made this simulation?

A. First, I used a computer program called "ED-SMAC," which is an acronym for "Engineering Dynamics Simulation Model of Automobile Collisions." "Engineering Dynamics" is the company that produces this software.

Q. Could you tell us what this computer program is and a little about how it works?

A. The ED-SMAC program produces a graphical display showing how an accident happened, based on the physics involved in the collision. You enter, as variables, the physical characteristics of the two vehicles—weight, size, shape—and the conditions of the road where the collision took place. The program then solves the various engineering equations that describe how the vehicles would move before, during, and after the collision.

Q. Is this computer program one on which experts in your field generally rely in simulating automobile collisions?

A. Yes.

Q. How does a computer simulation differ from a computer animation?

A. A computer animation is much more superficial, like a drawing, or a cartoon. When you make a computer animation, you don't have to input any data about the vehicles or road conditions, because an animation does not use physics or equations.

Q. Are you familiar with how to use the ED-SMAC program?

A. Yes.

Q. Can you tell us how you used this program to make the simulation?

A. I entered all the relevant data for the two vehicles, and the road conditions, and the program produced the simulation that's on that DVD disc.

Q. Where did you obtain the data?

A. The depositions of the two drivers told me some of the information about where the vehicles were located before the collision and which directions they were facing. The characteristics of the vehicles were based on their makes and models, which were contained in the accident report. I estimated the speeds of the two vehicles based on photographs of skid marks and the deposition testimony of the two drivers.

Q. Is this underlying data accurate to a reasonable degree of scientific certainty, and was it entered into the computer correctly?

A. Yes.

Q. Is the computer simulation a true and accurate re-creation of the accident?

A. Yes.

Q Can you identify this compact disc previously marked as Plaintiff's Exhibit 17 for identification?

A. Yes, it is the simulation that we have been discussing.

**Plaintiff's Counsel:** Your honor, I offer Exhibit 17 for identification into evidence and I would like to show the simulation to the jury now.
**The Court:** Dim the lights and let's get started.

### Comment

A computer simulation depicts "the computer program's own conclusions drawn from data entered into it. Simulations, therefore, constitute substantive evidence[.]" *Commonwealth v. Serge*, 837 A.2d 1255, 1261 n.4 (Pa. Sup. 2003); *see* 5 JACK B. WEINSTEIN ET AL., WEINSTEIN'S FEDERAL EVIDENCE § 900.07[7][a] (2d ed. 2014); *Jochims v. Isuzu Motors, Ltd.*, 145 F.R.D. 507, 510, n.3 (S.D. Iowa 1992) (computer simulation of vehicle rollover was supported by voluminous experimental data); *State v. Farner*, 66 S.W.3d 188, 208 (Tenn. 2001); *Constans v. Choctaw Transport, Inc.*, 712 So. 2d 885, 901 (La. Ct. App. 1997) ("In a simulation the computer functions in a sense as an expert itself, rendering its own opinion based on internal calculations of how the accident occurred."). By contrast, computer animations are "demonstrative evidence used to explain or illustrate expert witness testimony[.]" *Serge,* 837 A.2d at 1261.

The hypothetical is based on *Hudson v. City of Chicago,* 881 N.E.2d 430 (Ill. App. 2007), in which the Appellate Court of Illinois upheld the trial court's decision to admit a computer simulation similar to the one in the example above.

Before admitting a simulation, "the courts require proof of the validity of the scientific principles and data." *State v. Tollardo,* 77 P.3d 1023, 1028 (N.M. App. 2003) (collecting cases); *see Clark v. Cantrell,* 529 S.E.2d 528, 535 n.2 (S.C. 2000); *Novartis Corp. v. Ben Venue Labs,* 271 F.3d 1043, 1051–55 (Fed. Cir. 2001) (excluding computer simulation because court was "left in the dark" as to how the model was created). In considering whether this threshold will be met, courts apply the principles set forth in *Daubert v. Merrell Dow Pharms., Inc.,* 509 U.S. 579 (1993).

The admission of expert testimony in federal court is governed by Fed. R. Evid. 702. Rule 702 provides that if "scientific, technical, or other specialized knowledge will assist the trier of fact to understand the evidence or to determine a fact in issue," a witness who is "qualified as an expert by knowledge, skill, experience, training or education" may offer expert testimony, in the form of an opinion or otherwise, if three conditions are met: "(1) the testimony is based upon sufficient facts or data, (2) the testimony is the product of reliable principles and methods, and (3) the witness has applied the principles and methods reliably to the facts of the case."

Rule 702 places a "gatekeeping" obligation on a trial court. In performing this obligation, the trial court considers first "whether proffered scientific evidence is valid and reliable" and second "whether it will help the trier of fact, which is generally a question of relevance, or 'fit': assuming the evidence is reliable, does it apply to the facts in the individual case under consideration." *Newman v. Motorola, Inc.,* 218 Supp. 2d 769, 772 (D. Md. 2002); *see Kumho Tire Co. v. Carmichael,* 526 U.S. 137, 141 (1999); *see United States v. Mooney,* 315 F.3d 54, 62 (1st Cir. 2002). This "gatekeeping" obligation "applies not only to testimony based on 'scientific' knowledge, but also to testimony based on 'technical' and 'other specialized' knowledge." *Kumho,* 526 U.S. at 142. The purpose of the gatekeeping obligation is "to make certain that an expert, whether basing testimony upon professional studies or personal experience, employs in the courtroom the same level of intellectual rigor that characterizes the practice of an expert in the relevant field." *Id.* at 152.

Reliability determinations must be tied to the facts of the particular case. *Id.* at 150. The test of reliability is flexible, and the court may use the factors set forth by the Supreme Court in *Daubert v. Merrell Dow Pharm.*, 509 U.S. 579 (1993): (1) whether the proffered technique can be and has been tested; (2) whether the technique or theory has been subject to peer review; (3) the known or potential rate of error; and (4) the general acceptance of a technique in the relevant community. *See Kumho*, 526 U.S. at 149; *United States v. Forrest*, 429 F.3d 73, 80 (4th Cir. 2005). This list of factors "neither necessarily nor exclusively applies to all experts or in every case." *Id.* at 141.

In assessing the reliability of a proffered expert's testimony, "the court's inquiry under *Daubert* focuses not on the substance of the expert's conclusions, but on the principles and methodology used to generate the conclusions." *Clarke v. LR Systems*, 219 F. Supp. 2d 323, 332 (E.D.N.Y. 2002). "It is for the jury, not the Court, to determine whether an expert's opinions are suspect because facts upon which he relied were shown to be inaccurate or unproven." *S.E.C. v. Johnson*, 525 F. Supp. 2d 70, 76 (D.D.C. 2007).

An expert's qualifications are relevant to the reliability inquiry. *See United States v. Lopez-Medina*, 461 F.3d 724, 743 (6th Cir. 2006). But disputes about the strength of an expert's credentials, faults in an expert's decision to use a particular methodology, or the lack of textual authority for an expert's opinion "go to the weight, not the admissibility, of his testimony." *Clarke*, 219 F. Supp. 2d at 333. Acceptance of the methodology by the other party's expert may give additional credence to the reliability of the proffered testimony. *Correa v. Cruisers, a Div. of KCS Int'l, Inc.*, 298 F.3d 13, 26 (1st Cir. 2002).

Rule 702 was amended in the year 2000, in response to the Supreme Court's decision in *Daubert v. Merrell Dow Pharm.*, 509 U.S. 579 (1993). Advisory Committee Notes, 2000 Amendments, Fed. R. Evid. 702. The amended Rule 702 "reflects an attempt to liberalize the rules governing the admission of expert testimony. The rule clearly is one of admissibility rather than exclusion." *Sappington v. Skyjack, Inc.*, 512 F.3d 440, 448 (8th Cir. 2008) (citations omitted). As the Advisory Committee Notes state: "A review of the case law after Daubert shows that the rejection of expert testimony is the exception rather than the rule."

## E. DIGITAL IMAGES

Plaintiff Jane Sherman was injured in an automobile accident as she was driving south on Seventh Avenue toward its intersection with Fifth Street. Plaintiff brings a negligence suit against the driver of the vehicle that collided with hers. At trial, plaintiff calls a private investigator she hired to take pictures of the accident scene.

### Defense Counsel:

Q. Please introduce yourself to the jury.

A. My name is Fred Dawkins and I am a freelance professional photographer and Web site designer.

Q. As part of your work, do you take digital photographs?

A. I do.

Q. How is a digital photograph different from a traditional photograph?

A. A traditional camera records an image on a piece of film, creating a "negative." A digital camera doesn't have film; instead, it has a light-sensitive sensor. When light from an image strikes this sensor, the sensor converts the image into tiny dots called pixels. Each pixel represents a "point" of a specific color. When enough pixels are placed in their proper positions on a two-dimensional grid, in columns and rows, the pixels appear to form a particular image. When you take a picture with a digital camera, it creates a computer file containing all the pixels needed to reproduce the image, and how to arrange those pixels properly.

Q. Did you have occasion to take digital photographs of the intersection of Fifth Street and Seventh Avenue?

A. Yes.

Q. Describe the circumstances.

A. You engaged me to take pictures of what that intersection looked like during morning rush hour on a weekday.

Q. And did you make such photographs?

A. Yes.

Q. Tell us when and the circumstances of your making those photographs.

A. On September 24, 2014, around 8:30 a.m., I drove south on Seventh Avenue toward its intersection with Fifth Street. Before I reached

Fifth Street, I pulled over, got out of the car, and took three pictures of the intersection in front of me.

Q. What type of camera did you use?

A. A nine megapixel Canon PowerShot camera

Q. Is the digital camera you used generally accepted as standard equipment by digital photographers?

A. Yes.

Q. Was the digital camera functioning properly that day?

A. Yes.

Q. Where did each image go after you "captured" it?

A. The image is stored on a memory card that is inserted into the camera.

Q. What did you do with the memory card after taking your pictures?

A. I put the memory card in a device that attaches to my computer and allows the computer to read the files stored on the card. I then used a computer program to open the files stored on the card and view the images contained in those files.

Q. Is there any way to tell that the image you took with the camera is the same image displayed on the computer screen?

A. Yes.

Q. Could you describe how you can confirm that the image on the computer is the same image captured by the camera?

A. I explained earlier how the digital camera works. When a digital camera creates the file containing the image, records in that file certain information about the image, which is called "metadata." For example, the camera records the time and date the image was taken, and the camera model and settings that were used. If someone has made changes to the image, using editing software on the computer for example, the metadata will show that these changes were made.

Q. How can one know that the metadata has not been tampered with, to make it appear the image has not been altered, when in fact changes were made to the image?

A. There is an encryption feature that prevents tampering with the metadata for the images taken by the camera and recorded on the memory card.

Q. I would like you to look at the projector screen and identify what you see.

A. That is a projected image of one of the three pictures I took of the intersection of Fifth Street and Seventh Avenue.

Q. Is it a true and accurate representation of what you observed when you took the picture?

A. Yes it is.

Q. Has the image file being displayed been edited or modified in any way since its creation?

A. No.

Q. Please tell us how you can be sure.

A. The metadata recorded in the image file show that it has not been altered since the moment it was taken.

## Comment

Digital photographs fall within three categories: "original digital images, digitally converted images, and digitally enhanced images." *Lorraine v. Markel American Ins. Co.*, 241 F.R.D. 534, 561 (D. Md. 2007).

An original digital image "'may be authenticated the same way as a film photo, by a witness with personal knowledge of the scene depicted who can testify that the photo fairly and accurately depicts it.'" *Id.* (quoting Edward J. Imwinkelried, *Can This Photo Be Trusted?*, TRIAL, October 2005, at 49); *see, e.g.*, *Owens v. State*, 214 S.W.3d 849, 854 (Ark. 2005) ("[W]e do not agree that this court should impose a higher burden of proof for the admissibility of digital photographs merely because digital images are easier to manipulate."); *People v. Goldsmith*, 59 Cal. 4th 258, 326 P.3d 239, *cert. denied sub nom. Goldsmith v. California*, 135 S. Ct. 763, 190 L. Ed. 2d 629 (2014); *Almond v. State*, 553 S.E.2d 803, 805 (Ga. 2001) ("We are aware of no authority, and appellant cites none, for the proposition that the procedure for admitting pictures should be any different when they were taken by a digital camera.") "If a question is raised about the reliability of digital photography in general, the court likely could take judicial notice of it under Rule 201." *Lorraine*, 241 F.R.D. at 561 (quoting Edward J. Imwinkelried, *Can This Photo Be Trusted?*, TRIAL, October 2005, at 49). But some commentators have urged courts to apply stricter foundation requirements to digital photographs than they do to traditional photographs. *See* Jill Witkowski, Note, CAN JURIES REALLY BELIEVE WHAT THEY SEE? NEW FOUNDATIONAL REQUIREMENTS FOR AUTHENTICATION OF DIGITAL IMAGES, 10 WASH. U. J. L. & POL'Y 267 (2002).

A digitally converted image is an image that has been converted from film, or some other non-digital medium, to digital format. Courts have held that where a witness testifies that he or she created an original non-digital image, and that the resulting digital image is a "fair and accurate depiction" of the original, a sufficient foundation is laid for admission of the digitally converted image, even if the witness did not personally perform the conversion. *Macaluso v. Pleskin*, 747 A.2d 830, 837 (N.J. Super. App. Div. 2000); *see Archanian v. State*, 145 P.3d 1008 (Nev. 2006). On the other hand, where the creator of the original image is unavailable, courts have held that the proponent of the digitally converted image must establish its reliability through testimony by a person "with some degree of computer expertise, who has sufficient knowledge to be examined and cross-examined about the functioning of the computer." *Rodd v. Raritan Radiologic Assoc., P.A.*, 860 A.2d 1003, 1012 (N.J. Super. App. Div. 2004).

At least one court, in considering the admissibility of digitally converted images, has applied the rule that a duplicate recording "is admissible to the same extent as an original unless (1) a genuine question is raised as to the authenticity of the original or (2) in the circumstances it would be unfair to admit the duplicate in lieu of the original." *See State v. Brown*, 739 N.W.2d 716, 722 (Minn. 2007). The *Brown* court upheld the admission of a digitally converted video because the State had offered testimony of the officer who performed the conversion. This officer had expertise in the conversion process, described the process, and explained that she used a system "used by various government and business entities, including the FBI, ATF, CIA, IRS, and Target Corporation." *Id.* at 721. But, the *Brown* court also warned prosecutors to be "on notice that the trial court has broad discretion to exclude digital copies if defense counsel is not provided with adequate notice and opportunity either to observe the conversion process or retain an independent expert to make a similar conversion or, in the alternative, to allow the court to arrange for supervision of the process." *Id.* at 722. The purpose for which the digital image is offered, and its centrality to the case, are key factors in any court's analysis of the admissibility issue. *See Rodd*, 860 A.2d 1003 (a malpractice case in which the jury was to resolve the question of whether the defendant radiologist should have seen a tumor on an X ray).

The hypothetical above concerns the third category of digital images: digitally enhanced images. "Enhancement" means that the original image, which could have been in either digital or non-digital format, has been altered in some way. The alteration can be intentional, as in *State v. Swinton,* 847 A.2d 921 (2004) (in which forensic scientists superimposed one digitally created image over another), or unintentional, as in *Rodd, supra*, 860 A.2d 1003 (in which a plaintiff offered a digital image converted from an original X ray, but the conversion process magnified the original image).

In *Swinton*, a murder case, the prosecution had admitted a digital image of bite marks found on a murder victim, on which a digital image of the defendant's teeth had been superimposed. This enhanced image, the appellate court held, had been erroneously admitted because the state had failed to lay a proper foundation. Specifically, the State failed to offer the "testimony [of] a person with some degree of computer expertise, who has sufficient knowledge to be examined and cross-examined about the functioning of the computer." *Swinton*, 847 A.2d at 941. The *Swinton* court offered six factors for the authentication of computer-enhanced evidence, *Id.* at 942:

1. The computer equipment is accepted in the field as standard and competent and was in good working order.
2. Qualified computer operators were employed.
3. Proper procedures were followed in connection with the input and output of information.
4. A reliable software program was utilized.
5. The equipment was programmed and operated correctly.
6. The exhibit is properly identified as the output in question.

*See also State v. Hartman*, 754 N.E.2d 1150 (Ohio 2001) (applying the *Frye* standard to digitally enhanced evidence, holding that the prosecution's expert was qualified and that the prosecution's digitally enhanced evidence was reliable) (citing *Frye v. United States*, 293 F. 1013 (C.A.D.C.1923)); *accord, State v. Hayden*, 950 P.2d 1024 (Wash. App. 1998).

The best course of action is for the proponent of digitally enhanced evidence to call as a witness the individual who performed the enhancement, establish the individual's knowledge of and expertise in the process he or she employed, and have the individual describe in detail each step of that process. This approach was endorsed by the Eighth Circuit in *United States v. Seifert,* 445 F.3d 1043 (8th Cir. 2006). The United States brought a federal arson charge against the defendant and offered in evidence a digitally enhanced surveillance video. The United States offered testimony from Jack Hunter, an expert in electronic surveillance and video analysis. Hunter "described the computer program that enhanced the image[,]" detailed the adjustments he made, and testified (on cross-examination) "that he simply enhanced the original video and did not manipulate it." *Id.* at 1045. The trial court admitted the video over the defendant's objections, and the Eighth Circuit affirmed.

## F. DIAGRAM NOT TO SCALE

A plaintiff sues a defendant for personal injuries received in an automobile accident. Counsel for the plaintiff seeks to have a witness draw, in court, a sketch depicting the relative positions of the automobiles involved in the collision.

### Plaintiff's Counsel:

Q. Mrs. Jones, where were you standing when you saw the collision?

A. I was standing in front of my husband's store on the northwest corner of South and Third Streets.

Q. Tell us what you saw?

A. I saw a red Ford pickup truck turn right, and almost at the same time I saw this blue Ford go through a yellow light, and the red pickup truck and the blue Ford collided.

Q. At this point, Your Honor, I would like permission to have Mrs. Jones step down from the witness stand and draw freehand on the easel a diagram of the intersection where this accident occurred.

**The Court:** Proceed.

Q. Can you first draw the intersection?

**Plaintiff's Counsel:** Let the record reflect the witness drew the intersection.

Q. Now, place by drawing an "X," if you will, the position of your husband's store with respect to the intersection.

**Plaintiff 's Counsel:** Let the record reflect that the witness marked an "X" reflecting the position of the store with respect to the intersection.

Q. Show us where the automobiles collided by marking the spot with a "Z." (Witness complies.)

**Plaintiff's Counsel:** Let the record reflect that the witness marked with a "Z" the spot where the automobiles collided.

## Comment

Drawings, plats, maps, and graphs are admissible in the discretion of the trial judge when shown to accurately represent what they purport to depict. *United States v. Ogba*, 526 F.3d 214 (5th Cir. 2008) ("Summary charts are properly admitted only if they accurately reflect the underlying records or testimony, particularly when they are based, in part, on the government's factual assumptions.") (citation omitted). *Accord, United States v. Lasko*, 146 Fed. Appx. 530, 532 (2d Cir. 2005) (unreported); *United States v. Velasquez*, 304 F.3d 237, 240 (3rd Cir. 2002); *United States v. Emmons*, 24 F.3d 1210, 1216 (10th Cir. 1994); *United States v. Chavez*, 979 F.2d 1350, 1355 (9th Cir. 1992); *Kenney v. Lewis Revels Rare Coins, Inc.*, 741 F.2d 378, 383 (11th Cir. 1984); *United States v. Hardin*, 710 F.2d 1231, 1237 (7th Cir.), *cert. denied*, 464 U.S. 918 (1983).

Sketches or diagrams need not be drawn to scale as a qualification for admissibility if the scene presented reasonably depicts the site. *See United States v. Espinosa*, 771 F.2d 1382 (10th Cir.), *cert. denied sub nom. Foreman v. United States*, 474 U.S. 1023 (1985); *United States v. D'Antonio*, 324 F.2d 667 (3d Cir. 1963), *cert. denied*, 376 U.S. 909 (1964); *In re Complaint of Nautilus Motor Tanker Co.*, 862 F. Supp. 1251, 1259 (D.N.J. 1994); *Cardullo v. General Motors Corp.*, 378 F. Supp. 890, 892 (E.D. Pa. 1974), *aff'd*, 511 F.2d 1392 (3d Cir. 1975). *See generally* GREGORY P. JOSEPH, MODERN VISUAL EVIDENCE Ch. 9 (2014), in which the author devotes considerable attention to the use of diagrams, charts, and graphs. Admissibility of this type of evidence is commonplace and depends on whether the evidence fairly and accurately depicts that which it purports to depict. *See United States v. Williams*, 657 F.2d 199 (8th Cir. 1981).

Moreover, such diagrams need not be introduced in evidence if counsel desires the sketch simply to serve as an aid to the witness's testimony. *See United States v. Ricks*, 475 F.2d 1326, 1328 (D.C. Cir. 1973); *Weller Mfg. Co. v. Wen Prods., Inc.*, 135 F. Supp. 121, 129 (N.D. Ill. 1955), *aff'd*, 231 F.2d 795 (7th Cir. 1956). Diagrams of accident scenes, particularly from police reports, are admissible when based upon the personal observation of the police officer or of the authenticating witness. *See supra* Chapter 3.I. pertaining to police reports and diagrams contained therein. Police composite sketches based on eyewitness accounts are also admissible pursuant to Federal Rule of Evidence 801(d)(1)(C), which renders as non-hearsay statements of identification made by a witness who testifies at trial and is subject to cross-examination.

Counsel can also use a traffic board, and the witness can place model cars on the traffic board to correspond with the positions of the vehicles involved in an accident. As the witness places the model on the traffic board, it would be appropriate for counsel to state for the record that the witness is placing the model on the board in a position in which the witness testified that he had observed the object or motor vehicle. Counsel can also place the model on the board as the witness testifies and state for the record where he is placing the model. It may be desirable to introduce in evidence the sketch or a photograph of the sketch, although resorting to the sketch or diagram during trial does not require that it be admitted. Even if the sketch is not introduced, it may be prudent to obtain a stipulation as to a photograph of it, or mark the sketch for identification, so that the appellate court can see what the jury saw, even if what they saw was not introduced as an exhibit. Whatever the jury sees should be in the record on appeal.

## G. DIAGRAM TO SCALE

A plaintiff institutes a negligence suit against a defendant for damages resulting from an injury sustained when the defendant's automobile struck the plaintiff, a pedestrian, at the intersection of Charles and Baltimore Streets. Plaintiff's attorney seeks to introduce a scaled diagram of the intersection and then request subsequent witnesses to depict the position of the motor vehicles on either side of the street, and particularly the defendant's vehicle in relationship to the plaintiff, at the time of the collision.

### Plaintiff's Counsel:

Q. Would you state your name, please?
A. John Bastelle.
Q. What is your occupation?
A. Surveyor.
Q. Mr. Bastelle, at my request, did you go to Charles and Baltimore Streets for purposes of preparing a diagram?
A. Yes, I did.
Q. When did you visit that intersection?
A. January 1, 2014.
Q. What time of day did you go to that intersection?
A. 6:00 a.m.

Q. What did you do when you arrived at the scene?

A. I measured the width of Charles Street, the width of Baltimore Street, and took measurements in all directions as well as sketched a diagram of the intersection.

Q. Did there come a time when you prepared a diagram based upon your observations and sketch?

A. Yes.

Q. Do you have that diagram with you?

A. Yes, I do. (Witness hands diagram to counsel.)

Q. Can you tell us how you prepared this diagram?

A. It was drawn to scale. I measured the distance involved and made a rough sketch while I was at the scene, and subsequently I prepared the scaled diagram.

Q. What was the scale?

A. 1 inch to 15 feet.

Q. What is meant by a scale of 1 inch to 15 feet?

A. That means that the distance measured as 1 inch on this diagram or model is equal to 15 feet on the streets of Baltimore and Charles.

Q. Is this drawing a true and correct diagram of the intersection as you saw it on January 1, 2014, drawn to the scale of 1 inch to 15 feet?

A. Yes, it is.

**Plaintiff 's Counsel**: We offer the diagram in evidence as Plaintiff's Exhibit No. 3.

## Comment

*See supra* Chapter 5.F. for comment on drawings not to scale.

## H. MODEL OF ACCIDENT SCENE

The same facts apply as stated in the previous pattern, except the plaintiff's attorney seeks to introduce a model of the intersection. Counsel first introduces a scaled diagram as in the previous pattern and proceeds as follows:

### Plaintiff's Counsel:

Q. What did you do after you prepared the scaled diagram?

A. I constructed a model from it.

Q. I show you Plaintiff's Exhibit No. 4 for identification and ask whether or not this is the model to which you referred?

A. Yes.

Q. Does this model accurately reflect the highway and the measurements according to the scale of your diagram?

A. Yes.

Q. Does Plaintiff's Exhibit No. 4 for identification clearly and accurately portray the intersection of Baltimore and Charles Streets?

A. Yes.

Q. We offer Plaintiff's Exhibit No. 4 for identification in evidence.

### Comment

It is not necessary to introduce in evidence the diagram from which the model was made (if a diagram exists, as one did in this case). *See United States v. Bugg*, 483 F. App'x 166, 172 (6th Cir. 2012) ("we have previously approved the use of models or replicas under Rule 403 to illustrate events for the jury where the prosecutor clarifies that the object was not used in the offense and the court gives an appropriate limiting instruction."). Models, as well as drawings, plats, and other demonstrative evidence, can be excluded by the court in its discretion. *See In re Air Crash Disaster*, 86 F.3d 498, 531 (6th Cir. 1996); *Finchum v. Ford Motor Co.*, 57 F.3d 526, 530 (7th Cir. 1995); *Pestel v. Vermeer Mfg. Co.*, 64 F.3d 382, 384 (8th Cir. 1995); *United States v. Chavez*, 979 F.2d 1350, 1355 (9th Cir. 1992); *United States v. Rockwell*, 781 F.2d 985, 987 (3d Cir. 1986); *Petty v. Ideco*, 761 F.2d 1146, 1150 (5th Cir. 1985), *abrogated on other grounds*, *United States v. Fisher*, 106 F.3d 622 (5th Cir. 1997); *Green v. Bock Laundry March Co.*, 490 U.S. 504 (1989); *Daskarolis v. Firestone Tire & Rubber Co.*, 651 F.2d 937, 939 (4th Cir. 1981); *Shepard v. General Motors Corp.*, 423 F.2d 406 (1st Cir. 1970); *Colon v. BIC USA*, 2001 U.S. Dist. LEXIS 21037, at *39 (S.D.N.Y. Dec. 19, 2001); L.S. Tellier, ANNOTATION, PROPRIETY, IN TRIAL OF CIVIL ACTION, OF USE OF MODEL OR INSTRUMENTALITY, OR OF SITE OR PREMISES, INVOLVED IN THE ACCIDENT OR INCIDENT, 69 A.L.R.2d 424 (1960 & Supps. 1984, 1995). *See generally Milanowicz v. Raymond Corp.*, 148 F. Supp. 2d 525, 533–37 (D. N.J. 2001). *See also United States v. Aldaco*, 201 F.3d 979, 986 (7th Cir. 2000) (replica of destroyed shotgun allowed jury to see what officer saw when he observed defendant holding a shotgun); *Roland v. Langlois*, 945 F.2d 956 (7th Cir. 1991) (the court held that it was not an abuse of discretion to admit a life-size model of an amusement ride that injured the plaintiff); *In re Beverly Hills Fire Litig.*, 695 F.2d

207 (6th Cir. 1982), *cert. denied*, 461 U.S. 929 (1983), *on remand*, 583 F. Supp. 1163 (E.D. Ky. 1984) (illustrates the wide discretion of the court in admitting models and other demonstrative evidence). *See also* Mark A. Dombroff, DOMBROFF ON DEMONSTRATIVE EVIDENCE (1983, Supp. 1990).

## I. ANATOMICAL MODEL

In a personal injury case, plaintiff's expert doctor is to refer to an anatomical model.

### Plaintiff's Counsel:

Q. Dr. Jones, in the study of medicine and in the practice of medicine, are visual aids used to help members of your profession teach and work with various structures of the human body?

A. Yes.

Q. What types of aids are used?

A. Charts, diagrams, films, and models.

Q. Have you brought with you today an anatomical model of the leg of a human being?

A. Yes, I have.

Q. Would the use of this model aid you in explaining to the jury the injuries received by Billy Jones?

A. Yes.

Q. Doctor, may I see the model that you have brought?

A. Yes. (Witness hands model to the plaintiff's counsel.)

Q. Doctor, what does this model show?

A. Well, it is the model of a leg reflecting the various bones, cartilage, and joints.

Q. Does this model accurately portray the human leg and how its various parts fit and operate together?

A. Yes.

**Plaintiff's Counsel:** I offer this model in evidence as Plaintiff's Exhibit No. 32.

## Comment

Anatomical models are admissible in the discretion of the court. *See Flanagan v. Redondo*, 595 N.E.2d 1077 (Ill. App. 1992), where the trial court properly admitted into evidence a skeletal model after the doctor had testified that the model was a true and accurate representation of the skeletal anatomy it purported to represent; *Smith v. Ohio Oil Co.*, 134 N.E.2d 526 (Ill. App. 1956); *Padgett v. S. Ry. Co.*, 396 F.2d 303, 308 (6th Cir. 1968); *Honeywell v. Rogers*, 251 F. Supp. 841, 845 (W.D. Pa. 1966). *See* L.S. Tellier, Annotation, *Propriety, in Trial of Civil Action, of Use of Skeleton or Model of Human Body or Part*, 58 A.L.R.2d 689 (1958 & Supp. 1994); B. Finberg, Annotation, *Propriety, in Trial of Criminal Case, of Use of Skeleton or Model of Human Body or Part*, 83 A.L.R. 2d 1097 (1962 & Supp. 1986, 1991, 1995).

Models or replicas may be used as visual aids, in the same manner as drawings and charts. *See United States v. Wanoskia*, 800 F.2d 235, 237 (10th Cir. 1986). In *Wanoskia*, the court permitted a demonstration by an animate human model to determine the distance from her head to the gun held by her, as her arms were exactly the same length as that of the deceased victim. *Id. See also United States v. Turner*, 528 F.2d 143, 167 (9th Cir.), *cert. denied*, 423 U.S. 996 (1975).

## J.  CHARTS OR SUMMARIES

The plaintiff instituted an employment discrimination action, under 42 U.S.C. § 2000(e) et seq., against the defendant school board, on the basis that she was denied promotion to a department chairmanship solely on the basis of race. Defendant's counsel seeks to introduce a tabulation of all instructors appointed as chairman of a home economics department in each of the board's schools since plaintiff's affiliation with the school. The tabulations showed, *inter alia*, the starting salary, raises in salary, and qualifications of each employee promoted to a department chairmanship. The tabulation summarized information obtained by Clara Jones, the supervisor of all departments of home economics, from personnel files and other board data contained in the personnel department.

### Defense Counsel:

Q.  Mrs. Jones, why did you not appoint Joan Brown to the position of home economics chairman in one of the schools of the White Marsh County school system?

A.  She did not meet the qualifications for the position, and there were others who did, and they were appointed.

**Defense Counsel:** Please have this document marked as Defense Exhibit No. 13 for identification.

Q. I show you what purports to be Defendant's Exhibit No. 13 for identification and ask if you can identify it.

A. Yes I can.

Q. Can you explain to us what is represented by this document?

A. This is a summary from information that is in the files of the supervisor of all of the home economic departments within the school system, of those individuals who were appointed to home economics department chairman positions from 2010 to 2014. The information includes the name of the individual, the race of the individual, the sex of the individual, the starting salary when the individuals first began employment with the school system, each raise in salary the individual received, the date of appointment to the position of department chairman, and the qualifications of that person.

Q. Who prepared this summary?

A. I did.

Q. Where did you obtain the information appearing in the summary?

A. From the records and files of the Board of Education.

Q. Does the tabulation accurately summarize the information from which it was compiled?

A. Yes.

Q. Does it accurately state the substance of the Board's records as to the matters set out in the tabulation?

A. Yes.

**Defense Counsel**: We offer Defendant's Exhibit No. 13 for identification in evidence at this time.

## Comment

Contents of writings, recordings, or photographs that cannot be conveniently examined in court may be presented in the form of a chart or summary, provided the chart or summary is properly authenticated. Fed. R. Evid. 1006. "When a summary is admitted pursuant to Rule 1006, the summary itself becomes substantive evidence for the trier of fact to consider." *United States v. Stone*, 852 F.Supp 2d 820, 828 (E.D. Mich. 2012). *See United States v. Appolon*, 715 F.3d 362, 364 (1st Cir. 2013) ("Federal

Rule of Evidence 1006 does not require that the documents being summarized also be admitted"); *United States v. Williams*, 264 F.3d 561, 575 (5th Cir. 2001); *7-UP Bottling Co. v. Archer Daniels Midland Co.*, 191 F.3d 1090, 1102 (9th Cir. 1999), *cert. denied sub nom. Gangi Bros. Packing Co. v. Cargill, Inc.*, 529 U.S. 1037 (2000); *United States v. Harmas*, 974 F.2d 1262, 1269 (11th Cir. 1992); *United States v. Williams*, 952 F.2d 1504, 1519 (6th Cir. 1991); *Fagiola v. National Gypsum Co. A.C. & S., Inc.*, 906 F.2d 53 (2d Cir. 1990); *United States v. Duncan*, 919 F.2d 981 (5th Cir. 1990), *cert. denied*, 500 U.S. 926 (1991); *United States v. Briscoe*, 896 F.2d 1476 (7th Cir.), *cert. denied sub nom. Usman v. United States*, 498 U.S. 863 (1990); *United States v. Nivica*, 887 F.2d 1110, 1125 (1st Cir. 1989), *cert. denied*, 494 U.S. 1005 (1990); *United States v. Possick*, 849 F.2d 332 (8th Cir. 1988); *United States v. Poschwatta*, 829 F.2d 1477 (9th Cir. 1987), *cert. denied*, 484 U.S. 1064 (1988), *overruled on other grounds*, *Cheek v. United States*, 498 U.S. 192 (1991), *overruling recognized*, *United States v. Wood*, 943 F.2d 1048 (9th Cir. 1991); *United States v. Porter*, 821 F.2d 968 (4th Cir. 1987), *cert. denied*, 485 U.S. 934 (1988); *United States v. Lemire*, 720 F.2d 1327, 1347 (D.C. Cir. 1983), *cert. denied*, 467 U.S. 1226 (1984); *United States v. Behrens*, 689 F.2d 154 (10th Cir.), *cert. denied sub nom. Wilkett v. United States*, 459 U.S. 1088 (1982); *United States v. Weaver*, 281 F.3d 228, 232 (D.D.C. 2002); *BD v. DeBuono*, 193 F.R.D. 117, 129–30 (S.D.N.Y. 2000) (inaccuracy of summary goes to weight, not admissibility, of evidence); *United States v. Thompson*, 518 F.3d 832, 858–59 (10th Cir. 2008); *United States v. Hemphill*, 514 F.3d 1350, 1358 (D.C. Cir. 2008); *United States v. Moon*, 513 F.3d 527, 545 (6th Cir. 2008); *United States v. Nguyen*, 504 F.3d 561, 572 (5th Cir. 2007); *Eichhorn v. AT&T Corp.*, 484 F.3d 644, 650 (3d Cir. 2007); *United States v. Milkiewicz*, 470 F.3d 390, 395–96 (1st Cir. 2006); *Judson Atkinson Candies, Inc. v. Latini-Hohberger Dhimantec*, 529 F.3d 371, 382 (7th Cir. 2008); *NRRM, LLC v. Mepco Fin. Corp.*, 2015 WL 1501897 (N.D. Ill. March 27, 2015). *See also* GREGORY P. JOSEPH, MODERN VISUAL EVIDENCE Ch. 9 (2014); 4 JOHN HENRY WIGMORE, WIGMORE ON EVIDENCE § 1230 (Chadbourn Rev. 1972 & Supp. 2014).

In addition to providing notice and the summary to opposing counsel, the proponent should also provide the original data prior to trial at a reasonable time and place. When possible, questions pertaining to the accuracy of the chart should be resolved during pretrial conferences or by stipulation. The court has discretion to order the underlying data to be produced in court. Significantly, the rules governing the admissibility of summaries and charts do not require that it be impossible to examine the records, but only that it would be inconvenient to do so. *See United States v. Meshack*, 225 F.3d 556, 582 (5th Cir. 2000), *cert. denied*, 122 S. Ct. 142 (2001), *amended on rehearing in part*, 244 F.3d 367 (5th Cir. 2001), *overruled on other grounds recognized by United States v. Runyan*, 62 Fed. Appx. 557 (N.D. Tx. 2003); *United States v. Osum*, 943 F.2d 1394, 1405 (5th Cir. 1991); *United States v. Campbell*, 845 F.2d 1374 (6th Cir.), *cert. denied*, 488 U.S. 908 (1988); *United States v. Possick*, 849 F.2d 332 (8th Cir. 1988); *R & R Assoc., Inc. v. Visual Scene, Inc.*, 726 F.2d 36, 37–38 (1st Cir. 1984); *Keith v. Volpe*, 618 F. Supp. 1132 (C.D. Cal. 1985); *Doninger Metal Prods. Corp. v. United States*, 50 Fed. Cl. 110, 130 (Fed. Cl. 2001). Moreover, the data contained in the summary must be admissible, unless they serve as the basis of an expert's opinion. *See Fraser v. Major League Soccer, LLC*, 284 F.3d 47, 67 (1st Cir. 2002); *Certain Underwriters at Lloyds v. Sinkovich*, 232 F.3d 200, 205 n.4 (4th Cir. 2000); *United States v. Filippi*, 1999 U.S. App. LEXIS 2840, at *19–20 (4th Cir. Feb. 23, 1999), *cert. denied*, 528 U.S. 846 (1999); *AMPAT/Midwest, Inc. v. Illinois Tool Works, Inc.*, 896 F.2d 1035, 1045 (7th Cir. 1990); *United States v. Dorta*, 783 F.2d 1179 (4th Cir.), *cert. denied*, 477 U.S. 905 (1986); *Hackett v. Housing Auth.*, 750 F.2d 1308 (5th Cir.), *cert. denied*, 474 U.S. 850 (1985); *Paddack v. Dave Christensen, Inc.*, 745 F.2d 1254 (9th Cir. 1984); *Ford Motor Co. v. Auto Supply Co.*, 661 F.2d 1171 (8th Cir. 1981); *United States v. Scales*, 594 F.2d 558, 562 (6th Cir.), *cert. denied*, 441 U.S. 946 (1979); *United States v. Conlin*, 551 F.2d 534, 538 (2d Cir.), *cert. denied*, 434 U.S. 831 (1977); *United States v. Demjanjuk*, 2002 U.S. Dist. LEXIS 6999, at *61–62 (N.D. Ohio Apr. 22, 2002); *Fisher v. Sellas*, 2002 Bankr. LEXIS 253, at *22–*23 (Bankr. N.D. Ill. Jan. 11, 2002); *Tucker v. Ohtsu Tire & Rubber Co.*, 49 F. Supp. 2d 456, 462 (D. Md. 1999); *Fujsawa Pharm. Co. v. Kapoor*, 1999 U.S. Dist. LEXIS 11381, at *35–36 (N.D. Ill. July 21, 1999); 6A Lynn McLain, Maryland Evidence: State and Federal § 1006.2 (2d ed. 2001 & Supp. 2009). Charts and diagrams highlighting specific facts in evidence may be used to illustrate testimony, as well as in closing argument.

When the foundation requirements are not met, the court may exclude the chart or summary. For examples of instances where the chart or summary was excluded, *see United States v. North American Reporting, Inc.*, 740 F.2d 50 (D.C. App. 1984) (a chart that collected a "jumble of the defendant's wishes, guesses and undocumented recollections" was not admissible) and *United States v. Pelullo*, 964 F.2d 193 (3d Cir. 1992) (a government agent's summary of defendant's financial activity was not admissible because the underlying materials were out-of-court statements).

It is important to keep in mind the difference between charts or summaries presented under Rule 1006 on the one hand and those that are simply used to demonstrate or explain on the other. The former are admissible in evidence; the latter are not. *White Indus. v. Cessna Aircraft Co.*, 611 F. Supp. 1049 (W.D. Mo. 1985) contains a good discussion of the differences, distinguishing between a Rule 1006 summary (which is admitted as substantive evidence) and a so-called "pedagogical" summary (which is a demonstrative aid shown to the factfinder but not admitted into evidence).

Counsel may also want to consider introducing summary evidence through the testimony of a witness. Cases discussing and permitting such evidence include *United States v. Mortimer*, 118 F.2d 266 (2d Cir. 1941) (stating general rule that statements compiled from voluminous records are admissible on the testimony of the supervising agent); *Diamond Shamrock Corp. v. Lumbermens Mutual Casualty Co.*, 466 F.2d 722 (7th Cir. 1972) ("it is not necessary . . . that every person who assisted in the preparation of the original records or summaries be brought to the witness stand"); *United States v. Soulard*, 730 F.2d 1292 (9th Cir. 1984) (testimony of an agent to present a summary analysis is admissible); *O'Dillon v. State*, 265 S.E.2d 18 (Ga. 1980) (admitting a sheriff's testimony as "summarizing witness"); *United States v. Johnson*, 54 F.3d 1150 (4th Cir. 1995) (summary testimony admissible pursuant to Rule 611(a)); *United States v. Baker*, 10 F.3d 1374 (9th Cir. 1993), *overruled on other grounds, United States v. Nordby*, 225 F.3d 1053 (9th Cir. 2000) (summary chart and summary testimony are properly admissible).

## K. TANGIBLE OBJECTS

The State institutes a criminal prosecution against John Jones, who is charged with stealing Sam Smith's wallet. The wallet was in Jones's possession when he was arrested and eventually was placed in a property envelope at the police station, where it remained until trial. The wallet was brought to trial by Officer Williams, who had not been involved in the arrest. The prosecutor attempts to introduce the wallet in evidence through Officer Williams.

### Prosecuting Attorney:

Q. Officer Williams, you have with you a wallet that we have marked for identification as State's Exhibit 4. Please tell us how you came to possess this wallet.

A. I went to the evidence room at police headquarters and signed out a large envelope marked as containing items that were in the possession of Mr. Jones at the time of his arrest.

Q. Were you involved in the arrest of Mr. Jones?

A. No.

Q. Were you involved in placing items found in the possession of John Jones into the property envelope you just discussed?

A. No.

Q. Are you able to account for and describe to us the custody of the wallet prior to the time you took it from the envelope?

A. No.

Q. Let me ask you to open the wallet and describe to us its contents.

A. The wallet contains an identification card stating it is the property of Sam Smith. It also contains several photographs of an individual I know to be Sam Smith.

**Prosecuting Attorney:** Your Honor, the State would at this time offer the Exhibit 4 wallet into evidence.

**Defense Attorney:** Objection, Your Honor, the State has failed to establish chain of custody with respect to the wallet.

**The Court:** The objection is overruled and the wallet will be admitted. While I agree that the State has not established a proper chain of custody, the wallet itself possesses characteristics that are fairly unique and that have been identified. In such a circumstance it is unnecessary to establish a chain of custody.

### Comment

Assuming relevance, to gain admission of a tangible object into evidence, the proponent must authenticate or identify it. Federal Rule of Evidence 901 states that the requirement is satisfied "by evidence sufficient to support a finding that the matter in question is what its proponent claims." The rule also provides several examples of authentication or identification that meet the requirement. The first is testimony by a witness with knowledge "that a matter is what it is claimed to be." Another is "appearance, contents, substance, internal patterns, or other distinctive characteristics, taken in conjunction with circumstances."

"Tangible objects . . . are admissible in evidence only when identified and shown to be in materially the same condition as at the time [at issue]." *Lockhart v. Texas Dept. of Corrections*, 782 F.2d 1275, 1280–81 (5th Cir. 1986); *see* 2 MCCORMICK ON EVIDENCE § 213 at 13-17 (Kenneth S. Broun ed., 7th ed. 2013). As McCormick notes, "If the condition of the item of real evidence is important to its identity, the unchanged condition is part of the authentication requirement. It could be the subject of testimony from a percipient witness, or even inferred from the object being relatively impervious to change." *Id.* at 11–12. *See also United States v. Kelly*, 14 F.3d 1169 (7th Cir. 1994) (gap in chain of custody occurring after the testing is treated more permissively), and *United States v. Thomas*, 987 F.2d 1298 (7th Cir. 1993) (in cases where the evidence is unique and resistant to change—Korean-made sawed-off shotgun—the chain of custody is relatively unimportant); *United States v. Miller*, 994 F.2d 441 (8th Cir. 1993) (one-year gap in the chain of custody goes to the weight of the evidence and not the admissibility); *United States v. Brooks*, 727 F.3d 1291 (10th Cir. 2013) (finding that chain of custody of zip ties used to bind robbery victims was sufficient to permit admission of the ties even though crime scene investigators could not say whether they were contaminated by DNA of other persons); *United States v. Collado*, 957 F.2d 38 (1st Cir. 1992) (the unique characteristic approach to authentication of real evidence is provided for by Fed. R. Evid. 901(b)(4) and the chain of custody analysis by rule 901(b)(1)); *United States v. Clonts*, 966 F.2d 1366 (10th Cir. 1992) ("the degree of proof needed to establish an uninterrupted chain of custody depends upon the nature of the evidence at issue"); *United States v. Roberson*, 897 F.2d 1092 (11th Cir. 1990) (gaps in the chain of custody go to the weight of the evidence and not the admissibility); *United States v. Hon*, 904 F.2d 803 (2d Cir. 1990) (deficiencies—such as incorrectly labeled evidence, evidence bags left open, and no written records—in the government's chain of custody go to the weight of the evidence and not the admissibility); *United States v. Browne*, 891 F.2d 389 (1st Cir. 1989) (the trial court must be able to determine that it is reasonably probable that there was no material alteration of the evidence after it came into the custody of the proponent); *United States v. Casamanto*, 887 F.2d 1141 (2d Cir. 1989) (the chain of custody from the seizure of the substance to the analysis is subject to stricter scrutiny, and deficiencies render the evidence inadmissible); *United States v. Mahone*, 537 F.2d 922 (7th Cir. 1976) (quoting *United States v. Blue*, 440 F.2d 300, 303 (7th Cir. 1971)) ("The chain of custody is not relevant when a witness identifies the object as the actual object about which he has testified."); *United States v.*

*Panczko*, 353 F.2d 676 (7th Cir. 1965), *overruled on other grounds*; *United States v. Arciniega*, 574 F.2d 931 (7th Cir. 1978) (a chain of custody must be proved when the condition of the object at a prior time is in issue); *United States v. Combs*, 369 F.3d 925, 938 (6th Cir.), *cert. denied*, 128 S. Ct. 1646 (2008); *United States v. Lee*, 502 F.3d 691, 697 (7th Cir.), *cert. denied*, 128 S.Ct. 1316 (2008); *United States v. Chapman*, 345 F.3d 360, 367 (8th Cir.), *cert. denied,* 541 U.S. 955 (2004); *United States v. Carlos Cruz*, 352 F.3d 499, 506 (1st Cir.), *cert. denied,* 543 U.S. 857 (2004); *United States v. Inserra*, 34 F.3d 83, 90 (2d Cir. 1994); *United States v. Smith*, 481 F.3d 259, 265 (5th Cir.), *cert. denied*, 127 S. Ct. 2288 (2007) (In a criminal trial, any proposed break in the chain of custody goes to weight, not admissibility); *United States v. Jones*, 356 F.3d 529, 535–36 (4th Cir.), *cert. denied*, 541 U.S. 942 (2004) ("A 'missing link' in the chain of custody 'does not prevent the admission of real evidence, so long as there is sufficient proof that the evidence is what it purports to be and has not been altered in any material respect.' *United States v. Ricco*, 52 F.3d 58, 61–62 (4th Cir. 1995)").

# Opinions of the Lay Witness 6

## A. LAY OPINION, GENERALLY

The United States indicts the local director of a federally funded program for willful misapplication of funds. The defendant places in issue the question of his willfulness, claiming he did not know and understand the particular requirements of the program that he is charged with violating. The government calls the director's secretary, seeking to obtain her testimony on whether, in her opinion, the director fully understood the requirements of the program.

### U.S. Attorney:

Q. State your name, please.

A. Gwendolyn Jackson.

Q. Where are you employed?

A. The office of Federal Support for Wild Animals.

Q. What is the office of Federal Support for Wild Animals?

A. It is a federally funded program to protect wild animals from cruelty.

Q. What is your position in that department?

A. I am secretary to the director, Mr. Smith.

Q. How long have you served as his secretary?

A. For the past three years.

Q. What are your responsibilities as his secretary?

A. General typing, administrative work, and serving as a liaison between other members in the office and the director.

Q. During the course of your employment as the director's secretary, do you have occasion to work with him on projects?

A. Yes, I do.

Q. Do you have occasion to attend meetings with him?

A. Yes, I do.

Q. Do you have occasion to observe him as he performs his responsibilities?

A. Yes, I do.

Q. Do you ever have occasion to attend meetings with him where the purposes and rules of operating the office are explained and discussed?

A. Yes, many times.

Q. Do you have an opinion on whether Mr. Smith knew and understood the requirements of the program as to eligibility to receive federal funds?

A. Yes, I do.

Q. And what is that opinion?

A. Mr. Smith fully appreciated and understood the rules and requirements of the program with regard to awarding and applying federal funds to those who were eligible.

## Comment

Generally, lay witnesses may not state opinions in court. Nevertheless, the prevailing practice with regard to the admission of the opinions of lay witnesses manifests itself not as a rule of absolute prohibition, but rather as a preference for non-opinion testimony. *See* 1 McCormick on Evidence § 11 (Kenneth S. Broun ed., 7th ed. 2013). Federal Rule of Evidence 701, in conjunction with Rule 602, provides that a lay witness may testify in the form of an opinion if the opinion is rationally based on the perception of the witness, is helpful to a clear understanding of the testimony or the determination of a fact in issue, and is not based on scientific, technical, or specialized knowledge within the scope of Rule 702.

Lay witnesses have been permitted to express opinions on a wide variety of topics, including "[t]he appearance of person or things, identity, the manner of conduct, competency of a person, feelings, degrees of light or darkness, sound, size, weight, distance, and an endless number of things that cannot be described factually . . . ." Ladd, Expert Testimony, 5 Vand L. Rev. 414, 415–17 (1952). *See United States v. Min*, 704 F.3d 314, 324–25 (4th Cir. 2013) (meaning of drug slang words that defendant spoke to police officer); *United States v. Santana*, 342 F.3d 60, 68–69 (1st Cir. 2003) (witness permitted to testify that he smelled marijuana); *Christopher Phelps and Associates, LLC v. Galloway*, 492 F.3d 532, 542 (4th Cir. 2007); *Lifewise Master Funding v. Telebank*, 374 F.3d 917, 929 (10th Cir. 2004); *Nationwide Transport Finance v. Cass Information Systems, Inc.*, 523 F.3d 1051, 1059–60 (9th Cir. 2008) (excluding testimony as unhelpful where the lay witness merely told the jury what result to reach); *Brazos River Authority v. GE Ionics, Inc.*, 469 F.3d 416, 435 (5th Cir. 2006); *Tampa Bay Shipbuilding and Repair Co. v. Cedar Shipping Company, LTD*, 320 F.3d 1213, 1223 (11th Cir. 2003) (a lay witness can testify as to the value of his or her own services); *United States v. Mendoza-Paz*, 2002 U.S. App. LEXIS 6550, at *20–*21 (9th Cir. Apr. 10. 2002); *United States v. Nelson*, 2002 U.S. App. LEXIS 3628, at *13–*14 (9th Cir. Mar. 5, 2002) (no requirement that expert testimony be presented in child pornography cases to establish age of children in pictures); *United States v. Caballero*, 277 F.3d 1235, 1247 (10th Cir. 2002) (possible for same witness to provide both lay and expert testimony in same case); *Research Sys. Corp. v. IPSOS Publicite*, 276 F.3d 914, 924 (7th Cir. 2001) (lay testimony that product was not unique in the industry); *Walton v. Nalco Chem. Co.*, 272 F.3d 13, 29–30 (1st Cir. 2001) (court upheld exclusion of lay opinion of district sales manager as to company's net profits lost); *Meyers v. Wal-Mart Stores, Inc.*, 257 F.3d 625, 630 (6th Cir. 2001) (combination of both expert and lay testimony sufficient under Michigan law to present triable issue for jury; "before and after" lay testimony competent evidence on issue of damages); *Mattison v. Dallas Carrier Corp.*, 947 F.2d 95 (4th Cir. 1991) (a lay witness was permitted to testify that emergency flashers on a vehicle did not provide sufficient warning); *Asplundh Mfg. Div. v. Benton Harbor Eng'g*, 57 F.3d 1190 (3d Cir. 1995); *United States v. Newman*, 49 F.3d 1 (1st Cir. 1995), *superseded by statute as stated in United States v. Hensley*, 91 F.3d 274 (1st Cir. 1996); *Duluth Lighthouse for the Blind v. C.G. Bretting Mfg. Co.*, 199 F.R.D. 320, 325–26 (D. Minn. 2000) (discusses amended Rule 701 and advisory committee notes thereto).

Most often, lay witnesses are called upon to render opinions on speed, height and distance, sobriety, mental capacity, and the value of property. Lay witnesses can also testify that another person appeared nervous, *United States v. Mastberg*, 503 F.2d 465 (9th Cir. 1974); or excited, *Asplundh Mfg. Div. v. Benton Harbor Eng'g*, 57 F.3d 1190, 1196 (3d Cir. 1995); or about their own physical symptoms, *Smolen v. Chater*, 80 F.3d 1273 (9th Cir. 1996); or intoxicated, *United States v. Horn*, 185 F. Supp. 2d 530, 560 (D. Md. 2002); *EEOC v. Oak-Rite Mfg. Corp.*, 2001 U.S. Dist. LEXIS 15621, at *8–*9 (S.D. Ind. Aug. 27, 2001); or depressed, *Farfaras v. Citizens Bank and Trust of Chicago*, 433 F.3d 558, 565 (7th Cir. 2006). *See also Tufariello v. Long Island Railroad Co.*, 458 F.3d 80, 90 (2d Cir. 2006) (permitting lay witness to testify that a train's blasts were so loud he had to cover his ears, and that it made his ears ring).

Counsel must be careful to elicit responses from the witness that demonstrate that the opinion is rationally based on the observation. *See, e.g., DIJO, Inc. v. Hilton Hotels Corp.*, 351 F.3d 679, 685 (5th Cir. 2003) (lay opinion testimony must be based on firsthand observation and knowledge); *Eichorn v. AT&T Corp.*, 484 F.3d 644, 649–50 (3d Cir. 2007) (refusing to admit testimony of lay witness who would testify about a spreadsheet. The spreadsheet was prepared by the witness's son, and therefore the witness had no personal knowledge of it.); *JGR, Inc. v. Thomasville Furniture Industry, Inc.*, 370 F.3d 519, 526 (6th Cir. 2004); *Bandera v. City of Quincy*, 344 F.3d 47, 54 (1st Cir. 2003); *United States v. Cox*, 633 F.2d 871 (9th Cir. 1980), *cert. denied*, 454 U.S. 844 (1981). When the opinion encompasses a legal conclusion or testimony that the court believes is not helpful, the court properly may exclude the opinion. *See United States v. McIver*, 470 F.3d 550, 562 (4th Cir.) ("opinion testimony that states a legal standard or draws a legal conclusion by applying law to the facts is generally inadmissible"), *cert. denied*, 127 S. Ct. 2276 (2007); *Sims v. Great American Life Insurance Co.*, 469 F.3d 870, 890 (10th Cir. 2006) (excluding officer's lay opinion testimony when it was not of aid to the jury); *King v. Harrington*, 447 F.3d 531, 534 (7th Cir. 2007) (refusal to allow lay witness to testify was proper when the witness did not add anything to what the jury already knew and testimony was not helpful); *United States v. Roy*, 881 F.2d 1070 (4th Cir. 1989); *United States v. Ness*, 665 F.2d 248 (8th Cir. 1981); *United States v. Phillips*, 600 F.2d 535 (5th Cir. 1979). *See also* Fed. R. Evid. 104(a) and 403.

Certainly, superfluous opinions are rejected in favor of hearing testimony about underlying facts. Thus, for example, a witness's opinion about the believability of another witness's testimony is not admissible. *See Engesser v. Dooley*, 457 F.3d 731, 736 (8th Cir.) ("An expert may not opine on another witness's credibility."), *cert. denied*, 127 S. Ct. 1284 (2007); *United States v. Hill*, 749 F.3d 1250 (10th Cir. 2014). On the other hand, lay witnesses called as character witnesses may render opinions as to another witness's character traits for veracity.

While the federal rules express a preference for non-opinion testimony, there should be a natural inclination on the part of the trial attorney to avoid naked opinion testimony in the first place. The more concrete description, pushing a jury to infer the desired opinion, is more persuasive than an abstract, naked opinion. *See* 1 McCormick on Evidence § 11 (Kenneth S. Broun ed., 7th ed. 2013); Fed. R. Evid. 701 Advisory Committee's Note.

In this example, the witness is asked to express an opinion concerning another individual's state of mind. *See United States v. Fowler*, 932 F.2d 306 (4th Cir. 1991), where the court permitted officials to render opinions that a person with defendant's experience would know the rules about classified documents not being available to contractors; *United States v. Smith*, 550 F.2d 277 (5th Cir.), *cert. denied sub nom. Wallace v. United States*, 434

U.S. 841 (1977); *Gossett v. Oklahoma ex rel. Bd. of Regents for Langston Univ.*, 245 F.3d 1172, 1179 (10th Cir. 2001) (testimony as to pattern of discrimination against men); *Xiangyuan Zhu v. Countrywide Realty Co.*, 165 F. Supp. 2d 1181, 1187 n.5 (D. Kan. 2001) (testimony about intent to deceive); *United States v. Mirama Enters.*, 2002 U.S. Dist. LEXIS 1888, at *19–*20 (S.D. Cal. Jan. 24, 2002), *summ. judgment granted (plaintiff)*, 185 F. Supp. 2d 1148 (S.D. Cal. 2002). Even if the lay opinion focuses on the ultimate issue of a case, Federal Rule of Evidence 704 would permit the opinion, subject to the discretion of the court. *See* Fed. R. Evid. 403.

Different judges could reach different determinations when confronted with the same facts. *See* 4 JACK B. WEINSTEIN ET AL., WEINSTEIN'S FEDERAL EVIDENCE § 701.06 (2d ed. 2014). The rules, however, relax the traditional view that lay opinions are not admissible, and relax the foundation requirements for the admissibility of those opinions.

## B. VALUE OF PERSONAL PROPERTY

Plaintiff Margaret Sands institutes suit against John Smith, claiming that Smith was responsible for damages to her automobile in a collision that allegedly occurred as a result of defendant's negligence. Counsel for plaintiff seeks to elicit the plaintiff's opinion as to the value of her automobile at the time of the accident.

Q. Mrs. Sands, when did you purchase the automobile that you were driving and that was involved in the collision?

A. 2012.

Q. And what was the purchase price of the car?

A. $700.

Q. Did you make any improvements to the automobile at the time or after you purchased it?

A. Yes.

Q. Tell us what type of improvements you made?

A. I equipped the automobile with new tires and had other work done to it, such as installing a stereo sound system.

Q. Do you have an opinion as to the value of the automobile at the time of the accident?

A. Yes.

Q. Can you tell us what that opinion is?

A. The car was worth approximately $1,000 at the time of the accident.

## *Comment*

Generally, lay witnesses may not state opinions in court. Nevertheless, the prevailing practice with regard to the admission of the opinions of lay witnesses manifests itself not as a rule of absolute prohibition, but rather as a preference for non-opinion testimony. *See* 1 McCormick on Evidence § 11 (Kenneth S. Broun ed., 7th ed. 2013). Federal Rule of Evidence 701, in conjunction with Rule 602, provides that a lay witness may testify in the form of an opinion if the opinion is rationally based on the perception of the witness and helpful to a clear understanding of the testimony or the determination of a fact in issue and is not based on scientific, technical, or specialized knowledge within the scope of Rule 702. *See, e.g., State v. Sherman*, 13 A.3d 1138, 1152 (Conn. App. 2012) (witness permitted to testify regarding the value of his personal property).

Lay witnesses have been permitted to express opinions on a wide variety of topics, including "[t]he appearance of person or things, identity, the manner of conduct, competency of a person, feelings, degrees of light or darkness, sound, size, weight, distance, and an endless number of things that cannot be described factually. . . ." Ladd, *Expert Testimony*, 5 Vand L. Rev. 414, 415–17 (1952). *See Christopher Phelps and Assoc., LLC v. Galloway*, 492 F.3d 532, 542 (4th Cir. 2007); *Lifewise Master Funding v. Telebank*, 374 F.3d 917, 929 (10th Cir. 2004); *Nationwide Transport Finance v. Cass Information Systems, Inc.*, 523 F.3d 1051, 1059–60 (9th Cir. 2008) (excluding testimony as unhelpful where the lay witness merely told the jury what result to reach); *Brazos River Authority v. GE Ionics, Inc.*, 469 F.3d 416, 435 (5th Cir. 2006); *Tampa Bay Shipbuilding and Repair Co. v. Cedar Shipping Co., LTD*, 320 F.3d 1213, 1223 (11th Cir. 2003) (a lay witness can testify as to the value of his or her own services); *United States v. Mendoza-Paz*, 2002 U.S. App. LEXIS 6550, at \*20–\*21 (9th Cir. Apr. 10, 2002); *United States v. Nelson*, 2002 U.S. App. LEXIS 3628, at \*13–\*14 (9th Cir. Mar. 5, 2002) (no requirement that expert testimony be presented in child pornography cases to establish age of children in pictures); *United States v. Caballero*, 277 F.3d 1235, 1247 (10th Cir. 2002) (possible for same witness to provide both lay and expert testimony in same case); *Research Sys. Corp. v. IPSOS Publicite*, 276 F.3d 914, 924 (7th Cir. 2001) (lay testimony that product was not unique in the industry); *Walton v. Nalco Chem. Co.*, 272 F.3d 13, 29– 30 (1st Cir. 2001) (court upheld exclusion of lay opinion of district sales manager as to company's net profits lost); *Meyers v. Wal-Mart Stores, Inc.*, 257 F.3d 625, 630

(6th Cir. 2001) (combination of both expert and lay testimony sufficient under Michigan law to present triable issue for jury; "before and after" lay testimony competent evidence on issue of damages); *Asplundh Mfg. Div. v. Benton Harbor Eng'g*, 57 F.3d 1190 (3d Cir. 1995); *United States v. Newman*, 49 F.3d 1 (1st Cir. 1995), *superseded by statute as stated in United States v. Hensley*, 91 F.3d 274 (1st Cir. 1996); *Mattison v. Dallas Carrier Corp.*, 947 F.2d 95 (4th Cir. 1991) (a lay witness was permitted to testify that emergency flashers on a vehicle did not provide sufficient warning); *Duluth Lighthouse for the Blind v. C.G. Bretting Mfg. Co.*, 199 F.R.D. 320, 325–26 (D. Minn. 2000) (discussing amended Rule 701 and advisory committee notes thereto).

As a general rule, an owner of personal property is permitted to express an opinion on the value of that property. The rationale for the rule is somewhat disputed, sometimes leading to slightly different applications of the rule. *See District of Columbia Redev. Land Agency v. Thirteen Parcels of Land*, 534 F.2d 337 (D.C. Cir. 1976). One line of authority holds that the owner may give an opinion without qualification because of the close relationship he has to the property. *Id.* at 339. The owner is not draped in a cloak of expertise, but rather testifies from the unique position as the individual who stands to gain or lose the most from the tribunal's valuation of his property. *Id.* at 340. "The weight of such testimony is, of course, affected by the owner's knowledge of circumstances which affect value, and as an interested witness, it is for the jury to evaluate the credibility of his testimony." *Berkshire Mut. Ins. Co. v. Moffett*, 378 F.2d 1007, 1011 (5th Cir. 1967) (footnotes omitted). *See Neff v. Kehoe*, 708 F.2d 639, 643–44 (11th Cir. 1983); *J & H Auto Trim Co., Inc. v. Bellefonte Ins. Co.*, 677 F.2d 1365, 1368 (11th Cir. 1982); *In re Brown*, 244 B.R. 603, 611–12 (Bankr. W.D. Va. 2000); *Ty Inc. v. Softbelly's Inc.*, 353 F.3d 528, 534 (7th Cir. 2003) (allowing lay witness to testify about his personal knowledge about whether consumers considered a toy name to be generic); *Christopher Phelps and Assoc., LLC v. Galloway*, 492 F.3d 532, 542 (4th Cir. 2007) (courts follow common-law assumption that property owner is capable of testifying about the value of his own property); *Loughridge v. Chiles Power Supply Co., Inc.*, 431 F.3d 1268,1281 (10th Cir. 2005) (lay witness could testify to the value of his house that contained a defective heating system).

The other line of authority holds that the owner may give an opinion as to the value of his property based on his "quasi-expert" status. *District of Columbia Redev. Land Agency v. Thirteen Parcels of Land*, 534 F.2d 337

(D.C. Cir. 1976). That is, the owner is presumed to be qualified to give a valuation opinion based on his special knowledge arising out of ownership. This knowledge must rest on "some independent, competent, and relevant basis, such as experience in buying or selling [property], general knowledge of [property] values . . . , or some particular knowledge relating to the [property] in question." *Id.* at 347. Where a lack of such knowledge is affirmatively shown, such as "where the opinion rest[s] on hypothesized facts or speculation on circumstances not in existence," the owner's opinion will be held inadmissible. *Id.*; *see Robinson v. Watts Detective Agency, Inc.*, 685 F.2d 729, 739 (1st Cir. 1982), *cert. denied*, 459 U.S. 1204 (1983).

While not clearly defined in the circuits, most federal courts align themselves within this second ideological camp. *See Asplundh Mfg. Div. v. Benton Harbor Eng'g*, 57 F.3d 1190, 1198 (3d Cir. 1995); *Robinson v. Watts Detective Agency, Inc.*, 685 F.2d 729, 738 (1st Cir. 1982), *cert. denied*, 459 U.S. 1204 (1983); *Dietz v. Consol. Oil & Gas, Inc.*, 643 F.2d 1088, 1093–94 (5th Cir.), *cert. denied*, 454 U.S. 968 (1981); *Greenwood Ranches, Inc. v. Skie Constr. Co.*, 629 F.2d 518, 522 (8th Cir. 1980); *Rich v. Eastman Kodak Co.*, 583 F.2d 435, 437 (8th Cir. 1978); *Runge v. Lee*, 441 F.2d 579, 582 (9th Cir.), *cert. denied*, 404 U.S. 887 (1971); *Insurance Co. of Pa. v. Smith*, 435 F.2d 1029, 1031 (10th Cir. 1971); *Lee Shops, Inc. v. Schatten-Cypress Co.*, 350 F.2d 12, 17 (6th Cir. 1965), *cert. denied*, 382 U.S. 980 (1966); *Knuppel v. American Ins. Co.*, 269 F.2d 163, 166 (7th Cir. 1959); *In re Smith*, 267 B.R. 568, 573 (Bankr. S.D. Ohio 2001); *Lubecki v. Omega Logging, Inc.*, 674 F. Supp. 501, 509–10 (W.D. Pa. 1987); *Granholm v. TFL Express*, 576 F. Supp. 435, 452 (S.D.N.Y. 1983).

## C. VALUE OF REAL PROPERTY

Henry Armco, in a condemnation trial, wishes to demonstrate that the fair market value of his home, which the city wants to acquire for a highway, is $200,000.

### Plaintiff's Counsel:

Q. Mr. Armco, when did you acquire the premises known as 210 Madison Street?

A. 1999.

Q. What did you pay for the premises?

A. $120,000.

Q. Have you lived on the premises since the time you purchased it?

A. Yes, I have.

Q. Are you familiar with the real estate values in the vicinity of your home?

A. Yes, I am.

Q. What is the basis of your familiarity?

A. I have talked to neighbors living in similar type homes and they told me what their homes have sold for.

Q. When have you had these conversations?

A. Throughout the last five years.

Q. When did the sales that you discussed occur?

A. From 1999 to 2005.

Q. How many occurred during the past three years?

A. Five.

Q. Do you have an opinion on the fair market value of your premises as of July 1, 2005?

A. Yes, I do.

Q. Please state your opinion of that value as of July 1, 2005.

A. $200,000.

### Comment

Generally, lay witnesses may not state opinions in court. Nevertheless, the prevailing practice with regard to the admission of the opinions of lay witnesses manifests itself not as a rule of absolute prohibition, but rather as a preference for non-opinion testimony. *See* 1 MCCORMICK ON EVIDENCE § 11 (Kenneth S. Broun ed., 7th ed. 2013). Federal Rule of Evidence 701, in conjunction with Rule 602, provides that a lay witness may testify in the form of an opinion, if the opinion is rationally based on the perception of the witness and helpful to a clear understanding of the testimony or the determination of a fact in issue, and is not based on scientific, technical, or specialized knowledge within the scope of Rule 702. *See, e.g., Eberle v. Eberle*, 783 N.W. 2d 254, 260 (N.D. 2010) ("an owner of real property may testify as to the value of the land without further qualification or special knowledge").

Lay witnesses have been permitted to express opinions on a wide variety of topics, including "[t]he appearance of person or things, identity, the manner of conduct, competency of a person, feelings, degrees of light or darkness, sound, size, weight, distance, and an endless number of things that cannot be described factually. . . ." Ladd, *Expert Testimony*, 5 Vand L. Rev. 414, 415–17 (1952). *See Christopher Phelps and Assoc., LLC v. Galloway*, 492 F.3d 532, 542 (4th Cir. 2007); *Lifewise Master Funding v. Telebank*, 374 F.3d 917, 929 (10th Cir. 2004); *Nationwide Transport Finance v. Cass Information Systems, Inc.*, 523 F.3d 1051, 1059–60 (9th Cir. 2008) (excluding testimony as unhelpful where the lay witness merely told the jury what result to reach); *Brazos River Authority v. GE Ionics, Inc.*, 469 F.3d 416, 435 (5th Cir. 2006); *Tampa Bay Shipbuilding and Repair Co. v. Cedar Shipping Company, LTD*, 320 F.3d 1213, 1223 (11th Cir. 2003) (a lay witness can testify as to the value of his or her own services); *United States v. Mendoza-Paz*, 2002 U.S. App. LEXIS 6550, at *20–*21 (9th Cir. Apr. 10, 2002); *United States v. Nelson*, 2002 U.S. App. LEXIS 3628, at *13–*14 (9th Cir. Mar. 5, 2002) (no requirement that expert testimony be presented in child pornography cases to establish age of children in pictures); *United States v. Caballero*, 277 F.3d 1235, 1247 (10th Cir. 2002) (possible for same witness to provide both lay and expert testimony in same case); *Research Sys. Corp. v. IPSOS Publicite*, 276 F.3d 914, 924 (7th Cir. 2001) (lay testimony that product was not unique in the industry); *Walton v. Nalco Chem. Co.*, 272 F.3d 13, 29–30 (1st Cir. 2001) (court upheld exclusion of lay opinion of district sales manager as to company's net profits lost); *Meyers v. Wal-Mart Stores, Inc.*, 257 F.3d 625, 630 (6th Cir. 2001) (combination of both expert and lay testimony sufficient under Michigan law to present triable issue for jury; "before and after" lay testimony competent evidence on issue of damages); *Mattison v. Dallas Carrier Corp.*, 947 F.2d 95 (4th Cir. 1991) (a lay witness was permitted to testify that emergency flashers on a vehicle did not provide sufficient warning); *Asplundh Mfg. Div. v. Benton Harbor Engineering*, 57 F.3d 1190 (3d Cir. 1995); *United States v. Newman*, 49 F.3d 1 (1st Cir. 1995); *Duluth Lighthouse for the Blind v. C.G. Bretting Mfg. Co.*, 199 F.R.D. 320, 325–26 (D. Minn. 2000) (discussing amended Rule 701 and advisory committee notes thereto).

As a general rule, an owner of real property is permitted to express an opinion on the value of that property. The rationale for the rule is somewhat disputed, sometimes leading to slightly different applications of the rule. *See Christopher Phelps and Assoc., LLC v. Galloway*, 492 F.3d 532, 542 (4th Cir. 2007); *District of Columbia Redev. Land Agency v. Thirteen Parcels of Land*, 534 F.2d 337 (D.C. Cir. 1976). One line of authority holds that the owner may give an opinion without qualification because of the close relationship he has to the property. *Id.* at 339. The owner is not draped in a cloak of expertise, but rather testifies from the unique position as the individual who stands to gain or lose the most from the tribunal's valuation of his property. *Id.* at 340. "The weight of such testimony is, of course, affected by the owner's knowledge of circumstances which affect value, and as an interested witness, it is for the jury to evaluate the credibility of his testimony." *Berkshire Mut. Ins. Co. v. Moffett*, 378 F.2d 1007, 1011 (5th Cir. 1967). *See LaCombe v. A-T-O, Inc.*, 679 F.2d 431 (5th Cir. 1982); *District of Columbia Redev. Land Agency v. Thirteen Parcels of Land*, 534 F.2d 337, 339 (D.C. Cir. 1976); *In re Brown*, 244 B.R. 603, 611–12 (Bankr. W.D. Va. 2000).

The other line of authority holds that the owner may give an opinion as to the value of his property based on his "quasi-expert" status. *District of Columbia Redev. Land Agency v. Thirteen Parcels of Land*, 534 F.2d 337 (D.C. Cir. 1976). That is, the owner is presumed to be qualified to give a valuation opinion based on his special knowledge arising out of ownership. This knowledge must rest on "some independent, competent, and relevant basis, such as experience in buying or selling land, general knowledge of land values . . . , or some particular knowledge relating to the land in question." *Id.* at 347. Where a lack of such knowledge is affirmatively shown, such as "where the opinion rest[s] on hypothesized facts or speculation on circumstances not in existence," the owner's opinion will be held inadmissible. *Id.* at 347; *Robinson v. Watts Detective Agency, Inc.*, 685 F.2d 729, 739 (1st Cir. 1982), *cert. denied*, 459 U.S. 1204 (1983). While not clearly defined in the circuits, most federal courts align themselves within this second ideological camp. *See White v. Atlantic Richfield Co.*, 945 F.2d 1130, 1132–33 (9th Cir. 1991); *United States v. 7.92 Acres of Land*, 769 F.2d 4, 12 (1st Cir. 1985), *cert. denied*, 484 U.S. 1011 (1988); *LaCombe v. A-T-O, Inc.*, 679 F.2d 431, 434 (5th Cir. 1982); *Justice v. Pennzoil Co.*, 598 F.2d 1339, 1344 (4th Cir.), *cert. denied sub nom. McKinney v. Pennzoil Co.*, 444 U.S. 967 (1979); *United States v. 534.28 Acres of Land*, 442 F. Supp. 82, 84 (M.D. Pa. 1977); *United States v. 3698.63 Acres of Land*, 416 F.2d 65, 67 (8th Cir. 1969); *United States v. Sowards*, 370 F.2d 87, 92 (10th Cir. 1966); *Kinter v. United States*, 156 F.2d 5, 7 (3d Cir. 1946); *In re Smith*, 267 B.R. 568, 573 (Bankr. S.D. Ohio 2001); *In re Jamison*, 93 B.R. 595, 596 (Bankr. S.D. Ohio 1988); *Loughridge v. Chiles Power Supply Co., Inc.*, 431 F.3d 1268, 1281 (10th Cir. 2005).

## D. HANDWRITING IDENTIFICATION

Patio, Inc. institutes suit against a general contractor, alleging cost delays caused by the contractor's failure to coordinate the operations of a subcontractor. The theory of Patio, Inc.'s case is that the general contractor warranted to Patio, Inc. that it would issue no change orders to the subcontractor without first obtaining the approval of Patio, Inc. and that the general contractor breached this aspect of its contract. Plaintiff's counsel seeks to introduce in evidence through the president of plaintiff corporation a change order, issued by the general contractor's resident engineer, that was not shown to plaintiff and that resulted in delays, causing damages to plaintiff. The president of the plaintiff corporation, who is examined as to the source of the change order, is not a handwriting expert.

### Plaintiff's Counsel:

Q. Mr. Johnson, are you familiar with the signature of the general contractor's resident engineer on the project that is the subject of this lawsuit?

A. Yes.

Q. Can you tell us the basis of your familiarity with his signature?

A. In my capacity as president of Patio, Inc., I have seen the resident engineer's signature on hundreds of change orders and other documents over the last five years.

Q. Would you recognize that signature if you saw it today?

A. Yes.

**Plaintiff's Counsel:** Please mark this document as Plaintiff's Exhibit No. 32 for identification.

Q. Mr. Johnson, I show you what has been marked as Plaintiff's Exhibit No. 32 for identification and ask you if you can identify the signature at the bottom of that document.

A. It is the signature of Tom Morrow, the general contractor's resident engineer.

Q. Can you identify the document?

A. It is a change order issued by the general contractor's resident engineer requesting the sewer contractor to move a sewer line.

**Plaintiff's Counsel:** Your Honor, we offer Plaintiff's Exhibit No. 32 for identification in evidence.

## *Comment*

Generally, lay witnesses may not state opinions in court. Nevertheless, the prevailing practice with regard to the admission of the opinions of lay witnesses manifests itself not as a rule of absolute prohibition, but rather as a preference for non-opinion testimony. *See* 1 McCormick on Evidence § 11 (Kenneth S. Broun ed., 7th ed. 2013). Federal Rule of Evidence 701, in conjunction with Rule 602, provides that a lay witness may testify in the form of an opinion if the opinion is rationally based on the perception of the witness and helpful to a clear understanding of the testimony or the determination of a fact in issue, and is not based on scientific, technical, or specialized knowledge within the scope of Rule 702.

Lay witnesses have been permitted to express opinions on a wide variety of topics, including "[t]he appearance of person or things, identity, the manner of conduct, competency of a person, feelings, degrees of light or darkness, sound, size, weight, distance, and an endless number of things that cannot be described factually. . . ." Ladd, *Expert Testimony*, 5 Vand L. Rev. 414, 415–17 (1952). *See Christopher Phelps and Assoc., LLC v. Galloway*, 492 F.3d 532, 542 (4th Cir. 2007); *Lifewise Master Funding v. Telebank*, 374 F.3d 917, 929 (10th Cir. 2004); *Nationwide Transport Finance v. Cass Information Systems, Inc.*, 523 F.3d 1051, 1059–60 (9th Cir. 2008) (excluding testimony as unhelpful where the lay witness merely told the jury what result to reach); *Brazos River Authority v. GE Ionics, Inc.*, 469 F.3d 416, 435 (5th Cir. 2006); *Tampa Bay Shipbuilding and Repair Co. v. Cedar Shipping Company, LTD*, 320 F.3d 1213, 1223 (11th Cir. 2003) (a lay witness can testify as to the value of his or her own services); *United States v. Mendoza-Paz*, 2002 U.S. App. LEXIS 6550, at *20–*21 (9th Cir. Apr. 10, 2002); *United States v. Nelson*, 2002 U.S. App. LEXIS 3628, at *13–*14 (9th Cir. Mar. 5, 2002) (no requirement that expert testimony be presented in child pornography cases to establish age of children in pictures); *United States v. Caballero*, 277 F.3d 1235, 1247 (10th Cir. 2002) (possible for same witness to provide both lay and expert testimony in same case); *Research Sys. Corp. v. IPSOS Publicite*, 276 F.3d 914, 924 (7th Cir. 2001) (lay testimony that product was not unique in the industry); Walton v. Nalco Chem. Co., 272 F.3d 13, 29–30 (1st Cir. 2001) (court upheld exclusion of lay opinion of district sales manager as to company's net profits lost); *Meyers v. Wal-Mart Stores, Inc.*, 257 F.3d 625, 630 (6th Cir. 2001) (combination of both expert and lay testimony sufficient under Michigan law to present triable issue for jury; "before and after" lay testimony competent evidence on issue of damages); *Mattison v. Dallas Carrier Corp.*, 947 F.2d 95 (4th Cir. 1991) (a lay witness was permitted to testify that emergency flashers on a vehicle did not provide sufficient warning); *Asplundh Mfg. Div. v. Benton Harbor Engineering*, 57 F.3d 1190 (3d Cir. 1995); *United States v. Newman*, 49 F.3d 1 (1st Cir. 1995); *Duluth Lighthouse for the Blind v. C.G. Bretting Mfg. Co.*, 199 F.R.D. 320, 325–26 (D. Minn. 2000) (discussing amended Rule 701 and advisory committee notes thereto).

A lay witness is permitted to testify as to the genuineness of handwriting based upon his or her familiarity with that handwriting, provided that the familiarity is not acquired for purposes of litigation. Fed. R. Evid. 901(b)(2). Fed. R. Ediv. 901(b)(2) provides for authentication by: "[a] nonexpert's opinion that handwriting is genuine, based on a familiarity with it that was not acquired for the current litigation." *See also* 5 JACK B. WEINSTEIN ET AL., WEINSTEIN'S FEDERAL EVIDENCE § 901.04 (2d ed. 2014); *United States v. Ali*, 616 F.3d 745, 753–54 (8th Cir. 2010) (requiring satisfaction of both Rule 901(b)(2) and 701 to authenticate document based on lay testimony identifying signature). The minimum foundation requires the witness to testify that he or she is familiar with the handwriting in question and to describe the circumstances giving rise to that familiarity. Counsel should take care not to over-prepare a witness with regard to handwriting exemplars so as to create a familiarity based on trial preparation. In the case of *Murray v. United States*, 247 F. 874 (4th Cir. 1917), which predated the Federal Rules of Evidence, the court held that a lay opinion on handwriting was admissible based on the witness's observation of the questioned handwriting on only one other occasion. *Cf. United States v. Pitts*, 569 F.2d 343 (5th Cir.), *cert. denied*, 436 U.S. 959 (1978) (one-shot comparison does not meet standard of familiarity).

In *United States v. Barron*, 707 F.2d 125 (5th Cir. 1983), the court permitted a lay witness to testify that the defendant forged another's signature. *See also Hall v. United Insurance Co. of America*, 367 F.3d 1255, 1260–61 (11th Cir. 2004) (refusing to admit lay witness testimony on handwriting because the witness did not provide sufficiently detailed information on how she became familiar with the handwriting); *United States v. Samet*, 466 F.3d 251, 254 (2d Cir. 2006); *United States v. Apperson*, 441 F.3d

1162, 1200 (10th Cir.), *cert. denied*, 127 S. Ct. 1024 (2007); *United States v. Chandler*, 2001 U.S. App. LEXIS 3099, at *14–*15 (10th Cir. Mar. 1, 2001), *cert. denied*, 122 S. Ct. 120 (2001); *United States v. Scott*, 270 F.3d 30, 48–49 (1st Cir. 2001), *cert. denied*, 2002 U.S. LEXIS 2662 (U.S. Apr. 15, 2002); *United States v. Dozie*, 27 F.3d 95 (4th Cir. 1994); *United States v. Tipton*, 964 F.2d 650 (7th Cir. 1992); *United States v. Binzel*, 907 F.2d 746 (7th Cir. 1990) (witness may testify in non-absolute terms such as "I believe" or "the writing is similar to"); *United States v. Barker*, 735 F.2d 1280 (11th Cir.), *cert. denied*, 469 U.S. 933 (1984); *United States v. Carriger*, 592 F.2d 312 (6th Cir. 1979); *United States v. Pitts*, 569 F.2d 343 (5th Cir.), *cert. denied*, 436 U.S. 959 (1978); *United States v. Kilgore*, 518 F.2d 496 (5th Cir. 1975), *cert. denied*, 430 U.S. 905 (1977); *United States v. Dreitzler*, 577 F.2d 539 (9th Cir. 1978), *cert. denied*, 440 U.S. 921 (1979); *United States v. Gallagher*, 576 F.2d 1028 (3d Cir. 1978), *cert. denied sub nom. McCarthy v. United States*, 444 U.S. 1043 (1980); *United States v. Standing Soldier*, 538 F.2d 196 (8th Cir.), *cert. denied*, 429 U.S. 1025 (1976); *Ryan v. United States*, 384 F.2d 379 (1st Cir. 1967).

## E. VOICE IDENTIFICATION—LAY WITNESS

Newstime, Inc. sues Easy Wax Car Wash, claiming fees for advertisements placed in Newstime's publications. The defense is that the advertisements were never authorized. Plaintiff calls the vice president of Newstime, Inc. to prove that the president of Easy Wax Car Wash personally placed the advertisements by telephone.

### Plaintiff's Counsel:

Q. Who placed these advertisements?

A. John Jones, president of Easy Wax Car Wash.

Q. How did he place these advertisements?

A. By telephone.

Q. Who called whom?

A. He called me.

Q. Did you recognize the voice of the person who telephoned you on each of these occasions?

A. Yes, I did.

Q. Do you remember the date of the first telephone call to place an ad?

A.  Yes, January 13, 2014.

Q.  Had you spoken to John Jones on the telephone prior to the date of January 13, 2014?

A.  Yes, many times.

Q.  On this occasion and the other occasions, did he identify himself as John Jones to you?

A.  Yes.

Q.  Did you ever telephone him?

A.  Yes.

Q.  Now, on each of the calls that he placed to you requesting that advertisements be published in Newstime publications, what did he say to you?

## Comment

Generally, lay witnesses may not state opinions in court. Nevertheless, the prevailing practice with regard to the admission of the opinions of lay witnesses manifests itself not as a rule of absolute prohibition, but rather as a preference for non-opinion testimony. *See* 1 MCCORMICK ON EVIDENCE § 11 (Kenneth S. Broun ed., 7th ed. 2013). Federal Rule of Evidence 701, in conjunction with Rule 602, provides that a lay witness may testify in the form of an opinion if the opinion is rationally based on the perception of the witness and helpful to a clear understanding of the testimony or the determination of a fact in issue, and is not based on scientific, technical, or specialized knowledge within the scope of Rule 702. *See United States v. Diiaz-Arias*, 717 F.3d 1 (1st Cir. 2013) (state trooper's lay opinion identifying defendant as speaker on intercepted telephone conversations was properly admitted based on trooper's familiarity with defendant's voice and knowledge of Spanish language); *United States v. Rollins*, 544 F.3d 820, 831–32 (7th Cir. 2008) (law enforcement officer permitted to testify as to identity of the voices in recorded calls and about the meaning that the callers gave to certain words).

Lay witnesses have been permitted to express opinions on a wide variety of topics, including "[t]he appearance of person or things, identity, the manner of conduct, competency of a person, feelings, degrees of light or darkness, sound, size, weight, distance, and an endless number of things that cannot be described factually. . . ." Ladd, *Expert Testimony*, 5 VAND L. REV. 414, 415–17 (1952). *See Christopher Phelps and Assoc., LLC v. Galloway*, 492 F.3d 532, 542 (4th Cir. 2007); *Lifewise Master Funding v. Telebank*, 374 F.3d 917, 929 (10th Cir. 2004); *Nationwide Transport Finance v. Cass Information Systems, Inc.*, 523 F.3d 1051, 1059–60 (9th Cir. 2008) (excluding testimony as unhelpful where the lay witness merely told the jury what result to reach); *Brazos River Authority v. GE Ionics, Inc.*, 469 F.3d 416, 435 (5th Cir. 2006); *Tampa Bay Shipbuilding and Repair Co. v. Cedar Shipping Company, LTD*, 320 F.3d 1213, 1223 (11th Cir. 2003) (a lay witness can testify as to the value of his or her own services); *United States v. Mendoza-Paz*, 2002 U.S. App. LEXIS 6550, at \*20–\*21 (9th Cir. Apr. 10, 2002); *United States v. Nelson*, 2002 U.S. App. LEXIS 3628, at \*13–\*14 (9th Cir. Mar. 5, 2002) (no requirement that expert testimony be presented in child pornography cases to establish age of children in pictures); *United States v. Caballero*, 277 F.3d 1235, 1247 (10th Cir. 2002) (possible for same witness to provide both lay and expert testimony in same case); *Research Sys. Corp. v. IPSOS Publicite*, 276 F.3d 914, 924 (7th Cir. 2001) (lay testimony that product was not unique in the industry); *Walton v. Nalco Chem. Co.*, 272 F.3d 13, 29–30 (1st Cir. 2001) (court upheld exclusion of lay opinion of district sales manager as to company's net profits lost); *Meyers v. Wal-Mart Stores, Inc.*, 257 F.3d 625, 630 (6th Cir. 2001) (combination of both expert and lay testimony sufficient under Michigan law to present triable issue for jury; "before and after" lay testimony competent evidence on issue of damages); *Mattison v. Dallas Carrier Corp.*, 947 F.2d 95 (4th Cir. 1991) (a lay witness was permitted to testify that emergency flashers on a vehicle did not provide sufficient warning); *Asplundh Mfg. Div. v. Benton Harbor Engineering*, 57 F.3d 1190 (3d Cir. 1995); *United States v. Newman*, 49 F.3d 1 (1st Cir. 1995), *superseded by statute as stated in United States v. Hensley*, 91 F.3d 274 (1st Cir. 1996); *Duluth Lighthouse for the Blind v. C.G. Bretting Mfg. Co.*, 199 F.R.D. 320, 325–26 (D. Minn. 2000) (discussing amended Rule 701 and advisory committee notes thereto).

Federal Rule of Evidence 901(b)(5) provides that voice identification may be made by opinion evidence based upon hearing the voice at any time under circumstances connecting it with the alleged speaker. *See United States v. Bush*, 405 F.3d 909, 915 (10th Cir. 2005); *United States v. Garcia*, 413 F.3d 201, 207 n.3 (2d Cir. 2005); *United States v. Norman*, 415 F.3d 466, 472 (5th Cir. 2005); *United States v. Bakal*, 2001 U.S. App. LEXIS 21482, at \*4 (2d Cir. Oct. 3, 2001); *United States v. Tropeano*, 252 F.3d 653, 661 (2d Cir. 2001); *United States v. Jordan*, 2000 U.S. App. LEXIS 15489, at \*7–\*8 (7th Cir. June 29, 2000); *United States v. Duran*,

4 F.3d 800 (9th Cir. 1993), *cert. denied*, 510 U.S. 1078 (1994), *appeal after remand*, 46 F.3d 1146 (9th Cir.), *cert. denied*, 514 U.S. 1135 (1995); *United States v. Puentes*, 50 F.3d 1567 (11th Cir.), *cert. denied*, 516 U.S. 933 341 (1995); *United States v. Cooper*, 868 F.2d 1505 (6th Cir.), *cert. denied*, 490 U.S. 1094 (1989); *United States v. Vega*, 860 F.2d 779 (7th Cir. 1988), *abrogated on other grounds*, *United States v. Durrive*, 902 F.2d 1221 (7th Cir. 1990); *United States v. Cambindo Valencia*, 609 F.2d 603 (2d Cir. 1979), *cert. denied sub nom. Prado v. United States*, 446 U.S. 940 (1980); *United States v. Vitale*, 549 F.2d 71 (8th Cir.), *cert. denied*, 431 U.S. 907 (1977); *United States v. Watson*, 594 F.2d 1330 (10th Cir.), *cert. denied sub nom. Brown v. United States*, 444 U.S. 840 (1979); *United States v. DiMuro*, 540 F.2d 503 (1st Cir. 1976), *cert. denied*, 429 U.S. 1038 (1977); *Millender v. Adams*, 187 F. Supp. 2d 852, 869 (E.D. Mich. 2002); *United States v. Robinson*, 707 F.2d 811 (4th Cir. 1983); *United States v. Verlin*, 466 F. Supp. 155 (N.D. Tex. 1979); *United States v. Whitaker*, 372 F. Supp. 154 (M.D. Pa.), *aff'd sub nom. Appeal of Nicola*, 503 F.2d 1399 (3d Cir.), *aff'd*, 503 F.2d 1400 (3d Cir. 1974), *cert. denied*, 419 U.S. 1113 (1975).

McCormick on Evidence discusses the foundation for telephone voice identification, which requires preliminary testimony to establish the identity of the other person. 2 McCormick on Evidence § 228 (Kenneth S. Broun ed., 7th ed. 2013). McCormick also discusses the nature of the authentication requirements for identification of a voice. Authentication can arise from the witness's familiarity with and recognition of the voice. It can also arise from the circumstances. These circumstances can include a situation where the call was a return call in response to a message left for the caller, or a conversation during which the caller displayed knowledge of facts that only the caller would have, or the caller demonstrated a familiarity with facts that the person in question would likely know. The requisite familiarity may be acquired either before or after hearing the voice to be identified, and it may be acquired for the purpose of litigation. *See* 7 Michael H. Graham, Handbook of Federal Evidence § 901:5 (7th ed. 2012); 6A Lynn McClain, Maryland Evidence, State and Federal § 901.17 (3d ed. 2013). Sound recordings are also admissible in evidence. Proper foundation requires the following testimony: that the recording device was capable of taking the conversation offered in evidence; that the operator of the device was competent to operate the device; that the recording is authentic and correct; that changes, additions, or deletions have not been made in the recording; that the recording has been preserved in a manner that is shown to the court; an identification of the speakers; and that the conversation elicited was made voluntarily and in good faith, without any kind of inducement. *See United States v. McKeever*, 169 F. Supp. 426, 430 (S.D.N.Y. 1958), *rev'd on other grounds*, 271 F.2d 669 (2d Cir. 1959). *See also United States v. Green*, 175 F.3d 822, 830 (10th Cir. 1999), *reprinted in full*, *United States v. Browne*, 2000 U.S. App. LEXIS 6773 (10th Cir. Apr. 13, 2000); *United States v. Rengifo*, 789 F.2d 975 (1st Cir. 1986); *United States v. Rochan*, 563 F.2d 1246 (5th Cir. 1977); 5 JACK B. WEINSTEIN ET AL., WEINSTEIN'S FEDERAL EVIDENCE §§ 901.06-901.07 (2d ed. 2014). *But see United States v. Garrett*, 292 Fed. Appx. 3, 6 (11th Cir. 2008) ("Although the government should produce evidence regarding the competence of a recording machine operator, the fidelity of the equipment, the absence of alterations to the recorded media, and the identity of the speakers, 'the trial court has broad discretion to allow [media] into evidence without such a showing so long as there is independent evidence of accuracy.'") (quoting *United States v. Reed*, 887 F.2d 1398, 1405 (11th Cir. 1989)). Courts are given broad discretion to decide whether transcripts of the recordings should be provided to the jury. *United States v. Nunez*, 532 F.3d 645, 650–51 (7th Cir. 2008). *See also United States v. Khattab*, 536 F.3d 765, 766–67 (7th Cir. 2008) (allowing the government to introduce a translated transcript of a recording when the government had laid the proper foundation by producing an agent who identified the voice of the defendants as well as a linguist who testified that the translation from Arabic was accurate); *United States v. Gonzalez Perez*, No. 07-10485, 283 Fed. Appx. 716, 723–24 (11th Cir. 2008) ("The proponent who seeks to introduce written transcripts of audio tapes must introduce 'some evidence that the transcripts are accurate, that the words are accurately reproduced, and the voices accurately identified.' Moreover, when the transcript contains a translation into English of conversations spoken in a foreign language, the proponent must introduce the testimony of a qualified witness to authenticate and verify the translation.") (quoting *United States v. Rochan*, 563 F.2d 1246, 1251 (5th Cir. 1977)).

## F. INTOXICATION—LAY WITNESS

Sam Sailor, employed aboard the vessel *Vagabond*, fell off the boat's ladder while attempting to climb it and broke his arm. He sued Olaf Yachter, the owner of the boat, for his injuries, claiming that the ladder was negligently maintained and that boat was unseaworthy. Yachter defended on the ground that Sailor's injuries were due solely to Sailor's own intoxication. John Jones happened upon Sam Sailor shortly after his fall.

### Defendant's Attorney:

Q.  Where were you, Mr. Jones?

A.  I was patrolling the dock at the Wilson Marina. It was part of my job as a night watchman there.

Q.  What, if anything, unusual happened that evening?

A.  Well, I saw this fellow, who I later learned was Sam Sailor, staggering down the dock toward the Vagabond.

Q.  Did he make it to the Vagabond?

A.  He did. I watched him the whole way down the dock.

Q.  Then what happened?

A.  I watched him climb aboard the Vagabond. The next thing I heard was a big thud and then some frightful yelling and cursing.

Q.  What did you do?

A.  I ran to the Vagabond and found Sam Sailor stumbling around on the deck of the boat, holding his arm and cursing.

Q.  How close did you get to him?

A.  A foot or two. I wanted to see if he was okay.

Q.  What kind of lighting was in the area?

A.  There were plenty of lights. I could see well.

Q.  What did you observe?

A.  He smelled of alcohol. There was a look in his eye—on his face—the best way I can describe it is the relaxed muscles that an intoxicated person's face has and red, watery eyes.

Q.  Do you have an opinion as to whether Sam Sailor was intoxicated?

A.  Yes. In my opinion he was very intoxicated. He was dead drunk.

## *Comment*

Lay opinions on intoxication are governed by Federal Rules of Evidence 701 and 704 and comparable with state evidentiary rules. Such opinions generally are permitted, as long as the proponent of the evidence establishes that the witness had sufficient opportunity to observe the person in question. *See Sparrow v. Demonico*, 960 N.E. 2d 296, 305 (Mass. 2012) ("a non-expert is competent to testify to the physical appearance and condition and acts of a person both for their probative value for the jury and for the purpose of furnishing facts as the basis of hypothetical questions for experts"); *United States v. Denny*, 48 Fed. Appx. 732, 737 (10th Cir. 2002) (unreported) (holding that district court properly permitted lay opinion of intoxication); *Whitehead v. Book*, 641 F. Supp. 2d 549 (M.D. La. 2008) ("[O]pinion evidence is often admitted on the issue of the intoxication or sobriety of the defendant. It has been held that such an opinion may be given by a lay witness . . . , and that the witness may describe the facts and circumstances that led to his or her opinion—that is, he or she may give details as to the appearance and conduct of the defendant as derived from observation, and then testify whether the defendant was intoxicated or sober." (citation omitted)). *See also Trousdale v. State*, 500 So. 2d 1329 (Ala. Crim. App. 1986) (a police officer may "give his opinion as to sobriety vel non of the appellant"); *Jolly v. State*, 395 So. 2d 1135 (Ala. Crim. App. 1981) (lay opinion of intoxication is allowed to go to jury as evidence of intoxication); *Loof v. Sanders*, 686 P.2d 1205 (Alaska 1984) (lay witness can give opinion testimony on the issue of intoxication); *Esquivel v. Nancarrow*, 104 P.2d 399 (Ariz. 1969) ("the rule is well-settled, and nearly universal, that lay witnesses who have had a sufficient opportunity to observe a person may testify as to whether that person appears to be intoxicated . . ."); *State v. Lummus*, 950 P.2d 1190 (Ariz. 1997) (urges to apply caution in allowing testimony on the ultimate issue of intoxication; however, testimony on the degree of intoxication is admissible); *State v. English*, 575 S.W.2d 761 (Mo. App. 1978) (lay witnesses may give an opinion on the intoxication of another if preceded by evidence of conduct and appearance observed by them to support that opinion); *State v. Locklear*, 136 S.E.2d 716 App. 2000) (lay witness may give opinion as of the intoxication or sobriety of another); *State v. Wargo* (Oct. 31, 1997), 1997 Ohio App. LEXIS 4846 (a police officer may provide lay testimony as to his or her opinion concerning a defendant's state of intoxication); *Commonwealth v. Giehl*, 32 Pa. D.&C.3d 282 (Pa. 1983) (opinion as to defendant's intoxication is admissible, as intoxication is a matter of common observation); *People v. Williams*, 751 P.2d 395 (Cal. 1988) (lay opinion as to drug-induced intoxication is admissible); *State v. Lamme*, 563 A.2d 1372 (Conn. App. 1989) (lay opinion on the issue of intoxication is admissible); *State v. Bebb*, 53 P.3d 1198 (Haw. App. 2001) ("lay point of view" of police officer as to intoxication is admissible); *State v. Carlton*, 785 P.2d

184 (Kan. App. 1989) (lay opinions on the issue of intoxication are admissible); *State v. Turkowski* (Jan. 15, 2002), 2002 Minn. App. LEXIS 62 ("A lay witness may give an opinion as to another person's state of intoxication based on an observation of that person's breath, walk, and speech."); *State v. Slayton*, 367 A.2d 575 (N.H. 1976) ("lay opinion testimony as to state of intoxication has always been admissible").

# *Opinions of the Expert* 7

## A. QUALIFYING THE EXPERT

Counsel for the plaintiff qualifies an expert to render an opinion in the following manner:

### Plaintiff's Counsel:

Q. Doctor Sill, are you licensed to practice medicine in the state of Maryland?

A. Yes, I am.

Q. When were you so licensed, Doctor?

A. In 1972.

Q. And from what medical school did you graduate?

A. From St. Andrews University in Scotland.

Q. In what year?

A. In 1967.

Q. Doctor, when did you come to this country to practice medicine?

A. In 1968.

Q. What were the reasons that you came to this country?

A. I had an opportunity to do an internship at Johns Hopkins University here in Baltimore.

Q. Doctor, did you in fact complete that internship?

A. Yes, I did.

Q. For how long did that internship last, Doctor Sill?

A. Two years.

Q. What other postgraduate education did you undertake?

A. My postgraduate education spanned approximately four years. The first year I was an intern, which is the title given to recent graduates of medical school who remain in the hospital to continue their training. My internship lasted for two years. The third year I became a first-year resident, and in the fourth year I became the chief resident.

Q. In what field, if any, did you do your internship and residency?

A. General surgery.

Q. Doctor Sill, have you followed any particular specialty within your profession?

A. Yes. During the years following my internship and residency and thereafter, I have done traumatic surgery almost exclusively.

Q. What does that specialty involve?

A. Soft tissue surgery for injuries due to trauma, or violent bodily damage from any external cause.

Q. In addition to attending medical school and serving as an intern and resident, were there any other aspects of your training that further prepared you for your specialty?

A. I spent ten years doing emergency surgery and several years doing research in the field of trauma and shock.

Q. Doctor Sill, are you now in the private practice of medicine?

A. Yes, I am.

Q. For how long have you been in private practice?

A. For seven years.

Q. Approximately how many patients have you treated for traumatic injury?

A. Thousands.

Q. Did that treatment include surgery?

A. Yes.

Q. Are you affiliated with any hospitals?

A. Yes, I am affiliated with Fallston General Hospital, Johns Hopkins Hospital, and the Children's Hospital.

Q. Can you tell us what it means to be affiliated with a hospital as you are?

A. It means that I have the privilege of examining and treating patients at the hospital and performing necessary surgical operations.

Q. How does one become affiliated with a particular hospital?

A. He applies for the affiliation.

Q. What other hospitals have you been affiliated with in the course of your career in this country?

A. Only two other hospitals, Sinai Hospital and Greater Baltimore Medical Center.

Q. Doctor Sill, do you hold any teaching positions in your specialty?

A. I was an associate professor of surgery at Johns Hopkins Hospital for five years, from 1990 to 1995, and I am still an adjunct professor and on the surgical staff at that hospital.

Q. Have you had occasion to deliver lectures to professional groups or organizations concerning your specialty?

A. Yes.

Q. How often and to whom?

A. I have given about 100 lectures over the last four years, in almost every state, to medical students and doctors at seminars and medical association meetings.

Q. Of what professional organizations and honorary societies are you a member?

A. I am a member of several medical societies.

Q. Can you name just a few for us?

A. I am a member of the International Trauma Society, of which I was a co-founder; a member of the Medical and Chirurgical Faculty, which is the official name of the Maryland State Medical Society; the Surgical Research Society; the Atlantic Society for Experimental Medicine, and others.

Q. Have you written any articles or books in your specialty?

A. I have written about 200 articles and I have completed a book on general traumatic surgery.

Q. Thank you, Doctor Sill. Mr. Jones, defendant's counsel, now has a right to ask you any questions he may have about your qualifications. Does Mr. Jones have any questions about the doctor's qualifications as an expert in general traumatic surgery before I ask the doctor his opinion on this case?

## *Comment*

The admission of expert testimony in federal court is governed by Federal Rule of Evidence 702. Rule 702 provides that if "scientific, technical, or other specialized knowledge will assist the trier of fact to understand the evidence or to determine a fact in issue," a witness who is "qualified as an expert by knowledge, skill, experience, training or education" may offer expert testimony, in the form of an opinion or otherwise, if three conditions are met: "(1) the testimony is based upon sufficient facts or data, (2) the testimony is the product of reliable principles and methods, and (3) the witness has applied the principles and methods reliably to the facts of the case."

Rule 702 places a "gatekeeping" obligation on a trial court. In performing this obligation, the trial court considers first "whether proffered scientific evidence is valid and reliable," and second "whether it will help the trier of fact, which is generally a question of relevance, or 'fit': assuming the evidence is reliable, does it apply to the facts in the individual case under consideration." *Newman v. Motorola, Inc.*, 218 F. Supp. 2d 769, 772 (D. Md. 2002); *Belk, Inc. v. Meyer Corp.*, 679 F.3d 146, 161–63 (4th Cir. 2012) (expert was properly qualified to testify as an expert in marketing, consumer behavior, and evaluative studies at trial on trade dress infringement and unfair trade practices claims, although expert has not previously conducted trade dress or trademark surveys; expert had previously conducted extensive market research studies in various contexts); *Kumho Tire Co. v. Carmichael*, 526 U.S. 137, 141 (1999); *see United States v. Mooney*, 315 F.3d 54, 62 (1st Cir. 2002). This "gatekeeping" obligation "applies not only to testimony based on 'scientific' knowledge, but also to testimony based on 'technical' and 'other specialized' knowledge." *Kumho*, 526 U.S. at 142. The purpose of the gatekeeping obligation is "to make certain that an expert, whether basing testimony upon professional studies or personal experience, employs in the courtroom the same level of intellectual rigor that characterizes the practice of an expert in the relevant field." *Id.* at 152.

Reliability determinations must be tied to the facts of the particular case. *Id.* at 150. The test of reliability is flexible, and the court may use the factors set forth by the Supreme Court in *Daubert v. Merrell Dow Pharm.*, 509 U.S. 579 (1993): (1) whether the proffered technique can be and has been tested; (2) whether the technique or theory has been subject to peer review; (3) the known or potential rate of error; and (4) the general acceptance of a technique in the relevant community. *See Kumho*, 526 U.S. at 149; *United States v. Forrest*, 429 F.3d 73, 80 (4th Cir. 2005). This list of factors "neither necessarily nor exclusively applies to all experts or in every case." *Id.* at 141.

In assessing the reliability of a proffered expert's testimony, "the court's inquiry under Daubert focuses not on the substance of the expert's conclusions, but on the principles and methodology used to generate the conclusions." *Clarke v. LR Systems*, 219 F. Supp. 2d 323, 332 (E.D.N.Y. 2002). *See United States v. Stafford*, 721 F.3d 380, 393–94 (6th Cir. 2013) (to determine testimony's reliability, court does not determine whether opinion is correct, but rather determines whether it rests on a reliable foundation). "It is for the jury, not the Court, to determine whether an expert's opinions are suspect because facts upon which he relied were shown to be inaccurate or unproven." *S.E.C. v. Johnson*, 525 F. Supp. 2d 70, 76 (D.D.C. 2007).

An expert's qualifications are relevant to the reliability inquiry. *See United States v. Lopez-Medina*, 461 F.3d 724, 743 (6th Cir. 2006). But disputes about the strength of an expert's credentials, faults in an expert's decision to use a particular methodology, or the lack of textual authority for an expert's opinion "go to the weight, not the admissibility, of his testimony." *Clarke*, 219 F. Supp. 2d at 333. Acceptance of the methodology by the other party's expert may give additional credence to the reliability of the proffered testimony. *Correa v. Cruisers, a Div. of KCS Int'l, Inc.*, 298 F.3d 13, 26 (1st Cir. 2002).

Rule 702 was amended in the year 2000 in response to the Supreme Court's decision in *Daubert v. Merrell Dow Pharm.*, 509 U.S. 579 (1993). Advisory committee notes, 2000 Amendments, Fed. R. Evid. 702. The amended Rule 702 "reflects an attempt to liberalize the rules governing the admission of expert testimony. The rule clearly is one of admissibility rather than exclusion." *Sappington v. Skyjack, Inc.*, 512 F.3d 440, 448 (8th Cir. 2008) (citations omitted). As the advisory committee notes state: "A review of the case law after *Daubert* shows that the rejection of expert testimony is the exception rather than the rule."

Notwithstanding these statements, some categories of expert testimony have fared better than others under *Daubert*, *Kumho*, and Rule 702. For example, testimony of doctors, toxicologists, and epidemiologists is often proffered to show a causal link between a product or substance and a particular disease. Such evidence has been, more often than not, excluded by federal trial courts. *See, e.g., General Elec. Co. v. Joiner*, 522 U.S. 136 (1997) (excluding witnesses from testifying as experts on the question of the causation of lung cancer by exposure to potential carcinogens); *Amorgianos v. Nat'l R.R. Passenger Corp.*, 303 F.3d 256 (2d Cir. 2002) (affirming exclusion of toxicology expert testimony concerning link between xylene exposure and neurological symptoms); *Junk v. Terminix Int'l Co. Ltd. P'Ship*, 594 F. Supp. 2d 1062 (S.D. Iowa 2008) (excluding as unreliable testimony concerning link between in-home pesticide treatments and neurological deficits in fetus); *In re Methyl Tertiary Butyl Ether (MTBE) Products Liability Litig.*, 593 F. Supp. 2d 549 (S.D.N.Y. 2008) (court excluded proposed expert testimony about the level at which people could perceive MTBE in their water because of its odor or taste, as the testimony did not satisfy any of the four non-exclusive Daubert factors); *Grant v. Pharmative, LLC*, 452 F. Supp. 2d 903 (D. Neb. 2006) (excluding expert testimony of a link between a herbal supplement and liver disease, as the proposed witness had not tested his hypothesis of a link, which contradicts the body of research regarding the issue); *Burleson v. Glass*, 268 F. Supp. 2d 699 (W.D. Tex. 2003) (physician's opinion that exposure to thoriated tungsten welding rods causes lung and/or throat cancer was not reliable or relevant); *Newman v. Motorola, Inc.*, 218 F. Supp. 2d 769 (D. Md. 2002) (excluding proffered expert testimony that cellular phone use caused brain tumors, after concluding that expert's papers purporting to show this causal link were suspect due to recall bias, lack of any demonstrated dose-response relationship, and other methodological flaws); *Awad v. Merck & Co., Inc.*, 99 F. Supp. 2d 301 (S.D.N.Y. 1999) (non-epidemiological studies did not support expert's opinion that rubella vaccine caused chronic arthritis in adult female, where three large-scale epidemiological studies provided strong evidence that there was no causal relationship between vaccine and chronic joint pain), *aff'd*, 213 F.3d 627 (2d Cir. 2000).

By contrast, federal courts have been much more receptive to the admission of expert testimony in criminal cases from forensic scientists and law enforcement experts. *See, e.g., United States v. Hicks*, 389 F.3d 514 (5th Cir. 2004), *cert. denied*, 126 S. Ct. 1022 (2006) (upholding admission of cartridge-firearm ballistics comparisons); *United States v. Trala*, 386 F.3d 536 (3d Cir. 2004), *vacated on other grounds*, 126 S. Ct. 1078 (2006) (upholding reliability of PCR/STR DNA typing method); *United States v. Garcia-Morales*, 382 F.3d 12 (1st Cir. 2004) (upholding prosecution expert's testimony on nature and structure of typical drug distribution conspiracies); *United States v. Patterson*, 277 F.3d 709 (4th Cir. 2002) (upholding admission of testimony concerning fingerprints obtained with a laser imaging device); *but see United States v. Willock*, 696 F. Supp.2d 536 (D. Md. 2010) (prohibiting a ballistics comparison expert from expressing his opinions to "a reasonable degree of certainty in the ballistics field.") (For a thorough analysis of Daubert's application in the federal courts from 2000 through 2005, *see* Peter Nordberg, Daubert on the Web, at www.daubertontheweb.com.).

A question arises whether Rule 702 requires a proponent of expert testimony to elicit, on direct examination, testimony from the expert that specifically addresses the criteria promulgated in the rule. In most instances, this approach will not be necessary. Usually the expert's testimony will encompass the criteria, if not specifically, at least sufficiently to satisfy the court that the criteria of the rule have been satisfied. For example, when during the examination of the expert at trial the proponent asks, "What is the basis of that opinion?," the answer will include a recitation of facts sufficient to justify an opinion. The testimony will also encompass explanations relating to the reliability of the methods used to form the opinion and to the applicability of the opinion to the facts of the case. If there is any doubt, then the proponent should pose specific questions to satisfy the rule, *e.g.*, "What methods or principles did you use to form your opinion? Are these methods or principles accepted or recognized within the industry?

Did you apply the methodology you adopted in a proper manner?" While arguably these questions go to the ultimate issue of admissibility, the answers they seek go to the heart of the criteria established by the rule to evaluate the admissibility of the testimony. In many instances, if doubt exists about the admissibility of the expert testimony, opposing counsel will most likely seek a so-called *"Daubert* hearing" prior to trial for purposes of obtaining a pretrial ruling to exclude the expert from giving testimony. Even if a *Daubert* hearing is not conducted, the court, acting as "gatekeeper" to assess reliability, can exclude the expert's testimony at trial. A cautious advocate will want to pay close attention to Rule 702 in conducting the direct examination of the expert.

In *Samuel v. Ford*, 96 F. Supp. 2d 491 (D. Md. 2000), Judge Paul Grimm, writing for the court, fashioned a *Daubert/Kumho Tire* "checklist," attached to the opinion as an appendix, that counsel should follow if seeking to challenge the admissibility of an expert's testimony at trial under *Daubert/Kumho Tire* standards. The checklist requires the following information: (1) the name of the expert whose opinion(s) is (are) challenged; (2) a brief summary of the opinion(s) challenged, including a reference to the source of the opinion (such as the Fed. R. Civ. P. 26(a)(2)(B) disclosure, deposition transcript, etc.); (3) a brief description of the methodology/reasoning used by the expert to reach the challenged opinion(s), including a reference to the source materials; (4) a brief explanation of the basis for the challenge to the reasoning/ methodology used by the expert, including a reference to the source material for the challenge; (5) a discussion of the known or potential error rate associated with the methodology employed by the expert, if known; (6) a summary of the relevant peer review material, if available, with citation to the source; and (7) a discussion of whether the methods/principles used have been generally accepted within the relevant scientific or technical community, with citation to references. *Samuel*, 96 F. Supp. 2d at 504.

While all courts may not expect counsel to follow such a detailed checklist to present an evidentiary challenge to proffered expert testimony, it is a good reference tool, as it highlights the various components that must be considered in making a *Daubert/Kumho Tire* challenge. Further, it underscores that the facts related to the *Daubert/ Kumho Tire* factors should be obtained during discovery. *See also* PAUL W. GRIMM, CHARLES S. FAX & PAUL MARK SANDLER, DISCOVERY PROBLEMS AND SOLUTIONS (2d ed. 2009).

The knowledge of the expert can be obtained from observation, experience, standard texts, or any other reliable source. The courts do have discretion in allowing expert testimony. *See United States v. Jordan*, 236 F.3d 953, 955 (8th Cir.), *cert. denied*, 122 S. Ct. 220 (2001) (trial court has broad discretion to admit or exclude expert testimony); *Brown v. Wal-Mart Stores, Inc.*, 1999 U.S. App. LEXIS 32031, at *5–*6 (6th Cir. Nov. 24, 1999) (expert is permitted wide latitude to offer opinions, including those not based on firsthand knowledge or observation); *United States v. Fosher*, 590 F.2d 381 (1st Cir. 1979); *Reno– West Coast Distrib. Co., Inc. v. Mead Corp.*, 613 F.2d 722 (9th Cir.), *cert. denied*, 444 U.S. 927 (1979); *Soo Line R.R. Co. v. Fruehauf Corp.*, 547 F.2d 1365 (8th Cir. 1977); *United States v. Dukagjini*, 326 F.3d 45, 52 (2d Cir.), *cert. denied*, 541 U.S. 1092 (2004); *Truck Ins. Exchange v. Magnetek, Inc.*, 360 F.3d 1206, 1210 (10th Cir. 2004). However, this discretion is not unbridled. In *Garrett v. Desa Indus., Inc.*, 705 F.2d 721 (4th Cir. 1983), the court reversed the trial court's ruling, which prohibited a mechanical engineer from opining on the unsafe design of a product. Consider *In re Hanford Nuclear Reservation Litig.*, 521 F.3d 1028, 1056 (9th Cir. 2008), *opinion amended and superseded*, 534 F.3d 986 (9th Cir. 2008) (finding that the lower court abused its discretion by excluding the testimony of the expert's expertise); *Kopf v. Skyrm*, 993 F.2d 374 (4th Cir. 1993). *See also Allison v. McGhan Med. Corp.*, 184 F.3d 1300, 1306 (11th Cir. 1999).

## B. INTRODUCTION OF EXPERT TESTIMONY IN FEDERAL COURT

A plaintiff seeks to have DNA fingerprinting analysis admitted in federal court. Defense counsel objects. The court conducts a full evidentiary hearing on the matter pursuant to the so-called *Daubert* test. Plaintiff's counsel qualifies an expert in the field and proceeds.

### Plaintiff's Counsel:

Q. Doctor August, what is DNA?

A. DNA is a genetic blueprint carried by every cell in the human body. It triggers the development of cells and outlines defining genetic features.

Q. Is the DNA in every human being unique?

A. When taken as a whole, every human being has unique DNA, with the exception of identical twins.

Q. Can DNA be used as a tool to identify people, much like a fingerprint?

A. Yes, when subject to appropriate testing.

Q. How does that testing process work?

A. We use tests that break the DNA into a series of fragments that can be identified and charted. Probes are used to look at particular parts of the DNA that are usually different in different human beings. Once a significant number of probes has been done, the results from the probes can be matched against the DNA taken from a specific subject.

Q. If you have two DNA probe samples from two different people, will they necessarily be unique?

A. If you compare only one probe sample, then no, they will not necessarily be unique.

Q. Why not?

A. Every human being has unique DNA when you are comparing all of the DNA; however, a probe sample only compares a small portion of DNA. Any one particular probe sample might match anywhere from 10 to 90 percent of the population at large. As you do more and more probe samples of DNA, the number of persons that match all of the DNA probes becomes smaller and smaller.

Q. Can DNA testing prove conclusively that one person is the only match for a particular DNA?

A. No, the testing does not prove that one person is the only match; instead, it rules out most of the population to the extent that you can have a very small number of potential matches.

Q. How are those numbers of matches calculated?

A. Through statistical formulas.

Q. Are those statistical formulas that you used generally accepted in the scientific community?

A. Yes.

Q. Have those statistical formulas been subjected to peer review publication?

A. Yes, many times.

Q. And have guidelines been established for the use of these statistical formulas?

A. Yes.

Q. What are those guidelines?

A. Basically, DNA data should be interpreted using the statistical formulas most favorable to the defendant in a criminal case. In a civil case, the formulas should favor the party against whom the evidence is sought to be used.

Q. With regard to the tests involved in extracting the DNA samples, are these tests generally reliable when correctly administered?

A. Yes.

Q. Have these testing procedures been subject to peer review publication?

A. Yes, many times.

Q. Have reliability parameters been developed for these testing procedures?

A. Yes, they have.

Q. And what are those parameters?

A. They vary based on the number of probes taken and the quality or rareness of those probes. They can range from a low of one match in a million people to a high of one match in a billion people.

Q. Do set standards and controls exist for carrying out these tests?

A. Yes.

Q. Is the process by which you match a sample DNA to the control DNA generally reliable?

A. Yes. The odds of the matching procedure incorrectly matching two samples is about one in a million.

Q. Thank you, Doctor.

**Plaintiff's Attorney:** Your Honor, we request that the court find that DNA fingerprint testing meets the factors set forth in the *Daubert* case, and that plaintiff be allowed to lay a foundation for admitting such evidence in this case.

**The Court:** The ruling will be reserved subject to cross-examination by defendant's counsel.

## Comment

The admission of expert testimony in federal court is governed by Fed. R. Evid. 702. Rule 702 provides that if "scientific, technical, or other specialized knowledge will assist the trier of fact to understand the evidence or to determine a fact in issue," a witness who is "qualified as an expert by knowledge, skill, experience, training or education" may offer expert testimony, in the form of an opinion or otherwise, if three conditions are met: "(1) the testimony is based upon sufficient facts or data, (2) the testimony is the product of reliable principles and methods, and (3) the witness has applied the principles and methods reliably to the facts of the case."

Rule 702 places a "gatekeeping" obligation on a trial court. In performing this obligation, the trial court considers first "whether proffered scientific evidence is valid and reliable," and second "whether it will help the trier of fact, which is generally a question of relevance, or 'fit': assuming the evidence is reliable, does it apply to the facts in the individual case under consideration." *Newman v. Motorola, Inc.*, 218 F. Supp. 2d 769, 772 (D. Md. 2002); *see Kumho Tire Co. v. Carmichael*, 526 U.S. 137, 141 (1999); *see United States v. Mooney*, 315 F.3d 54, 62 (1st Cir. 2002). This "gatekeeping" obligation "applies not only to testimony based on 'scientific' knowledge, but also to testimony based on 'technical' and 'other specialized' knowledge." *Kumho*, 526 U.S. at 142. The purpose of the gatekeeping obligation is "to make certain that an expert, whether basing testimony upon professional studies or personal experience, employs in the courtroom the same level of intellectual rigor that characterizes the practice of an expert in the relevant field." *Id.* at 152.

Reliability determinations must be tied to the facts of the particular case. *Id.* at 150. The test of reliability is flexible and the court may use the factors set forth by the Supreme Court in *Daubert v. Merrell Dow Pharm.*, 509 U.S. 579 (1993): (1) whether the proffered technique can and has been tested; (2) whether the technique or theory has been subject to peer review; (3) the known or potential rate of error; and (4) the general acceptance of a technique in the relevant community. *See Kumho*. 526 U.S. at 149; *United States v. Forrest*, 429 F.3d 73, 80 (4th Cir. 2005). This list of factors "neither necessarily nor exclusively applies to all experts or in every case." *Id.* at 141.

In assessing the reliability of a proffered expert's testimony, "the court's inquiry under *Daubert* focuses not on the substance of the expert's conclusions, but on the principles and methodology used to generate the conclusions." *Clarke v. LR Systems*, 219 F. Supp. 2d 323, 332 (E.D.N.Y. 2002). "It is for the jury, not the Court, to determine whether an expert's opinions are suspect because facts upon which he relied were shown to be inaccurate or unproven." *S.E.C. v. Johnson*, 525 F. Supp. 2d 70, 76 (D.D.C. 2007).

An expert's qualifications are relevant to the reliability inquiry. *See United States v. Salva-Morales*, 660 F.3d 72, 76 (1st Cir. 2011) (information regarding the proposed expert's qualifications was best elicited by direct examination; trial judge did not abuse discretion in refusing to admit the expert's curriculum vitae where the direct examination showed that the witness was qualified as an expert). *United States v. Lopez-Medina*, 461 F.3d 724, 743 (6th Cir. 2006). But disputes about the strength of an expert's credentials, faults in an expert's decision to use a particular methodology, or the lack of textual authority for an expert's opinion "go to the weight, not the admissibility, of his testimony." *Clarke*, 219 F. Supp. 2d at 333. Acceptance of the methodology by the other party's expert may give additional credence to the reliability of the proffered testimony. *Correa v. Cruisers, a Div. of KCS Int'l, Inc.*, 298 F.3d 13, 26 (1st Cir. 2002).

Rule 702 was amended in the year 2000, in response to the Supreme Court's decision in *Daubert v. Merrell Dow Pharm.*, 509 U.S. 579 (1993). Advisory committee notes, 2000 Amendments, Fed. R. Evid. 702. The amended Rule 702 "reflects an attempt to liberalize the rules governing the admission of expert testimony. The rule clearly is one of admissibility rather than exclusion." *Sappington v. Skyjack, Inc.*, 512 F.3d 440, 448 (8th Cir. 2008) (citations omitted). As the advisory committee notes state: "A review of the case law after *Daubert* shows that the rejection of expert testimony is the exception rather than the rule."

Notwithstanding these statements, some categories of expert testimony have fared better than others under *Daubert*, *Kumho*, and Rule 702. For example, testimony of doctors, toxicologists, and epidemiologists is often proffered to show a causal link between a product or substance and a particular disease. Such evidence has been, more often than not, excluded by federal trial courts. *See, e.g., General Elec. Co. v. Joiner*, 522 U.S. 136 (1997) (excluding witnesses from testifying as experts on the question of the causation of lung cancer by exposure to potential carcinogens); *Amorgianos v. Nat'l R.R. Passenger Corp.*, 303 F.3d 256 (2d Cir. 2002) (affirming exclusion of toxicology expert testimony concerning link between xylene exposure and neurological symptoms); *Junk v. Terminix Intern. Co. Ltd. P'Ship*, 594 F. Supp. 2d 1062 (S.D. Iowa 2008) (excluding as unreliable testimony concerning link between in-home pesticide treatments and neurological deficits in fetus); *In re Methyl Tertiary Butyl Ether (MTBE) Products Liability Litig.*, 593 F. Supp. 2d 549 (S.D.N.Y. 2008) (court excluded proposed expert testimony about the level at which people could perceive MTBE in their water because of its odor or taste, as the testimony did not satisfy any of the four non-exclusive *Daubert* factors); *Grant v. Pharmative, LLC*, 452 F. Supp. 2d 903 (D. Neb. 2006) (excluding expert testimony of a link between an herbal supplement and liver disease, as the proposed witness had not tested his hypothesis of a link, which contradicts the body of research regarding the issue); *Burleson v. Glass*, 268 F. Supp. 2d 699 (W.D. Tex. 2003) (physician's opinion that exposure to thoriated tungsten welding rods causes lung and/or throat cancer was not reliable or relevant); *Newman v. Motorola, Inc.*, 218 F. Supp. 2d 769 (D. Md. 2002) (excluding proffered expert testimony that cellular phone use caused brain tumors, after concluding that expert's papers purporting to show this causal link were suspect due to recall bias, lack of any demonstrated dose-response relationship, and other methodological flaws); *Awad v. Merck & Co., Inc.*, 99 F. Supp. 2d 301 (S.D.N.Y. 1999) (non-epidemiological studies did not support expert's opinion that rubella vaccine caused chronic arthritis in adult female, where three large-scale epidemiological studies provided strong evidence that there was no causal relationship between vaccine and chronic joint pain), *aff'd*, 213 F.3d 627 (2d Cir. 2000).

By contrast, federal courts have been much more receptive to the admission of expert testimony in criminal cases from forensic scientists and law enforcement experts. *See, e.g., United States v. Hicks*, 389 F.3d 514 (5th Cir. 2004), *cert. denied*, 126 S. Ct. 1022 (2006) (upholding admission of cartridge-firearm ballistics comparisons); *United States v. Trala*, 386 F.3d 536 (3d Cir. 2004), *vacated on other grounds*, 126 S. Ct. 1078 (2006) (upholding reliability of PCR/STR DNA typing method); *United States v. Garcia-Morales*, 382 F.3d 12 (1st Cir. 2004) (upholding prosecution expert's testimony on nature and structure of typical drug distribution conspiracies); *United States v. Patterson*, 277 F.3d 709 (4th Cir. 2002) (upholding admission of testimony concerning fingerprints obtained with a laser imaging device). (For a thorough analysis of *Daubert*'s application in the federal courts from 2000 through 2005, *see* Peter Nordberg, *Daubert on the Web*, at www.daubertontheweb.com.).

A question arises whether Rule 702 requires a proponent of expert testimony to elicit, on direct examination, testimony from the expert that specifically addresses the criteria promulgated in the rule. In most instances, this approach will not be necessary. Usually the expert's testimony will encompass the criteria, if not specifically, at least sufficiently to satisfy the court that the criteria of the rule have been satisfied. For example, when during the examination of the expert at trial the proponent asks, "What is the basis of that opinion?," the answer will include a recitation of facts sufficient to justify an opinion. The testimony will also encompass explanations relating to the reliability of the methods used to form the opinion and to the applicability of the opinion to the facts of the case. If there is any doubt, then the proponent should pose specific questions to satisfy the rule, *e.g.,* "What methods or principles did you use to form your opinion? Are these methods or principles accepted or recognized within the industry? Did you apply the methodology you adopted in a proper manner?" While arguably these questions go to the ultimate issue of admissibility, the answers they seek go to the heart of the criteria established by the rule to evaluate the admissibility of the testimony. In many instances, if doubt exists about the admissibility of the expert testimony, opposing counsel will most likely seek a so-called "*Daubert* hearing" prior to trial for purposes of obtaining a pretrial ruling to exclude the expert from giving testimony. Even if a *Daubert* hearing is not conducted, the court acting as "gatekeeper" to assess reliability can exclude the expert's testimony at trial. A cautious advocate will want to pay close attention to Rule 702 in conducting the direct examination of the expert.

In *Samuel v. Ford*, 96 F. Supp. 2d 491 (D. Md. 2000), Judge Paul Grimm, writing for the court, fashioned a *Daubert/Kumho Tire* "checklist," attached to the opinion as an appendix, that counsel should follow if seeking to challenge the admissibility of an expert's testimony at trial under *Daubert/ Kumho Tire* standards. The checklist requires the following information: (1) the name of the expert whose opinion(s) is (are) challenged; (2) a brief summary of the opinion(s) challenged, including a reference to the source of the opinion (such as the Fed. R. Civ. P. 26(a)(2)(B) disclosure, deposition transcript, etc.); (3) a brief description of the methodology/reasoning used by the expert to reach the challenged opinion(s), including a reference to the source materials; (4) a brief explanation of the basis for the challenge to the reasoning/methodology used by the expert, including a reference to the source material for the challenge; (5) a discussion of the known or potential error rate associated with the methodology employed by the expert, if known; (6) a summary of the relevant peer review material, if available, with citation to the source; and (7) a discussion of whether the methods/principles used have been generally accepted within the relevant scientific or technical community, with citation to references. *Samuel*, 96 F. Supp. 2d at 504.

While all courts may not expect counsel to follow such a detailed checklist to present an evidentiary challenge to proffered expert testimony, it is a good reference tool, as it highlights the various components that must be considered in making a *Daubert/Kumho Tire* challenge. Further, it underscores that the facts related to the *Daubert/ Kumho Tire* factors should be obtained during discovery. *See also* PAUL W. GRIMM, CHARLES S. FAX & PAUL MARK SANDLER, DISCOVERY PROBLEMS AND SOLUTIONS (2d ed. 2009).

The knowledge of the expert can be obtained from observation, experience, standard texts, or any other reliable source. The courts do have discretion in allowing expert testimony. *See United States v. Jordan*, 236 F.3d

953, 955 (8th Cir.), *cert. denied*, 122 S. Ct. 220 (2001) (trial court has broad discretion to admit or exclude expert testimony); *Brown v. Wal-Mart Stores, Inc.*, 1999 U.S. App. LEXIS 32031, at \*5–\*6 (6th Cir. Nov. 24, 1999) (expert is permitted wide latitude to offer opinions, including those not based on first-hand knowledge or observation); *United States v. Fosher*, 590 F.2d 381 (1st Cir. 1979); *Reno–West Coast Distrib. Co., Inc. v. Mead Corp.*, 613 F.2d 722 (9th Cir.), *cert. denied*, 444 U.S. 927 (1979); *Soo Line R.R. Co. v. Fruehauf Corp.*, 547 F.2d 1365 (8th Cir. 1977); *United States v. Dukagjini*, 326 F.3d 45, 52 (2d Cir.), *cert. denied*, 541 U.S. 1092 (2004); *Truck Ins. Exchange v. Magnetek, Inc.*, 360 F.3d 1206, 1210 (10th Cir. 2004). However, this discretion is not unbridled. In *Garrett v. Desa Indus., Inc.*, 705 F.2d 721 (4th Cir. 1983), the court reversed the trial court's ruling, which prohibited a mechanical engineer from opining on the unsafe design of a product. *Consider In re Hanford Nuclear Reservation Litig.*, 521 F.3d 1028, 1056 (9th Cir. 2008) (finding that the lower court abused its discretion by excluding the testimony of the expert's expertise); *Kopf v. Skyrm*, 993 F.2d 374 (4th Cir. 1993). *See also Allison v. McGhan Med. Corp.*, 184 F.3d 1300, 1306 (11th Cir. 1999).

As distinguished from the federal courts, many state courts still follow the more strict *Frye* test in considering the admissibility of scientific evidence. Consider *People v. Leahy*, 882 P.2d 321 (Cal. 1994), where the California Supreme Court, in determining whether the results of a horizontal gaze nystagmus (HGN) field sobriety test were admissible, held that the *Kelly/Frye* test of admissibility, which had been modeled after the *Frye* test, had survived *Daubert*.

The application of the different state and federal tests for determining the admissibility of evidence, including scientific evidence, can produce conflicting results in factually similar cases. Such was the case in Arizona, where two cases involving the admissibility of DNA evidence initially produced different results at the state and federal levels. The Court of Appeals of Arizona found DNA evidence linking Mr. Hummert to a crime inadmissible under the *Frye* test in *Arizona v. Hummert*, 905 P.2d 493 (Ariz. 1994), *opinion vacated*, 933 P.2d 1187 (Ariz. 1997). That same month, in an Arizona case where DNA evidence was to be used similarly to link Mr. Chischilly to a crime, the federal court of appeals found DNA evidence admissible. *United States v. Chischilly*, 30 F.3d 1144 (9th Cir. 1994), *cert. denied*, 513 U.S. 1132 (1995), *overruled on other grounds, United States v. Preston*, 751 F.3d 1008 (9th Cir. 2014); *see also* JAMES PODGERS, DECISIONS SPLIT ON DNA ADMISSIBILITY, A.B.A. J., Dec. 1994, at 54.

For a discussion of the admissibility of DNA evidence under *Daubert* and *Frye*, *see* Barry C. Scheck, *DNA and Daubert*, 15 Cardozo L. Rev. 1959 (1994); Leonard J. Deftos, *Daubert & Frye*: *Compounding the Controversy Over the Forensic Use of DNA Testing*, 15 Whittier L. Rev. 955 (1994).

## C. DIRECT OBSERVATION—TREATING PHYSICIAN

Plaintiff, suing for personal injuries, wishes to elicit testimony from a surgeon as to the cause of the injuries.

### Plaintiff's Counsel:

Q. Doctor, do you know the plaintiff in this case, Joan Smith?

A. Yes.

Q. Have you seen her professionally?

A. Yes.

Q. When?

A. On May 1, 2014.

Q. Where did you see her?

A. At the emergency room of University Hospital.

Q. What was the occasion?

A. She was admitted to the emergency room having been brought to the hospital in an ambulance.

Q. How long after her arrival did you first see her?

A. Almost immediately.

Q. What were the circumstances?

A. Joan Smith was met immediately upon her arrival at the hospital emergency room by a team of doctors from the Shock Trauma Unit, nurses and anesthesiologists of which I was in charge. These individuals, including myself, immediately performed specific tests and administered procedures according to a preset protocol.

Q. Can you tell us what that protocol involved with regard to Joan Smith?

A. Automatically she received intravenous fluid, a blood pressure monitor, pulse rate monitor, respiratory rate monitor, and various tubes placed into her throat and bladder.

Q. Doctor, at the time Joan Smith was admitted to the emergency room was a history taken by a responsible member of the hospital staff?

A. Yes.

Q. Who?

A. The nurse in charge.

Q. What do you mean by history?

A. The facts leading up to the injury, as well as the medical chronology of the patient.

Q. Who provided the history in this instance, if you know?

A. The child's mother.

Q. What was the pertinent history?

Q. Joan Smith was a three-year-old child who had fallen from a fire escape.

Q. Doctor, did you personally examine Joan Smith in the emergency room after she was administered the tests to which you referred?

A. Yes.

Q. What did that examination consist of?

A. (Witness explains in detail.)

Q. Did you make a diagnosis?

A. Yes.

Q. What was that diagnosis?

A. The patient exhibited internal bleeding, multiple fractures of limbs, including the forefinger of the left hand, the lower limb of the right arm, and the lower left leg, a basilar skull fracture, and lacerations on the forehead.

Q. Doctor, did there come a time when you performed surgery on Joan Smith?

A. Yes. Approximately three hours after she was admitted to the hospital, I performed an operation to stop the internal bleeding.

Q. Why did you wait three hours before performing surgery?

A. Other tests had to be administered to the patient.

Q. Do you have an opinion, Doctor Sill, based upon reasonable medical certainty, as to what caused the injuries that you diagnosed?

A. Yes. It is my opinion that the injuries I described were caused by the child's fall from the fire escape.

Q. What was the basis of that opinion?

A. My examination of the patient in the Shock Trauma Unit and the history as reported in the medical records taken by the nurse in charge for purposes of my review as an aid for diagnosing the child's condition.

Q. Why did you reach that conclusion on that basis?

A. These were precisely the kind of injuries that such a fall would normally cause, and there was no other possible reason that could have produced these injuries.

Q. Are you satisfied that you had sufficient opportunity to observe Joan Smith in the shock trauma unit and to review her history?

A. Yes, of course.

## *Comment*

Expert witnesses may render opinions at trial using the following methods: firsthand knowledge, as in this case; hearsay, or a combination of firsthand knowledge and hearsay; facts related in the testimony of others; facts related to the expert in a hypothetical question (*see infra* Chapter 7.G., 7.H.; and even hearsay that the expert learned before trial, provided that the hearsay is of a type reasonably relied on by experts in the field (*see infra* Chapter 7.I.; Fed. R. Evid. 703); *see* 1 McCormick on Evidence § 13-15 (Kenneth S. Broun ed., 7th ed. 2013); 3 Michael H. Graham, Handbook of Federal Evidence § 702:1 (7th ed. 2012). *See supra* pp. 152–163 for discussion of Fed. R. Evid. 702 and the criteria for evaluation of the admissibility of expert testimony. Rule 702 codifies the U.S. Supreme Court decisions in *Daubert v. Merrell Dow Pharmaceuticals, Inc.*, 509 U.S. 579 (1993); *Joiner v. General Electric Co.*, 522 U.S. 136 (1997); and *Kumho Tire Co. v. Carmichael*, 526 U.S. 137 (1999). The rule requires that expert testimony be based upon sufficient facts or data, that the testimony be derived from reliable principles and methods, and that the principles and methods used be reliably applied to the facts of the case on which the expert will testify. Whether the proponent of expert testimony will ask the witness specific questions embracing the language of Rule 702 will be determined on a case-by-case basis. In this pattern counsel did pose a last question to the expert relating to whether he had a sufficient basis to form his opinion.

Federal Rule of Evidence 704 provides that the opinion of an expert that embraces the ultimate issue is not inadmissible merely on that basis. *See In re Actos (Pioglitazone) Products Liability Litigation*, 2014 WL 120973 at *13 (W.D. La. 2014); *United States v. Barile*, 2002 U.S. App. LEXIS 7149, at *24 (4th Cir. Apr. 18, 2002); *Crawford v. Bundick*, 2002 U.S. App. LEXIS 5923, at *4 (8th Cir. Apr. 2, 2002); *United States v. Caballero*, 277 F.3d 1235, 1249 (10th Cir. 2002); *Bonner v. ISP Techs, Inc.*, 259 F.3d 924, 929 (8th Cir. 2001) (neither Rule 702 nor *Daubert* requires that an expert's opinion resolve an ultimate issue of fact to a scientific absolute in order to be admissible); *United States v. Glover*, 265 F.3d 337, 345 (6th Cir. 2001), *cert. denied*, 122 S. Ct. 1103 (2002) ("expert was only drawing on common sense when he gave his opinion as to the ultimate issue, and the jury was informed that it could accept or reject the expert's test, as it could with any other witness"); *NutraSweet Co. v. X-L Eng'g Co.*, 227 F.3d 776, 789 (7th Cir. 2000); *United States v. McSwain*, 197 F.3d 472, 483 (10th Cir. 1999), *cert. denied*, 529 U.S. 1138 (2000); *In re Air Disaster at Lockerbie, Scotland*, 37 F.3d 804 (2d Cir. 1994), *cert. denied*, 513 U.S. 1126 (1995), *implied overruling on other grounds recognized in Brink's Ltd. v. South African Airways*, 93 F.3d 1022 (2nd Cir. 1996); *United States v. Simpson*, 7 F.3d 186 (10th Cir. 1993); *United States v. Dunn*, 846 F.2d 761 (D.C. Cir. 1988); *Salas v. Wang*, 846 F.2d 897 (3d Cir. 1988); *Adalman v. Baker, Watts & Co.*, 807 F.2d 359 (4th Cir. 1986); *Torres v. County of Oakland*, 758 F.2d 147 (6th Cir. 1985); *Haney v. Mizell Mem'l Hosp.*, 744 F.2d 1467 (11th Cir. 1984); *United States v. Fosher*, 590 F.2d 381 (1st Cir. 1979); *United States v. Scavo*, 593 F.2d 837 (8th Cir. 1979); *United States v. Masson*, 582 F.2d 961 (5th Cir. 1978); *Case & Co., Inc. v. Board of Trade*, 523 F.2d 355 (7th Cir. 1975). *But see Cottom v. Town of Seven Devils*, 2002 U.S. App. LEXIS 3711, at *14 (4th Cir. Mar. 8, 2002) (expert simply assumed the truth of plaintiffs' allegations and concluded that police conduct was improper); *C P Interests, Inc. v. Cal. Pools, Inc.*, 238 F.3d 690 (5th Cir. 2001) (neither Rule 702 nor Rule 704 permits experts to offer conclusions of law); *Anderson v. Suitors*, 499 F.3d 1228, 1237 (10th Cir. 2007); *United States v. Daizy*, 403 F.3d 1147, 1171 (10th Cir. 2005) ("an expert may not simply tell the jury what result it should reach without providing any explanation of the criteria on which that opinion is based or any means by which the jury can exercise independent judgment"); *United States v. Verduzco*, 373 F.3d 1022, 1034 (9th Cir.), *cert. denied*, 543 U.S. 992 (2004).

Federal Rule of Evidence 704(b), on the issue of expert testimony with respect to the mental state of a defendant in a criminal case, differs from the practice in many state rules, which permit opinion testimony on the ultimate issue of criminal responsibility. Federal Rule of Evidence 704 does not. *See United States v. Watson*, 260 F.3d 301, 308 (3d Cir. 2001); *United States v. Boyd*, 55 F.3d 667 (D.C. Cir. 1995); *United States v. Gastiaburo*, 16 F.3d 582 (4th Cir.), *cert. denied*, 513 U.S. 829 (1994); *United States v. Simmons*, 923 F.2d 934 (2d Cir.), *cert. denied*, 500 U.S. 919 (1991);

*United States v. Kessi*, 868 F.2d 1097 (9th Cir. 1989); *United States v. Angiulo*, 847 F.2d 956 (1st Cir.), *cert. denied*, 488 U.S. 928 (1988), *abrogated on other grounds, United States v. Marino*, 277 F.3d 11 (1st Cir. 2002); *United States v. Newman*, 849 F.2d 156 (5th Cir. 1988); *United States v. Cox*, 826 F.2d 1518 (6th Cir. 1987), *cert. denied*, 484 U.S. 1028 (1988); *United States v. Pohlot*, 827 F.2d 889 (3d Cir. 1987), *cert. denied*, 484 U.S. 1011 (1988); *United States v. Felak*, 831 F.2d 794 (8th Cir. 1987); *United States v. Esch*, 832 F.2d 531 (10th Cir. 1987), *cert. denied*, 485 U.S. 991 (1988); *United States v. Windfelder*, 790 F.2d 576 (7th Cir. 1986); *United States v. Alexander*, 805 F.2d 1458 (11th Cir. 1986); *United States v. Price*, 458 F.3d 202, 211-212 (3d Cir.), *cert denied*, 127 S. Ct. 1014 (2007); *United States v. Johnson*, 488 F.3d 690, 699 (6th Cir. 2007); *see also* 1 McCormick on Evidence § 12 at 87-90 (Kenneth S. Broun ed., 7th ed. 2013). *But see United States v. Dixon*, 185 F.3d 393, 401–02 (5th Cir. 1999); *United States v. Alvarez*, 837 F.2d 1024, 1030–31 (11th Cir.) (holding that an expert, while precluded under Federal Rule of Evidence 704(b) from expressing an opinion or inference as to the defendant's state of mind, can testify with respect to the defendant's mental state if the expert leaves the inference of the mental state to be drawn by the trier of fact), *cert. denied*, 486 U.S. 1026 (1988); *accord, United States v. Brown*, 32 F.3d 236 (7th Cir. 1994); *United States v. Bailey*, 319 F.3d 514, 521 (D.C. Cir. 2003) (allowing expert witness testimony that no innocent person would go along on a drug transaction, because the expert was testifying solely from general criminal practices); *United States v. Blount*, 502 F.3d 674, 679 (7th Cir. 2007) (finding that when the "rule is applied to law enforcement experts testifying about the criminal nature of a defendant's actions, it takes on a more limited role" and allows them to testify as long as it is made clear that the expert's opinion is based on knowledge of common criminal practices).

In this pattern, the treating physician expressed his opinion concerning the cause of injuries based on his personal observations and firsthand knowledge. Fed. R. Evid. 703; *see McGuire v. Davis*, 437 F.2d 570 (5th Cir. 1971); *see also Power v. Arlington Hosp. Ass'n*, 42 F.3d 851 (4th Cir. 1994); *Graham v. Wyeth Lab., Div. of Am. Home Prods. Corp.*, 906 F.2d 1399 (10th Cir.), *cert. denied*, 498 U.S. 981 (1990); *Coleman v. De Minco*, 730 F.2d 42 (1st Cir. 1984); *United States v. McCoy*, 539 F.2d 1050 (5th Cir. 1976), *cert. denied*, 431 U.S. 919 (1977); *Sulesky v. United States*, 545 F. Supp. 426 (S.D. W.Va. 1982). Federal Rule of Evidence 705 permits the expert to give his or her opinion without disclosure of the underlying data or basis of that opinion. Nevertheless, strategically, counsel frequently will prefer to elicit the underlying data or basis of an expert's opinion before asking the expert to express the opinion. In other instances, the furnishing of the basis of the opinion is deferred until after the expert renders the opinion.

In this pattern, the expert related his familiarity with the patient and the circumstances of his personal knowledge of her condition. Following the request by counsel for the expert to express his opinion, wrap-up questions were asked requesting the witness to specify not only the basis of his opinion, but also the reasons for his conclusion. Simply eliciting from the witness the basis of his opinion is not enough. Reasons are what persuade the trier of fact.

In this pattern, counsel asked the witness to express his opinion in terms of "certainty." However, all that is required is "probability." *See United States v. Rahm*, 993 F.2d 1405 (9th Cir. 1993); *United States v. Baller*, 519 F.2d 463 (4th Cir.), *cert. denied*, 423 U.S. 1019 (1975); *see also DaSilva v. American Brands, Inc.*, 845 F.2d 356 (1st Cir. 1988). Counsel should appreciate that if an expert cannot express an opinion in terms of reasonable "medical certainty," the term "medical probability" should be used. However, if the expert can state an opinion in terms of reasonable "medical certainty," the question should be phrased in those terms, because the more strongly expressed the opinion, the more impact it is likely to have on the trier of fact. Federal cases, like state court cases, are unclear as to what degree of certainty is required from the expert in the expression of an opinion—particularly when the witness is a medical expert. *See, e.g., Mayhew v. Bell S.S. Co.*, 917 F.2d 961 (6th Cir. 1990) (expert testimony was excluded on the basis of speculation, because the doctor did not testify to any degree of certainty); *Snodgrass v. Ford Motor Co.*, 2001 U.S. Dist. LEXIS 18555, at *14 (D. N.J. Sept. 4, 2001) (while absolute certainty is not required, expert opinion typically is excluded when testimony is speculative, using language such as "possibility"); *Hollander v. Sandoz Pharms. Corp.*, 95 F. Supp. 2d 1230, 1235 (W.D. Okla. 2000) (plaintiffs' expert's testimony insufficient when expert listed only "possible" ways drug could cause hypertension and study cited "presented only some suggestive evidence"). *But see Omar v. Sea-Land Service Inc.*, 813 F.2d 986 (9th Cir. 1987) (allowing admission of physician's speculative testimony as to causation because jury was aware of the hypothetical nature of the testimony, and other medical evidence was offered); *In re Prempro Products Litig.*, 514 F.3d 825, 831 (8th Cir. 2008) (expert's testimony as to hypothetical question was admissible).

Nevertheless, opinions expressed in terms of "could" and "most probably" are admitted. *Williams v. Wal-Mart Stores, Inc.*, 922 F.2d 1357 (8th Cir. 1990) (what could have caused back pain was proper subject for expert testimony); *DaSilva v. American Brands, Inc.*, 845 F.2d 356 (1st Cir. 1988) (holding that medical expert's testimony as to causation, expressed in terms of "my belief" and "could have," was sufficient to reflect a reasonable degree of medical certainty); *United States v. Longfellow*, 406 F.2d 415 (4th Cir.), *cert. denied*, 394 U.S. 998 (1969); *see City of Greenville v. W.R. Grace & Co.*, 827 F.2d 975, 980 n.2 (4th Cir. 1987). *But see Renaud v. Martin-Marietta Corp.*, 972 F.2d 304 (10th Cir. 1992).

In the Fourth Circuit there is no distinction between events that may occur in the future and those that may have occurred in the past. Expert opinion must be expressed in terms of "probably," rather than "possibly," regardless of whether the expert is testifying to future events, *see Standard Oil Co. v. Sewell*, 37 F.2d 230 (4th Cir. 1930), or to past events, *Sakaria v. TransWorld Airlines*, 8 F.3d 164 (4th Cir. 1993), *cert. denied*, 511 U.S. 1083, *reh'g denied*, 512 U.S. 1247 (1994); *Rohrbough v. Wyeth Labs., Inc.*, 916 F.2d 970 (4th Cir. 1990); *Crinkley v. Holiday Inns, Inc.*, 844 F.2d 156 (4th Cir. 1988); *Fitzgerald v. Manning*, 679 F.2d 341 (4th Cir. 1982); *City of Richmond v. Atlantic Co.*, 273 F.2d 902 (4th Cir. 1960); *Ralston Purina Co. v. Edmunds*, 241 F.2d 164 (4th Cir.), *cert. denied*, 353 U.S. 974 (1957); *Leakas v. Columbia Country Club*, 831 F. Supp. 1231 (D. Md. 1993). *See also* Phillip E. Hassman, Annotation, ADMISSIBILITY OF EXPERT MEDICAL TESTIMONY AS TO FUTURE CONSEQUENCES OF INJURY AS AFFECTED BY EXPRESSION IN TERMS OF PROBABILITY OR POSSIBILITY, 75 A.L.R.3d 9 (1977 & Supp. 2014).

## D. DIRECT OBSERVATION—NON-TREATING PHYSICIAN

Plaintiff, suing for personal injuries, wishes to elicit testimony from a non-treating orthopedic surgeon as to the cause of the injuries.

### Plaintiff's Counsel:

Q. Doctor, do you know the plaintiff in this case, Joan Smith?

A. Yes.

Q. Have you seen her professionally?

A. Yes.

Q. When?

A. On May 23, 2014.

Q. What were the circumstances of your seeing her?

A. At your request, she made an appointment to see me for an orthopedic examination.

Q. Did you in fact examine Miss Smith on May 23, 2014, Doctor?

A. Yes.

Q. Did you take a history before you examined her, Doctor?

A. Yes.

Q. What did that history consist of?

**Defense Counsel:** Objection; may we approach the bench? [At bench conference.]

**Defense Counsel:** If the court please, this doctor is a non-treating physician who examined Miss Smith in order to qualify as an expert witness, and he cannot present the history and subjective symptoms of the plaintiff as distinguished from symptoms he uncovered as a result of his examination of the plaintiff.

**The Court:** Overruled. Rule 803(4) of the Federal Rules of Evidence has abolished the distinction between treating and non-treating physicians. The history and subjective symptoms as related to the non-treating doctor may be introduced as substantive evidence.

[Bench conference concluded.]

### Plaintiff's Counsel:

Q. What did the history consist of, Doctor?

A. Miss Smith was involved in an automobile accident at the intersection of Calvert and Redwood Streets on May 3, 2014, when she was a passenger in the back seat of a car that was struck from behind. Since the accident she has experienced severe lower back pain, which she never experienced prior to the accident. She has difficulty walking, running, and participating in any sports activities. She feels more severe pain when she lifts objects, regardless of their weight, and her pain in her lower back frequently "shoots into her legs."

Q. What did your examination consist of, Doctor?

A. I did a gross orthopedic and neurological examination of the patient's body, upper and lower extremities.

Q. What does that mean?

A. I examined the musculoskeletal system, which includes the neck and back areas of the patient.

Q. As a result of the examination did you make a diagnosis?

A. Yes.

Q. What was that diagnosis?

A. (Witness responds with details of the diagnosis.)

Q. Do you have an opinion based upon reasonable medical certainty as to what caused the injuries that you diagnosed?

A. Yes.

Q. What is that opinion?

A. It is my opinion that the injuries that I described were caused by the automobile accident in which the plaintiff was involved on May 3, 2014.

Q. What is the basis of that opinion?

A. My examination of the patient, the history that she gave to me, as well as the subjective symptoms she reported to me.

Q. Why did you reach that conclusion on that basis?

A. These were precisely the kind of injuries that such an automobile accident would normally produce when the patient was in a rear-end-type collision in which she was sitting in the back seat of the automobile, and there is no other possible cause in this case to produce these injuries.

## Comment

*See* pp. 152–163 *supra* for discussion of Fed. R. Evid. 702 and the criteria for evaluation of the admissibility of expert testimony. Rule 702 codifies the U.S. Supreme Court decisions in *Daubert v. Merrell Dow Pharmaceuticals, Inc.*, 509 U.S. 579 (1993); *Joiner v. General Electric Co.*, 522 U.S. 136 (1997); and *Kumho Tire Co. v. Carmichael*, 526 U.S. 137 (1999). The rule requires that expert testimony be based upon sufficient facts or data, that the testimony be derived from reliable principles and methods, and that the principles and methods used be reliably applied to the facts of the case in which the expert will testify. Whether the proponent of expert testimony will ask the witness specific questions embracing the language of Rule 702 will be determined on a case-by-case basis.

Frequently, in cases requiring testimony of medical experts, a non-treating physician is engaged to examine a patient, not for the purpose of treatment, but in order to qualify as an expert witness. This non-treating physician is often asked to testify as to his or her medical conclusions and the information, including the history and subjective symptoms, received from the patient that provide the basis of the conclusions. Federal Rule of Evidence 803(4) provides that statements made for purposes of medical diagnosis are not excluded on the basis of the hearsay rule, and effectively abolishes the traditional view excluding from evidence the non-treating physician's testimony relating a patient's history and subjective symptoms as reported by the patient. *See O'Gee v. Dobbs Houses, Inc.*, 570 F.2d 1084 (2d Cir. 1978) (non-treating physician may present history of patient as related to treating physician, if basis of opinion and history can be considered as substantive evidence); *see generally McCollum v. McDaniel*, 2002 U.S. App. LEXIS 4825, at *12 (4th Cir. Mar. 25, 2002); *United States v. Gabe*, 237 F.3d 954, 957 (8th Cir. 2001); *United States v. Edward J.*, 224 F.3d 1216, 1219 (10th Cir. 2000); *United States v. Console*, 13 F.3d 641 (3d Cir. 1993), *cert. denied sub nom. Curcio v. United States*, 511 U.S. 1076, *cert. denied sub nom. Markoff v. United States*, 513 U.S. 812 (1994); *United States v. Farley*, 992 F.2d 1122 (10th Cir. 1993); *Navarro de Cosme v. Hospital Pavia*, 922 F.2d 926 (1st Cir. 1991); *Rock v. Huffco Gas & Oil Co.*, 922 F.2d 272 (5th Cir. 1991); *Morgan v. Foretich*, 846 F.2d 941 (4th Cir. 1988); *Cook v. Hoppin*, 783 F.2d 684 (7th Cir. 1986); *United States v. Castaneda-Reyes*, 703 F.2d 522 (11th Cir.), *cert. denied*, 464 U.S. 856 (1983); *United States v. Iron Shell*, 633 F.2d 77 (8th Cir. 1980), *cert. denied*, 450 U.S. 1001 (1981); *United States v. Nick*, 604 F.2d 1199 (9th Cir. 1979); *Drayton v. Jiffee Chem. Corp.*, 591 F.2d 352 (6th Cir. 1978); *United States v. Lechoco*, 542 F.2d 84 (D.C. Cir. 1976), *abrogated on other grounds*, *In re Sealed Case*, 352 F.3d 409 (D.C. Cir. 2003); *Floradori v. Harris*, 523 F.3d 477, 509 (5th Cir. 2008) (expert witness physician's testimony was not admissible when he had never treated the plaintiff and relied on questionable data); *Crowe v. Marchland*, 506 F.3d 13, 17 (1st Cir. 2007); *see also White v. Illinois*, 502 U.S. 346 (1992).

## E. EXPERT OPINION—BASED ON INADMISSIBLE FACTS AND DATA

The plaintiff, a gasoline dealer, instituted an antitrust suit against defendant oil company, claiming damages resulting from the oil company's refusal to sell gasoline to the plaintiff. The plaintiff calls an economist to express an opinion on the market value of the plaintiff's business. After qualifying the witness, counsel proceeds as follows:

### Plaintiff's Counsel:

Q. Do you have an opinion as to the market value of plaintiff's gasoline station as of January 1, 2014?

A. Yes.

Q. What is that opinion?

A. $220,000.

Q. Can you tell us the basis of that opinion?

A. The history of the gasoline station from 2005 to 2014, consisting of information that was supplied to me by the proprietor; a survey of traffic flow on Baltimore Street by the Department of Transportation; and various service station problems that I was advised of when I interviewed representatives from the oil company.

Q. Can you tell us whether it is customary and reasonable for economists to rely on this type of information in formulating opinions on market values of gasoline stations?

A. Absolutely, it is the custom and practice in the field.

Q. What are the reasons upon which you base your conclusions?

A. (The witness gives his reasons.)

### *Comment*

Federal Rule of Evidence 703 provides that the facts and data relied upon by the expert in reaching his or her opinion need not themselves be admissible in evidence, if they are of a type reasonably relied upon by experts in the particular field in forming opinions on the subject. *See Monsanto Co. v. David*, 516 F.3d 1009 (Fed. Cir. 2008); *Burek v. Valley Camp Coal Co.*, 2001 U.S. App. LEXIS 13695, at *10 (4th Cir. 2001), *cert. denied*, 122 S. Ct. 927 (2002); *United States v. Feliciano*, 223 F.3d 102, 121 (2d Cir. 2000), *cert. denied*, 532 U.S. 943 (2001); *Brennan v. Reinhart Institutional Foods*, 211 F.3d 449, 450–51 (8th Cir. 2000); *Tyger Constr. Co. v. Pensacola Constr. Co.*, 29 F.3d 137 (4th Cir. 1994), *cert. denied*, 1513 U.S. 1080 (1995); *Engebretsen v. Fairchild Aircraft Corp.*, 21 F.3d 721 (6th Cir. 1994); *University of Rhode Island v. A.W. Chesterton Co.*, 2 F.3d 1200 (1st Cir. 1993); *United States v. Locascio*, 6 F.3d 924 (2d Cir. 1993), *cert. denied*, 511 U.S. 1070 (1994); *South Cent. Petroleum, Inc. v. Long Bros. Oil Co.*, 974 F.2d 1015 (8th Cir. 1992); *United States v. Elkins*, 885 F.2d 775 (11th Cir. 1989), *cert. denied*, 494 U.S. 1005 (1990); *United States v. Wright*, 783 F.2d 1091 (D.C. Cir. 1986); *United States v. Affleck*, 776 F.2d 1451 (10th Cir. 1985);

*Paddack v. Dave Christensen, Inc.*, 745 F.2d 1254 (9th Cir. 1984); *United States v. Lawson*, 653 F.2d 299 (7th Cir. 1981), *cert. denied*, 454 U.S. 1150 (1982); *United States v. Genser*, 582 F.2d 292 (3d Cir. 1978), *cert. denied*, 444 U.S. 928 (1979); *United States v. Williams*, 447 F.2d 1285 (5th Cir. 1971), *cert. denied*, 405 U.S. 954, *reh'g denied*, 405 U.S. 1048 (1972); *In re Lake States Commodities, Inc.*, 272 B.R. 233, 242–43 (Bankr. N.D. Ill. 2002); *Crowe v. Marchland*, 506 F.3d 13, 17–18 (1st Cir. 2007) (Expert witness physician's reliance on X rays and medical reports was sufficient, and her testimony was admissible, despite the fact that she had never seen the patient, because physicians commonly base their opinions on reports made by other doctors); *Turner v. Burlington Northern Santa Fe Ry. Co.*, 338 F.3d 1058, 1061 (9th Cir. 2003); *Pineda v. Ford Motor Co.*, 520 F.3d 237, 246 (3d Cir. 2008); *Monsanto Co. v. David*, 516 F.3d 1009, 1016 (Fed. Cir. 2008); *see also Dura Auto. Sys. of Ind., Inc. v. CTS Corp.*, 285 F.3d 609 (7th Cir. 2002) (expert witness is permitted to use assistants in formulating expert opinion, and usually the assistants need not testify). Thus, for example, expert testimony based on public opinion polls is admissible even though the poll itself may not be admissible. *See Baumholser v. Amax Coal Co.*, 630 F.2d 550 (7th Cir. 1980). Under the rules, counsel need not, as a matter of evidentiary requirement, prove the opinions and diagnoses of other doctors by calling them to the stand. *See In re "Agent Orange" Prod. Liab. Litig.*, 611 F. Supp. 1223 (E.D.N.Y. 1985); *see also United States v. Mann*, 712 F.2d 941 (4th Cir. 1983). In this pattern, counsel need not prove the "traffic flow" on Baltimore Street to enable the expert to state that he relied upon that information as a basis for his or her opinion.

Query: Can the economist in this pattern or any expert actually relate or disclose the otherwise inadmissible data he reasonably relied upon and received from others to form an opinion? Under Federal Rule of Evidence 703, courts may not permit the expert to express or relate this information. The information can only be used as a basis for the opinion without specifically being presented to the jury. If, however, a request is presented to the court to allow such inadmissible data to be presented, such evidence at the discretion of the court may be admissible if the court determines that the probative value of the evidence substantially outweighs its prejudicial effect. *See Brennan v. Reinhart Institutional Foods*, 211 F.3d 449, 451 (8th Cir. 2000); *Boone v. Moore*, 980 F.2d 539 (8th Cir. 1992); *United States v. Sims*, 514 F.2d 147 (9th Cir.), *cert. denied*, 423 U.S. 845 (1975); *United States v. DeSimone*, 488 F.3d 561, 576 (1st Cir. 2007); however, Federal

Rule of Evidence 705 provides that on cross-examination the expert may be required to disclose the underlying facts of an opinion. *See O'Gee v. Dobbs Houses, Inc.*, 570 F.2d 1084 (2d Cir. 1978); *see also University of Rhode Island, supra*, 2 F.3d at 1217; *Wright, supra*, 783 F.2d at 1101.

The question asked of the economist in this pattern—"Can you tell us whether it is customary and reasonable for economists to rely on this type of information in formulating opinions on market values of filling stations?"—is not a question required to establish a foundation for the opinion of the expert based on the inadmissible data. In fact, it is a self-serving-type question, because the standard of reasonableness that the court applies in determining whether to permit the expert to rely on the otherwise inadmissible facts is a judicial one. *See* Fed. R. Evid. 104(a); Fed. R. Evid. 703 advisory committee's note. However, if the court wants guidance from the expert on what is reasonably relied upon by an expert in that particular field in forming opinions, the question may be of some benefit. *See also* 5 MICHAEL H. GRAHAM, HANDBOOK OF FEDERAL EVIDENCE § 703.1 at 554 (7th ed. 2012). As Professor Graham points out, the advisory committee's note to Federal Rule of Evidence 703 stresses that reasonable reliance is a vital standard. Therefore, in accordance with the note, the opinion of an "accidentologist" as to the point of impact would not be admissible if that opinion were based on the statements of bystanders. *Id.*

A question arises as to whether reasonably reliable "facts or data" include opinions. The answer is in the affirmative. *See* James W. McElhaney, Expert Witnesses and the Federal Rules of Evidence, 28 MERCER L. REV. (1977), for an enlightening discussion of the federal rules as they pertain to experts. *See also* Fed. R. Evid. 703 advisory committee's note; *American Universal Ins. Co. v. Falzone*, 644 F.2d 65 (1st Cir. 1981), abrogation on other grounds recognized by *Smith v. Kmart Corp.*, 177 F.3d 19 (1st Cir. 1999); *Nanda v. Ford Motor Co.*, 509 F.2d 213 (7th Cir. 1974); *Ries v. CSX Transp., Inc.*, 2000 U.S. Dist. LEXIS 4763, at *6 (E.D. Pa. Mar. 29, 2000); 5 MICHAEL H. GRAHAM, HANDBOOK OF FEDERAL EVIDENCE § 703.1 (7th ed. 2012).

In *Wilson v. Merrell Dow Pharms., Inc.*, 893 F.2d 1149 (10th Cir. 1990), the Tenth Circuit Court of Appeals clearly ruled that expert testimony may be based on inadmissible hearsay when such information is the type customarily relied upon by experts in the field. The court recognized that such information may be admissible to show the basis of the expert's opinion, but not as substantive evidence. Furthermore, counsel may not use the experts' testimony as a ruse to get in hearsay evidence that would otherwise be inadmissible; the expert cannot merely repeat the hearsay without "applying any expertise whatsoever." *United States v. Lombardozzi*, 491 F.3d 61, 73 (2d Cir. 2007). Counsel should appreciate that such evidence could still be excluded on the basis of its prejudicial effect. *See also United States v. Tipton*, 269 Fed. Appx. 551, 559–60 (6th Cir. 2008); *United States v. Leeson*, 453 F.3d 631 (4th Cir. 2006). *See Emigh v. Consol. Rail Corp.*, 710 F. Supp. 608 (W.D. Pa. 1989) (holding that although Federal Rule of Evidence 703 allows an expert to base an opinion on otherwise inadmissible evidence, Federal Rule 403 precludes the use of Rule 703 as a device to put such evidence before the jury when the evidence would be more prejudicial than probative).

## F. EXPERT OPINION WITHOUT DISCLOSURE OF DATA UNDERLYING OPINION

Don Smith institutes suit against Harry Stone. Smith claims Stone's deed from Smith's father should be set aside, because Smith's father lacked the mental capacity to transfer the property. Plaintiff has retained a world-renowned psychiatrist as an expert witness. The witness will be asked to express an opinion on whether the plaintiff's father possessed sufficient mental capacity to execute a valid deed. Plaintiff's counsel is unsure as to whether a factual basis exists for the expert's opinion that would be deemed sufficient, because the expert never examined the grantor. Therefore, counsel does not examine the witness with regard to underlying facts or data in support of the opinion. Immediately after qualifying the expert and eliciting testimony that the expert discussed the grantor's condition with the plaintiff for the first time on the eve of trial, the following questions are asked.

### Plaintiff's Counsel:

Q. Doctor, do you have an opinion based upon reasonable medical certainty as to whether Mr. Smith was of sound and disposing mind, capable of signing a deed, with an understanding of the nature of his act, its effect, and the natural objects of his bounty?

A. Yes.

Q. What is your opinion?

A. He was totally lacking in such mental capacity.

Q. What are your reasons for that opinion?

A. (Witness furnishes reasons.)

Q. Thank you, Doctor. That is all.

## *Comment*

Federal Rule of Evidence 705 permits the expert to testify in terms of an opinion and give reasons, without first testifying to the underlying facts unless the court otherwise requires. *See Guidroz-Brault v. Mo. Pac. R.R.*, 254 F.3d 825, 831–32 (9th Cir. 2001); *United States v. Havvard*, 260 F.3d 597, 601 (7th Cir. 2001); *Ambrosini v. Labarraque*, 966 F.2d 1464 (D.C. Cir. 1992); *Symbol Techs. Inc. v. Opticon, Inc.*, 935 F.2d 1569 (Fed. Cir. 1991); *Monks v. General Elec. Co.*, 919 F.2d 1189 (6th Cir. 1990); *Lewis v. Rego Co.*, 757 F.2d 66 (3d Cir. 1985); *Bulthuis v. Rexall Corp.*, 789 F.2d 1315 (9th Cir. 1985); *Evers v. General Motors Corp.*, 770 F.2d 984 (11th Cir. 1985); *Deitchman v. E.R. Squibb & Sons, Inc.*, 740 F.2d 556 (7th Cir. 1984); *Rock Island Improv. Co. v. Helmerich & Payne, Inc.*, 698 F.2d 1075 (10th Cir.), *cert. denied*, 461 U.S. 944 (1983); *United Roasters, Inc. v. Colgate-Palmolive Co.*, 649 F.2d 985 (4th Cir.), *cert. denied*, 454 U.S. 1054 (1981); *N.V. Maatschappij Voor Industriele Waarden v. A.O. Smith Corp.*, 590 F.2d 415 (2d Cir. 1978); *United States v. Santarpio*, 560 F.2d 448 (1st Cir.), *cert. denied*, 434 U.S. 984 (1977); *Bryan v. John Bean Div. of FMC Corp.*, 566 F.2d 541 (5th Cir. 1978); *Polk v. Ford Motor Co.*, 529 F.2d 259 (8th Cir.), *cert. denied*, 426 U.S. 907 (1976); *Reis v. Barley, Snyder, Senft & Cohen LLC*, No. 05-CV-01651, 2008 WL 2653670, at *5 (E.D. Pa. July 3, 2008).

The rule in effect abolishes the requirement for the hypothetical question, because experts may render opinions pursuant to the rule without discussing the basis of the opinion. The expert may have no firsthand knowledge but nevertheless be permitted to render an opinion without a hypothetical question. However, the rule can be a trap for the unwary litigator. Assume the expert renders an opinion, pursuant to Federal Rule of Evidence 705, relying on otherwise inadmissible information received from third parties. Although the expert relies on this information, he does not disclose this on direct examination. On cross-examination, however, the basis of the opinion is elicited pursuant to the rules, and the court subsequently concludes that the expert's "reliance" was not reasonable. *See supra*, Chapter 7.E., discussing Fed. R. Evid. 703; *see also* James W. McElhaney, Expert Witnesses and the Federal Rules of Evidence, 28 MERCER L. REV. 463 (1977). *Consider*

*Smith v. Ford Motor Co.*, 626 F.2d 784 (10th Cir. 1980), *cert. denied*, 450 U.S. 918 (1981), where the court commented that Federal Rule of Evidence 705 places upon opposing counsel the burden of exploring, through cross-examination, the facts and assumptions that serve as the basis of an expert's opinion. *Accord, Bryan v. John Bean Div. of FMC Corp.*, 566 F.2d 541 (5th Cir. 1978); *see also Polk v. Ford Motor Co.*, 529 F.2d 259 (8th Cir.), *cert. denied*, 426 U.S. 907 (1976). *Consider Studiengesellschaft Kohle v. Dart Inds., Inc.*, 862 F.2d 1564 (Fed. Cir. 1988) (holding that Fed. R. Evid. 705 does not require a court or trier of fact to automatically credit an expert's testimony that is not cross-examined). Hence, careful pretrial discovery is important so that counsel can prepare for cross-examination of the expert witness at trial.

## G. THE LONG FORM—HYPOTHETICAL

Don Smith institutes suit against Henry Stone. Smith claims a deed to Stone, signed by Smith's father on June 6, 2014, should be set aside, because Smith's father lacked the mental capacity to transfer the property. Plaintiff has retained as an expert witness a psychiatrist who did not examine Smith's father or hear any of the evidence. After qualifying the expert, the following examination occurs:

### Plaintiff's Counsel:

Q. Doctor, I will ask you what is known as a hypothetical question. This question will request that you give an opinion based on facts as submitted in this case. Please follow closely the statement of facts that I present to you, assume them to be true, and then I will ask you to express an opinion upon those facts. Are you ready, sir?

A. Yes, sir.

Q. Assume a man 89 years of age cannot stand up straight and needs a cane. He suffered a stroke at the age of 87, and since that time he constantly babbles and talks to himself. He professes frequently that he is Abraham Lincoln reincarnated. Now, Doctor, assuming all these facts and conditions as being true, do you have an opinion based on reasonable medical certainty as to whether this man, on June 6, 2014, was of sound and disposing mind, capable of signing a deed with an understanding of the nature of his act, its effect, and the natural objects of his bounty?

A. Yes, I do.

Q. What is your opinion, Doctor?

A. My opinion is that the gentleman did not have a sound and disposing mind, and was incapable of signing a deed with an understanding of the nature of his act, its effect, and the natural objects of his bounty.

Q. What is the basis of that opinion?

A. The details suggested about the patient's state of mind—that is, his constant babbling, his belief that he is Abraham Lincoln reincarnated, the fact that he had a stroke several years before, and his age.

Q. Why did you reach that conclusion on that basis?

A. The facts related by you indicate that the man has lost touch with reality and is incapable of the rational thinking necessary for one to understand the nature and extent of his property and the consequences of his transferring the property.

## *Comment*

Experts are permitted to express opinions based not only on direct observation, but also on hypothetical questions. *See United States v. Mancillas*, 183 F.3d 682 (7th Cir. 1999), *cert. denied*, 529 U.S. 1005 (2000); *United States v. Harley*, 990 F.2d 1340 (D.C. Cir. 1993), *cert. denied*, 510 U.S. 885 (1993); *Toucet v. Maritime Overseas Corp.*, 991 F.2d 5 (1st Cir. 1993); *Williams v. Jader Fuel Co., Inc.*, 944 F.2d 1388 (7th Cir. 1991), *cert. denied*, 504 U.S. 957 (1992); *Samples v. City of Atlanta*, 916 F.2d 1548 (11th Cir. 1990); *Taylor v. Burlington N. R.R.*, 787 F.2d 1309 (9th Cir. 1986); *Ramsey v. Culpepper*, 738 F.2d 1092 (10th Cir. 1984); *United States v. Mann*, 712 F.2d 941 (4th Cir. 1983); *Teen-Ed, Inc. v. Kimball Int'l, Inc.*, 620 F.2d 399 (3d Cir. 1980); *United States v. Kreimer*, 609 F.2d 126 (5th Cir. 1980); *Iconco v. Jensen Constr. Co.*, 622 F.2d 1291 (8th Cir. 1980); *Cunningham v. Gans*, 507 F.2d 496 (2d Cir. 1974); *Garza v. Indiana & Michigan Elec. Co.*, 338 F.2d 623 (6th Cir. 1964); *Holland v. Horn*, 150 F. Supp. 2d 706, 745 (E.D. Pa. 2001); *Certain Underwriters at Lloyds London v. Sinkovich*, 232 F.3d 200, 203 (4th Cir. 2000); *see also Barefoot v. Estelle*, 463 U.S. 880, *reh'g denied*, 464 U.S. 874 (1983), *superseded by statute as stated in Slack v. McDaniel*, 529 U.S. 473 (2000); *but see Duluth Lighthouse for the Blind v. C.G. Bretting Mfg. Co.*, 199 F.R.D. 320, 324 (D. Minn. 2000) (if a person is a lay witness and not an expert witness, he cannot respond to hypothetical questions, even if he relies on specialized knowledge to form his opinions); *United States v. Henderson*, 409 F.3d 1293, 1300 (11th Cir. 2005) ("the ability to answer hypothetical questions is the essential difference between expert and lay witnesses"); Under Federal Rule of Evidence 705, counsel is no longer required to use hypothetical questions to obtain an opinion from an expert who does not have firsthand knowledge of facts upon which the expert bases an opinion. One of the primary reasons for the adoption of these rules was to free counsel from the burden of asking complex and lengthy hypothetical questions. *See* 1 McCormick on Evidence § 16 at 137-139 (Kenneth S. Broun ed., 7th ed. 2013). Nevertheless, these questions can be very effective and are admissible in the court's discretion. *See Newman v. Hy-Way Heat Sys., Inc.*, 789 F.2d 269 (4th Cir. 1986); *Taylor, supra*, 787 F.2d 1309; *United States v. Kreimer*, 609 F.2d 126 (5th Cir. 1980).

One technique for avoiding objections during trial to a complex hypothetical is to review the hypothetical with opposing counsel prior to presenting it in trial. For this reason, and also so that counsel's presentation in court can be smooth and complete, it is helpful to write out the hypothetical question prior to trial. Either of two forms of hypothetical questions can be utilized: the long form, as illustrated by this pattern, and the short form, as illustrated in Chapter 7.G., *infra*.

The long form of hypothetical question requires counsel to state for the witness such facts as are essential to the foundation of an opinion, and ask the witness to assume the truth of the facts so stated, and then to render an opinion based upon them. The question must contain a fair summary of the material facts in evidence that are essential to the formulation of a rational opinion concerning the subject matter. *See Iconco v. Jensen Constr. Co.*, 622 F.2d 1291 (8th Cir. 1980); *see also Theriot v. Bay Drilling Co.*, 783 F.2d 527, 537 n.8 (5th Cir. 1986) (noting that a hypothetical question must utilize a fair, undistorted collection of facts); *Logsdon v. Baker*, 517 F.2d 174 (D.C. Cir. 1975). However, the long-form hypothetical question need not contain all the facts in evidence, if it contains a fair summary of the facts. *See Iconco v. Jensen Constr. Co.*, 622 F.2d 1291 (8th Cir. 1980); *Twin City Plaza, Inc. v. Central Sur. & Ins. Corp.*, 409 F.2d 1195 (8th Cir. 1969); *United States v. Aspinwall*, 96 F.2d 867 (9th Cir. 1938); *Napier v. Greenzweig*, 256 F. 196 (2d Cir. 1919). If the question is framed inadequately, the court can require counsel to include additional facts. *Minneapolis, St. Paul & Sault Ste. Marie R.R. v. Metal-Matic, Inc.*, 323 F.2d 903 (8th Cir. 1963).

On occasion it becomes necessary to ask a hypothetical question based on facts assumed to be true but not in evidence when the question is asked.

This procedure can be adopted, when necessary, if counsel sufficiently satisfies the court by a proffer and assurances of definite intent to "connect up." *See* 1 McCORMICK ON EVIDENCE § 14 (Kenneth S. Broun ed., 7th ed. 2013). This concept of "connecting up" is particularly important when the facts not in evidence are not within the reasonable reliance provision of Federal Rule of Evidence 703. *See Vermont Food Indus., Inc. v. Ralston Purina Co.*, 514 F.2d 456 (2d Cir. 1975); 3 MICHAEL H. GRAHAM, HANDBOOK OF FEDERAL EVIDENCE § 705.2 (7th ed. 2012). It may be argued that connecting up is not necessary, since federal rules do not require the expert to state the factual basis for his or her opinion on direct examination. However, it is suggested that if counsel resorts to the hypothetical question as a technique to prove the case, then the traditional rules applying to the hypothetical question should govern. *See generally* 1 McCORMICK ON EVIDENCE § 11 (Kenneth S. Broun ed., 7th ed. 2013); Federal Rule of Evidence 705 allows the court, at its discretion, to require the expert to testify to the factual basis on direct examination. *See* 5 MICHAEL H. GRAHAM, HANDBOOK OF FEDERAL EVIDENCE § 705.2 (7th ed. 2012); Fed. R. Evid. 705 advisory committee's note.

Concerning the use of the phrase "reasonable medical certainty" as opposed to "reasonable probability," *see supra* Chapter 7.C.

## H. THE SHORT FORM—HYPOTHETICAL

Mr. Silver, son of the late Wilson Bonds, instituted suit against his cousin to set aside a deed transferring Bonds's Eastern Shore Estate, on the grounds that Bonds was incompetent to execute a deed at the time the land was conveyed.

Plaintiff's attorney called a psychiatrist as an expert witness. The psychiatrist attended the trial and listened to portions of the testimony. After he was qualified as an expert, counsel presented the psychiatrist with a hypothetical question in the following manner:

Q. Doctor, have you heard certain testimony in this case?

A. Yes, sir.

Q. Assuming the truth of all that testimony and excluding from that testimony any inferences, expressions of opinion, and conclusions of others, do you have any opinion based upon reasonable medical certainty whether or not Mr. Bonds was of sound and disposing mind, capable of signing a deed, with an understanding of the nature of his act, its effect, and the natural objects of his bounty?

A. Yes, sir.

Q. What is that opinion, Doctor?

A. My opinion is that the gentleman did not have a sound and disposing mind, and was incapable of signing a deed with an understanding of the significance of his act, its effect, and the natural objects of his bounty.

Q. What is the basis of that opinion?

A. The details suggested about the patient's state of mind—that is, his constant babbling, his belief that he is Abraham Lincoln reincarnated, the fact that he had a stroke several years before, and his age.

Q. Why did you reach that conclusion on that basis?

A. The testimony of Messrs. James and Collins, which I heard, indicate that the man had lost touch with reality and was incapable of the rational thinking necessary for one to understand the nature and extent of his property and the consequences of transferring the property.

## Comment

The hypothetical question may be asked in either of two ways: the long-form method, *see supra* Chapter 7.G., and the short-form method, reflected in this pattern, sometimes referred to as the "bare bones" method. A few jurisdictions are hesitant to allow the short-form method, and several others provide the trial court with a great degree of discretion to restrict and limit the practice. *See* 32 C.J.S. *Evidence* § 554 (1964 & Supp. 1996). The short-form method requires that the expert predicate his opinion upon uncontradicted evidence heard or read and assumed to be true. *See id.*; 1 McCormick on Evidence § 11 (Kenneth S. Broun ed., 7th ed. 2013); *see also Bosse v. Ideco Div. of Dresser Indus., Inc.*, 412 F.2d 567 (10th Cir. 1969); *Frankel v. Lull Eng'g Co., Inc.*, 334 F. Supp. 913 (E.D. Pa. 1971), *aff'd*, 470 F.2d 995 (3d Cir. 1973) (allowing an expert witness to answer a short-form hypothetical question that assumed as factual the testimony of a previous witness, after the court had determined that the question was intelligible to the jury). Counsel should take care to request that the expert exclude from consideration any inferences, expressions of opinion, or conclusions of others, unless reliance upon the aforesaid information is customary in the expert's particular specialty. Fed. R. Evid. 703; *see also Concerned Area Residents for the Environment v. Southview Farm*, 834 F. Supp. 1422 (W.D.N.Y. 1993), *rev'd on other grounds*, 34 F.3d 114 (2d Cir. 1994), *cert. denied*, 514 U.S. 1082 (1995).

The witness need not have heard all the evidence before giving an opinion in response to the short form; the witness must, however, have heard the evidence on which an opinion is sought. *See* 1 MCCORMICK ON EVIDENCE § 11 (Kenneth S. Broun ed., 7th ed. 2013). Concerning the use of the phrase "reasonable medical certainty," *see supra* Chapter 7.C.

## I.  EXPERT WITNESS—HANDWRITING COMPARISON

In a criminal matter, the Government's case hinges upon the fact that the defendant, Kirby Hempel, endorsed a check in the name of John Pelhem, which Hempel allegedly received for distributing contraband. The Government lawyer desires to prove through expert testimony the genuineness of the defendant's signature on the check. He proceeds as follows:

### Government:

Q.  Agent Hubbel, at the time the defendant was arrested, did you advise him of his rights?

A.  Yes, I did.

Q.  What, if anything, resulted after you advised the defendant of his rights?

A.  He waived those rights.

Q.  Did he sign a written waiver?

A.  Yes.

**Government:** I wish to have this document marked as the State's Exhibit No. 1 for identification.

Q.  Now, Agent, do you recognize this document?

A.  Yes, this is the waiver of rights form that the defendant signed.

Q.  Do you recognize the signature on the righthand side of this card at the bottom?

A.  Yes, it is the defendant's signature.

Q.  How do you know it is the defendant's signature?

A.  I was present when he signed the statement and saw him do it.

**Government:** We offer this waiver as Government's Exhibit No. 1.

\* \* \*

We now call to the witness stand Johnson Heightford Teton. (The witness is thereupon qualified as a handwriting expert.)

**Government:** We would like to have this check, which purports to bear the signature of the defendant as an endorsement, marked as Government's Exhibit No. 2 for identification.

Q. Mr. Teton, I show you State's Exhibit No. 1, which is a statement signed by the defendant in this case, and I also show you Government's Exhibit No. 2 for identification, which is a check that purports to bear the signature of John Pelhem endorsed upon it, and I ask you if you have seen these documents before.

A. Yes, I have.

Q. What were the circumstances of your seeing these documents before today?

A. You requested that I examine these documents to determine if I could express an opinion on whether the check, Exhibit No. 2 for identification, was signed by the same person who signed Exhibit No. 1.

Q. What did your examination consist of?

A. I examined them microscopically as to line quality and slant and letter forms.

\* \* \*

(Counsel requests that the expert explain each procedure and requests the expert to make use of enlarged photographs to illustrate his point.)

\* \* \*

Q. Now, Mr. Teton, do you have an opinion based on reasonable certainty as to whether the same person who signed "Kirby Hempel" to Government's Exhibit No. 1 also signed "John Pelhem" to State's Exhibit No. 2 for identification?

A. Yes, I do.

Q. What is that opinion?

A It is my opinion that the person who signed Exhibit No. 2 was the same person who signed Exhibit No. 1.

Q. What, sir, is the basis of that opinion?

A. My examination of the documents and comparisons that I made.

Q. What are the reasons upon which you base your conclusion?

A. (The witness explains his reasons in detail.)

### Comment

Genuineness of a disputed signature may be established by comparison of any writing proved to be genuine with the signature on the contested document. *See, e.g., United States v. Henry*, 164 F.3d 1304, 1309 (10th Cir.), *cert. denied*, 527 U.S. 1029 (1999); *NLRB v. General Wood Preserving Co.*, 905 F.2d 803 (4th Cir.), *cert. denied*, 498 U.S. 1016 (1990); *Ona Corp. v. NLRB*, 729 F.2d 713 (11th Cir. 1984); *United States v. Clifford*, 704 F.2d 86 (3d Cir. 1983); *United States v. Mauchlin*, 670 F.2d 746 (7th Cir. 1982);

*United States v. Brink*, 648 F.2d 1140 (8th Cir.), *cert. denied*, 454 U.S. 1031 (1981); *United States v. Mangan*, 575 F.2d 32 (2d Cir.), *cert. denied*, 439 U.S. 931 (1978); *United States v. Turquitt*, 557 F.2d 464 (5th Cir. 1977); *Scharfenberger v. Wingo*, 542 F.2d 328 (6th Cir. 1976); *United States v. Greiser*, 502 F.2d 1295 (9th Cir. 1974); *United States v. Wagner*, 475 F.2d 121 (10th Cir. 1973); *Easterday v. United States*, 292 F. 664 (D.C. Cir.), *cert. denied*, 263 U.S. 719 (1923); *Overnight Transp. Co.*, 334 N.L.R.B. 134 (2001); *Cogburn Healthcare Ctr.*, 335 N.L.R.B. 105 (2001).

In this pattern, the prosecutor introduced a document with the genuine signature of the defendant and then requested the expert to compare the authenticated genuine specimen with the signature on the contested document. The initial document that bears the genuine signature of the party need not be a document relevant to the case, but may be any document that is a genuine example of the writing of the person alleged to have written the contested document. Fed. R. Evid.901(3). *See United States v. Mauchlin*, 670 F.2d 746 (7th Cir. 1982); *Reece v. Reece*, 212 A.2d 468 (Md. 1965); *DiPietro v. State*, 356 A.2d 599 (Md. App. 1976); *Green v. State*, 329 A.2d 731 (Md. App. 1974), *cert. denied*, 274 Md. 728 (1975). *See also United States v. Wagner*, 475 F.2d 121 (10th Cir. 1973).

## J. EXAMINATION OF PSYCHIATRIST TO ESTABLISH INSANITY DEFENSE

Tom Jones is arrested for the murder of Mr. Apple. The homicide occurred on March 3, 2009. A plea of "not guilty by reason of insanity" is entered. At trial, testimony is sought from a psychiatrist as to the defendant's responsibility under the Insanity Defense Reform Act, codified at 18 U.S.C. § 17 (2006). Defense counsel, after qualifying a psychiatrist as an expert, proceeds as follows:

### Defense Counsel:

Q. Doctor, have you seen Tom Jones in your professional capacity?
A. Yes.
Q. Under what circumstances?
A. At your request, I interviewed Mr. Jones and administered various psychological tests.
Q. On how many occasions did you consult with Mr. Jones?
A. Four separate occasions.

Q. On what dates did those consultations occur?

A. During various days in June and July of 2014.

Q. How many hours of consultation did you spend with Mr. Jones?

A. Twelve hours.

Q. What was the purpose of your examination?

A. I conducted psychiatric examinations of Mr. Jones to determine whether I could form an opinion as to his responsibility under the Insanity Defense Reform Act, 18 U.S.C. § 17 (2006) for certain criminal conduct occurring on March 3, 2009.

Q. As a result of your consultation with Mr. Jones, were you able to form an opinion as to whether Mr. Jones, on March 3, 2014, had a mental disease or defect?

A. Yes.

Q. What is that opinion?

A. On March 3, 2014, Mr. Jones was suffering from a mental defect.

Q. Is the mental defect from which the defendant was suffering on March 3, 2014, the result of any psychiatric or neurological disorder?

A. Yes.

Q. What is the nature of the mental defect from which the defendant was suffering on March 3, 2014?

A. The defendant was suffering from a psychotic depressive reaction.

Q. Do you have an opinion whether this mental defect caused the defendant to lack substantial capacity either to appreciate the criminality of his conduct or to conform his conduct to the requirements of the law?

A. Yes.

Q. What is that opinion?

A. It is my opinion that the defendant, as a result of the described mental defect, did not lack substantial capacity to appreciate the criminality of his conduct, but did lack substantial capacity to conform his conduct to the requirements of the law.

Q. What is the basis of your opinion?

A. My examination of the defendant, review of psychological test results, and his personal history.

Q. What are the reasons upon which you base your conclusion?

A. [The psychiatrist or psychologist should then relate all the reasons supporting his or her opinion.]

## *Comment*

The American Law Institute (ALI) test expressed in the Insanity Defense Reform Act of 1984, 18 U.S.C. § 17 (2014), is followed by federal courts in determining insanity. *See United States v. Leister*, 393 F.2d 920 (4th Cir. 1968), and *United States v. Gillis*, 773 F.2d 549 (4th Cir. 1985). The test provides that "[I]t is an affirmative defense to a prosecution under any Federal statute that, at the time of the commission of the acts constituting the offense, the defendant, as a result of a severe mental disease or defect, was unable to appreciate the nature or quality of the wrongfulness of his acts. Mental disease or defect does not otherwise constitute a defense." All of the federal circuit courts have utilized some variation of the ALI test. *See generally United States v. Kimes*, 246 F.3d 800, 806 (6th Cir. 2001), *cert. denied*, 122 S. Ct. 823 (2002); *United States v. Vachon*, 869 F.2d 653 (1st Cir. 1989); *United States v. Pohlot*, 827 F.2d 889 (3d Cir. 1987), *cert. denied*, 484 U.S. 1011 (1988); *United States v. Cox*, 826 F.2d 1518 (6th Cir. 1987), *cert. denied*, 484 U.S. 1028 (1988); *United States v. Freeman*, 804 F.2d 1574 (11th Cir. 1986); *Wade v. United States*, 426 F.2d 64 (9th Cir. 1970), *appeal after remand*, *United States v. Wade*, 489 F.2d 258 (9th Cir. 1973); *United States v. Brawner*, 471 F.2d 969 (D.C. Cir. 1972), *superseded by statute*, *Shannon v. United States*, 512 U.S. 573 (1994); *Blake v. United States*, 407 F.2d 908 (5th Cir. 1969) (en banc), *superseded by statute as stated in United States v. Long,* 562 F.3d 325 (5th Cir. 2009); *United States v. Shapiro*, 383 F.2d 680 (7th Cir. 1967), *superseded by statute, United States v. Ewing*, 494 F.3d 607 (7th Cir. 1007); *Pope v. United States*, 372 F.2d 710 (8th Cir. 1967), *vacated on other grounds*, 392 U.S. 651 (1968); *United States v. Freeman*, 357 F.2d 606 (2d Cir. 1966); *Wion v. United States*, 325 F.2d 420 (10th Cir. 1963), *cert. denied*, 377 U.S. 946 (1964); *United States v. Agnello*, 158 F. Supp. 2d 285, 286–87 (E.D.N.Y. 2001); *United States v. Pendergraft*, 120 F. Supp. 2d 1339 (M.D. Fla. 2000), *vacated on other grounds*, *Spielvogel v. United States*, 543 U.S. 1109 (2005); *United States v. Baxt*, 74 F. Supp. 2d 436, 440 (D.N.J. 1999), *subsequent appeal*, 265 F.3d 1057 (3d Cir. 2001).

In federal court, the expert cannot be asked ". . . '[w]as the accused able to appreciate the nature and quality of his act or [w]as the accused able to appreciate the wrongfulness of his acts'?" Fed. R. Evid. 704(b) provides that in criminal cases in which the defendant raises the insanity defense, "an expert must not state an opinion about whether the defendant did or did not have a mental state or condition that constitutes an element of the crime charged or of a defense. Those matters are for the trier of fact alone." Accordingly, the question and answer in the pattern concerning whether the defendant lacked "substantial capacity" may run afoul of the prohibition set forth in Rule 704(b). However, the expert can be asked: "'Was the accused suffering from a mental disease or defect' or 'explain the characteristics of the mental disease and defect.'" 5 MICHAEL H. GRAHAM, HANDBOOK OF FEDERAL EVIDENCE § 704.2 (7th ed. 2012). Although an expert cannot be asked whether a particular defendant knew what he was doing was wrong, counsel may ask generally whether an individual suffering from the mental illness would know what he was doing was wrong. *See United States v. Brown*, 32 F.3d 236 (7th Cir. 1994); *United States v. Thigpen*, 4 F.3d 1573 (11th Cir. 1993), *cert. denied*, 512 U.S. 1238 (1994); *United States v. Kristiansen*, 901 F.2d 1463 (8th Cir. 1990); *United States v. Samples*, 456 F.3d 875, 884 (8th Cir. 2006); *United States v. Diekhoff*, 535 F.3d 611, 619–20 (7th Cir. 2008); *United States v. Eff*, 524 F.3d 712, 716–17 (5th Cir. 2008); *United States v. Cohen*, 510 F.3d 1114, 1123–24 (9th Cir. 2007).

## K. OPINION OF APPRAISER TO ESTABLISH FAIR MARKET VALUE OF REAL ESTATE

In a condemnation case, the defendant, Bernard Sabian, disputes the government's opinion about the fair market value of his property. On behalf of Mr. Sabian, counsel calls a real estate appraiser, Henry Hallock, to express his opinion about the fair market value of the landowner's property:

### Defense Counsel:

Q. Mr. Hallock, are you familiar with the property located at 1635 Oak Street in Perryville, Maryland?

A. Yes, I am.

Q. Did you recently perform an appraisal of that property at my request?

A. Yes, I did.

Q. Let me show you what has been marked for identification as Defendant's Exhibit No. 19, and ask whether you can identify this document.

A. Yes. This is my appraisal of that property.

Q. When did you perform this appraisal?

A.  I completed it on June 4, 2014.

Q.  What was the purpose of the appraisal?

A.  To arrive at the fair market value of the property.

Q.  What is meant by fair market value?

A.  The highest price estimated, in terms of money that a buyer would be warranted in paying and a seller justified in accepting, provided that both parties were fully informed, acting intelligently and voluntarily, and, further, that all rights and benefits inherent in or attributable to the property would be included in the transfer.

Q.  Tell us what was the first thing you did when you commenced your appraisal, Mr. Hallock?

A.  I visited the Land Records Office and reviewed the description of the property, the size, and the boundaries of the property involved; I reviewed assessment data from the County's Assessment Office; I reviewed the deeds for any unusual provisions; and I looked at maps at the Zoning Department.

Q.  What was your next step?

A.  I visited the property, observed the boundaries, and investigated the surrounding properties to determine their uses, types of buildings, and whether the neighborhood was improving or declining.

Q.  Please give a description of the property, including its location and size.

A.  The property consists of four acres with a home.

Q.  To what use was the property being put?

A.  It was and is the residence of Mr. and Mrs. Bernard Sabian.

Q.  After you examined the property, did you determine what, in your opinion, based on a reasonable degree of certainty, is the highest and best use of that property?

A.  Yes.

Q.  And what is the highest and best use?

A.  Residential.

Q.  Did you determine what in your opinion is the fair market value of that property?

A.  Yes.

Q.  What methods did you use in arriving at your opinion as to the fair market value?

A.  I used what is known as the market data approach, the cost approach, and the income approach.

Q. Would you describe briefly what is meant by the market data approach?

A. This approach involves consideration of a number of recent sales of comparable properties to determine the sales prices. They are adjusted up or down with regard to location, size, and shape of improvements and land, zoning, and topography to reflect the differences between those properties and the one owned by Mr. Sabian, and on that basis I determined the value of his property.

Q. Please describe what you mean by the cost approach.

A. This approach considers what it would cost to reproduce the structure or replace it with a building of equivalent utility, less an allowance for depreciation and obsolescence. I then add the value of the land to this figure to obtain a value for the entire property.

Q. And now, tell us what is meant by the income approach method of appraising.

A. I evaluate the rental value of property and apply this to determine the fair market value of the property. I take the gross rental income less a vacancy allowance to determine adjusted gross income, and then deduct the expenses incurred by the property owner to arrive at a net income figure. The net income figure is then capitalized at the current market rate to ascertain the value through the income approach.

Q. Did you rely equally on all of these approaches in your report and opinion, sir?

A. No. I relied primarily on the market data approach and used the cost approach as a check against that result. I did not use the income approach to form my opinion, although I discussed this approach in my report.

Q. Why did you rely primarily on the market data approach?

A. The market data approach is usually the most reliable one for properties for which there is an active market. In this case, a three-bedroom home in a suburban location, there was an active market for this type of property, so the market data approach was the best approach to use in this instance.

Q. Mr. Hallock, what comparable sales did you ascertain that relate to your opinion of the fair market value of Mr. Sabian's property?

A. I located four comparable sales. The first was the home seven blocks away owned by Mr. and Mrs. Jasper. The house was sold six months prior to my report for $150,000. It is a home site almost identical to the property in question. Three other home sites were within a square mile and also sold for $200,000, $175,000, and $145,000, respectively. These comparable sales are listed in my report.

Q. Why did you use these four specific properties in appraising Mr. Sabian's property?

A. Each of these comparable properties was sold on the open market at the comparable time of the valuation date. Also, these comparable sales involved properties similar to Mr. Sabian's property.

Q. How did you ascertain these comparable sales?

A. Through public records and interviews with the homeowners of these properties. I also consulted the Lusk Sales Reports, which is a weekly report service, and the Central Maryland Multiple Listing Service of the Real Estate Board, which provides a monthly wrap-up of all properties that have transferred through the real estate agents' hands.

Q. Now, tell us, did you form an opinion based upon a reasonable degree of certainty as to the fair market value of Mr. Sabian's home at the time of your valuation?

A. Yes.

Q. And what is that opinion?

A. My opinion is that the home is worth $250,000.

Q. What is the basis of your opinion?

A. My observation of the property, my review of the data we discussed, and the selection of the market data approach, which offers the most reliable method for determining value in this case.

Q. What are the reasons on which you base your conclusion?

A. Two of the three appraisal methods were considered, with the third approach—the income approach—not being used, because this was not an income-producing property. The cost approach depends on segregated valuations of land and improvements. The two segments are then combined to give an estimate of total value. The market data approach considers sales of similar style residential units, as total entities, currently taking place within the market area of the subject property. In this case, because the sales data are very recent and a very active market prevails, I selected the market data approach as the most accurate and reliable means to estimate the fair market value of the subject property.

**Defense Counsel**: We offer in evidence Mr. Hallock's appraisal.

## Comment

Broad discretion is vested in the trial court to determine if a witness qualifies to express an opinion on the value of real estate. It is essential, however, that the witness demonstrate an understanding of the meaning of market value. *See generally In re MDL-731-Tax Refund Litig. of Organizers and Promoters of Investment Plans*, 989 F.2d 1290 (2d Cir.), *cert. denied*, 510 U.S. 964 (1993); *United States v. L.E. Cooke Co.*, 991 F.2d 336 (6th Cir. 1993); *Frymire-Brinati v. KPMG Peat Marwick*, 2 F.3d 183 (7th Cir. 1993); *United States v. 68.94 Acres of Land*, 918 F.2d 389 (3d Cir. 1990); *United States v. 10,031.98 Acres of Land*, 850 F.2d 634 (10th Cir. 1988); *United States v. 0.161 Acres of Land*, 837 F.2d 1036 (11th Cir. 1988); *United States v. 329.73 Acres of Land*, 666 F.2d 281 (5th Cir. 1982); *United States v. 75.13 Acres of Land*, 693 F.2d 813 (8th Cir. 1982); *United States v. 10.48 Acres of Land*, 621 F.2d 338 (9th Cir. 1980); *United States v. Whitehurst*, 337 F.2d 765 (4th Cir. 1964); *Riley v. District of Columbia Redev. Land Agency*, 246 F.2d 641 (D.C. Cir. 1957); *United States v. 100.01 Acres of Land*, 2002 U.S. Dist. LEXIS 8133, at \*5–\*6 (W.D. Va. May 7, 2002); *Vector Pipeline, L.P. v. 68.55 Acres of Land*, 157 F. Supp. 2d 949, 956 (N.D. Ill. 2001).

Although slight variation may exist in the definition of fair market value, in condemnation cases under federal law, the expert's opinion must be in accordance with the general principles enunciated by the U.S. Supreme Court. Under Federal Rule of Civil Procedure 71A, an individual whose land is condemned may request a trial on the issue of just compensation. The Supreme Court, in *Olson v. United States,* 292 U.S. 246, 255 (1934), held that:

> [j]ust compensation includes all elements of value that inhere in the property, but it does not exceed market value fairly determined. The sum required to be paid the owner does not depend upon the uses to which he has devoted his land but is to be arrived at upon just consideration of all the uses for which it is suitable. The highest and most profitable use for which the property is adaptable and needed or likely to be needed in the reasonably near future is to be considered, not necessarily as the measure of value, but to the full extent that the prospect of demand for such use affects the market value while the property is privately held.

*See United States v. 158.24 Acres of Land*, 696 F.2d 559 (8th Cir. 1982).

## L. DIRECT EXAMINATION OF A PHYSICIAN USING MEDICAL TEXT AS AUTHORITY

Dr. Larry Fox, a physician specializing in lung disease, is called to testify as a defense witness in a case involving a claim for asbestos-related disease. Counsel wishes to establish that CT scans are the only reliable method used to diagnose lung obstructions, a method the plaintiff's physician failed to utilize.

### Counsel:

Q. Dr. Fox, are you familiar with diagnosing lung obstructions?

A. Yes. I have diagnosed lung obstructions, nearly one every day in my practice, for the last 13 years.

Q. How do physicians diagnose a lung obstruction?

A. By analysis of a CT scan, along with other more intrusive tests if necessary.

Q. Do you have an opinion based upon a reasonable degree of medical certainty whether the use of a CT scan is standard medical practice to diagnose a lung obstruction?

A. Yes.

Q. What is that opinion?

A. It is standard medical practice.

Q. What is the basis of your opinion?

A. I base my opinion on the education I have received, and upon Dr. Smythe's treatise, entitled Diagnosing Lung Obstructions.

Q. Is this a copy of Diagnosing Lung Obstructions?

A. Yes, it is.

Q. Do you recognize Dr. Smythe's treatise as authoritative in the field of diagnosing lung obstructions?

A. Yes, I do.

Q. Is Dr. Smythe's treatise used as a teaching textbook on lung obstructions in medical schools throughout this country?

A. Yes.

Q. Is Dr. Smythe a recognized authority on lung obstructions?

A. Yes.

Q. Doctor, on page 165, Dr. Smythe's treatise states that "only with a CT scan can a lung obstruction be properly detected." Do you agree with that statement, sir?

A. Yes, I do.

Q. If a doctor were to diagnose a lung obstruction without performing a CT scan, in your opinion, Doctor, would such a diagnosis be flawed?

A. Yes, sir, the diagnosis would be flawed and unreliable.

Q. Does your opinion conform with Dr. Smythe's writings?

A. Yes.

### Comment

Federal practice, governed by Federal Rule of Evidence 803(18), provides that textbooks and treatises can be used as substantive evidence on direct examination of an expert if the expert testifies that he or she relied on the treatise. *See In re Welding Fume Products Liability Litigation*, 534 F. Supp. 2d 761, 764–65 (N.D. Ohio 2008); *Costantino v. Herzog*, 203 F.3d 164, 172 (2d Cir. 2000) (some periodicals are sufficiently esteemed to justify a presumption in favor of admitting the articles accepted for publication therein); *Twin City Fire Ins. Co. v. Country Mut. Ins. Co.*, 23 F.3d 1175 (7th Cir. 1994); *Meschino v. North American Drager, Inc.*, 841 F.2d 429 (1st Cir. 1988); *Ward v. United States*, 838 F.2d 182 (6th Cir. 1988); *Schultz v. Rice*, 809 F.2d 643 (10th Cir. 1986); *Allen v. Safeco Ins. Co.*, 782 F.2d 1517, *aff'd in part, vacated in part on other grounds*, 793 F.2d 1195 (11th Cir. 1986); *Ellis v. Int'l Playtex, Inc.*, 745 F.2d 292 (4th Cir. 1984); *Tart v. McGann*, 697 F.2d 75 (2d Cir. 1982); *United States v. An Article of Drug*, 661 F.2d 742 (9th Cir. 1981); *Johnson v. William C. Ellis & Sons Iron Works, Inc.*, 609 F.2d 820 (5th Cir. 1980); *Maggipinto v. Reichman*, 607 F.2d 621 (3d Cir. 1979); *Brown v. United States*, 419 F.2d 337 (8th Cir. 1969); *United States v. Horn*, 185 F. Supp. 2d 530 (D. Md. 2002); *United States v. Norman*, 415 F.3d 466, 474 (5th Cir. 2005), *cert. denied*, 546 U.S. 1117 (2006).

If a textbook or treatise is so admitted, the statements from the book may be read into evidence but are not received as exhibits. The proper foundation for use of learned treatises as substantive evidence on direct examination includes establishing that the expert relied on the treatise or publication, and establishing that the witness recognizes the treatise as authoritative. An alternative approach is to ask the court to take judicial notice that the treatise is authoritative. *See* 2 McCORMICK ON EVIDENCE, § 321 (7th ed. 2012); FEDERAL EVIDENCE PRACTICE GUIDE § 6.11[16] (Joseph M. McLaughlin ed., Matthew Bender 1990). Alternatively, a party may seek to have a textbook or treatise recognized only as the basis for an expert's opinion, and use of the book for this purpose does not require the same foundation. However, if a foundation is not laid, the treatise cannot be considered as substantive evidence. *See* p. 263 *infra* for an example of cross-examination using authoritative treatises.

# *Character, Habit, and Custom*  8

## A. CHARACTER AS A MATERIAL PROPOSITION OR ESSENTIAL ELEMENT IN A CIVIL CASE

### i. *Reputation*

Jill Spender instituted suit against All Spray Exterminating Company for negligent entrustment of an automobile to John Jones, an All Spray employee, who was involved in an automobile collision with the plaintiff. Counsel for the defendant seeks to introduce evidence that the employee was a careful, courteous, and safe driver prior to being entrusted with his employer's car, because the issue is in dispute during the trial.

#### Defense Counsel:

Q. How long have you known John Jones?

A. For ten years.

Q. How close to John Jones do you live?

A. I am his next-door neighbor.

Q. What is your occupation, sir?

A. I am an Episcopal minister.

Q. How long have you been a minister?

A. For twenty-five years.

Q. Where, if you know, does Mr. Jones work?

A. At the school, three blocks from his home. He is now one of their custodians.

Q. Have you talked to people in the community about Mr. Jones?

A. Yes.

Q. Have you discussed with people in the community his driving an automobile?

A. Yes.

Q. Do you know whether or not as of January 2, 2014, Mr. Jones had a reputation in the community in which he lives and works with regard to his driving an automobile?

A. Yes, I do.

Q. Did he have such a reputation?

A. Yes, he did.

Q. What was that reputation?

A. He had a reputation for being a careful, courteous, and safe driver.

## *Comment*

Character evidence means evidence concerning a person's nature or disposition. *See* 3 MICHAEL H. GRAHAM, HANDBOOK OF FEDERAL EVIDENCE § 404.1 (7th ed. 2012). Federal Rule of Evidence 404 clearly provides that a person's character or trait of character is inadmissible to prove action in conformity with that character or trait. This policy is frequently referred to as the propensity rule. *See* 1A JOHN HENRY WIGMORE, WIGMORE ON EVIDENCE § 54.1 (Tillers rev. 1983 & Supp. 2014); *see also* 1 McCORMICK ON EVIDENCE §§ 186–188 (Kenneth S. Broun ed., 7th ed. 2013). *See, e.g.*, *Weitz Co LLC. v. MacKenzie House, LLC*, 665 F.3d 970, 974–75 (8th Cir. 2012) (evidence of other or prior acts inadmissible to prove the character of a person to prove conformity therewith; prior acts include prior lawsuits); *Housely v. Holquist*, 879 F. Supp. 2d 472, 486 (D. Md. 2011) (police officers' decisions before entering a residence were not admissible, in a § 1983 suit claiming unlawful entry and excessive force, to show that they had a propensity to act rashly); *Harriman v. Pullman Palace-Car Co.*, 85 F. 353 (8th Cir. 1898) (in defending civil negligence case, defendant porter was prohibited from showing that he was usually careful and attentive); *see also Sparks v. Gilley Trucking Co.*, 992 F.2d 50 (4th Cir. 1993) (prior speeding tickets inadmissible to show defendant was speeding at time of accident).

In *United States v. Hernandez*, 975 F.2d 1035 (4th Cir. 1992), the court explained that the propensity rule exists to prevent prejudice. *See also United States v. Arbelaez-Agudelo*, 2001 U.S. App. LEXIS 19490, at *9 (6th Cir. Aug. 27, 2001), *cert. denied*, 122 S. Ct. 1329 (2002) (Rule 404(b) not implicated when evidence of other crimes or wrongs is part of a continuing pattern of illegal activity); *Okai v. Verfuth*, 275 F.3d 606, 610 (7th Cir. 2001) (evidence of other crimes, wrongs, or acts admissible if offered for other purposes, such as motive, intent, plan, or opportunity); *United States v. Duckett*, 2000 U.S. App. LEXIS 23627, at *4 (4th Cir. Sept. 21, 2000) (Rule 404(b) is a rule of inclusion that allows all evidence of other crimes relevant to an issue in trial, except that which tends to prove only criminal disposition); *Neuren v. Adduci, Mastriani, Meeks & Schill*, 43 F.3d 1507 (D.C. Cir. 1995); *Moorhead v. Mitsubishi Aircraft Int'l, Inc.*, 828 F.2d 278 (5th Cir. 1987); *United States v. Dunn*, 805 F.2d 1275 (6th Cir. 1986); *Lataille v. Ponte*, 754 F.2d 33 (1st Cir. 1985); *McCluney v. Jos. Schlitz Brewing Co.*, 728 F.2d 924 (7th Cir. 1984); *Hirst v. Gertzen*, 676 F.2d 1252 (9th Cir. 1982); *Cmwlth. of Pa. v. Porter*, 659 F.2d 306

(3d Cir. 1981) (en banc), *cert. denied,* 458 U.S. 1121 (1982); *United States v. Salisbury,* 662 F.2d 738 (11th Cir. 1981), *cert. denied,* 457 U.S. 1107 (1982); *Hackbart v. Cincinnati Bengals, Inc.,* 601 F.2d 516 (10th Cir.), *cert. denied,* 444 U.S. 931 (1979), *modified sub nom. Perrin v. Anderson,* 784 F.2d 1040 (10th Cir. 1986); *St. Clair v. Eastern Air Lines, Inc.,* 279 F.2d 119 (2d Cir.), *cert. denied,* 364 U.S. 882 (1960); *Lombardo v. Stone,* 2002 U.S. Dist. LEXIS 1267, at *8–*9 (S.D.N.Y. Jan. 29, 2002); *United States v. Long,* 328 F.3d 655, 660 (D.C. Cir.), *cert. denied,* 540 U.S. 1075 (2003); *United States v. Whitney,* 524 F.3d 134, 141 (1st Cir. 2008); *United States v. Goosby,* 523 F.3d 632, 638 (6th Cir. 2008); *United States v. McKay,* 431 F.3d 1085, 1093 (8th Cir.), *cert. denied,* 127 S. Ct. 46 (2006) (evidence of membership in a gang could not be admitted purely for the purpose of showing that a defendant associated with unsavory characters); *United States v. Wantuch,* 525 F.3d 505, 517 (7th Cir. 2008) (allowing uncharged acts to be admitted at trial did not violate Rule 404 because the acts were "intricately related" to the charged crime); *United States v. Gregg,* 451 F.3d 930, 934 (8th Cir. 2006) (victim's violent character was not an essential element of defendant's defense of self-defense, and thus, evidence of specific instances of victim's violent conduct was not admissible to prove victim was the aggressor in the altercation); *United States v. Perez,* 526 F.3d 543 (9th Cir. 2008).

Circumstantial use of character evidence to imply that a person's character or trait tends to make it more probable that the person acted in conformity with that character or trait is distinguishable from the permitted use of character evidence where character is in issue. *See* Fed. R. Evid. 405. Character is in issue when it is an essential element of a charge, claim, or defense in a civil or criminal case. When character is in issue, a person's possession of a particular trait or character is material to the resolution of the substantive rights and liabilities of the parties. The use of character evidence is always admissible when character is in issue. *Gibson v. Mayor and Council of City of Wilmington,* 355 F.3d 215, 231 (3d Cir. 2004) (because defendant did not make his character an essential element of the defense, his evidence of "good acts" was inadmissible); *Barnes v. City of Cincinnati,* 401 F.3d 729, 741 (6th Cir. 2005) (allowing statement of prior acts that were "probative of his intent" to demote plaintiff).

Court decisions most often recognize the materiality of character evidence—that is, they recognize that character is an issue where the focus of inquiry is essentially criminal. *See Doe v. Smith,* 470 F.3d 331

(7th Cir. 2006), *abrogation on other grounds recognized, Trentadue v. Redmon*, 619 F.3d 648 (7th Cir. 2010) (teacher's prior solicitation conviction was admissible); *Crumpton v. Confederation Life Ins. Co.*, 672 F.2d 1248 (5th Cir.), *reh'g denied*, 679 F.2d 250 (5th Cir. 1982) (in civil action on insurance policy for accidental death, character evidence as to peacefulness of decedent was admissible); *see also Perrin v. Anderson*, 784 F.2d 1040 (10th Cir. 1986). Consider *In re Aircrash in Bali*, 684 F.2d 1301 (9th Cir. 1982), *appeal after remand*, 871 F.2d 812 (9th Cir.), *cert. denied, Pan-American World Airways, Inc. v. Causey*, 493 U.S. 917 (1989); *Breeding v. Massey*, 378 F.2d 171 (8th Cir. 1967); *Skultin v. Bushnell*, 82 F. Supp. 2d 1258, 1260 (D. Utah 2000); 2 JACK B. WEINSTIN, ET AL., WEINSTEIN'S FEDERAL EVIDENCE § 404.02[2] (2d ed. 2014); 3 MICHAEL H. GRAHAM, HANDBOOK OF FEDERAL EVIDENCE § 405:2 (7th ed. 2012). However, character also can be at issue in civil cases, for example, as illustrated in this pattern, or in cases of negligent entrustment or defamation. *See, e.g., In re Aircrash in Bali*, 684 F.2d 1301 (9th Cir. 1982) (holding that training records of pilot were admissible to show that airline had notice of pilot's incompetence and was therefore negligent); *Weider v. Hoffman*, 238 F. Supp. 437 (M.D. Pa. 1965) (holding that testimony concerning character of plaintiff in libel action was admissible as part of defendant's defense of truth); *see also* 1 MCCORMICK ON EVIDENCE § 187 (Kenneth S. Broun ed., 7th ed. 2013).

Evidence of a character trait of an accused or of the victim of a crime is allowed under limited circumstances. *See* Fed. R. Evid. 404. Although the language of Federal Rule of Evidence 404(a) applies only to criminal cases, when the main issues of a civil case are criminal in nature, such as in civil assault, a defendant may use evidence of character as the basis for an inference that he did not commit the acts in question. *Perrin v. Anderson*, 784 F.2d 1040 (10th Cir. 1986); *Crumpton v. Confederation Life Ins. Co.*, 672 F.2d 1248 (5th Cir. 1982). Consider *In re Aircrash in Bali*, 684 F.2d 1301 (9th Cir. 1982), *appeal after remand*, 871 F.2d 812 (9th Cir.), *cert. denied, Pan-American World Airways, Inc. v. Causey*, 493 U.S. 917 (1989); *Breeding v. Massey*, 378 F.2d 171 (8th Cir. 1967). State practice may not be the same. Prior to the adoption of the state evidence code in Maryland, case law permitted such use. *See Bugg v. Brown*, 246 A.2d 235 (Md. 1968).

The practice of admitting evidence of character in these types of civil actions that involve a criminal issue, however, is a minority position. *See* 1 MCCORMICK ON EVIDENCE § 192 (Kenneth S. Broun ed., 7th ed. 2013);

22 CHARLES A. WRIGHT & KENNETH W. GRAHAM, JR., FEDERAL PRACTICE AND PROCEDURE: EVIDENCE § 5236 (1978 & Supp. 2014).

Federal Rule of Evidence 405 provides that the method of proving character includes reputation and opinion. A witness testifying about reputation or offering an opinion cannot testify about specific prior acts. *See* Fed. R. Evid. 405; *United States v. Marrero*, 904 F.2d 251 (5th Cir.), *cert. denied*, 498 U.S. 1000 (1990). *See also United States v. Talamante*, 981 F.2d 1153 (10th Cir. 1992), *cert. denied*, 507 U.S. 1041 (1993); *United States v. Camejo*, 929 F.2d 610 (11th Cir.), *cert. denied*, 502 U.S. 880 (1991); *United States v. Gravely*, 840 F.2d 1156 (4th Cir. 1988).

Of course, on cross-examination a reputation witness can be probed about relevant specific instances for purposes of impeachment. *See* Fed. R. Evid. 608(b); *United States v. Boone*, 279 F.3d 163, 174–75 (3d Cir. 2002); *United States v. Aronds*, 2000 U.S. App. LEXIS 4145, at *30 (6th Cir. Mar. 14, 2000) (if direct testimony addresses community reputation, inquiry made be made on cross-examination about conduct, or even charges, that might have come to the attention of the relevant community; however, cross-examiner must possess good-faith belief that the described events are of a type "likely to have become a matter of general knowledge, currency, or reputation in the community"), *citing United States v. Brugier*, 161 F.3d 1145, 1150 (8th Cir. 1998); *United States v. McHorse*, 179 F.3d 889, 901 (10th Cir.), *cert. denied*, 528 U.S. 944 (1999); *United States v. Pacione*, 950 F.2d 1348 (7th Cir. 1991), *cert. denied*, 505 U.S. 1229 (1992); *United States v. Coleman*, 805 F.2d 474 (3d Cir. 1986); *United States v. Reich*, 479 F.3d 179, 190–92 (2d Cir.), *cert denied*,128 S. Ct. 115 (2007).

For example, if a witness expresses a favorable opinion on direct examination about a defendant, counsel on cross can ask the witness "have you heard" of a particular instance of conduct relevant to the character trait in question, and if so, "would that alter your opinion?" However, it would be improper to ask the character witness whether his or her opinion would change if the witness assumed that the defendant actually committed the act with which the defendant is charged. *United States v. Mason*, 993 F.2d 406 (4th Cir. 1993); *United States v. Siers*, 873 F.2d 747 (4th Cir. 1989), *cert. denied*, 506 U.S. 1086 (1993); *see also United States v. Guzman*, 167 F.3d 1350, 1352 (11th Cir. 1999); *United States v. Wilson*, 983 F.2d 221 (11th Cir. 1993); *United States v. Velasquez*, 980 F.2d 1275 (9th Cir. 1992), *cert. denied*, 508 U.S. 979 (1993); *United States v. Oshatz*, 912 F.2d 534 (2d Cir. 1990), *cert. denied*, 500 U.S. 910 (1991); *United States v. Bartan*,

888 F.2d 1220 (8th Cir. 1989); *United States v. Page*, 808 F.2d 723 (10th Cir.), *cert. denied*, 482 U.S. 918 (1987); *United States v. McGuire*, 744 F.2d 1197 (6th Cir. 1984), *cert. denied*, 471 U.S. 1004 (1985); *United States v. Williams*, 738 F.2d 172 (7th Cir. 1984); *United States v. Curtis*, 644 F.2d 263 (3d Cir. 1981), *cert. denied*, 459 U.S. 1018 (1982); *United States v. Candelaria-Gonzalez*, 547 F.2d 291 (5th Cir. 1977); *Gibson v. Moskowitz*, 523 F.3d 657, 666 (6th Cir. 2008) (refusing to allow evidence on cross-examination of plaintiffs' prior bad acts when they were not relevant to the case at hand); *United States v. Chan*, 2002 U.S. Dist. LEXIS 1221, at *5 (S.D.N.Y. Jan. 25, 2002). *But see United States v. White*, 887 F.2d 267 (D.C. Cir. 1989) (holding that guilt-assuming hypotheticals may be asked of witnesses expressing a personal opinion as to a defendant's character, but not to witnesses testifying as to the defendant's reputation in the community).

Nevertheless, in cases where character is an essential issue, as in this pattern, proof of specific instances is admissible on direct examination. Fed. R. Evid. 405(b); *United States v. Smith*, 230 F.3d 300, 307 (7th Cir. 2000), *cert. denied*, 531 U.S. 1176 (2001) (in the limited instance when a person's character is an essential element of a charge, claim, or defense, proof also can be made by specific instances of conduct); *United States v. Marrero*, 904 F.2d 251 (5th Cir.), *cert. denied*, 498 U.S. 1000 (1990); *United States v. Masters*, 622 F.2d 83 (4th Cir. 1980).

When counsel seeks to establish character through evidence of reputation, he or she should appreciate that, under some state rules of evidence, a character witness in state court is required to confine his or her testimony to the individual's reputation in the community in which the individual resided. Opinions about the individual's reputation at the individual's place of business are inadmissible. *See* 22 CHARLES A. WRIGHT & KENNETH W. GRAHAM, JR., FEDERAL PRACTICE AND PROCEDURE: EVIDENCE § 5264 (1980 & Supp. 2014). Under the federal rules, however, a character witness is allowed to opine on reputation where the individual works. *Blackburn v. UPS, Inc.*, 179 F.3d 81, 99 (3d Cir. 1999); *United States v. Oliver*, 492 F.2d 943 (8th Cir. 1974), *appeal after remand*, 525 F.2d 731 (8th Cir. 1975), *cert. denied*, 424 U.S. 973 (1976); *United States v. Mandel*, 591 F.2d 1347 (4th Cir. 1979), *aff'd on reh'g en banc*, 602 F.2d 653 (4th Cir. 1979), *cert. denied*, 455 U.S. 961 (1980). There is a general movement to allow testimony concerning an individual's reputation at work, as well as the individual's community reputation. *See* 2 STEPHEN A. SALTZBURG

ET AL., FEDERAL RULES OF EVIDENCE MANUAL § 405.02 (10th ed. 2011 & Supp. June 2014).

The witness must demonstrate familiarity with the defendant's reputation and competence to testify about it. The testimony, furthermore, must relate to the accused's reputation at the time of the acts charged and to character traits pertinent to the offense in question. *See* 2 JACK B. WEINSTEIN, ET AL., WEINSTEIN'S FEDERAL EVIDENCE § 405.03 (2d ed. 2014), and cases cited therein.

A person's reputation is the community's view or estimate of that person. 2 MICHAEL H. GRAHAM, HANDBOOK OF FEDERAL EVIDENCE § 404:1 (7th ed. 2012). Professor Graham points out that the failure to distinguish between character and reputation causes confusion. This confusion is exacerbated often, because reputation is one method of proving character. *Id.* Counsel should appreciate that, on cross-examination, circumstantial evidence of character is admissible to impeach or support other evidence of a witness's character for truthfulness. Fed. R. Evid. 607, 608, 609. *See* 2 MICHAEL H. GRAHAM, HANDBOOK OF FEDERAL EVIDENCE § 404:2 (7th ed. 2012); *infra*, Chapter 8.B.–D.

Federal Rule of Evidence 608 provides that, if a witness's character has been attacked for truthfulness by means of reputation or opinion testimony, the character of that witness can be supported on redirect examination by reputation or opinion evidence. Specific instances are not provable. *United States v. Smith*, 277 Fed. Appx. 870, 871–72 (11th Cir. 2008). *See infra* Chapter 8.A.iv.

Habit and custom, as distinguished from character, should also be considered. Federal Rule of Evidence 406 provides for the admission of evidence of habit and custom. *See infra* Chapter 8.E.–G.

### ii. *Opinion*

The same facts apply as stated in the previous pattern, except counsel for defendant seeks to introduce opinion evidence that the employee was known as a careful, courteous, and safe driver prior to being entrusted with the employer's car.

### Defense Counsel:

Q. How long have you known John Jones?
A. For ten years.

Q. How close to John Jones do you live?

A. I am his next-door neighbor.

Q. What is your occupation, sir?

A. I am an Episcopal minister.

Q. How long have you been a minister?

A. For twenty-five years.

Q. Where, if you know, does Mr. Jones work?

A. At the school, three blocks from his home. He is one of their custodians.

Q. Have you ever had occasion to drive with John Jones?

A. Yes, I have.

Q. On more than one occasion?

A. Yes, I have driven with him many, many times.

Q. Do you have an opinion as to whether or not he was a careful, courteous, and safe driver of an automobile as of January 2, 2014?

A. Yes, I do.

Q. What is that opinion?

A. I think he is an excellent driver, and he always has been.

### *Comment*

*See* Fed. R. Evid. 405. When character is in issue or is an essential element of a claim or defense, it can be proved by opinion, reputation, or by specific instances. When character is not in issue and is sought to be proved, counsel must use the method of opinion or reputation. Fed. Evid. 405; *supra* Chapter 8.A.i.–ii.; *see also United States v. Plumman*, 409 F.3d 919, 928 (8th Cir. 2005); *United States v. Talamante*, 981 F.2d 1153 (10th Cir. 1992), *cert. denied*, 507 U.S. 1041 (1993); *United States v. Camejo*, 929 F.2d 610 (11th Cir.), *cert. denied*, 502 U.S. 880 (1991); 2 STEPHEN A. SALTZBURG ET AL., FEDERAL RULES OF EVIDENCE MANUAL § 405.02 (10th ed. 2011 & Supp. June 2014).

This pattern illustrates the opinion method. The court can conclude, as a matter of discretion, that the character witness lacks a sufficient basis to render an opinion. *United States v. McMurray*, 20 F.3d 831 (8th Cir. 1994); *United States v. Dotson*, 799 F.2d 189 (5th Cir. 1986); *United States v. Nedza*, 880 F.2d 896 (7th Cir.), *cert. denied*, 493 U.S. 938 (1989); *United States v. Tedder*, 403 F.3d 836, 839 (7th Cir. 2005).

### iii. *Opinion with Specific Instance*

The same facts apply as stated in the previous pattern, but counsel relies on opinions and specific facts to illustrate the opinion.

#### Defense Counsel:

Q. How long have you known John Jones?

A. For ten years.

Q. How close to John Jones do you live?

A. I am his next-door neighbor.

Q. What is your occupation, sir?

A. I am an Episcopal minister.

Q. How long have you been a minister?

A. For twenty-five years.

Q. Where, if you know, does Mr. Jones work?

A. At the school, three blocks from his home. He is one of their custodians.

Q. Have you ever had occasion to drive with him?

A. Yes, I have.

Q. On more than one occasion?

A. Yes, I have driven with him many times.

Q. Do you have an opinion as to whether he is a careful, courteous, and reliable driver of an automobile?

A. Yes, I do.

Q. What is that opinion?

A. I think he is an excellent driver, and he always has been.

Q. Can you tell us of any particular instances when you have driven with him?

A. Well, one example that comes to mind was when he gave me a ride to pick up my automobile from the shop when it was being repaired.

Q. Can you tell us what you observed about his driving at that time?

A. He always stopped at stop signs. He didn't make those running-type stops that you often see—that is, where people slow down but do not come to a full stop. He came to a full stop. He would stop at all traffic lights; he never sped. There is one country road where the speed limit is only 30 miles per hour and almost everyone speeds, but Mr. Jones, I observed, maintained the speed limit.

## Comment

*See* Fed. R. Evid. 405. In this pattern, if character were not in issue, testimony about specific instances would not be proper on direct examination. *Cf. Kanida v. Gulf Coast Medical Personnel LP*, 363 F.3d 568, 582 (5th Cir. 2004); *United States v. Keiser*, 57 F.3d 847 (9th Cir.) (for specific instances to be admissible, relevant question is whether an element of the charge or claim involves a character trait), *cert. denied*, 516 U.S. 1029 (1995); *Perrin v. Anderson*, 784 F.2d 1040 (10th Cir. 1986) (specific incidents permitted only when rights of parties were affected by existence of character trait). *See United States v. Kellogg*, 510 F.3d 188 (3rd Cir. 2007) (in mail fraud prosecution, government's question on cross-examination of character witness as to whether the witness had any knowledge about the way defendant ran his business was admissible as testimony regarding witness's knowledge of specific instances of defendant's conduct and was not impermissibly guilt-assuming.

### iv. *Specific Instances*

The same facts apply as stated in the previous pattern, except counsel uses only specific acts to demonstrate character.

#### Defense Counsel:

Q. Have you ever had occasion to drive with Mr. Jones?

A. Yes, I have.

Q. Can you tell us of any particular instances when you have driven with him?

A. I recall an occasion when he gave me a ride to pick up my automobile from the shop.

Q. What did you observe about his driving at that time?

A. He always stopped at stop signs. He didn't make those running-type stops that you often see, that is, where people slow down but do not come to a full stop. He came to a full stop. He would stop at all traffic lights; he never sped. There is one country road where the speed limit is only 30 miles per hour and almost everyone speeds, but Mr. Jones, I observed, maintained the speed limit.

Q. No further questions.

## Comment

*See* Fed. R. Evid. 405. When character is in issue or is an essential element of a claim or defense, it can be proved by opinion, reputation, or specific instances. *United States v. Marrero*, 904 F.2d 251 (5th Cir.), 498 U.S. 1000 (1990). *See also United States v. Morris*, 2002 U.S. App. LEXIS 3870, at *10 (10th Cir. Mar. 12, 2002); *United States v. Taken Alive*, 262 F.3d 711, 714 (8th Cir. 2001); *United States v. Smith*, 230 F.3d 300, 307 (7th Cir. 2000), *cert. denied*, 531 U.S. 1176 (2001); *United States v. Saenz*, 1999 U.S. App. LEXIS 1080, at *2 (9th Cir. Jan. 22, 1999), *subsequent appeal*, 179 F.3d 686 (9th Cir. 1999); *United States v. Keiser*, 57 F.3d 847 (9th Cir. 1995), *cert. denied*, 516 U.S. 1029 (1995); *United States v. Hill*, 40 F.3d 164 (7th Cir. 1994), *cert. denied*, 514 U.S. 1029 (1995); *United States v. Piche*, 981 F.2d 706 (4th Cir. 1992), *cert. denied*, 508 U.S. 916 (1993), *superseded by statute*, *United States v. Ziadeh*, 104 Fed. Appx. 869 (4th Cir. 2004); *United States v. Waloke*, 962 F.2d 824 (8th Cir. 1992); *Perrin v. Anderson*, 784 F.2d 1040 (10th Cir. 1986); *United States v. Wallach*, 935 F.2d 445 (2d Cir. 1991), *on remand*, 788 F. Supp. 739 (S.D.N.Y.), *aff'd*, 979 F.2d 912 (2d Cir. 1992), *cert. denied*, 508 U.S. 939 (1993); *United States v. Frost*, 914 F.2d 756 (6th Cir. 1990); *United States v. Gully*, 526 F.3d 809, 818 (5th Cir. 2008); *United States v. Yong Ping Liu*, 288 Fed. Appx. 193, 204 (5th Cir. 2008).

## B. CHARACTER OF ACCUSED—REPUTATION METHOD

John Witherspoon is indicted for a robbery allegedly committed on January 3, 2010. He calls a witness to testify to his good character, to support his contention that he did not commit the robbery. His attorney proceeds as follows:

### Defense Counsel:

Q. How long have you known Mr. Witherspoon?
A. For ten years.
Q. How close to John Witherspoon do you live?
A. I am his next-door neighbor.
Q. What is your occupation, sir?
A. I am a physician.
Q. How long have you been a physician?

A.  Twenty years.

Q.  Have you met John Witherspoon either socially or professionally?

A.  Yes, many times socially, but not professionally.

Q.  Have you spoken to him or heard others speak about him in your community?

A.  Yes.

Q.  Do you know if he has a reputation in the community for truthfulness?

A.  Yes.

Q.  Are you acquainted with that reputation in the community for truth and veracity?

A.  Yes, I am.

Q.  Do you have an opinion as to that reputation?

A.  Yes.

Q.  What is your opinion concerning his reputation?

A.  His reputation is excellent.

Q.  Would you believe him under oath?

A.  Absolutely.

* * *

If Witherspoon had been indicted for assault, defense counsel might pose the question as follows:

Q.  Have you spoken about him or heard others speak about him in your community?

A.  Yes.

Q.  Do you know if he has a reputation in the community for being a peaceable and law-abiding citizen?

A.  Yes, I do.

Q.  Can you tell us what that reputation is?

A.  He has a reputation for being peaceful, quiet, and law-abiding.

## Comment

Federal Rule of Evidence 404(a)(1) allows evidence of a pertinent trait of the character of an accused to be offered by the accused for the purpose of proving that the accused did not commit the crime charged. *United States v. Han*, 230 F.3d 560, 564 (2d Cir. 2000); *United States v. Maiben*, 2000 U.S. App. LEXIS 15777, *2 (9th Cir. July 6, 2000) (once introduced, government can impeach with questions about past bad acts); *United*

*States v. Moore*, 27 F.3d 969 (4th Cir.), *cert. denied*, 513 U.S. 979 (1994); *United States v. Santana-Camacho*, 931 F.2d 966 (1st Cir. 1991); *United States v. Pujana-Mena*, 949 F.2d 24 (2d Cir. 1991); *United States v. Cortez*, 935 F.2d 135 (8th Cir. 1991), *cert. denied*, 502 U.S. 1062 (1992); *United States v. Barry*, 814 F.2d 1400 (9th Cir. 1987); *United States v. Troutman*, 814 F.2d 1428 (10th Cir. 1987); *Virgin Islands v. Grant*, 775 F.2d 508 (3d Cir. 1985); *United States v. Reed*, 700 F.2d 638 (11th Cir. 1983); *United States v. West*, 670 F.2d 675 (7th Cir.), *cert. denied, King v. United States*, 457 U.S. 1124, *cert. denied, Jeffers v. United States*, 457 U.S. 1139 (1982), *overruled on other grounds, United States v. Green*, 258 F.3d 683 (7th Cir. 2001); *United States v. Jackson*, 588 F.2d 1046 (5th Cir.), *cert. denied*, 442 U.S. 941 (1979); *United States v. Cylkouski*, 556 F.2d 799 (6th Cir. 1977); *United States v. Lechoco*, 542 F.2d 84 (D.C. Cir. 1976), *abrogated on other grounds, In re Sealed Case*, 352 F.3d 409 (D.C. Cir. 2003); *United States v. Gully*, 526 F.3d 809, 818 (5th Cir. 2008); *United States v. Yarbrough*, 527 F.3d 1092, 1101 n.5 (10th Cir. 2008); *United States v. Ortiz*, 2015 WL 4773021 (D.P.R. Aug. 13, 2015).

The rules also permit the prosecutor to use character evidence to rebut similar evidence offered by the accused to prove a character trait in question. Fed. R. Evid. 404(a)(1); *see United States v. Moore*, 27 F.3d 969 (4th Cir.), *cert. denied*, 513 U.S. 979 (1994); *United States v. Reed*, 700 F.2d 638 (11th Cir. 1983); *but see United States v. Hands*, 184 F.3d 1322, 1328 (11th Cir. 1999) (government cannot bootstrap irrelevant evidence into trial by using it to impeach answers to irrelevant questions). In addition, when the accused offers character evidence about the victim, the prosecutor may offer similar character evidence about the accused. Fed. R. Evid 404(a)(1). The rules provide that character can be established by evidence of reputation or by opinion evidence. Fed. R. Evid. 405(a). However, Federal Rule of Evidence 405(b) provides that, if character or a trait of character of the accused is an essential element of the charge, counsel may prove character by specific instances. Since character is not an essential element of the charge of robbery or assault in this pattern, proof of character by specific instances is prohibited.

When counsel seeks to establish character through evidence of reputation, he or she should appreciate that, prior to the adoption of state rules of evidence, a character witness in state court was required to confine his or her testimony to the individual's reputation in the community in which the individual resided. *See* 22 CHARLES A. WRIGHT & KENNETH

W. GRAHAM, JR., FEDERAL PRACTICE AND PROCEDURE: EVIDENCE § 5264 (1978 & Supp. 2014). Under the federal rules, a character witness is allowed to opine on reputation where the individual works, in addition to the community where the individual resides. *Blackburn v. UPS, Inc.*, 179 F.3d 81, 99 (3d Cir. 1999); *United States v. Mandel*, 591 F.2d 1347 (4th Cir. 1979), *aff'd on reh'g en banc*, 602 F.2d 653 (4th Cir. 1979), *cert. denied*, 455 U.S. 961 (1980); *United States v. Oliver*, 492 F.2d 943 (8th Cir. 1974), *appeal after remand*, 525 F.2d 731 (8th Cir. 1975), *cert. denied*, 424 U.S. 973 (1976).

The witness must demonstrate familiarity with the defendant's reputation and competence to testify about it. The testimony, furthermore, must relate to the accused's reputation at the time of the acts charged, and to character traits pertinent to the offense in question. *See* 2 JACK B. WEINSTEIN, ET AL., WEINSTEIN'S FEDERAL EVIDENCE §§ 405.03 (2d ed. 2014), and cases cited therein; *see also* 22 CHARLES A. WRIGHT & KENNETH W. GRAHAM, JR., FEDERAL PRACTICE AND PROCEDURE: EVIDENCE § 5264 (1978 & Supp. 2014).

Although the language of Federal Rule of Evidence 404(a) applies only to criminal cases, when the main issues of a civil case are criminal in nature, such as in civil assault, a defendant may use evidence of character as the basis for an inference that he did not commit the acts in question. *Perrin v. Anderson*, 784 F.2d 1040 (10th Cir. 1986).

## C. CHARACTER OF ACCUSED—OPINION METHOD

John Witherspoon is indicted for robbery. He calls a witness to testify to his good character to prove he could not have committed the robbery. His attorney proceeds as follows:

### Defense Counsel:

Q. How long have you known John Witherspoon?
A. For ten years.
Q. How close to John Witherspoon do you live?
A. I am his next-door neighbor.
Q. What is your occupation, sir?
A. I am a physician.
Q. How long have you been a physician?
A. For ten years.

Q. Have you had any occasion to socialize or see John Witherspoon on occasions prior to this morning?

A. Yes, many, many times.

Q. Do you have an opinion as to whether or not Mr. Witherspoon is honest and truthful, law-abiding and peaceful [depending on crime charged]?

A. Yes, I do.

Q. And what is that opinion?

A. My opinion is that he is a very truthful and honest individual [or peaceful and law-abiding].

Q. Would you believe him under oath?

A. Yes, I would.

## Comment

*See supra* Chapter 8.A.ii.–iii.; *United States v. McDonald*, 688 F.2d 224 (4th Cir. 1982), *cert. denied*, 459 U.S. 1103 (1983) (psychiatric character testimony); *Virgin Islands v. Petersen*, 553 F.2d 324 (3d Cir. 1977) (opinion testimony, like reputation testimony, is based on the witness's observation of the defendant's conduct over a period of time). In *Petersen*, the court instructed that the best means to elicit opinion testimony is simply to inquire directly about the witness's opinion of the character trait in question. Of course, if counsel is using the opinion method of proving character, the witness can offer an opinion even if the witness is unfamiliar with the defendant's reputation. *See United States v. Polsinelli*, 649 F.2d 793 (10th Cir. 1981). Although a witness must have an adequate basis to testify about an individual's reputation or to give an opinion of the individual's character, this does not permit the witness to describe specific instances. Fed. R. Evid. 405.

## D. EVIDENCE OF GOOD CHARACTER AND CONDUCT OF A WITNESS

During the course of a murder trial, defendant calls an alibi witness, who testifies that defendant was with him playing cards at the time when the State claims defendant was participating in the bank robbery in which the victim was killed. On cross-examination, the government attacks the witness's truthfulness by obtaining an admission from him that he was convicted of forgery nine years ago, when he was 21 years old. On rebuttal, defendant calls the leader of a youth group of which the alibi witness was a member from the ages of 18 to 28, to support the credibility of the alibi witness. He elicits the following testimony:

### Defense Counsel:

Q. Mr. Smith, tell us your education.

A. I'm a college graduate, University of Maryland, and majored in sociology.

Q. What is your present occupation?

A. I am the youth leader of the Rolling Mills Recreation Center.

Q. What is the Rolling Mills Recreation Center?

A. It is an organization funded by the community of Rolling Mills, which serves as a focal point for young people from the ages of 13 to 30 to participate in sports activities and community affairs.

Q. How is the recreation center organized?

A. We have a director, which I have been serving as for the past eight years. Before that, I was the assistant director. We also have positions of assistant director, secretary, and treasurer.

Q. How are the people selected to fill these positions?

A. The manager appoints the people to these positions.

Q. Do you know John Smith, who resides at 212 Rolling Mills Road?

A. Yes, I do.

Q. How do you know him?

A. John Smith has been a member of the recreation center since 2004, and I have had occasion to work with him and supervise him and watch him grow up.

Q. Did you have occasion to observe him when he participated in various sports activities?

A. Yes, I did. I also had the opportunity to help teach him to play basketball and baseball and to swim.

Q. Do you have an opinion as to whether or not Mr. Smith is a truthful person?

A. Yes, I do.

Q. Can you tell us what that opinion is?

A. I think he's one of the most truthful, honorable young men I have ever met.

## Comment

Federal Rule of Evidence 608 permits the credibility of a witness to be supported by reputation or opinion evidence, provided that the evidence refers only to the witness's character for truthfulness or untruthfulness, and provided further that the witness's character has been previously attacked. *See United States v. Whitmore*, 359 F.3d 609 (D.C. Cir. 2009); *United States v. Balsam*, 203 F.3d 72, 87, n.18 (1st Cir.), *cert. denied*, 530 U.S. 1250 (2000) (Rule 608(b) does not provide for admission of physical evidence, such as a tape recording); *United States v. Hashisaki*, 1999 U.S. App. LEXIS 30139, at *5 (9th Cir. Nov. 17, 1999), *cert. denied*, 529 U.S. 1043 (2000) (testimony regarding a person's job performance does not implicate the person's character for truthfulness and is not admissible under Rule 608); *United States v. McMurray*, 20 F.3d 831 (8th Cir. 1994); *United States v. Williams*, 986 F.2d 86 (4th Cir.), *cert. denied*, 509 U.S. 911 (1993); *United States v. Dring*, 930 F.2d 687 (9th Cir. 1991), *cert. denied*, 506 U.S. 836 (1992) (trial court has discretion to determine what constitutes attack on witness's character for being truthful); *United States v. Bowie*, 892 F.2d 1494 (10th Cir. 1990); *United States v. McNeill*, 887 F.2d 448 (3d Cir. 1989), *cert. denied*, 493 U.S. 1087 (1990); *United States v. Candoli*, 870 F.2d 496 (9th Cir. 1989); *United States v. Hilton*, 772 F.2d 783 (11th Cir. 1985); *Stokes v. Delcambre*, 710 F.2d 1120 (5th Cir. 1983); *United States v. Angelini*, 678 F.2d 380 (1st Cir. 1982); *Beard v. Mitchell*, 604 F.2d 485 (7th Cir. 1979); *United States v. Medical Therapy Sciences, Inc.*, 583 F.2d 36 (2d Cir. 1978), *cert. denied*, 439 U.S. 1130 (1979); *United States v. Cylkouski*, 556 F.2d 799 (6th Cir. 1977). *Consider United States v. Truslow*, 530 F.2d 257 (4th Cir. 1975), for a discussion of the right of defense counsel to show the bad reputation of a prosecution witness for truth and veracity by asking a defense witness whether he was familiar with the general reputation of the prosecution witness for truth and veracity.

In rendering opinion testimony on character, the witness may state a reasonable basis for his or her testimony but may not testify about specific instances. Although Federal Rule of Evidence 608 does not specifically use the term "reasonable basis," the basis for reputation or opinion evidence as to character usually involves the witness's having heard the reputation discussed by others or having been involved directly in discussions of the reputation. *See* 4 MICHAEL H. GRAHAM, HANDBOOK OF FEDERAL EVIDENCE § 608:3 (7th ed. 2012); *cf. United States v. Thomas*, 768 F.2d 611 (5th Cir. 1985) (upholding a trial court's refusal to admit a polygraphist's testimony as to the truthfulness of the defendant/witness, because such testimony fell outside of the meaning of "opinion" evidence in Rule 608). Frequently, a follow-up question is asked after the witness renders his or her opinion: "Would you believe him or her under oath?" *See United States v. Yarbrough*, 527 F.3d 1092, 1100–03

(10th Cir. 2008) (good character evidence regarding accused's integrity and law-abiding status was admissible despite the fact that the sole issue of the case was obstruction of justice); *United States v. Skelton*, 514 F.3d 433, 441–42 (5th Cir. 2008); *United States v. McMurray*, 20 F.3d 831 (8th Cir. 1994).

A curious distinction exists between federal and some state practices with regard to a character witness being able to testify about whether another witness testified truthfully. Maryland Rule 5–608(a)(3)(A) prohibits such testimony. *United States v. Davis*, 639 F.2d 239 (5th Cir. 1981), expresses a contrary view.

## E. HABIT, USUAL METHOD OF PRACTICE

Mrs. Smith institutes an employment discrimination suit, pursuant to 42 U.S.C. § 2000(e) et seq., against Raisin, Inc., claiming sex discrimination. She testifies that during the course of her hiring interview the company's agent asked her whether or not she could lift a weight over 50 pounds, and that she was also asked questions concerning her marital status, whether she had children, whether she was divorced, and whether she received child support. Defendant's agent has no specific recollection of interviewing the plaintiff, and cannot remember specifically that he did not ask the questions plaintiff alleges. He does know, however, that it was his usual practice not to ask questions of that nature when interviewing any applicants, female or male, and he is asked to so testify.

### Defense Counsel:

Q. Mr. Jones, how long were you department director for Raisin, Inc., in the food sales division?

A. Twelve years.

Q. Was one of the things you did as director the hiring of personnel for the division?

A. Yes, it was.

Q. Would you outline your procedure in recruiting applicants to fill any vacant positions in 2013?

A. We would first advertise in the newspaper and send notification to recruitment offices at local schools and employment agencies. After we received the responses, we would send application forms to the individuals who responded. After we received the completed application forms, we would interview the applicants.

Q. In 2013, did you advertise a position in the food sales division of Raisin, Inc.'s Baltimore division?

A. Yes.

Q. Did you receive responses to those ads?

A. Yes.

Q. Did you forward application forms to those who responded?

A. Yes, we did.

Q. Did you conduct any interviews that year?

A. Absolutely.

Q. How many interviews did you conduct, if you remember?

A. Approximately 200 interviews.

Q. Do you remember conducting an interview with the plaintiff in this case, Renee Smith?

A. I'm sorry. I do not have any recollection of meeting her, although my notes reflect that I did interview her.

Q. Do you remember what happened during your interview?

A. I'm sorry. I do not remember.

Q. Do you recall whether or not you asked her any specific questions?

A. I do not.

Q. In addition to the 200 interviews that you conducted for the position that Mrs. Smith applied for, how many other interviews have you conducted as a representative of Raisin, Inc.?

A. At least 1,500 interviews.

Q. Did you ever ask a question during any interview concerning a female applicant's ability to lift over a particular number of pounds, or did you ever ask whether a female applicant was married, divorced, or receiving child support or alimony?

A. Absolutely not. It was not my practice to ask any questions of that type.

Q. How can you be so sure?

A. Because at the many seminars that I attended on how to conduct interviews within the company, we were instructed never to ask questions of that type.

Q. When did you attend those seminars?

A. Twice a year. From 2006 up to this very time. We have seminars that deal with interview techniques.

## *Comment*

Federal Rule of Evidence 406 provides that "[e]vidence of the habit of a person or of the routine practice of an organization, whether corroborated or not and regardless of the presence of eyewitnesses, is relevant to prove that the conduct of the person or organization on a particular occasion was in conformity with the habit or routine practice." *See Leonard v. Nationwide Mut. Ins. Co.*, 499 F.3d 419, 442 (5th Cir. 2007) (habit is a "specific reaction to a specific set of stimuli that is reflexive, repeated, and invariable in nature") (quoting *Pursley v. Dretke*, 114 Fed. Appx. 630, 634 (5th Cir. 2004)). Proof of habit is better received than proof of character because "the uniformity of one's response to habit is far greater than the consistency with which one's conduct conforms to character." *Williams v. Security Nat'l Bank of Sioux City, Iowa*, 358 F. Supp. 2d 782, 812 (N.D. Iowa 2005) (citation omitted); *see Jones v. Southern Pacific R.R.*, 962 F.2d 447, 449 (5th Cir. 1992). For a detailed discussion of what constitutes a "habit" under Rule 406, *See Fecho v. Eli Lilly & Co.*, 914 F. Supp.2d 130, 137–42 (D. Mass. 2012) (proponent failed to establish that physician had a habit of reading and heeding drug manufacturer's warnings and sharing them with patients).

To establish evidence of habit, a party must show that the pertinent actions "were 'semi-automatic,' such as 'the habit of going down a particular stairway two stairs at a time, or of giving the hand-signal for a left turn, or of alighting from railway cars while they are moving.'" *Friend v. Time Mfg. Co.*, 2006 WL 2135807 (D. Ariz. Jul. 28, 2006) (quoting advisory committee notes to Fed. R. Evid. 406). Rule 406 evidence must "rest on an analysis of instances numerous enough to [support] an inference of systematic conduct and to establish one's regular response to a repeated specific situation." *Bell v. Consol. Rail Corp.*, 299 F. Supp. 2d 795, 800 (N.D. Ohio 2004). There is no precise formula for determining when behavior may become so consistent as to rise to level of habit, but "'adequacy of sampling and uniformity of response' are controlling considerations[.]" *Goldsmith v. Bagby Elevator Co., Inc.*, 513 F.3d 1261, 1285 (11th Cir. 2008) (quoting advisory committee notes to Fed. R. Evid. 406). *See United States v. Santos*, 65 F. Supp. 2d 802, 821 (E.D. Ill. 1999) (requirement that party establish the degree of specificity and frequency of uniform response and to show more than a mere tendency to act in a given manner helps prevent attempts to "sneak in" inadmissible character evidence under Rule 404, *i.e.*, evidence used to establish a party's propensity to act in conformity with her general character, as habit), *subsequent appeal, remanded*, 201 F.2d 953 (7th Cir. 2000).

The following cases offer examples of types of behavior that were offered as habit evidence: *S.E.C. v. Lyon*, 605 F. Supp. 2d 531 (S.D.N.Y. 2009) (SEC established evidence of habit where deponents testified to having "process" or "procedures" or "a script to read" to ensure that potential investors agreed to keep identity of issuer confidential before being brought "over the wall," and testified to frequency with which practice was followed); *United States ex rel. El-Amin v. George Washington Univ.*, 533 F. Supp. 2d 12 (D.D.C. 2008) (holding that parties failed to establish habitual or routine character of conduct of hospital's anesthesiologists, where the proponents did not indicate whether habit or routine practice evidence they sought to introduce concerned individual anesthesiologists or all of hospital's anesthesiologists, did not identify time period over which habit or routine practice occurred, did not identify which of steps mandated by Medicare regulations were implicated by alleged habit or routine practice, and did not proffer evidence establishing reliability of routine or habit); *Goldsmith v. Bagby Elevator Co., Inc.*, 513 F.3d 1261, 1285 (11th Cir. 2008) (evidence of four other dismissals of black employees under different circumstances was not "habit" evidence, but was admissible under 404(b) as proof of intent to discriminate); *United States v. Angwin*, 271 F.3d 786, 800 (9th Cir. 2001) (evidence that police officer takes a non-confrontational course of action in dangerous situations is not habit evidence probative of how he acted on a specific occasion), *overruled on other grounds, United States v. Lopez*, 484 F.3d 1186 (9th Cir. 2007).

The method of proving habit, that is, reputation, opinion, or specific instances, is within the discretion of the trial judge. *See, e.g., United States v. Warner*, 498 F.3d 666, 692–93 (7th Cir. 2007) (holding that district court did not abuse its discretion in excluding evidence proffered as habitual). Evidence of habit is more readily received than that of character because the uniformity of one's response to habit is far greater than the consistency with which one's conduct conforms to character. *See* 1 MCCORMICK ON EVIDENCE § 195 (Kenneth S. Broun ed., 7th ed. 2013); *see also Meyer v. United States*, 638 F.2d 155 (10th Cir. 1980).

This pattern could also be viewed as testimony supporting "usual method of practice," which is frequently admitted for purposes of showing a person's standard of care. Although in some instances "usual method of practice" is indistinguishable from habit, these are two areas of conduct that are separate and distinct. A third separate concept is known as "custom and usage." This concept refers to a habitual or customary practice among certain groups of people—for example, trades or neighborhoods. *See infra* Chapter 8.G. However, the federal rules explicitly combine habit or routine practice in business under one rule and make no separate provision for "usual method of practice," although the doctrine is recognized. *See also Columbia Nitrogen Corp. v. Royster Co.*, 451 F.2d 3 (4th Cir. 1971); U.C.C. §§ 1-205, 2-208.

## F. ROUTINE PRACTICE (CUSTOM) IN BUSINESS

John Baines institutes suit against his landlord for negligence in failing to repair a porch, which collapsed and caused the plaintiff's son serious injury. To show knowledge on the part of the landlord that the porch was in need of repair, Mr. Baines's attorney introduces documents of the Department of Housing reflecting that the porch was inspected by a housing inspector, that the inspector indicated on his report that the porch was in need of repair, and that after the report was completed by the housing inspector it was mailed to the landlord.

### Plaintiff's Counsel:

Q. Mr. Richards, please tell us your occupation?
A. Regional manager of the Worcester Housing Authority.
Q. I show you Exhibit 32 and ask you if you are familiar with it.
A. Yes, this is a housing report used by our inspectors when they visit homes to conduct housing inspections.
Q. What premises are reflected in this report?
A. 16 Omaha Street.
Q. Do you recognize the signature at the bottom of the report?
A. Yes, it is Inspector Thomas's signature.
Q. Where is Inspector Thomas today, if you know?
A. He died last year.
Q. Directing your attention to Item 16 on the report, do you see the item "porch"?
A. Yes.
Q. What else do you see with regard to that item?
A. I note that the column "needs repair" is checked.

Q. How long have you been affiliated with the Housing Authority?

A. Five years.

Q. During your five years with the Housing Authority, have you become familiar with the routine practice [custom] with regard to the inspection of houses by the Department?

A. Yes, I have.

Q. During the year 2014, was there a routine practice or custom concerning the inspection of houses?

A. Yes.

Q. What was that routine practice [custom]?

A. That year, each landlord in the southeast section of the city received a notice from our department advising that within sixty days one of our inspectors would visit his rental property for purposes of conducting a general, overall inspection.

Q. What did this inspection consist of?

A. The inspectors went to the premises and generally reviewed the plumbing, heating, and related facilities, as well as checked structural conditions, and in general looked for unsafe or unhealthy conditions within the premises.

Q. What routine practice or custom, if any, would the inspector follow with regard to reporting defects?

A. He would indicate on his report that the particular improvement or repair was necessary.

Q. Does the department have a routine practice or custom with regard to processing the reports taken or made by the housing inspectors of the Authority?

A. Yes.

Q. What is that practice?

A. After the housing inspector completes his report, he files a copy with us in the central office. The central office then makes five additional copies for placement in the file and one is forwarded by mail to the landlord.

Q. Do your agency's records reflect whether Mr. Herbert, the landlord in this case, received a copy of Mr. Thomas's report?

A. They do not.

Q. Why not?

A. Because of a fire that destroyed our records for that time.

Q. How was the routine that you described established?

A. The supervisor of the department promulgated this policy at least six years ago and it appears in the department's policy manual.

Q. How is the routine enforced?

A. By supervisory checks and administrative seminars, which all appropriate individuals attend.

Q. Is the routine practice and custom of the Housing Authority adhered to in every case?

A. Yes, to the best of my knowledge it is.

## Comment

Federal Rule of Evidence 406 treats routine practice of a business exactly as it does evidence of habit. *See S.E.C. v. Lyon*, 605 F. Supp. 2d 531 543 (S.D.N.Y. 2009) ("Evidence of an organization's routine practice is admissible provided the proponent of the evidence establishes that the organization acted with 'regularity over substantially all occasions or with substantially all other parties with whom the [organization] has had similar business transactions.'") (citing *Mobil Exploration & Producing U.S., Inc. v. Cajun Constr. Servs., Inc.*, 45 F.3d 96, 100 (5th Cir. 1995)). *See, e.g., United States v. Rangel-Arreola*, 991 F.2d 1519 (10th Cir. 1993); *Rosenburg v. Lincoln Am. Life Ins. Co.*, 883 F.2d 1328 (7th Cir. 1989); *United States Football League v. National Football League*, 842 F.2d 1335 (2d Cir. 1988); *O'Brien v. Papa Gino's of Am., Inc.*, 780 F.2d 1067 (1st Cir. 1986); *Mathes v. The Clipper Fleet*, 774 F.2d 980 (9th Cir. 1985); *G.M. Brod & Co. v. U.S. Home Corp.*, 759 F.2d 1526 (11th Cir. 1985); *Cmwlth. of Pa. v. Porter*, 659 F.2d 306 (3d Cir. 1981) (en banc), *cert. denied*, 458 U.S. 1121 (1982); *United States v. Callahan*, 551 F.2d 733 (6th Cir. 1977), *appeal after remand*, 579 F.2d 398 (6th Cir. 1978); *Wiles v. Nationwide Life Ins. Co.*, 334 F.2d 296 (4th Cir. 1964); *ECDC Envtl., L.C. v. N.Y. Marine & Gen'l Ins. Co.*, 1999 U.S. Dist. LEXIS 9836, at *38 (S.D.N.Y. June 30, 1999); *Morris v. Travelers Indemnity Co. of Am.*, 518 F.3d 755, 761 (10th Cir. 2008) (witness's testimony of common business practice without more evidence (such as written documentation) was not enough to establish a common business practice); *Leonard v. Nationwide Mutual Insurance Co.*, 499 F.3d 419, 442 (5th Cir. 2007) (evidence of conversations with five other policy holders was not sufficient to establish habit evidence); *United States v. Warner*, 498 F.3d 666, 692 (7th Cir. 2007); *see also Weil v. Seltzer*, 873 F.2d 1453 (D.C. Cir. 1989).

## G. CUSTOM AND USAGE

JBX, a partnership, purchased a large shipment of film from Columbia Film Company for the purpose of preparing a feature film. When numerous actors breached their contracts with JBX, the partnership sought to return the film and obtain a refund. The film company declined. The partnership instituted suit, calling an expert witness to testify that the contract between the parties, when construed in light of usage of the trade and course of dealings between the parties, imposed a duty on the film company to accept the return of the film and to refund the partnership's payment allocable to the film returned.

### Plaintiff's Counsel:

(John Smith, having been qualified as a film expert, testified as follows.)

Q. Is there a custom, practice, or usage within the trade and industry of film merchandising with regard to the sale of film to be used in the production of full-length motion pictures?

A. Yes.

Q. Are you familiar with that custom, practice, or usage?

A. Yes.

Q. What is the custom, practice, or usage with regard to refunds when film footage is not used?

A. Frequently the film industry overestimates the amount of film necessary to shoot various scenes planned to be incorporated within full-length feature films. Film companies, therefore, traditionally accept the return of the film quite readily, and agree to refund the price of the returned film to a motion picture company.

Q. Do you have any personal knowledge as to whether or not defendant Columbia Film Company habitually observes this custom of accepting the return of unused film and refunding the purchase price?

A. Yes, I do.

Q. What do you know about that?

A. They do observe that custom. I know for a fact that they have observed it with Paramount Pictures and Metro Goldwyn Mayer on dozens of occasions.

## *Comment*

Evidence of custom and usage is frequently admitted in cases dealing with contracts. *See Precision Fitness Equip., Inc. v. Nautilus, Inc.* 2011 U.S. Dist. LEXIS 13576 (D. Colo. 2011) (evidence of trade usage and course of dealing is admissible under the Uniform Commercial Code unless such evidence is "carefully negated" by the contracting parties); *Hugo Boss Fashions Inc. v. Federal Ins. Co.*, 252 F.3d 608, 617 (2d Cir. 2001); *Carey Canada, Inc. v. Columbia Cas. Co.*, 940 F.2d 1548 (D.C. Cir. 1991); *H&W Indus., Inc. v. Occidental Chem. Corp.*, 911 F.2d 1118 (5th Cir. 1990); *Walk-In Medical Centers, Inc. v. Breuer Capital Corp.*, 818 F.2d 260 (2d Cir. 1987); *A.J. Cunningham Packing Corp. v. Florence Beef Co.*, 785 F.2d 348 (1st Cir. 1986); *In re Pearson Bros. Co.*, 787 F.2d 1157 (7th Cir. 1986); *Kern Oil & Refining Co. v. Tenneco Oil Co.*, 792 F.2d 1380 (9th Cir. 1986), *cert. denied*, 480 U.S. 906 (1987); *G.M. Brod & Co., Inc. v. U.S. Home Corp.*, 759 F.2d 1526 (11th Cir. 1985); *Ralph's Distrib. Co. v. AMF, Inc.*, 667 F.2d 670 (8th Cir. 1981); *Brunswick Box Co. v. Coutinho, Caro & Co.*, 617 F.2d 355 (4th Cir. 1980); *Sunbury Textile Mills, Inc. v. Comm'r of Internal Revenue*, 585 F.2d 1190 (3d Cir. 1978); *Major v. Bishop*, 462 F.2d 1277 (10th Cir. 1972); *In re Worldcorp, Inc.*, 252 B.R. 890, 896 (Bankr. D. Del. 2000); *Trent Partners & Assocs. v. Digital Equip. Corp.*, 120 F. Supp. 2d 84, 99 (D. Mass. 1999); *Allapattah Servs. v. Exxon Corp.*, 61 F. Supp. 2d 1300, 1304 (S.D. Fla. 1999).

# General Interest

## A.  IMMUNIZING THE WITNESS

During a wrongful death case, the plaintiff's eyewitness to the collision is on the witness stand. The witness is expected to testify that she saw the defendant run the red light. Previously during a deposition, the witness had testified that she had doubts about whether the light was yellow or red. Counsel wants to take the sting out of cross-examination by eliciting the witness's prior testimony on direct examination and having her explain it before cross-examination.

### Plaintiff's Counsel:

Q. Did you see the collision?

A. Yes.

Q. Tell us exactly what you saw occur.

A. Mr. Smith ran the red light and collided with the car operated by the late Mrs. Duncan.

Q. Are you sure the light was red?

A. Yes.

Q. Did you ever testify differently in the past about what color you believed the light to be?

**Defense Counsel:** Objection. Counsel is about to impeach her own witness.

**The Court:** Overruled.

A. Yes.

Q. When?

A. Last year in a deposition in this case I testified that I could not remember if the light were yellow or red.

Q. Do you remember now?

A. Yes, the light was definitely red.

Q. Why did you testify differently in the deposition?

A. At the time of the deposition, I was experiencing cluster migraine headaches. I was taking certain medicines that affected my ability to remember.

Q. Do you have any doubt now about what color the light was at the time in question.

A. No, I do not. It was red.

Q. Thank you. No further questions.

## *Comment*

Although at common law a party could not ordinarily impeach her own witness, modern practice adopts a different approach. Federal Rule of Evidence 607 and many state evidence codes now permit the credibility of a witness to be attacked by any party calling that witness.

The opportunity to impeach one's own witness offers counsel the ability to call a witness for favorable testimony. Then counsel can elicit the unfavorable testimony in a less harmful way than by simply turning the witness over for cross-examination. Taking the sting out of what could be a lethal cross-examination is a strategic technique well worth considering. *See United States v. Buffalo*, 358 F.3d 519 (8th Cir. 2004); *United States v. Darden*, 70 F.3d 1507, 1539 (8th Cir. 1995); *United States v. Marroquin*, 885 F.2d 1240 (5th Cir. 1989). *See also* 2 SALTZBURG, MARTIN & CAPRA, FEDERAL RULES OF EVIDENCE MANUAL at 607–17 (10th ed. 2011 & Supp. June 2014).

The extent to which counsel can rehabilitate her witness after introducing the harmful evidence is a matter of discretion with the court. Thus, the questions to the witness about whether the witness is now sure that the light was red, although not improper, may be objected to on the basis of "asked and answered."

## B. PRESENT SENSE IMPRESSION AND EXCITED UTTERANCE

Sam Shopper has sued the Green Grocery Store in negligence for injuries he sustained in a slip and fall at the store. He has called Wendy Williams as a witness to testify to certain out-of-court statements she heard that tend to prove the existence of a dangerous condition on the premises and that the Green Grocery Store had prior knowledge of the condition.

### Plaintiff's Attorney:

Q. Where were you at the time Mr. Shopper fell, Mrs. Williams?

A. I was in the dairy section of the store, looking for yogurt.

Q. What, if anything, do you recall?

A. Well, as I pushed my shopping cart toward where the yogurt is displayed, I passed a woman and her young daughter who were also shopping in the dairy section. A second or two later, I heard a young girl's voice—it must have been the daughter—say, "Mommy, look! There's milk all over the floor!"

Q. What happened after that?

A. The next thing I know I heard a smack, like the palm of your hand against concrete, and then I heard a man screaming. I turned and saw a man, who I later found out was Mr. Shopper, writhing in pain on the floor.

Q. What happened after that?

A. I went over to see if Mr. Shopper was injured, and a store manager came over as well.

Q. Did anyone else attend to Mr. Shopper?

A. Yes, a young woman came over and she had her cell phone with her. She called 911 and asked for an ambulance.

Q. How long did you stay with Mr. Shopper?

A. For as long as it took for the paramedics to arrive—probably no more than 10 or 15 minutes.

Q. What, if anything, do you recall happening when the paramedics arrived?

A. Mr. Shopper looked like he was in a lot of pain. The woman who called 911 was holding his hand and holding his hat, which I guess had come off in the fall. When the paramedics loaded him onto the stretcher, the woman said, "I can't believe nobody cleaned that floor. I saw milk on it over a half an hour ago."

## Comment

The Federal Rules of Evidence codify the different, but closely related, common-law hearsay exceptions for present sense impressions and excited utterance. According to the rules, the former applies to a "statement describing or explaining an event or condition made while the declarant was perceiving the event or condition, or immediately thereafter." Rule 803(1). The excited utterance exception applies to a "statement relating to a startling event or condition made while the declarant was under the stress of excitement caused by the event or condition." Rule 803(2). *See United States v. Shoup*, 476 F.3d 38, 42–43 (1st Cir. 2007) (911 call fell within both the present sense impression and excited utterance exceptions to the hearsay rule).

Each exception has a "time" element that must be satisfied before the proffered statement may be admitted. Present sense impression carries the more restrictive temporal measurement, with the declarant having to make the statement at the exact time he or she is perceiving the event or "immediately thereafter." The advisory committee note to Rule 803 speaks of event-statement contemporaneity, with only a "slight lapse" permitted between the two. *E.g.*, *United States v. Ibisevic*, 675 F.3d 342 (4th Cir. 2012) (in prosecution for smuggling, mother's testimony that defendant told her about customs officers' questioning of defendant was admissible as present sense impression, because defendant made statement to his mother immediately after conversation with officers); *United States v. Green*, 556 F.3d 151 (3rd Cir. 2009) (holding that delay of 50 minutes did not meet standard of "substantial contemporaneity"); *United States v. Parker*, 936 F.2d 950 (7th Cir. 1991) (underlying rationale of present sense impression is that substantial contemporaneity of event and statement minimizes unreliability due to defective recollection or conscious fabrication); *Pau v. Yosemite Park and Curry Co.*, 928 F.2d 880 (9th Cir. 1991) (statement made about accident two days after occurrence held not admissible under present sense impression exception); *but see Schindler v. Seiler*, 474 F.3d 1008, 1012 (7th Cir. 2007) (because there was time for the declarant to think over the statement, and because no evidence was presented demonstrating "the statement's immediacy," the present sense impression exception did not apply).

By contrast, an excited utterance need not be made contemporaneously with the happening of a startling event, as long as the declarant made it at a time when he or she remained under the stress or excitement caused by it. *United States v. Boyce*, 742 F.3d 792, 798 (7th Cir. 2014) (911 call by mother of a defendant's children in which she answered dispatcher's question by stating that defendant had a gun and had assaulted her was an excited utterance even though made in response to dispatcher's question); *McCurdy v. Greyhound Corp.*, 346 F.2d 224 (3d Cir. 1965) ("excited utterance" admissible as part of the "res gestae" is made by a participant in the event during a period when he was, for any reason, incapable of reasoned reflection about the occurrence); *Murphy Auto Parts Co., Inc. v. Ball*, 249 F.2d 508 (D.C. Cir. 1957) (existence of an exciting event and an utterance prompted by the event without time to reflect, "i.e., dominated by the excitement of the event," are required for admissibility). *See Brunsting v. Lutsen Mountains Corp.*, 601 F.3d 813, 817 (8th Cir. 2010) ("one well-recognized exception to the hearsay rule is found in Rule 803(2), which excepts from the hearsay rule any statement relating to a startling event or condition made while the declarant was under the stress of excitement caused by the event or condition."). There is no specific cutoff point. Rather, courts will look to the totality of the circumstances to determine if the statement was made at a time when the declarant was so under the influence of the shock and excitement produced by the event as to hinder the declarant's ability to reflect on the incident. *United States v. Fell*, 531 F.3d 197, 231 (2d Cir. 2008) (excited utterance "need not be contemporaneous with the startling event to be admissible"; instead, the pertinent question is whether the declarant was still under the "stress of excitement caused by the event or condition") (quoting *United States v. Jones*, 299 F.3d 103, 112 (2d Cir. 2002)); *Morgan v. Foretich*, 846 F.2d 941 (4th Cir. 1988) (when deciding whether declarant was under stress of event at time of utterance, court will look to (1) the lapse of time between the event and the statement, (2) the age of the declarant, (3) physical and mental state of declarant, (4) characteristics of the event, and (5) the subject matter of the statement); *see also Pau v. Yosemite Park and Curry Co.*, 928 F.2d 880 (9th Cir. 1991) (court did not abuse discretion denying admissibility on excited utterance exception; record does not clearly indicate decedent was under stress of accident when statement allegedly made). Also, the startling event need not be an unexpected event, such as an accident or a criminal act, as long as it affects the declarant's ability to reflect upon the statement. *United States v. Moore*, 791 F.2d 566 (7th Cir. 1986) (startling event need not be totally unexpected happening, as long as it has startling effect upon the declarant).

The advisory committee note, in acknowledging that the two exceptions overlap, recognized that the "most significant practical difference" between the two is in the allowable time lapse between the event and the statement.

Another common foundational requirement for the two exceptions is the relatedness of the statement to the event. To qualify as a present sense impression, the statement must "describe or explain" the event or condition, Rule 803(1); *United States v. Campbell*, 782 F. Supp. 1258 (N.D. Ill. 1991), whereas an excited utterance must merely "relate to" the startling event or condition, a standard that encompasses a much broader category of statements. Rule 803(2); *United States v. Moore*, 791 F.2d 566 (7th Cir. 1986).

In a criminal case, the extent to which the Confrontation Clause of the Sixth Amendment applies to the two exceptions is unclear. In *Crawford v. Washington*, 541 U.S. 36 (2004), the Supreme Court restricted the admissibility of testimonial hearsay statements where the declarant is not available to testify. Whether a statement is "testimonial" depends on such factors as whether the declarant's purpose was to provide evidence for use in a prosecution, the level of formality in the making of the statement, and whether the declarant was facing an ongoing emergency. *See Davis v. Washington*, 547 U.S. 813, 826–27 (2006). Most courts have found that present sense impressions are non-testimonial. *See, e.g., United States v. Thomas*, 453 F.3d 838, 841, 844 (7th Cir. 2006); *United States v. Danford*, 435 F.3d 682, 687 (7th Cir. 2005); *State v. Price*, 952 So. 2d 112, 121 (La. App. 2006); *People v. Coleman*, 16 A.D.3d 254, 254–55, 791 N.Y.S.2d 112 (N.Y. App. Div. 2005); *Salt Lake City v. Williams*, 128 P.3d 47, 49–50, 53–54, 54 n.6 (Utah Ct. App. 2005); *but see People v. Dobbin*, 6 Misc. 3d 892, 898, 791 N.Y.S.2d 897 (N.Y. Sup. Ct. 2004).

## C. DYING DECLARATION

John Wilson, M.D., treated Daniel Davis in the emergency room at Community Hospital after Mr. Davis's vehicle left the roadway and struck a utility pole, gravely injuring him. Mr. Davis's estate has sued the Great Dane Bus Company as a result of the accident, and has called Dr. Wilson to testify at trial regarding statements Mr. Davis made in the emergency room.

### Plaintiff's Attorney:

Q. Dr. Wilson, did you treat Mr. Davis on May 5th?
A. Yes I did.
Q. What was his condition when you treated him?
A. Mr. Davis was suffering from massive internal bleeding and was slipping into shock.
Q. Were you ever able to stabilize him?
A. Unfortunately not. The trauma to Mr. Davis's abdomen was so great that it was impossible to find and stop all of the bleeding. We realized after not too long that we would not be able to save Mr. Davis.
Q. What, if anything, did Mr. Davis say in the emergency room?
A. He said that he was cold, and that he was going to die.
Q. When Mr. Davis made that statement, how did he sound?
A. He said it, like, in a resigned fashion, and sounded sad.
Q. What if anything else did Mr. Davis say?
A. He said that a Great Dane bus had killed him. He said the bus crossed the center line and forced him off the road.

## *Comment*

Dying declarations are an exception to the hearsay rule, and are governed by Federal Rule of Evidence 804(b)(2), which states:

> The following are not excluded by the rule against hearsay if the declarant is unavailable as a witness: . . . In a prosecution for homicide or in a civil case, a statement made by a declarant, while believing the declarant's death to be imminent, made about its cause or circumstances.

At common law, the exception was only applicable to homicide prosecutions; the federal rules have expanded it to now include civil proceedings.

Courts look to the state of the declarant's mind at the time the statement was made. It is not enough that a declarant fear or believe her illness may end in death. There "must be a 'settled hopeless expectation' that death is near at hand, and what is said must be spoken in the hush of its impending presence." *Shepard v. United States*, 290 U.S. 96, 100 (1933). *United States v. Shields*, 497 F.3d 789, 793 (8th Cir. 2007) (dying declaration exception did not apply because declarant's wounds did not appear to be life-threatening, no one expected him to die, and there was no indication that the declarant felt his death was imminent); *Pippin v. Dretke*, 434 F.3d 782, 793 (5th Cir. 2005); *People v. Nieves*, 492 N.E.2d 109, 113 (N.Y. 1986) (support for the dying declaration exception to the hearsay rule is now generally based in the alleged psychological effect that awareness of impending death has on the declarant, as such knowledge is presumed to remove from the mind all motivation and inclination to lie). If it can be reasonably inferred from the state of the wound or the state of the illness that the dying person was aware of his danger, then the requirement of impending death is met. *State v. Quintana*, 644 P.2d 531, 534 (N.M. 1982). *But see Crabbe v. Troublefield*, 888 F.2d 1385 (4th Cir. 1989 (per curiam) statement excluded where declarant's doctors testified that he was slipping in and out of consciousness and probably was incapable of speaking coherently).

The Supreme Court has not determined whether the Confrontation Clause of the Sixth Amendment applies to a dying declaration under the standards the Court set forth in *Crawford v. Washington*, 541 U.S. 36 (2004). In dicta, however, the *Crawford* Court opined:

> The one deviation we have found involves dying declarations. The existence of that exception as a general rule of criminal hearsay law cannot be disputed. Although many dying declarations may not be testimonial, there is authority for admitting even those that clearly are. We need not decide in this case whether the Sixth Amendment incorporates an exception for testimonial dying declarations. If this exception must be accepted on historical grounds, it is *sui generis*.

547 U.S. at 56 n.6.

Many state court decisions have held that *Crawford* creates a dying declaration exception to the Confrontation Clause. *See, e.g., People v. Monterroso*, 34 Cal.4th 743, 764–65 (2004); *Commonwealth v. Nesbitt*, 452 Mass. 236, 249–51 (2008); *People v. Taylor*, 275 Mich. App. 177, 183 (2007); *State v. Martin*, 695 N.W.2d 578, 585–86 (Minn. 2005), *abrogation on other grounds recognized by Arredondo v. State*, 754 N.W. 2d 566 (Minn. 2008); *Harkins v. State*, 143 P.3d 706, 710–11 (Nev. 2006); *State v. Calhoun*, 657 S.E.2d 424, 427–428 (N.C. 2008). Several lower federal courts, however, have disagreed. *See United States v. Mayhew*, 380 F. Supp. 2d 961, 964–65 (S.D. Ohio 2005); *United States v. Jordan*, 2005 WL 513501, at *3–*4 (D. Colo. 2005).

## D. SUBSEQUENT REMEDIAL MEASURES

The plaintiff, driver of an automobile, collided with a truck on State Highway 64. He was westbound and the truck was eastbound. They met head-on. Both the plaintiff and the truck driver were unconscious after the impact and did not recall how the accident happened, and so there was no direct evidence of its cause. At a bridge on Highway 64, there was a dangerous narrowing of the highway from 24 feet to 18 feet. Plaintiff sued not the state, but rather a highway construction contractor with which the state had a contract to widen the section of Highway 64 on which the plaintiff was traveling. The defendant contractor argued that the dangerous condition existed on a portion of the highway excluded from the construction contract, and therefore the contractor had no duty to post a warning sign. On cross-examination of a representative of the defendant contractor, who had denied on direct that the contractor controlled the section of the highway where the accident occurred, plaintiff's attorney asks him about subsequent remedial measures taken after the accident.

### Plaintiff's Counsel:

Q. After the accident, did your company install any warning signs or devices in the portion of the highway where the accident occurred?

**Defense Attorney:** Objection.

**The Court:** What's the basis of the objection?

**Defense Attorney:** The basis of the objection is that under Federal Rule of Evidence 407, remedial measures taken after an accident are not admissible to prove negligence, culpable conduct, or a need for a warning or instruction.

**The Court:** Overruled. Evidence of subsequent remedial measures as proof of an admission of fault is excluded. Nevertheless, exclusion is called for only when the evidence of subsequent remedial measures is offered as proof of negligence or culpable conduct. The rule does not require the exclusion of evidence of subsequent measures when offered for another purpose, such as proving ownership, control or feasibility of precautionary measures, if controverted, or for impeachment. Here, evidence that the defendant put out warning signs after the accident is admissible to show that the defendant contractor was in control of the site.

## *Comment*

Federal Rule of Evidence 407 provides that evidence of subsequent remedial measures, taken after an injury or harm allegedly caused by an event, is not admissible as proof of "negligence; culpable conduct; a defect in a product or its design; or a need for a warning or instruction." However, Rule 407 allows the court to admit this evidence "for another purpose, such as impeachment or—if disputed—proving ownership, control, or the feasibility of precautionary measures." *See, e.g., Mahaney ex-rel. estate of Kyle v. Novartis Pharmaceuticals Corp.*, 835 F. Supp. 2d 299 (W.D. Ky 2011) (pharmaceutical company labeling change on drugs used to combat advanced cancers that have presented themselves in patients' bones, which mentioned osteonecrosis of the jaw under the subsection "Warnings and Precautions", encouraged patients taking the drugs to maintain good oral hygiene and urged patients to avoid invasive dental procedures, was not admissible in action alleging failure to warn as evidence of a defect in the original warning or instruction). As the advisory committee note to Rule 407 explains, the rule rests on two grounds. First, the conduct is not in fact an admission, since the conduct is equally consistent with injury by mere accident or through contributory negligence. As Baron Bramwell put it, the rule rejects the notion that "because the world gets wiser as it gets older, therefore it was foolish before." *Hart v. Lancashire & Yorkshire Ry. Co.*, 21 L.P.R. N.S. 261, 263 (1869). The second ground for exclusion rests on a social policy of "encouraging people to take, or at least not discouraging them from taking, steps in furtherance of added safety." Advisory committee note to Rule 407. The courts have applied the principle embodied in Rule 407 to exclude evidence of subsequent repairs, installation of safety devices, changes in company rules, and discharge of employees. Advisory committee note to Rule 407.

There are exceptions to the rule of exclusion. Exclusion is required only when the evidence of subsequent remedial measures is offered as proof of negligence or other culpable conduct. The rule of exclusion prevents the inference that fault is admitted by engaging in subsequent repairs. Other purposes are, however, allowable, including ownership or control; existence of duty; feasibility of precautionary measures, if controverted; and impeachment. *Id.* In addition, Rule 407 does not require "exclusion of policy changes made not in response to a sense of social responsibility or a desire to remedy an injury, but rather in response to the dictates of a higher authority." *Gilanian v. City of Boston*, 431 F. Supp. 2d 172, 177 (D. Mass. 2006); *see Herndon v. Seven Bar Flying Service, Inc.*, 716 F.2d 1322, 1331 (10th Cir. 1983); *Cowden v. BNSF Ry. Co.*, 690 F.3d 884, 897 (8th Cir. 2012); *Rozier v. Ford Motor Co.*, 573 F.2d 1332, 1343 (5th Cir. 1978). "The proper purposes set forth in the rule are not exhaustive. *See Pineda v. Ford Motor Co.*, 520 F. 3d 237, 246–47 (3d Cir. 2008) (reversible error to preclude plaintiff's expert from relying on language of defendant's subsequent safety recall instructions as part of the Fed. R. Ediv. 703 basis for expert's opinion that earlier warnings were inadequate)." 5 Lynn McClain, Maryland Evidence, State and Federal § 407:2, n.12 (3d ed. 2013).

The example above is drawn from *Powers v. J. B. Michael & Co.*, 329 F.2d 674 (6th Cir. 1964), an action against a road contractor for negligent failure to put out warning signs. There, the court allowed testimony that the defendant subsequently put out signs to show that the portion of the road in question was under the defendant's control.

The requirement that the other purpose "be controverted" calls for automatic exclusion of the subsequent repairs evidence "unless a genuine issue be present" and allows the opposing party to lay the ground work for exclusion by making an admission. Otherwise, the factors of undue prejudice, confusion of issues, misleading the jury, and waste of time remain for consideration under Federal Rule of Evidence 403. Advisory committee note to Rule 407.

The 1997 amendments to Rule 407 made two changes in the rule. First, the amendment clarifies that the rule applies only to changes made after the occurrence that produced the damages giving rise to the action. Evidence of measures taken by the defendant prior to the "event" causing "injury or harm" are not excluded even if they occurred after the manufacture or design of the product.

Rule 407 was also amended to provide that evidence of subsequent remedial measures may not be used to prove "a defect in a product or its design, or that a warning or instruction should have accompanied a product." This amendment adopts the view of a majority of the federal circuits that have interpreted Rule 407 to apply to products liability actions. Advisory committee notes to the 1997 Amendments to Rule 407.

## E. INITIAL EXAMINATION OF A CHILD

James Watson, a 5½-year-old boy, witnessed a vehicle matching the description of one driven by a criminal defendant leaving the scene of a homicide at the approximate time of the homicide. The prosecution has called young James to testify at the murder trial in an attempt to place the defendant at the scene of the crime.

### Prosecutor:

Q. Jimmy, how old are you today?

A. Five and a half.

Q. When will you be six?

A. November 29th.

Q. Jimmy, do you know the difference between telling the truth and telling a lie?

A. Yeah.

Q. Is it o.k. to tell a lie?

A. No.

Q. What happens if you tell a lie, Jimmy?

A. My Mom and Dad said I will be in trouble. I will get a punishment.

Q. Did your Mom and Dad tell you to tell the truth today?

A.  Yes.

Q.  When that man over there asked you to raise your hand, do you know what he was asking you to do?

A.  To tell the truth.

Q.  And do you promise to tell the truth in court today, Jimmy?

A.  Uh huh.

Q.  Where do you live, Jimmy?

A.  With Mom and Dad.

Q.  Do you live in a house?

A.  Yes.

Q.  Do you know your address?

A.  Yeah, it's 15 Springfield Road.

Q.  Jimmy, are you in school?

A.  Kindergarten.

Q.  What is the name of your kindergarten?

A.  It's called Fairview School.

Q.  How do you get to school in the morning?

A.  I ride the school bus.

Q.  Where does the school bus pick you up?

A.  It comes right in front of my house.

Q.  What time does it come to pick you up?

A.  After breakfast. I look out the window.

Q.  Do you remember the morning the police cars came to the house across your street?

A.  Yes.

Q.  Do you remember what the weather was like the morning the police cars came to the house across the street?

A.  It was raining.

Q.  Were you looking out the window before the police cars came?

A.  Yeah. I saw a big green truck.

Q.  Where did you see the truck?

A.  It was in the driveway across the street.

Q.  Did you see the truck go anywhere?

A.  I saw it drive down our street really fast. It made a lot of noise.

## Comment

Fed. R. Evid. 601 provides that "[e]very person is competent to be a witness unless these rules provide otherwise." The rule abolished age as making a person incompetent as a witness. Notes of Committee on the Judiciary, House Report No. 93–650. 18 U.S.C. § 3509(c), the Federal Victims Rights Act, provides that a child "is presumed to be competent." A competency examination regarding a child witness "may be conducted by the court only upon written motion and offer of proof of incompetency by a party" if the court "determines, on the record, that compelling reasons exist. A child's age alone is not a compelling reason." *See United States v. Allen J.*, 127 F.3d 1292, 1295 (10th Cir. 1997).

The enactment of Fed. R. Evid. 601 and 18 U.S.C. § 3509 modified the long-standing rule on child witnesses set forth in *Wheeler v. United States*, 159 U.S. 523 (1895). In Wheeler, the trial court permitted the 5½-year-old son of the murder victim to testify against the defendant, which the defendant claimed was error. Writing for the court, Justice Brewer held:

> That the boy was not by reason of his youth, as a matter of law, absolutely disqualified as a witness is clear. While no one should think of calling as a witness an infant only two or three years old, there is no precise age which determines the question of competency. This depends on the capacity and the intelligence of the child, his appreciation of the difference between truth and falsehood, as well as of his duty to tell the former. The decision of this question rests primarily with the trial judge, who sees the proposed witness, notices his manner, his apparent possession or lack of intelligence, and may resort to an examination which will tend to disclose his capacity and intelligence, as well as his understanding of the obligation of an oath. As many of these matters cannot be photographed into the record, the decision of the trial judge will not be disturbed on review, unless from that which is preserved it is clear that it was erroneous.

*Wheeler*, 159 U.S. at 524–25. Although *Wheeler* no longer completely states the applicable standard for determining the competency of a child witness, it may inform any examinations taking place pursuant to 18 U.S.C. § 3509(c) and may help explain the type of evidence necessary to demonstrate a compelling reason for such an examination. *See Mersereau v. State*, 286 P.3d 97, 104–05 (Wyo. 2012), for an example of a competency hearing where the court found that the child witness was not competent to testify. The child testified to verifiably untrue matters such as the number of grandparents and pets he had.

In examining a child witness, whether to assess competency or otherwise, it is permissible for counsel to employ leading questions on direct examination. Although Federal Rule of Evidence 611(c) prohibits the use of leading questions on direct examination, the 1972 committee notes to subdivision (c) acknowledge that the examination of a child witness is a recognized exception. *See State v. Isom*, 2015 UT App 160, 354 P.3d 791 (Utah Ct. App. 2015); *Flores v. State*, No. 04-14-00915-CR, 2015 WL 5730263 (Tex. App. Sept. 30, 2015); *State v. Diaz*, 2015 WL 5472288 (Tenn. Crim. App. Sept. 18, 2015); *United States v. Callahan*, No. 14-3771, 2015 WL 5202925 (6th Cir. Sept. 8, 2015).

## F.  LIFT OF STAY EXAMINATION

Thomas C. Rodriguez represents XYZ Bank, which made a loan to Mr. Roger Jones for the purchase of a Jeep. The bank took a lien on the Jeep to secure payment of the loan obligation. At the inception of the loan and for 12 months thereafter, Mr. Jones made payments on the loan in accordance with the agreement. Then Mr. Jones filed a Chapter 7 bankruptcy petition and ceased making all payments to the bank.

The bank has asked Rodriguez to obtain relief from the automatic stay of section 362 of the Bankruptcy Code so that the bank may exercise its non-bankruptcy law rights in the Jeep, such as repossession and public or private sale.[1] The automatic stay precludes the exercise of such rights absent an order of the bankruptcy court, and specifically precludes any act to obtain possession of property of the bankruptcy estate or to exercise control over property of the bankruptcy estate. The Jeep is property of the bankruptcy estate.

The bank calls Mr. John Smith, its consumer loan officer, to the stand.

Q.  Please state your name.
A.  John Smith.
Q.  Where do you live?
A.  12 South Green Street, Baltimore, Maryland.
Q.  What is your occupation?
A.  I am the consumer loan officer for XYZ Bank

---

1. Any deficiency amounts remaining due will likely be discharged in bankruptcy, absent Mr. Smith having perpetrated a fraud on the bank, which would require a separate adversary proceeding by the bank against Mr. Smith.

Q. What are your responsibilities in that position?

A. I receive, review, and approve consumer loan applications and monitor such loans once made. Also, in the event of a default, I take all necessary steps to collect the defaulted loans and recover any collateral securing such loans.

Q. Does the bank keep books and records in the ordinary course of business?

A. Yes

Q. Are entries made into the books and records in the ordinary course of business?

A. Yes

Q. Is it the ordinary course of business for XYZ Bank to make entries into its books and records?

A. Yes.

Q. Are you familiar with the account of Roger Jones?

A. Yes.

Q. What type of transaction did Mr. Jones enter into with XYZ Bank?

A. The bank made a loan to Mr. Jones for his purchase of a Jeep. In connection with that loan, the bank obtained a lien on the Jeep.

Q. Did you review the books and records before coming to court today?

A. Yes.

Q. Other than providing the books and records to me for purposes of court today, have they remained under your dominion and control?

A. Yes.

Q. I would like to hand you a document which has been pre-marked as Movant's Exhibit 1 for identification. Would you please review this document?

Q. Can you identify the document?

A. Yes.

Q. What is it?

A. It is a Note and Security Agreement from Roger Jones to XYZ Bank.

Q. Have you seen this document before?

A. Yes.

Q. Who signed the documents?

A. Mr. Jones.

(Authentication of Note and Security Agreement, enter into evidence.)

Q. What are Mr. Jones's obligations under the note?

A. He is to make monthly payments in the amount of $450 for a term of five years.

Q. What is the status of Mr. Jones's payments under the note?

A. Default. Mr. Jones paid his note payments for twelve months, but has not made a single payment in the five months since he filed bankruptcy.

Q. Mr. Smith, I would like to hand you a document pre-marked as Movant's Exhibit 2. Please review that document. Can you identify this document?

A. Yes. It is a Loan Payoff Statement for Mr. Jones's loan.

(Authenticate document as business record; enter into evidence.)

Q. Pursuant to the Loan Payoff Statement, how much does Mr. Jones currently owe under the loan?

A. $19,000 plus an additional $1,500 in outstanding interest and late fees.

Q. As part of the transaction with Mr. Jones, what, if any, collateral did the bank take a lien upon?

A. Pursuant to the Note and Security Agreement, Mr. Jones granted XYZ Bank a security interest in the 2012 Jeep Cherokee, VIN# 1J4G278Y3VC61723. (Exhibit—Security interest filing statement or title to vehicle depending upon local law for perfection of security interest in a vehicle)

Q. Is the Jeep depreciating in value?

A. Yes. All cars other than collectors' items depreciate in value, and this is not a collectors' item.

Q. What is the current value of the Jeep?

A. $12,500 at retail; $10,500 at wholesale.

Q. How do you know that?

A. Based on the value listed in the Kelley Blue Book. It is commonly used in the industry as a guide for the valuation of used automobiles.

## Comment:

To prevail, Rodriguez must prove that there is (i) "cause," including that the bank is not adequately protected by its collateral (in this case, the

Jeep), or (ii) there is no equity in the property (again, the Jeep) and the property is not necessary to an effective reorganization. By this example, we are seeking relief on the latter ground, namely, that there is no equity in the Jeep (its value is less than the debt it secures) and it is not necessary to an effective reorganization (because this a Chapter 7 case, which is a liquidation case, there will be no opportunity for reorganization; this portion of the relief is saved for argument to the court).

Section 362 of the Bankruptcy Code governs relief from the stay. A decision to lift the stay under section 362 is a matter within the discretion of the court. *In re Robbins*, 964 F.2d 342, 345 (4th Cir. 1992); *In re Myers*, 491 F.3d 120, 128 (3d Cir. 2007). Pursuant to section 362, the court may lift the stay "for cause." 11 U.S.C. § 362. The Fourth Circuit set forth several factors to consider when determining whether to lift the stay to allow state court litigation to proceed: "The factors that courts consider in deciding whether to lift the automatic stay include (1) whether the issues in the pending litigation involve only state law, so the expertise of the bankruptcy court is unnecessary, (2) whether modifying the stay will promote judicial economy and whether there would be greater interference with the bankruptcy case if the stay were not lifted because matters would have to be litigated in the bankruptcy court, and (3) whether the estate can be protected properly by a requirement that creditor seek enforcement of any judgment through the bankruptcy court." *In re Robbins*, 964 F.2d 342, 345 (4th Cir. 1992).

*In re Kaplan Breslaw Ash, LLC*, 264 B.R. 309 (Bankr. S.D.N.Y. 2001) (secured creditor seeking relief from the stay to exercise its rights in collateral, based upon debtor's alleged lack of equity therein, must show (1) amount of claim, (2) that claim is secured by valid, perfected lien in property of the estate, and (3) that debtor lacks equity in property).

*In re Rogers*, 239 B.R. 883 (Bankr. E.D. Tex. 1999) (To establish prima facie case of cause for relief from stay due to lack of adequate protection for its interests, movant must initially demonstrate that it holds claim, which is secured by valid, perfected lien upon estate property, and that decline in value of collateral is either occurring or threatened, against which creditor is precluded from protecting its interests due to existence of automatic stay; once movant presents such a prima facie case, burden shifts to debtor to prove that collateral is not declining in value or that the secured creditor is adequately protected.).

## G. EXAMINATION OF CREDITOR ON THE "ORDINARY COURSE OF BUSINESS" EXCEPTION TO PREFERENTIAL TRANSFER

Since 2002, ABC Tool & Die Company (ABC) has manufactured and sold gear shafts to General Motors for use in various GM models. After GM filed for bankruptcy protection in the U.S. Bankruptcy Court, ABC received a letter from GM's counsel making a demand for repayment of $105,350 that GM paid to ABC within the 90 days prior to GM's bankruptcy filing. The letter stated that, based upon counsel's preliminary investigation, the amount to be repaid constituted a preferential transfer under section 547 of the Bankruptcy Code.

George Young, ABC's counsel, responded to GM's counsel that ABC had been selling gear shafts to GM for more than seven years, that the payments being attacked as preferences were "made in the ordinary course of business" within the meaning of section 547(c)(2) of the Bankruptcy Code, and that therefore the payments are not recoverable by GM as preferences.

The parties were unable to reach a settlement and the matter was set for trial. At trial, George Young calls ABC's controller as a witness for the defense.

Q. Please state your name for the record.
A. Jacob Sarkozy.
Q. And what is your occupation?
A. I am the controller for ABC Tool & Die Company.
Q. What are your responsibilities in that position?
A. I maintain records of the company's accounts payable and accounts receivable, and I manage the company's financial records and transactions.
Q. How long have you been in that position?
A. Since 2001.
Q. Does ABC keep financial books and records in the ordinary course of business?
A. Yes.
Q. Is it the ordinary course of business for ABC to make entries into its books and records?
A. Yes.
Q. Are you familiar with the account of General Motors?
A. Yes, ABC has been doing business with GM since 2002.

Q. Can you describe the nature of the business conducted between ABC and GM?

A. Yes, since 2002, ABC has been manufacturing and selling specialized gear shafts to GM for use in GM cars and trucks.

Q. Did you review the entries in ABC's books and records relating to GM before coming to court today?

A. Yes.

Q. Other than providing the books and records to me for purposes of court today, have they remained under your dominion and control?

A. Yes.

Q. I would like to hand you a document which has been premarked as Defendant's Exhibit 1 for identification. Would you please review this document?

A. Certainly.

Q. Can you identify this document?

A. Yes.

Q. What is it?

A. It's an accounts receivable aging report showing activity on the ABC-GM account.

Q. Does this report accurately reflect all charges incurred and all payments made by GM in connection with ABC's sale of gear shafts to GM?

A. Yes.

Q. Can you tell me if, based on this report, GM has established a regular timeline for the payment of ABC's invoices?

A. Yes, they have.

Q. And can you describe for the court what is GM's regular timeline for the payment of ABC's invoices?

A. Since 2001, GM has always paid ABC's invoices within 20 to 29 days after the date of the invoice.

Q. Are you aware that GM filed for bankruptcy protection in June 1, 2009?

A. Yes, I am aware of that. GM was a large part of our business, so all of us at ABC were well aware of the bankruptcy when it was filed.

Q. Are you also aware that ABC is being sued by GM in this case to recover $105,350 that ABC purportedly received from GM within the ninety-day period prior to GM's bankruptcy filing?

A. Yes, I am aware of that.

Q. Is it true that ABC received $105,350 from GM within the ninety-day period prior to GM's bankruptcy filing?

A. Yes.

Q. Was the timing of the payments that ABC received from GM within the ninety-day period prior to GM's bankruptcy filing consistent with GM's regular practice of paying ABC's invoices within 20 to 29 days?

A. Yes, there was no change in GM's payment practices for the payments made within 90 days prior to GM's bankruptcy filing. In fact, the three payments that ABC received during that 90-day period were made 22, 24, and 26 days after the dates of ABC's invoices.

Q. Are you familiar with payment terms generally for parts suppliers in the automotive industry?

A. Yes. Parts suppliers, such as ABC, generally obtain a "net 30 days" term for their invoices.

Q. And what does "net 30 days" mean?

A. That credit term means that the full amount of the invoice is due from the purchaser thirty days after the date shown on the invoice.

Q. What was the credit term that applied to ABC's invoices to GM?

A. Net 30 days.

Q. I'd like to show you a group of documents that have been marked, collectively, as Defendant's Exhibit 2. Could you review these documents?

A. Sure.

Q. Can you identify these documents?

A. Yes, these are ABC's invoices to GM for the period from June 1, 2008, through June 1, 2009.

Q. Can you tell the court what credit terms applied to these invoices?

A. Yes, it's shown at the bottom of each invoice. The terms for all of these ABC invoices are "net 30 days."

Q. And was GM's regular practice of paying ABC invoices within 20 to 29 days after the date of the invoice consistent with the "net 30 days" term shown on the invoices?

A. Yes.

## Comment

Preferences are governed by section 547 of the Bankruptcy Code. 11 § 547 (2010). One of the most commonly invoked exceptions to a preference is the "ordinary course of business" exception that is codified in Section 547(c)(2). This exception provides that a transfer is not a preference if the transfer was in payment of a debt incurred in the ordinary course of business or financial affairs of the debtor and the transferee, and the transfer was either:

    a.   Made in the ordinary course of business or financial affairs of the debtor and the transferee; or

    b.   Made according to ordinary business terms.

[Note: Prior to the amendment to the Bankruptcy Code in 2005, the defendant had to prove both elements A and B above in order to invoke the defense. The 2005 amendments modified section 547(c)(2) to create a disjunctive test by changing the "and" to an "or." As a result, although the operative statutory language did not change, practitioners should exercise care in relying on opinions interpreting the law in actions commenced before October 7, 2005 (the effective date of the amendments).]

Section 547(c)(2)(A) sets forth a subjective test, asking whether payments were made in ordinary course of dealings between parties. *See In re Daedalean, Inc.*, 193 B.R. 204 (D. Md. 1996). Section 547(c)(2)(B) sets forth an objective test, concerning itself with industry-wide practices as opposed to the relationship between parties, encompassing a broad range of terms in industry, and allowing the creditor considerable latitude in defining what the relevant industry is. *Id.* In practical application, the separate defenses may overlap, and courts, prior to 2005, often focused primary attention on the first prong.

In the examination above, ABC relies upon the exception set forth in section 547(c)(2)(A) to prove that the payments made to it by GM within 90 days prior to the bankruptcy case are not preferences.

In preference litigation, the creditor bears the burden of proving that the payment(s) were within the ordinary course of business in the relevant industry. *See Gulf City Seafoods, Inc. v. Ludwig Shrimp Co. (In re Gulf City Seafoods, Inc.)*, 296 F.3d 363 (5th Cir. 2002) (interpreting the law prior to the 2005 amendment, the court concluded that a creditor who failed to offer evidence of industry payment standards failed to sustain its burden of proving defense that the payments were made in the ordinary course of business).

Payments on long-term debt may qualify for the ordinary course of business exception. *Union Bank v. Wolas*, 502 U.S. 151, 162 (1991).

## H. EXAMINATION OF DEBTOR TO DECLARE DEBT NON-DISCHARGEABLE

In June 2007, John Smith obtained a credit card from XYZ Bank. One week later, Smith lost his job as an accountant. The next day, instead of looking for work, Smith used his credit card to book a two-week vacation in the Caribbean. On the same day, he bought three rooms of new furniture at an expensive boutique. Smith charged more than $10,000 on his XYZ credit card for the vacation and the new furniture, exceeding his $5,000 credit limit. Four weeks later, still unemployed and without means to pay even the minimum amount due to XYZ Bank, Smith consults an attorney and files a Chapter 7 bankruptcy case.

XYZ Bank hires George Young as its attorney to represent its interests in the John Smith bankruptcy case. In the course of his investigation, Young discovers the suspicious circumstances surrounding Smith's use of the card to purchase the Caribbean vacation and the new furniture. Young files a complaint against Smith in the bankruptcy court to declare that Smith's debt to XYZ is non-dischargeable in Smith's bankruptcy case.

At trial, Young calls Smith as a witness in his case-in-chief and obtains permission from the trial judge to treat Smith as a hostile witness.

Q. Please state your name for the record.
A. John Smith
Q. Where do you live?
A. 2422 Maryland Avenue, Baltimore Maryland.
Q. Are you currently employed?
A. No.
A. When did you file this Chapter 7 bankruptcy case?
A. July 18, 2014.
Q. Were you employed on the date you filed this bankruptcy case?
A. No.
Q. Isn't it true that you lost your job as an accountant just about a month before you filed bankruptcy?
A. Yes, I was working as an accountant, but I was laid off on June 15, 2014.
Q. Are you familiar with XYZ Bank?
A. Yes, I used to have a credit card account with XYZ Bank.
Q. When did you first open that credit card account?
A. In early June of 2014.

Q. Did you use the credit card after you were laid off from your job?

A. Yes.

Q. What did you use the XYZ credit card to purchase after you had been laid off from your job?

A. I purchased a vacation package and some furniture.

Q. Isn't it true that you made those charges on the day after you were laid off?

A. Yes.

Q. At that point in time, had you begun looking for a new job?

A. No.

Q. And at that point in time, did you have any employment interviews or prospects of employment?

A. No.

Q. How much did you charge on the XYZ credit card for the vacation and the new furniture?

A. $10,525.

Q. Have you repaid any portion of those charges to XYZ?

A. No.

Q. Why not?

A. Well, I knew at the time I made the charges that the only way I would be able to repay them is if I found a new job. Since I wasn't able to find a new job, I consulted an attorney about filing bankruptcy.

Q. So at the time you incurred the charges on the XYZ account, you had no means of repaying the charges, correct?

A. Yes, that's correct.

Q. Did the charges you incurred on the XYZ credit card exceed your credit limit?

A. Yes. My card limit was $5,000.

## Comment

Section 523(a) of the Bankruptcy Code provides a laundry list of situations in which a debt may be declared non-dischargeable. A creditor may obtain a declaration of non-dischargeability by filing a complaint in the bankruptcy court against the debtor. This commences an adversary proceeding that is tracked as a separate lawsuit by the bankruptcy court. Discovery is available in adversary proceedings under the bankruptcy rules (which generally track the Federal Rules of Civil Procedure).

The example above relies upon section 523(a)(2) of the Bankruptcy Code, which provides that a debt is non-dischargeable if the debt is:

> (2) for money, property, services, or an extension, renewal, or refinancing of credit to the extent obtained by—
>     a.  false pretenses, a false representation, or actual fraud, other than a statement respecting the debtor's or an insider's financial condition; [or]
>     b.  use of a statement in writing—
>         i.   that is materially false;
>         ii.  respecting the debtor's or an insider's financial condition;
>         iii. on which the creditor to whom the debtor is liable for such money, property, services, or credit reasonably relied; and
>         iv.  that the debtor caused to be made or published with intent to deceive.

In addition, section 523(a)(2)(C) provides that "consumer debts owed to a single creditor and aggregating more than $650 for luxury goods or services incurred by an individual debtor on or within 90 days before the order for relief under this title are presumed to be nondischargeable."

In the example above, Young's examination of Smith sets forth the elements to satisfy the presumption of non-dischargeability in section 523(a)(2)(C). Generally, where this presumption is not applicable, a creditor must prove that a debt is non-dischargeable by a preponderance of the evidence. *Grogan v. Garner*, 498 U.S. 279, 287 (1991).

Because § 523(a)(2)(A) requires a determination of the debtor's intent, it is often helpful—even necessary—for the plaintiff to call the debtor as a witness. The Ninth Circuit has crafted a non-exclusive list of factors that may be considered in determining a debtor's subjective intent: (1) the length of time between the charges and the filing of bankruptcy; (2) whether or not an attorney has been consulted regarding the filing of bankruptcy before the charges were made; (3) the number of charges made; (4) the amount of the charges; (5) the debtor's financial condition at the time the charges are made; (6) whether the charges are above the credit limit of the account; (7) whether the debtor made multiple charges on the same day; (8) whether or not the debtor was employed; (9) the debtor's prospects for employment; (10) the financial sophistication of the debtor; (11) whether there was a sudden change in the debtor's buying habits; and (12) whether the purchases were made for luxuries or necessities. *See In re Ettell*, 188 F.3d 1141 (9th Cir. 1999) (citing *Citibank v. Dougherty (In re Dougherty)*, 84 B.R. 653, 657 (9th Cir. BAP 1996)). Although the list of factors varies from circuit to circuit, the determination of fraudulent intent generally requires the court to consider the totality of the circumstances on a case-by-case basis.

In most cases involving Section 523 claims, a creditor must establish that it relied upon false representations of the debtor. Justifiable reliance is required under section 523(a)(2)(A), and reasonable reliance is required under section 523(a)(2)(B). *See In re Sharp*, 340 F. App'x 899 (4th Cir. 2009) (discussing elements of section 523(a)(2) and requisite reliance); *In re Anastas*, 94 F.3d 1280 (9th Cir. 1996) (holding that the use of a credit card is a representation of an intent to repay, but is not a representation of the ability to repay the debt); *In re Mercer*, 246 F.3d 391 (noting that the theory of implied representation is applicable in the context of dischargeability action against debtor who obtained a preapproved credit card from the creditor); *but see First Nat'l Bank of Mobile v. Roddenberry*, 701 F.2d 927, 932 (11th Cir. 1983) (the mere use of a credit card is not an actual or implied representation of any fact or intent on the part of the debtor).

Sometimes a creditor will have obtained a fraud judgment against a debtor in state court prior to the debtor's bankruptcy filing. In those instances, collateral estoppel may apply in assisting the creditor to obtain a declaration that the debt is non-dischargeable. A state court judgment that the debtor committed fraud may be entitled to collateral estoppel effect when the issue of fraud was actually raised and litigated in the state court, the resolution of the issue was necessary to the outcome of the state court trial, and the debtor participated in all stages of the proceedings. *See Stoehr v. Mohamed Bin Bander Mohamed Bin Abdul Rahman Al Saud*, 244 F.3d 206 (1st Cir. 2001); *In re Bursack*, 65 F.3d 51 (6th Cir. 1995) (state court fraud judgment given preclusive effect even though debtor did not appear at trial); *In re Corey*, 583 F.3d 1249 (10th Cir. 2009) (state court fraud judgment entered by default was preclusive on the issue of fraud in subsequent adversary proceeding to determine dischargeability).

# Part 2

---

# Cross-Examination and Redirect

---

# Cross-Examination $\boldsymbol{10}$

## A. PURPOSE, FORM, AND STRUCTURE

Counsel on cross-examination takes advantage of the leading question, not ordinarily permitted in direct examination, to control the witness.

### Prosecutor:

Q. You were driving the red truck?
A. Yes.
Q. You stopped at the red light?
A. Yes.
Q. You then turned left after the light turned green?
A. Yes.

### *Comment*

The purpose of cross-examination, like the purpose of direct examination, is to argue or prove your case through questions to and answers from the witness. Whereas in direct examination counsel is more often than not asserting the facts proving the case, more often than not on cross-examination counsel is defending the case, but not always. Frequently helpful affirmative facts can be developed. Cross-examination is not always a crash and destroy exercise.

Cross-examination is usually limited to the subject matter of direct examination, and to matters affecting the credibility of the witness. But the court has discretion to allow inquiry into additional matters. *See, e.g.,* FRE 611(b). Often questions probing the credibility of the witness introduce matters beyond the scope of the direct examination. Some courts will permit an expansive cross-examination for convenience of the witness and the parties to eliminate the need to recall the witness.

Generally, the cross-examined witness does not want your client to prevail. With every question you ask, you take a certain risk of receiving an answer adverse to your case. The more finely honed the question, the lower the risk. Ultimately, it is a question of controlling the witness.

The best technique for control is the leading question, which is prohibited in direct examination, with limited exceptions, but permitted in cross. *See* FRE 611(a). A leading question suggests its answer. ("You saw the collision, isn't that true?" Even better: "You saw the collision?") Non-leading questions do not. ("Tell us whether or not you saw the collision.") Leading questions tend to be short, affirmative questions containing a statement that compels a favorable response. Use short, leading questions to control the witness. Strive for "Yes" or "No" answers, preferably "Yes." (See Chapter 1, *supra*, for discussion of direct examination and the differences between leading and non-leading questions.) Although there are many goals and techniques of cross-examination, some of the prominent ones are listed below and exemplified in this chapter.

The structure of cross-examination consists of a beginning, middle, and a conclusion. Once you determine that you are going to conduct take advantage of primacy and begin strong; save other strong points for the end. Here are some considerations for cross-examination.

- Decide whether you need to ask any questions at all on cross.
- Have a specific objective for the testimony you want to obtain.
- Use the appropriate style and delivery.
- Be selective in deciding what topics to cover.
- Use short leading questions to control the witness.
- Strive for "Yes" or "No" answers, preferably "Yes."
- Remember the doctrines of primacy and recency.
- Use adverse witness testimony to develop your own case independently.
- Reveal discrepancies between direct examination testimony and the facts.
- Use the testimony of the witness to corroborate the favorable testimony of other witnesses.
- Use the testimony of one witness to discredit the unfavorable testimony of another witness.
- Impeachment—discrediting the witness or witnesses' testimony.
- Know when to sit down

## B. REVEAL DISCREPANCIES BETWEEN DIRECT EXAMINATION AND THE FACTS

Plaintiff Mr. Smith testified on direct examination that defendant, David Jones, was fraudulently overcharging customers, and that Richard Thomas observed this misconduct. Defendant claims that Thomas was the one who was engaged in the misconduct, and was "throwing the defendant under the bus."

Defense counsel cross-examines Smith drawing upon helpful facts without attacking Smith.

Q. In the past, customers complained about Mr. Thomas?

A. Yes.

Q. Some complaints related to the proper procedures used prepare bills?

A. Yes.

Q. Some of the complaints related to Mr. Thomas making mistakes on the bills by overcharging?

A. Yes.

Q. Some customers complained that Mr. Thomas cheated them?

A. Yes.

Q. Complaints that he stole from them?

A. Yes.

Q. Do you know where Mr. Thomas now resides?

A. Yes.

Q. Where is that?

A. He is incarcerated.

Q. And is he incarcerated for conduct that relates to his is cheating customers by over-billing them?

A. Absolutely.

### Comment

In this cross-examination, counsel, controlling the witness with mostly leading questions, establishes facts deflecting the claim of the plaintiff. Interestingly counsel uses a non-leading question for effect knowing full well the answer:

Q. Do you know where Mr. Thomas now resides?

If the witness misstated the facts or feigned loss of recollection, counsel was prepared to either refresh the witness's recollection or impeach her. (*See* Sections L–N, *infra*.)

## C. USE THE TESTIMONY OF A WITNESS TO CORROBORATE THE FAVORABLE TESTIMONY OF OTHER WITNESSES

On cross-examination of the government's witness, Alice Hodge, defense counsel elicits favorable testimony about her client, David Jones.

Q. In your work with David Jones were you satisfied at the time, the year 2014, that he wanted to make sure that everything was done ethically and properly?

A. Yes.

Q. And would it be your testimony before the jury that he was always concerned about following the correct campaign finance protocol?

A. Yes.

To bolster the prior favorable testimony, defense counsel put similar questions to Christopher Marcus, another government witness, later in the trial.

Q. In all the years that you worked with David Jones, did he ever tell you or suggest that you do something illegal?

A. No.

Q. Did he ever tell you during the years you worked with him to do something unethical?

A. No.

## Comment

Eliciting favorable testimony to advance or defend your theme need not be confrontational. The term "hitchhiking" refers to the practice of using an adverse witness to argue your theme or to impress the judge or jury with the favorable attributes of the case.

This example calls to mind the doctrine of frequency or repetition. The more often the judge or jury hears positive testimony about your client, the better. This is particularly true when the positive testimony comes from an adverse witness.

## D. USE APPROPRIATE STYLE AND DELIVERY

Q. Good morning, Mrs. Jones. You know I have to ask you some questions in follow-up?

A. Yes, I do.

Q. If you need a break for any reason, let me know. I recognize your loss, but in a court of law, I am obligated to ask you some follow-up questions.

## *Comment*

The display of kindness and courtesy is not only inherently worthy, but also earns respect from judge or jury.

## E. ESTABLISH FLAWED CHARACTER—PRIOR BAD ACTS OR PRIOR CONVICTION

The government witness pled guilty to numerous crimes and hopes for some consideration from the government for testifying against the defendant. Defense counsel cross-examines to discredit the witness.

Q. I'd like to talk to you about the particular crimes to which you pled guilty.

A. Yes, sir.

Q. One of them was check kiting; is that correct?

A. That's correct.

Q. What was the average size of the check that you wrote in the check-kiting scheme?

A. The gross revenues of our company were $60 million that year, so there were a significant amount of checks. I couldn't tell you how many—2014 we grossed $60 million. So for me to be able to say that—we probably had some checks for $20,000 and we had some for millions of dollars.

Q. Okay. So you'd be writing checks for a million dollars, recognizing, in your heart, that it was wrong because it was violating the law; isn't that true?

A. Yes, sir.

Q. With your bank fraud crime, am I correct you had engaged a fictitious person to contact the bank to pretend that person had a valid contract with your company. Is that correct?

A. Yes, sir.

Q. And you knew at the time that was wrong?

A. Yes, sir.

Q. It was false?

A. Yes, sir.

Q. Fake?

A. Yes, sir.

Q. Made up?

A. Yes, sir.

Q. And you have a custom and practice for some reason that I don't have to get into of make-believing when it suits you; isn't that true?

A. I take full responsibility, sir.

Q. Do I understand correctly that you entered into a plea agreement with the Government before you pled guilty to the crimes you committed?

A. Yes.

Q. You are to be sentenced next month?

A. Yes.

Q. You are hoping for the lightest sentence you can get?

A. Yes.

Q. You had an attorney representing you in the plea discussions?

A. Yes.

Q. He had numerous discussions about your matter?

A. Yes.

Q. You spoke on numerous times with the Prosecutor?

A. Yes.

Q. These occasions were in person?

A. Yes.

Q. In the prosecutors' offices?

A. Yes.

### Comment

In the pattern, defense counsel hopes to show that the witness's testimony is not credible because the witness is motivated by the desire to curry favor with the government and thus receive lenient treatment. The Confrontation Clause of the Sixth Amendment guarantees the right of an accused in a criminal prosecution "to be confronted with the witnesses against him." The right of confrontation is secured for defendants in state as well as federal criminal proceedings. *Delaware v. Van Arsdall*, 475 U.S. 673, 678 (1986). The Supreme Court has held that "[t]he main and essential purpose of confrontation is to secure for the opponent the opportunity of cross-examination." *Davis v. Alaska*, 415 U.S. 308, 315–16 (1974). The exposure of a witness's motivation in testifying is a proper and important function of the constitutionally protected right of cross-examination. *Id.*, at 316–17.

A witness may be impeached by inquiring into his prior convictions. *United States v. Baldenegro-Valdez*, 703 F.3d 1117 (8th Cir. 2013), including about the fact of the witness's prior convictions, the statutory range of punishments, the minimum and maximum punishment he faces, the fact that he had a plea agreement with the government, the fact that he hopes to receive a lesser sentence by cooperating with the government, and the fact that he could receive a sentence under the statutory minimum if the government filed the requisite motion. *Id.* However, while the defense may cross-examine a cooperating witness in order to elicit the fact that the witness is hoping to please the government by testifying in order to receive a reduced sentence, it is generally not an abuse of discretion for the District Court "to limit counsel's technical arguments about the specific applications of mandatory minimums or the sentencing guidelines." *Id.*; *see also United States v. Walley*, 567 F.3d 354, 360 (8th Cir. 2009) (holding that there was no Sixth Amendment violation where the jury knew that without the government's sentencing motion, the defendant faced a "significant" sentence as opposed to the five-year mandatory minimum).

The Supreme Court has made it clear that the Confrontation Clause does not prevent a trial judge from imposing any limits on defense counsel's inquiry into the potential bias of a prosecution witness. As the Supreme Court has noted, "the Confrontation Clause guarantees an *opportunity* for effective cross-examination, not cross-examination that is effective in whatever way, to whatever extent, the defense might wish." *Delaware v. Fensterer*, 474 U.S. 15, 20 (1985) (per curiam) (emphasis in original). On the contrary, trial judges retain wide latitude to impose reasonable limits on such cross-examination based on concerns about, *inter alia*, "harassment, and prejudice, confusion of the issues, the witness' safety, or interrogation that is repetitive or only marginally relevant." *Delaware v. Van Arsdall*, 475 U.S. at 679.

A limitation on cross-examination does not violate the Sixth Amendment unless the defendant shows that a reasonable jury might have received a "significantly different impression" of the witness's credibility had defense counsel "been permitted to pursue his proposed line of cross-examination." *Delaware v. Van Arsdall*, 475 U.S. at 680.

## F. IMPEACHMENT BY EXAGGERATION OR IMPROBABILITY

Defense counsel cross-examines the witness to show that his testimony of wrongdoing by defendant was exaggerated and/or improbable based on his failure to report them to his principal when obligated to do so.

> Q. Well, when you were the eyes and ears of the President, was it to make sure everything went right?

A. Correct.

Q. Your job was to report any major problems?

A. Yes.

Q. So when you're at the gala, and you're telling the jury that there are all kinds of issues with cost over runs and that you were getting concerned that the costs were spiraling, was that significant to you?

A. Yes.

Q. And when it was significant to you, was it also significant to you that your dear friend the President of the United States was relying upon you to be his eyes and ears?

A. I don't know.

Q. Was it of significance to you that your dear friend the former President of the United States asked you to be his eyes and ears at this event?

A. It would be significant, yes.

Q. And how many times did you call or notify the President of the United States that things were amiss at the gala or the planning of the gala?

A. We had no conversations about it before the gala.

Q. So it's your testimony that you never reported to him that there was a problem, correct?

A. Correct.

## Comment

The goal here is to lead or allow the witness to testify in such a way that he or she exaggerates, thus causing the testimony to appear improbable. Here defense counsel would have the jury believe that the witness, if he had seen the problems about which he testified, would have reported to his principal. (*See Anatomy of a Trial, a Handbook for Young Lawyers, Second Edition*, Paul Mark Sandler, ABA Litigation Section (2014).)

## G. HISTORIC EXAMPLE OF CROSS-EXAMINATION REVEALING IMPROBABILITY

Chicago lawyer Weymouth Kirkland in the 1900s represented an insurance company defending a claim based on the death of a policyholder. Lloyd Paul Stryker recounts the following cross-examination in *The Art of Advocacy* as does Paul Mark Sandler in *Anatomy of a Trial A Handbook for Young Lawyers*. A key witness for the plaintiff was the ship's cook.

Q. How long had you known Peck (the policy holder)?

A. Fifteen years.

Q. You knew him well?

A. Yes, sir.

Q. How did you happen to see his body?

A. I looked out of the porthole.

Q. You recognized it beyond doubt as the body of Peck?

A. Yes, sir.

Q. Did you make any outcry when you saw the body?

A. No, sir.

Q. Did you ask the captain to stop the ship?

A. No, sir.

Q. What were you doing when you happened to look out the window and saw the body?

A. I was peeling potatoes.

Q. And when the body of your old friend, Peck, floated by, you just kept on peeling potatoes?

A. Yes, sir.

### *Comment*

Tying in a cross-examination with closing argument can be effective. Consider what Kirkland is reported to have argued:

> He did not argue that the cook's argument was false. Rather he took out from his pocket a potato, rested his foot on a chair and began to peel the potato. Doing so he said to the jury: "What ho! What have we here? Who is this floating past? As I live and breathe, if it isn't my old friend Peck! I shall tell the captain about this in the morning. In the meantime I must go on peeling my potatoes."

## H. EXTRINSIC EVIDENCE OF PRIOR INCONSISTENT ORAL STATEMENT

During a federal court trial for malicious prosecution, the plaintiff, a disc jockey, claims that the defendant radio station improperly prosecuted him for stealing records from the station. The plaintiff contends that as program director of the station, he was entitled to take as many duplicate records as he desired. The station coordinator testified that the plaintiff was never appointed program director.

Counsel for the plaintiff seeks to impeach the station coordinator by means of a prior inconsistent oral statement:

### Plaintiff's Counsel:

Q. Mrs. Smith, you were the station coordinator of WZBQ Radio Station in the year 2013, is that correct?

A. Yes.

Q. What were your responsibilities as station coordinator?

A. I was in charge of making all personnel appointments and coordinating those personnel.

Q. Was there a position of program director in 2013?

A. Yes.

Q. Would it be accurate to say that the plaintiff, John Reeves, was that director?

A. No, he was not.

Q. You did not appoint him director in the spring of 2013?

A. Absolutely not.

\* \* \*

(John Brown, a witness, being first duly sworn, is called to the stand.)

### Plaintiff's Counsel:

Q. Mr. Brown, what was your position at WZBQ Radio Station in 2013?

A. Disc jockey.

Q. Who was your immediate supervisor?

A. The program director.

Q. Who was that program director in the spring of 2013?

A. John Reeves.

Q. Do you know the circumstances under which John Reeves became that program director?

A. During a meeting of all staff personnel in May 2013, the station coordinator, Carol Smith, announced that John Reeves was appointed program director.

Q. No further questions.

## *Comment*

Federal Rule of Evidence 613 modifies the rule with regard to the use of prior inconsistent oral statements for impeachment purposes. The traditional approach required that the witness be confronted on the stand while under cross-examination as to whether he or she made the supposed inconsistent statement, and be provided with the substance of the statement, as well as the time, place, and person to whom it was made. Federal Rule of Evidence 613, however, eliminates the requirement that the witness be afforded this opportunity. *See* Fed. R. Evid. 613, advisory committee's note. Consider *United States v. Marks*, 816 F.2d 1207 (7th Cir. 1987) (trial court retains discretion to require disclosure prior to questioning).

Impeachment by prior inconsistent oral or written statement requires that: (a) the statement be inconsistent; (b) the inconsistency relate to a matter of sufficient relevancy; (c) there be compliance with the rule requiring disclosure of the prior statement to opposing counsel upon request and an opportunity for explanation, for denial, and for interrogation by the opposing party; and (d) the court instruct the jury as to the purpose of the inconsistent statement. *United States v. Allen*, 540 F.3d 821, 825 (8th Cir. 2008); *United States v. Richardson*, 515 F.3d 74, 84 (1st Cir. 2008); *Rahn v. Hawkins*, 464 F.3d 813, 821 (8th Cir. 2006), *overruled on other grounds recognized, Avichail v. St. John's Mercy Health System,* 686 F.3d 548 (2012) (plaintiff's questions regarding prior inconsistent statements contained in commendation report were admissible); *United States v. Crockett*, 435 F.3d 1305, 1313 (10th Cir. 2006); *Rush v. Illinois Central Railroad Co.*, 399 F.3d 705, 720 (6th Cir. 2005); *United States v. Avants*, 367 F.3d 433, 448–49 (5th Cir. 2004); *United States v. Barile*, 286 F.3d 749, 755 (4th Cir. 2002); *Cathron v. Jones*, 190 F. Supp. 2d 990 (E.D. Mich. 2002); *United States v. Gonzalez*, 142 F. Supp. 2d 1052, 1059 (N.D. Ill. 2001); 1 MCCORMICK ON EVIDENCE § 34 (Kenneth S. Broun ed., 7th ed. 2013) (discussing the degree of inconsistency required).

The instruction given by the court is important. The statement can be admissible for impeachment purposes only or as substantive proof, depending on the nature of the statement. Significantly, Federal Rule of Evidence 801(d)(1)(A) exempts from the hearsay rule a prior statement of a declarant who testifies at trial and is subject to cross-examination about the statement, if the prior statement is inconsistent and was given under oath, subject to the penalty of perjury, at a trial, hearing, or other proceeding, or in a deposition. These types of prior inconsistent statements are admissible as substantive proof in the case. *Cf.* Fed. R. Evid. 801(d)(1). Counsel should also bear in mind that treatment of a prior inconsistent statement on cross-examination is distinguished from treatment of a statement of a party opponent. The statement of a party opponent is also treated as substantive evidence, but it is governed by Federal Rule of Evidence 801(d)(2). Introduction of the statement of a party opponent under Federal Rule of Evidence 801(d)(2) does not require any foundation on cross-examination. *See generally* 2 MCCORMICK ON EVIDENCE § 254 (Kenneth S. Broun ed., 7th ed. 2013).

While the prior statement must be inconsistent, *United States v. Vasquez*, 635 F.3d 889, 897–98 (8th Cir. 2011), the prior statement need not have been made under oath. *United States v. Sanabria*, 645 F.3d 505, 513 (1st Cir. 2011). The test for determining inconsistency to permit impeachment is somewhat elastic. *See* 2 MICHAEL H. GRAHAM, HANDBOOK OF FEDERAL EVIDENCE § 613:3 (7th ed. 2012). Inconsistency exists if the witness states that he or she does not remember making the prior statement. Under that circumstance, the making of the statement can be proved by extrinsic evidence, *e.g.*, another witness. *United States v. Billue*, 994 F.2d 1562 (11th Cir. 1993), *cert. denied*, 510 U.S. 1099 (1994); *accord*, *United States v. Cline*, 570 F.2d 731 (8th Cir. 1978); *United States v. Sisto*, 534 F.2d 616 (5th Cir. 1976); *Williamson v. United States*, 310 F.2d 192 (9th Cir. 1962); *United States v. Gibson*, 84 F. Supp. 2d 784, 789 (S.D. W. Va.), *aff'd*, 92 F. Supp. 2d 562 (S.D. W. Va.), *aff'd*, 238 F.3d 416 (4th Cir. 2000), *reprinted in full*, 2000 U.S. App. LEXIS 29495 (4th Cir. Nov. 17, 2000). *But see United States v. Devine*, 934 F.2d 1325 (5th Cir. 1991), *cert. denied*, 502 U.S. 929, 502 U.S. 1047, 502 U.S. 1064, 502 U.S. 1065, 502 U.S. 1092, 502 U.S. 1104 (1992) (holding that the testimony of the witness that he did not remember making a prior statement did not constitute an inconsistent statement, and was therefore properly excluded as hearsay); *accord*, *United States v. Palumbo*, 639 F.2d 123 (3d Cir.), *cert. denied*, 454 U.S. 819 (1981); *United States v. DeSimone*, 488 F.3d 561, 571–72 (1st Cir. 2007) (witness's declaration that he could not remember making the prior statement did not constitute an inconsistent statement). However, if the witness admits making the prior inconsistent statement, the prevailing view is that counsel may not introduce extrinsic evidence to impeach. 2 MICHAEL H. GRAHAM, HANDBOOK OF FEDERAL EVIDENCE § 613:3 (7th ed. 2012); 1 MCCORMICK ON EVIDENCE § 37 (Kenneth S. Broun ed., 7th ed. 2013). Counsel may impeach with a prior inconsistent oral statement, even if that statement is reduced to writing. *See Jankins v. TDC Mgmt. Corp.*, 21 F.3d 436 (D.C. Cir. 1994).

Although Queen Caroline's Rule is abolished by court rule, strategic cross-examinations nevertheless establish traditional foundations to spring the trap. For example, in this pattern, counsel could have gone further to establish a foundation by inquiring: "In your capacity as director, you called many meetings of your staff. From time to time you made important announcements filling new positions at these meetings. You talked to your staff during these meetings about John Reeves. Didn't you announce at one of your staff meetings that you were appointing John Reeves to the position of program director?" Striking the balance between establishing enough foundation to lay the trap and too much so as to reveal the trap goes to the heart of the skill of the cross-examiner. This skill is innate and also may be acquired.

Federal Rule of Evidence 613(b) governs the use of extrinsic evidence of prior inconsistent statements. Extrinsic evidence refers to evidence presented by other witnesses or by documentary evidence not authenticated by the witness who is on the stand and who made the prior inconsistent statement. Thus, impeaching by a prior inconsistent statement that the witness authenticates is not impeaching by extrinsic evidence. Federal Rule of Evidence 613(b) requires that extrinsic evidence of a prior inconsistent statement by a witness is not admissible unless the witness is afforded an opportunity to explain or deny the statement. *See United States v. Sutton*, 41 F.3d 1257 (8th Cir. 1994), *cert. denied*, 514 U.S. 1072 (1995); *United States v. Hudson*, 970 F.2d 948 (1st Cir. 1992); *United States v. Bonnett*, 877 F.2d 1450 (10th Cir. 1989); *United States v. Holt*, 817 F.2d 1264 (7th Cir. 1987); *Wammock v. Celotex Corp.*, 793 F.2d 1518 (11th Cir. 1986), *substituted opinion*, 835 F.2d 818 (11th Cir. 1987); *United States v. Cutler*, 676 F.2d 1245 (9th Cir. 1982); *United States v. Lay*, 644 F.2d 1087 (5th Cir.), *cert. denied*, 454 U.S. 869 (1981); *Hilyer v. Howat Concrete Co., Inc.*, 578 F.2d 422 (D.C. Cir. 1978). *Cf. Udemba v. Nicoli*, 237 F.3d 8, 18 (1st Cir. 2001); *United States v. Young*, 248 F.3d 260, 267–68 (4th Cir.), *cert. denied*, 533 U.S. 961 (2001); *United States v. Winchenbach*, 197 F.3d 548, 557 (1st Cir. 1999); *United States v. Smith*, 13 Fed. R. Evid. Serv. 1258 (4th Cir. 1983). This opportunity need not be provided by counsel conducting the cross-examination, but may be left to counsel conducting redirect. 2 MICHAEL H. GRAHAM, HANDBOOK OF FEDERAL EVIDENCE § 613:3 (7th ed. 2012).

As a tactical device, counsel may wish to read Rule 613(b) to the court, after the extrinsic evidence is presented, and "remind his adversary that the witness has the right to resume the stand to explain or deny the extrinsic evidence." A problem is posed when the witness, who is impeached by extrinsic evidence, becomes unavailable to explain the inconsistency. In this situation, the court may exercise discretion to disallow the prior statement. *See Wammock v. Celotex Corp.*, 793 F.2d 1518 (11th Cir. 1986), *substituted opinion*, 835 F.2d 818 (11th Cir. 1987). If counsel for the proponent anticipates this problem, he or she might use the traditional method of confronting the witness or might introduce the extrinsic evidence prior to laying the foundation for the inconsistent statement. *See United States v. Bibbs*, 564 F.2d 1165 (5th Cir. 1977), *cert. denied*, 435 U.S. 1007 (1978); *Wammock v. Celotex Corp.*, 793 F.2d 1518 (11th Cir. 1986), *substituted opinion*, 835 F.2d 818 (11th Cir. 1987); *United States v. Wilson*, 490 F. Supp. 713 (E.D. Mich. 1980), *aff'd*, 639 F.2d 314 (6th Cir. 1981).

This latter approach was used in *United States v. Barrett*, 539 F.2d 244 (1st Cir. 1976), where it was held that the trial judge erred in preventing a second witness from testifying as to the prior inconsistent statement of a first witness. The first witness had not been questioned about the statement on cross-examination prior to the testimony of the second witness. According to the circuit court's view of the record, however, after the impeaching testimony there would still have been an opportunity for the first witness to explain or deny the contradictory statement. A witness clearly can be impeached by extrinsic proof, even if counsel does not question the witness about the matter. *See United States v. Glascoe*, 12 Fed. R. Evid. Serv. 1586 (4th Cir. 1983). *Cf. United States v. Saget*, 991 F.2d 702 (11th Cir.) (no impeachment with a third party's interpretation of a witness's prior oral statement unless the witness had adopted the third party's statement as his or her own), *cert. denied*, 510 U.S. 950 (1993); *United States v. Barile*, 2002 U.S. App. LEXIS 7149, at *18 (4th Cir. Apr. 18, 2002).

## I. EXAMINATION OF WITNESS ON PRIOR INCONSISTENT WRITTEN STATEMENT

Same facts as stated in previous pattern, except counsel for plaintiff seeks to impeach the station coordinator with a prior inconsistent written statement in federal court.

### Plaintiff's Counsel:

Q. Mrs. Smith, you were the station coordinator of WZBQ Radio Station in the spring of 2014, is that correct?

A. Yes.

Q. What were your responsibilities as station coordinator?

A. I was in charge of making all personnel appointments and coordinating the staff.

Q. Was there a position of program director at the station in 2014?

A. Yes.

Q. Who occupied that position?

A. It was vacant.

Q. Would it be accurate to say that the plaintiff, John Reeves, was the program director during the spring of 2014?

A. No, he was not.

Q. Did you appoint him program director in the spring of 2014?

A. No, I did not.

Q. Did you ever appoint him as program director of WZBQ?

A. No.

Q. Didn't you circulate a memorandum in the spring of 2014 announcing the appointment of Reeves to the position of program director?

A. No.

Q. Would the clerk please mark this document. Mrs. Smith, I show you what has been marked Plaintiff's Exhibit 1 for identification, and ask you to review the document and tell us whether or not your signature appears at the bottom.

A. Yes, it does.

Q. Did you prepare this document?

A. Yes, I did.

Q. What is the date at the top of the document?

A. May 1, 2014.

Q. Your Honor, we offer Plaintiff's Exhibit 1 for identification in evidence. Would you please read for us, Mrs. Smith, the first paragraph of Plaintiff's Exhibit 1?

A. "On this date, effective immediately, I appoint John Reeves as program director of WZBQ Radio Station. Please join with me in extending to him our congratulations."

Q. No further questions.

## *Comment*

Federal Rule of Evidence 613 modifies the rule enunciated in *Queen Caroline's Case*, 2 Br.&B. 284, 129 Eng. Rep. 976 (1820), which required that the witness be shown his own prior written statement before counsel could cross-examine the witness about that statement. Nevertheless, under the federal rule, disclosure to opposing counsel is required. This disclosure is designed to protect the witness from being misled by unwarranted insinuations that a statement has been made when, in fact, there has never been any such statement. *See United States v. Green*, 556 F.3d 151, 158 n.3 (3rd Cir. 2009).

Under the federal rule, there is no rigid requirement that the foundation for impeachment include the four elements traditionally required for that purpose, *i.e.*, whether the witness ever made a statement, whether it was made to a particular party, whether it was made at a particular time, and whether it was made at a particular place. The only foundation that is required under the federal rule is that the witness be given the opportunity at some time to explain or deny the prior statement. *United States v. Catalan-Roman*, 585 F.3d 453, 464 n.11 (1st Cir. 2009); *United States v. Santisteban*, 501 F.3d 873, 877 (8th Cir. 2007); *Rush v. Illinois Cent. RR. Co.*, 399 F.3d 705, 723 (6th Cir. 2005); *United States v. Sutton*, 41 F.3d 1257 (8th Cir. 1994), *cert. denied*, 514 U.S. 1072 (1995); *United States v. Hudson*, 970 F.2d 948 (1st Cir. 1992); *United States v. Bonnett*, 877 F.2d 1450 (10th Cir. 1989); *United States v. Holt*, 817 F.2d 1264 (7th Cir. 1987). *Cf. United States v. Young*, 248 F.3d 260, 267 (4th Cir.), *cert. denied*, 533 U.S. 961 (2001); *Udemba v. Nicoli*, 237 F.3d 8, 18 (1st Cir. 2001); *United States v. Chee*, 1999 U.S. App. LEXIS 8406, at *15–*16 (10th Cir. May 3, 1999), *cert. denied*, 528 U.S. 909 (1999); *United States v. Smith*, 13 Fed. R. Evid. Serv. 1258 (4th Cir. 1983); *Jones v. City of New York*, 2002 U.S. Dist. LEXIS 2052, at *11 (S.D.N.Y. Feb. 11, 2002); *Behler v. Hanlon*, 199 F.R.D. 553, 558–60 (D. Md. 2001) (discusses impeachment by contradiction—not explicitly set forth in federal rules—as well as by prior inconsistent statement). This opportunity need not be provided by counsel conducting the cross-examination, but may be left to counsel conducting redirect. 2 MICHAEL H. GRAHAM, HANDBOOK OF FEDERAL EVIDENCE § 613:3 (7th ed. 2012).

Impeachment by prior inconsistent oral or written statement requires that: (a) the statement be inconsistent; (b) the inconsistency relate to a matter of sufficient relevancy; (c) there be compliance with the rule requiring disclosure of the prior statement to opposing counsel upon request, as well as an opportunity for explanation, denial, and interrogation by the opposing party; and (d) the court must instruct the jury as to the purpose of the inconsistent statement. *Firemen's Fund Ins. Co. v. Thien*, 8 F.3d 1307 (8th Cir. 1993); *United States v. Rogers*, 549 F.2d 490 (8th Cir. 1976), *cert. denied*, 431 U.S. 918 (1977). *See also United States v. Larry Reed & Sons P'ship*, 280 F.3d 1212, 1215 (8th Cir. 2002); *Conte v. Gen'l Housewares Corp.*, 215 F.3d 628, 638 (6th Cir. 2000); *United States v. Winchenbach*, 197 F.3d 548, 557–59 (1st Cir. 1999) (explains dichotomy between Rule 613(b) and Rule 608(b)), *magistrate's recomm'n*, 2000 U.S. Dist. LEXIS 9219 (D. Me. June 30, 2000); *United States v. Turner*, 189 F. 3d 712, 718 (8th Cir. 1999) (prior inconsistent statement can be admissible for impeachment but not for the truth of the matter contained therein); *United States v. Causey*, 834 F.2d 1277 (6th Cir. 1987); *United States v. Grubbs*, 776 F.2d 1281 (5th Cir. 1985); *Bell v. City of Milwaukee*, 746 F.2d 1205 (7th Cir. 1984), *overruled on other grounds*, *Russ v. Watts*, 414 F.3d 783 (7th Cir. 2005); *United States v. Palumbo*, 639 F.2d 123 (3d Cir. 1981); *United States v. Miller*, 664 F.2d 94 (11th Cir. 1981), *cert. denied*, 459 U.S. 854 (1982); *United States v. Stahl*, 616 F.2d 30 (2d Cir. 1980); *United States v. Ling*, 581 F.2d 1118 (4th Cir. 1978); *Cathron v. Jones*, 190 F. Supp. 2d 990 (E.D. Mich. 2002); *United States v. Gonzalez*, 142 F. Supp. 2d 1052, 1059 (N.D. Ill. 2001); *Rahn v. Hawkins*, 464 F.3d 813, 821 (8th Cir. 2006) (plaintiff's questions regarding prior inconsistent statements contained in commendation report were admissible); *Rush v. Illinois Central Railroad Co.*, 399 F.3d 705, 720 (6th Cir. 2005); *United States v. Richardson*, 515 F.3d 74, 84 (1st Cir. 2008); *United States v. Barile*, 286 F.3d 749, 755 (4th Cir. 2002); *United States v. Avants*, 367 F.3d 433, 448–49 (5th Cir. 2004); *United States v. Crockett*, 435 F.3d 1305, 1313 (10th Cir. 2006). *See generally* 1 McCormick on Evidence § 34 at 149–154 (Kenneth S. Broun ed., 7th ed. 2013) (discussing the degree of inconsistency required).

The instruction given by the court is important. The statement can be admissible for impeachment purposes only, or as substantive proof, depending on the nature of the statement. Significantly, Federal Rule of Evidence 801(d)(1)(A) exempts from the hearsay rule a prior statement of a declarant who testifies at trial and is subject to cross-examination about the statement, if the prior statement is inconsistent and was given under oath subject to the penalty of perjury, at a trial, hearing, or other proceeding, or in a deposition. These types of prior inconsistent statements are admissible as substantive proof in the case. *Cf.* Fed. R. Evid. 801(d)(1). Counsel should also bear in mind that treatment of a prior inconsistent statement on cross-examination is distinguished from treatment of an admission of a party opponent. The admission is also treated as substantive evidence, but it is governed by Federal Rule of Evidence 801(d)(2). Introduction of the admission of a party opponent under Federal Rule of Evidence 801(d)(2) does not require any foundation on cross-examination, pursuant to Federal Rule of Evidence 613(b).

## J. CROSS-EXAMINATION UTILIZING AUTHORITATIVE TREATISES AND TEXTBOOKS

Dr. Willoughby Frund, a psychiatrist, has testified in a manner contrary to an authoritative and standard text in the field of psychiatry. The cross-examiner wishes to impeach Dr. Frund's testimony, using the standard text, and proceeds as follows:

### Counsel:

Q. Doctor, I show you the two-volume work captioned "Basic Psychiatry," by Friedman, Lipwitz, and Jones. Would you agree that this work is recognized in the field of psychiatry as authoritative?

A. Yes.

Q. This work is used in medical schools throughout the country as a text for instruction?

A. Yes.

Q. And the authors, Friedman, Lipwitz, and Jones, are recognized authorities in the field of psychiatry, is that not accurate?

A. Yes.

Q. And you have this work in your own medical library, do you not?

A. Yes.

Q. And from time to time you have occasion to refer to it, is that not correct?

A. Yes.

Q. Now, may I call your attention to the section on page 50, where the authors make this statement. (Statement is read.) Would you agree or disagree with that statement?

A. I would disagree.

Q. Are there any recognized authorities whose writings disagree with the statement of Doctors Friedman, Lipwitz, and Jones?

A. I don't recall any particular writing at this time.

## *Comment*

A "learned treatise" is "[a] treatise, periodical, or pamphlet on a subject of history, medicine, or other science or art . . . if it has been established as a reliable authority by the testimony of the expert who relied upon it or to whose attention it was called." *Fisher v. United States*, 78 Fed. Cl. 710, 713–14 (2007) (citation omitted). Learned treatises are used in cross-examination in three situations. First, when an expert relies on specific material from a treatise to reinforce an opinion on direct. Second, when an expert admits to having relied on general authorities, although not the particular material sought to be used for impeachment. Third, as in the pattern examination, when no reference is made to the particular textbook on direct examination, but the expert recognizes the particular materials as being authoritative. *See Johnson v. William C. Ellis & Sons Iron Works, Inc.*, 609 F.2d 820 (5th Cir. 1980); Annotation, *Use of Medical or Other Scientific Treatises in Cross-Examination of Expert Witness*, 60 A.L.R.2D 77 (1958). *See also* MICHAEL H. GRAHAN, HANDBOOK OF FEDERAL EVIDENCE, § 803.18 (7th ed. 2012); *In re Welding Fume Products Liability Litigation*, 534 F. Supp. 2d 761, 764–65 (N.D. Ohio 2008) ("authors of treatises have no bias in any particular case"), quoting 2 MCCORMICK ON EVIDENCE § 321 (6th ed. 2006).

The treatises themselves are not received as exhibits. *See* Fed. R. Evid. 803(18). *See also United States v. Mangan*, 575 F.2d 32 (2d Cir.), *cert. denied*, 439 U.S. 931 (1978).

Federal Rule of Evidence 803(18) provides that textbooks and treatises can be used as substantive evidence on direct examination of an expert, if the expert testifies that he or she relied on the treatise. The proper foundation for use of learned treatises as substantive evidence on direct examination includes: establishing that the expert relied on the treatise or publication, and establishing that the witness recognizes the treatise as authoritative. *Caruolo v. John Crane, Inc.*, 226 F.3d 46, 54–55 (2d Cir. 2000); *Costantino v. Herzog*, 203 F.3d 164,168–70 (2d Cir. 2000) (videotape of accepted obstetrical procedures properly admitted as visual version of a learned treatise); *United States v. Horn*, 185 F. Supp. 2d 530, 556 (D. Md. 2002); *United States v. Norman*, 415 F.3d 466, 473 (5th Cir. 2005), *cert. denied*, 546 U.S. 1117 (2006) (denying the defense the opportunity to cross examine an expert witness based on a learned treatise when a proper foundation for that treatise had not been laid). An alternative approach is to ask the court to take judicial notice that the treatise is authoritative.

*See* Fed. R. Evid. 201; *United States v. Horn*, 185 F. Supp. 2d 530, 556 (D. Md. 2002). Alternatively, a party may seek to have a textbook or treatise recognized only as the basis for an expert's opinion, and use of the book for this purpose does not require the same foundation. However, if a foundation is not laid, the treatise cannot be considered as substantive evidence. *See* Chapter 7.L., *supra*, for an example of direct examination using authoritative treatises.

## K. CROSS-EXAMINATION OF A CHARACTER WITNESS

Defendant is accused of aggravated sexual assault on a babysitter for his children. On direct examination, defendant's counsel calls Reverend Jones, who testifies to the defendant's good character. Defendant's counsel establishes that Reverend Jones has knowledge of the defendant's good reputation in the community and of the defendant's reputation for having a peaceful nature.

### Prosecuting Counsel:

Q. Reverend Jones, you testified that Danny Defendant has a good reputation in your community and that you have known the defendant to maintain a peaceful nature.

A. Yes.

Q. Are you aware that on June 28, 2013, January 23, 2014, and September 13, 2014, the police were called to Danny Defendant's home by his wife, who complained of being beaten by him?

A. No.

Q. Do you know that on March 30, 2010, Danny Defendant was arrested for assaulting a woman he was dating and spent 30 days in jail?

A. No.

Q. And have you ever seen this article, from page 1 of the Metro Section of the Washington Post, dated August 20, 2010, titled "Danny Defendant Gets 30 Days for Assaulting Date"?

A. No, I have not.

Q. Reverend, if you had read this article, and if you had known of Mr. Defendant's previous run-ins with the law, would you still hold the belief that Mr. Defendant is a peaceful person with a good reputation?

A. Well, yes, I would.

Q. Reverend, weren't you incarcerated for three days in the County Jail in 2008 for committing perjury?

A. Yes, but I was let out when the trial ended, and the charges were dropped.

## Comment

Federal Rule of Evidence 405 allows counsel on cross-examination to ask character witnesses about their knowledge of a defendant's specific acts. *See generally Michelson v. United States*, 335 U.S. 469 (1948). The Fourth Circuit has established the parameters of cross-examination of defense character witnesses as follows:

> Of course, the prosecutor is free upon cross-examination to inquire of the defendant's reputation witnesses whether they have heard particular rumors about the defendant or have heard about specific instances of misconduct on his part, but such inquiries are for the purpose of revealing inconsistencies between what the witness has heard and the conclusion about the defendant's reputation which the witness expressed upon direct examination, and not for the purpose of proving the defendant's bad reputation.

*United States v. Curry*, 512 F.2d 1299, 1305 (4th Cir.), *cert. denied*, 423 U.S. 832 (1975). *See also United States v. Skelton*, 514 F.3d 433, 444 (5th Cir. 2008); *United States v. Boone*, 279 F.3d 163, 174–75 (3d Cir. 2002). The government must have a good-faith belief that the specific incidents at issue actually occurred. *United States v. Kinsella*, 545 F. Supp. 2d 158, 162 (D. Me. 2008); *United States v. Guerrero*, 665 F.3d 1305, 1312 (D.C. Cir. 2011) (no error where prosecution cross-examined character witness based on undisputed facts showing defendant possessed drug paraphernalia and drugs). In addition, for a reputation witness "the prosecutor must possess a good faith belief that the described events are of a type likely to have become a matter of general knowledge, currency or reputation in the community." *United States v. Brugier*, 161 F.3d 1145, 1150 (8th Cir. 1998) (citation omitted). But with respect to a character witness who offers opinion testimony rather than testifying to a defendant's reputation, the government can ask about specific instances of misconduct regardless of whether they would be widely known in the defendant's community, because a "specific instance of misconduct, even if not of the kind generally known in the community, would be relevant to the witness's own opinion." *See United States v. Reich*, 479 F.3d 179, 190 (2d Cir. 2007).

The trial court has the discretion to allow the government to attempt to undermine a witness's credibility in situations where the witness has given testimony of the defendant's good character. The government may do so by asking if the witness has knowledge of the defendant's prior misconduct that is not consistent with the witness's direct testimony. *See United States v. Kellogg*, 510 F.3d 188, 194–95 (3d Cir. 2007) (government's cross-examination of defendant's character witness, which included questions about whether the witness knew how the defendant ran his business, was admissible); *United States v. Anderson*, 452 F.3d 66, 78 (1st Cir.), *cert. denied*, 127 S. Ct. 696 (2006); *United States v. Evans*, 569 F.2d 209 (4th Cir.), *cert. denied*, 435 U.S. 975 (1978).

There is a tendency for these types of cross-examination to impinge on Federal Rule of Evidence 403's standard that the probative value of the evidence should not be substantially outweighed by the danger of unfair prejudice. Therefore, important limitations are placed on judicial discretion in admitting inquiries concerning such prior misconduct. These limitations include the requirement of a threshold showing that the question is relevant to the character trait testified to by the witness on direct. This showing should be accomplished by a sidebar or proffer outside the hearing of the jury. The trial judge must determine that the probative value of the testimony will not be substantially outweighed by the danger of unfair prejudice. A cautionary instruction to the jury regarding the purpose of the evidence may be given. *See generally United States v. Bailey*, 505 F.2d 417 (D.C. Cir. 1974), *cert. denied*, 420 U.S. 961 (1975).

It is reversible error to permit a character witness to be asked on cross-examination if the witness's opinion of the defendant would change if the defendant had committed the crime for which he is on trial. Such guilt-assuming hypotheticals should not be asked of character witnesses. *United States v. Guzman*, 167 F.3d 1350, 1352 (11th Cir. 1999); *United States v. Damblu*, 134 F.3d 490, 494–95 (2d Cir. 1998); *United States v. Mason*, 993 F.2d 406 (4th Cir. 1993); *United States v. Chan*, 2002 U.S. Dist. LEXIS 1221, at *5 (S.D.N.Y. Jan. 25, 2002); *United States v. Brutus*, 505 F.3d 80, 85 (2d Cir. 2007) (guilt-assuming hypotheticals are prohibited despite their probative value because they create too much of a risk of impairing the presumption of innocence).

Improper cross-examination of a character witness, especially in a criminal law context, can be highly prejudicial. Merely asking questions suggesting past criminal acts committed by an accused is improper. *Michelson v. United States*, 335 U.S. 469, 481 (1948); *United States v. Senffner*, 280 F.3d 755, 762–66 (7th Cir. 2002); *United States v. Clark*, 2001 U.S. App. LEXIS 27023, *7–*8 (6th Cir. Dec. 14, 2001), *cert. denied*, 2002 U.S. LEXIS 2415 (2002); *United States v. Wilson*, 244 F.3d 1208 (10th Cir.), *cert. denied*, 533 U.S. 962 (2001); *United States v. Varoudakis*, 233 F.3d 113, 118–19 (1st Cir. 2000); *United States v. Schneider*, 157 F. Supp. 2d 1044, 1069–70 (court stated that the prosecutorial misconduct that permeated the trial demanded more than "ritualistic verbal spanking"). When a character witness testifies regarding a specific character trait, cross-examination must be limited to those crimes or acts of the defendant that evidence bad character for that specific character trait. *See United States v. Aronds*, 2000 U.S. App. LEXIS 4145, at *29 (6th Cir. Mar. 14, 2000); *United States v. Monteleone*, 77 F.3d 1086 (8th Cir. 1996); *United States v. Adair*, 951 F.2d 316 (11th Cir. 1992); *United States v. Bright*, 588 F.2d 504 (5th Cir. 1979); *United States v. Skelton*, 514 F.3d 433, 444 (5th Cir. 2008). For example, if a defendant is charged with embezzlement and calls character witnesses to testify to his good character for honesty, those witnesses should not be cross-examined about rumors of an illicit love affair. Such rumors, even if true, are not relevant to the character trait of honesty. *Aaron v. United States*, 397 F.2d 584 (5th Cir. 1968).

The character witness's prior criminal record and certain bad acts (whose commission would tend to establish the witness's lack of veracity or penchant for not telling the truth) are also admissible in impeaching the character witness. *See United States v. Pennix*, 313 F.2d 524 (4th Cir. 1963); *Henderson v. United States*, 202 F.2d 400 (6th Cir. 1953), *appeal after remand*, 218 F.2d 14 (6th Cir.), *cert. denied*, 349 U.S. 920 (1955); *Campbell v. United States*, 176 F.2d 45 (D.C. Cir. 1949).

The instruction given by the court is important. The statement can be admissible for impeachment purposes only or as substantive proof, depending on the nature of the statement. Significantly, Federal Rule of Evidence 801(d)(1)(A) exempts from the hearsay rule a prior statement of a declarant who testifies at trial and is subject to cross-examination about the statement, if the prior statement is inconsistent and was given under oath, subject to the penalty of perjury, at a trial, hearing, or other proceeding, or in a deposition. These types of prior inconsistent statements are admissible as substantive proof in the case. *Cf.* Fed. R. Evid. 801(d)(1). Counsel should also bear in mind that treatment of a prior inconsistent statement on cross-examination is distinguished from treatment of a statement of a party opponent. The statement of a party opponent is also treated as substantive evidence, but it is governed by Federal Rule of Evidence 801(d)(2). Introduction of the statement of a party opponent under Federal Rule of Evidence 801(d)(2) does not require any foundation on cross-examination. *See generally* 2 McCormick on Evidence § 254 (Kenneth S. Broun ed., 7th ed. 2013).

The test for determining inconsistency to permit impeachment is somewhat elastic. *See* 2 Michael H. Graham, Handbook of Federal Evidence § 613:3 (7th ed. 2012). Inconsistency exists if the witness states that he or she does not remember making the prior statement. Under that circumstance, the making of the statement can be proved by extrinsic evidence, *e.g.*, another witness. *United States v. Billue*, 994 F.2d 1562 (11th Cir. 1993), *cert. denied*, 510 U.S. 1099 (1994); *accord, United States v. Cline*, 570 F.2d 731 (8th Cir. 1978); *United States v. Sisto*, 534 F.2d 616 (5th Cir. 1976); *Williamson v. United States*, 310 F.2d 192 (9th Cir. 1962); *United States v. Gibson*, 84 F. Supp. 2d 784, 789 (S.D. W. Va.), *aff'd*, 92 F. Supp. 2d 562 (S.D. W. Va.), *aff'd*, 238 F.3d 416 (4th Cir. 2000), *reprinted in full*, 2000 U.S. App. LEXIS 29495 (4th Cir. Nov. 17, 2000). *But see United States v. Devine*, 934 F.2d 1325 (5th Cir. 1991), *cert. denied*, 502 U.S. 929, 502 U.S. 1047, 502 U.S. 1064, 502 U.S. 1065, 502 U.S. 1092, 502 U.S. 1104 (1992) (holding that the testimony of the witness that he did not remember making a prior statement did not constitute an inconsistent statement, and was therefore properly excluded as hearsay); *accord, United States v. Palumbo*, 639 F.2d 123 (3d Cir.), *cert. denied*, 454 U.S. 819 (1981); *United States v. DeSimone*, 488 F.3d 561, 571–72 (1st Cir. 2007) (witness's declaration that he could not remember making the prior statement did not constitute an inconsistent statement). However, if the witness admits making the prior inconsistent statement, the prevailing view is that counsel may not introduce extrinsic evidence to impeach. 2 Michael H. Graham, Handbook of Federal Evidence § 613:3 (7th ed. 2012); 1 McCormick on Evidence § 37 at 157–165 (Kenneth S. Broun ed., 7th ed. 2013). Counsel may impeach with a prior inconsistent oral statement, even if that statement is reduced to writing. See *Jankins v. TDC Mgmt. Corp.*, 21 F.3d 436 (D.C. Cir. 1994).

Although Queen Caroline's Rule is abolished by court rule, strategic cross-examinations nevertheless establish traditional foundations to spring the trap. For example, in this pattern, counsel could have gone further to establish a foundation by inquiring: "In your capacity as director, you called many meetings of your staff. From time to time you made important announcements filling new positions at these meetings. You talked to your staff during these meetings about John Reeves. Didn't you announce at one of your staff meetings that you were appointing John Reeves to the position of program director?" Striking the balance between establishing enough foundation to lay the trap and too much so as to reveal the trap goes to the heart of the skill of the cross-examiner. This skill is innate and also acquired.

Federal Rule of Evidence 613(b) governs the use of extrinsic evidence of prior inconsistent statements. Extrinsic evidence refers to evidence presented by other witnesses or by documentary evidence not authenticated by the witness who is on the stand and who made the prior inconsistent statement. Thus, impeaching by a prior inconsistent statement that the witness authenticates is not impeaching by extrinsic evidence. Federal Rule of Evidence 613(b) requires that extrinsic evidence of a prior inconsistent statement by a witness is not admissible unless the witness is afforded an opportunity to explain or deny the statement. *See United States v. Sutton*, 41 F.3d 1257 (8th Cir. 1994), *cert. denied*, 514 U.S. 1072 (1995); *United States v. Hudson*, 970 F.2d 948 (1st Cir. 1992); *United States v. Bonnett*, 877 F.2d 1450 (10th Cir. 1989); *United States v. Holt*, 817 F.2d 1264 (7th Cir. 1987); *Wammock v. Celotex Corp.*, 793 F.2d 1518 (11th Cir. 1986), *substituted opinion*, 835 F.2d 818 (11th Cir. 1987); *United States v. Cutler*, 676 F.2d 1245 (9th Cir. 1982); *United States v. Lay*, 644 F.2d 1087 (5th Cir.), *cert. denied*, 454 U.S. 869 (1981); *Hilyer v. Howat Concrete Co., Inc.*, 578 F.2d 422 (D.C. Cir. 1978). *Cf. Udemba v. Nicoli*, 237 F.3d 8, 18 (1st Cir. 2001); *United States v. Young*, 248 F.3d 260, 267–68 (4th Cir.), *cert. denied*, 533 U.S. 961 (2001); *United States v. Winchenbach*, 197 F.3d 548, 557 (1st Cir. 1999); *United States v. Smith*, 13 Fed. R. Evid. Serv. 1258 (4th Cir. 1983). This opportunity need not be provided by counsel conducting the cross-examination, but may be left to counsel conducting redirect. 2 MICHAEL H. GRAHAM, HANDBOOK OF FEDERAL EVIDENCE § 613:3 (7th ed. 2012).

As a tactical device, counsel may wish to read Rule 613(b) to the court, after the extrinsic evidence is presented, and "remind his adversary that the witness has the right to resume the stand to explain or deny the extrinsic evidence." A problem is posed when the witness, who is impeached by extrinsic evidence, becomes unavailable to explain the inconsistency. In this situation, the court may exercise discretion to disallow the prior statement.

*See Wammock v. Celotex Corp.*, 793 F.2d 1518 (11th Cir. 1986), *substituted opinion*, 835 F.2d 818 (11th Cir. 1987). If counsel for the proponent anticipates this problem, he or she might use the traditional method of confronting the witness or might introduce the extrinsic evidence prior to laying the foundation for the inconsistent statement. *See United States v. Bibbs*, 564 F.2d 1165 (5th Cir. 1977), *cert. denied*, 435 U.S. 1007 (1978); *Wammock v. Celotex Corp.*, 793 F.2d 1518 (11th Cir. 1986), *substituted opinion*, 835 F.2d 818 (11th Cir. 1987); *United States v. Wilson*, 490 F. Supp. 713 (E.D. Mich. 1980), *aff'd*, 639 F.2d 314 (6th Cir. 1981).

This latter approach was used in *United States v. Barrett*, 539 F.2d 244 (1st Cir. 1976), where it was held that the trial judge erred in preventing a second witness from testifying as to the prior inconsistent statement of a first witness. The first witness had not been questioned about the statement on cross-examination prior to the testimony of the second witness. According to the circuit court's view of the record, however, after the impeaching testimony there would still have been an opportunity for the first witness to explain or deny the contradictory statement. A witness clearly can be impeached by extrinsic proof, even if counsel does not question the witness about the matter. *See United States v. Glascoe*, 12 Fed. R. Evid. Serv. 1586 (4th Cir. 1983). *Cf. United States v. Saget*, 991 F.2d 702 (11th Cir.) (no impeachment with a third party's interpretation of a witness's prior oral statement unless the witness had adopted the third party's statement as his or her own), *cert. denied*, 510 U.S. 950 (1993); *United States v. Barile*, 2002 U.S. App. LEXIS 7149, at *18 (4th Cir. Apr. 18, 2002).

## L. IMPEACHMENT WITH PRIOR DEPOSITION TESTIMONY

An alleged witness to an accident is on the witness stand. The witness, June Smith, is the aunt of the infant, Mary Jones, who is the plaintiff in a suit for negligence against the landlord of June Smith's apartment. The infant plaintiff claims that the landlord negligently failed to repair a kitchen screen door. As a result of the landlord's negligence, the infant plaintiff, while playing in the kitchen, touched the screen door and fell off the second-story kitchen porch, suffering severe injuries. The witness is trying to show that the child touched the screen door, causing the door to fall, and that the door did not fall by other means or as a result of another child's activity. Cross-examination on behalf of the landlord proceeds in the following manner.

### Defense Counsel:

Q.  Is it your testimony that you saw the infant plaintiff touch the screen door and fall through the kitchen door onto the porch, and then from the porch onto the ground?

A.  Yes.

Q.  Miss Smith, do you recall that you were summoned to appear in my office over one year ago?

A.  Yes.

Q.  Do you remember coming to the office with an attorney?

A.  Yes.

Q.  Do you recall that we met in my library and that a court reporter was there who took down questions that I asked you and your answers to those questions?

A.  Yes.

Q.  The testimony that was taken down by the court reporter was taken down or recorded the same way as in this court, except there was no judge or jury present, is that correct?

A.  Yes.

Q.  And you were under oath then just as you are now?

A.  Yes.

Q.  The lawyer who accompanied you to my office for what was your deposition is the same lawyer who represents you now, is that correct?

A.  Yes.

Q.  When you finished testifying, your testimony was typed up by the court reporter word for word as you gave it and was submitted to you to read and to correct any mistakes, isn't that true?

A.  Yes.

Q.  Did you in fact read your deposition?

A.  Yes.

Q.  You did find mistakes in the transcript, did you not?

A.  Yes.

Q.  And you made notes of the corrections you felt had to be made, didn't you?

A.  Yes.

Q.  And then you signed your deposition as corrected by you before a Notary Public, isn't that true?

A.  Yes.

Q. Miss Smith, I am now going to read to you beginning at Line 7 on Page 81 of the transcript of the testimony as typed by the court reporter and corrected by you:

    Q. Prior to the accident involving the infant plaintiff, where were you, Miss Smith?

    A. I was in the bedroom looking after my little boy.

    Q. When was the last time you had seen the infant plaintiff prior to the accident?

    A. After we had breakfast, she was playing with the other children staying with me, and I went to nurse my baby.

    Q. Am I correct in understanding that your testimony is that after breakfast you left the infant plaintiff with the other children and that you went into the bedroom to nurse the baby and that you did not see the infant plaintiff until after she had the accident?

    A. Yes.

Q. Now, Miss Smith, what I have just read was your testimony under oath on April 14, 2014, wasn't it?

A. I cannot remember what I said at that time, but I suppose that what you read is what I said, if that's what it says.

Q. Well, you are not suggesting that what I read was anything but your previous testimony, are you?

A. No.

Q. Now, is your testimony today correct under oath, or was your testimony correct as you gave it in April of 2014?

A. I don't know.

## Comment

Once the witness testifies contrary to a prior statement, you have the basis to impeach. One of the most important steps in this situation is locking in the witness. As the situation allows, you might ask:

"Ms. Smith, is it your testimony that you saw the infant plaintiff touch the screen door, fall through the kitchen door onto the porch, and then from the porch onto the ground?"

In other words, have the witness reaffirm the testimony that is inconsistent with the prior statement. This approach allows you to strengthen the foundation for impeachment and gives the impression that you are being fair in giving the witness the opportunity to have his or her say. At

other times you may not want to allow the witness to repeat his contradictory assertions; it may be preferable to go directly to the impeachment
with the prior statement.

The National Institute for Trial Advocacy (NITA) and Judge Mark
Drummond characterize the steps of impeachment by prior inconsistent
statement as the three C's: Commit, Credit, and Confront. First commit the
witness to his or her trial testimony. For example "Did you just tell us you
saw the infant touch the screen door, fall through the kitchen door onto the
porch, and then from the porch onto the ground?"

Second, credit the prior testimony before trial; *e.g.*, "Do you recall that
we met in my library and that a court reporter was there who took down
questions that I asked you as well as your answers to those questions?"

Third, confront the witness with the prior inconsistent document or
statement, *e.g.*, I am now going to read to you beginning at line 7 on page
81 of the transcript of the testimony as typed by the court reporter and
corrected by you.

Or you can ask the witness to read. After the reading, you might ask:

"We can agree now that in April of 2014 you testified under oath in your
deposition that you did not see the child touch the door?" The response:

A. I guess so.
Q. Is that a "yes"?
A. Yes.

## M. IMPEACHMENT WITH PRIOR DEPOSITION
## TESTIMONY—BRIEFER TECHNIQUE

This same goal of impeachment could be achieved differently, more ef-
ficiently, and with less drama. Same facts as stated in the prior written
problem.

Q. Ms. Smith, you just testified that you saw the infant touch the
screen door and fall?
A. Yes.
Q. But you testified under oath over a year ago in your deposition that
you were—and I quote—at the time of the incident you were "in
another room looking after my little boy."
A. I do not recall that.

Q. You do remember that you gave a deposition last year?

A. Yes.

Q. Would it refresh your recollection if I were to read your testimony to you on this issue?

A. Sure.

Q. [Counsel reads the relevant deposition testimony.] Does that refresh your recollection that you did not see the child touch the screen door or fall?

A. I guess.

Q. Is that a "yes"?

A. Yes.

### Comment

This approach saves time and is best used if you do not want to be overbearing or you wish to save time, *e.g.*, the jury in your view appreciates that the witness is not too credible.

The techniques of impeachment cannot be mastered without appreciating the technicalities of the rules of impeachment.

Rules vary by jurisdiction, so be sure you are up to speed on them wherever you happen to be trying a case. Many state court rules provide that a prior written statement examined in state court must be shown to the witness, and the witness must be given an opportunity to explain or deny it before the end of the cross-examination.

On the other hand Rule 613(a) of the Federal Rules of Evidence does not require that the witness be shown a prior inconsistent written statement before the conclusion of the examination. Also, when impeaching with extrinsic evidence under the federal rule, you are not required to permit the witness to examine the statement. Under the federal rule, the opportunity for the witness to examine and explain the document may be left to counsel on redirect.

In addition to following the rules of evidence, counsel must adhere to ethical obligations concerning cross-examination. For example, the ABA Model Rules of Professional Conduct, Rule 3.4(e) prohibits you from stating any matter which you have no reasonable basis to believe is relevant to the case or will not be supported by admissible evidence. The American College of Trial Lawyers Code of Trial Conduct, Rule 20(g) provides that a lawyer should not ask improper questions or attempt to place before the jury any evidence that is improper.

In cases in which you have any doubt about the propriety of any disclosure to the jury, a request should be made to approach the bench and obtain a ruling out of the jury's hearing. You can be held in contempt for asking a question that calls for inadmissible evidence. For example, asking a question that implies that the plaintiff was drunk at the time of the accident, when there was no supporting evidence, would constitute a prejudicial error that could not be cured by a jury instruction. Similarly, a prosecutor's question on cross-examination that implies prior criminal conduct by a witness without any evidentiary foundation is improper under ethical standards.

There are numerous situations that can get you into trouble on cross. It would be improper for counsel to ask, "Isn't it true that you told X you saw Y shoot Z?," leaving the impression that such was the case and then not calling X to establish the fact when it was denied. It is a reversible error for the prosecutor to ask a question suggesting that the defendant has a long criminal record when she does not. It is improper for defense counsel to ask a rape victim if she had been raped before. In almost every case, there will be off-limit questions, and only broad familiarity with ethical obligations and rules will save you from making this kind of mistake.

Beware, too, of conflicts of interest. Sometimes an attorney will encounter adverse witnesses who are also clients, former clients, or expert witnesses he is using in another matter. It is unethical to skewer a client or former client on the witness stand in the interest of defending another client. A cross-examining lawyer is ethically prohibited from revealing client confidences or privileged information. A devastating cross of an opposing expert might boomerang against the cross-examiner's client in a second case in which the expert is serving the attorney. Fortunately, conflict situations like this are rare, but if a conflict arises, it should be recognized as early as possible so that it may be remedied by obtaining the consent of the client or former client to be cross-examined. If consent is not feasible, the attorney could raise the issue with the court and consider withdrawal from the case.

It is not always effective simply to ask the witness whether she recalls her deposition being taken on a previous occasion. Members of a jury may not know the significance of the deposition. Therefore, counsel should ask more detailed questions, as in pattern L., to illustrate the significance of the deposition and to emphasize the subsequent inconsistent trial testimony. *See generally Wood v. Stihl, Inc.*, 705 F.2d 1105, 1109 (9th Cir. 1983); *Coletti v. Cudd Pressure Control*, 165 F.3d 767, 774 (10th Cir. 1999); *Shearing v. Iolab Corp.*, 975 F.2d 1541 (Fed. Cir. 1992) (at trial, attempted impeachment of witnesses occurred when they had recollections that had not been mentioned in previous depositions); *Aetna Cas. & Sur. Co. v. Guynes*, 713 F.2d 1187 (5th Cir. 1983) (previous deposition testimony used to impeach trial witness testimony). *But see New Mexico S&L Ass'n v. United States Fid. & Guar. Co.*, 454 F.2d 328 (10th Cir. 1972) (party may not introduce deposition testimony as substantive evidence or to impeach when witness merely cannot remember facts to which the witness previously testified).

The last question, "Now, is your testimony today correct under oath, or was your testimony correct as you gave it in April of 2014?" is optional. Some prefer this type of question to dramatize the inconsistency during the testimony stage of the proceedings. Others prefer to end the examination with the inconsistency in place, thus reserving the opportunity in closing argument to emphasize and elaborate upon its significance. Both approaches are used in varying situations.

The advantage of the first approach is that the heightened dramatization can have a significant influence on the jury during the course of testimony. The weakness in this approach is that the witness, when confronted with the proverbial question "Are you lying now, or were you lying then?," is given the opportunity to explain away the inconsistency. *See* Fed. R. Evid. 613; Fed. R. Civ. P. 32(9).

Still another approach to impeachment using a transcript is to simply remind the witness that she just testified that she saw the incident, but in her deposition at a certain page and line she swore that she did not see the incident. *See*, for example, Herbert J. Stern, TRYING CASES TO WIN, CROSS-EXAMINATION, Wiley Law Publications (John Wiley & Sons, Inc. 1993).

## N. IMPEACHMENT USING INTERROGATORIES

Plaintiff sues defendant for damages resulting from an automobile collision. Plaintiff testified that his special damages were in excess of $50,000. Defendant's counsel proceeds as follows:

> **Defense Counsel:** Mr. Jones, you testified that your expenses, as a result of this occurrence, were in excess of $40,000, is that correct?

> A. Yes.
> Q. Do you recall that you were served with interrogatories or a series of questions in this case?

A. Yes.

Q. Do you recall that you helped your counsel write answers to these interrogatories?

A. Yes.

Q. And you reviewed the answers before they were filed in court?

A. Yes.

Q. You wanted them to be correct before you swore to them, didn't you?

A. Yes.

Q. And you appeared before a Notary Public, did you not, and made oath or declared under penalty of perjury that the answers were true to the best of your information and belief?

A. Yes.

Q. When you reviewed those answers, your lawyer advised or explained to you the significance of these questions and how they were being answered, didn't he?

A. Yes.

Q. And did you, in fact, review the answers to these interrogatories in the light of your counsel's explanation and advice before the answers were filed in court?

A. Yes.

Q. Would you please look at Exhibit 14 and the question and answer to interrogatory No. 27?

A. OK.

Q. Do you see the question and answer?

A. Yes.

Q. Would you please read them to us?

A. Witness reads the question and answer: Question 27: "Itemize the expenses paid or incurred by you as a result of the occurrence." "1. Property damage—$5,000. 2. Medical bills—$6,000."

**Defense Counsel:** Thank you.

## Comment

The use of interrogatories for impeachment is similar to the use of depositions for impeachment. *See* Fed. R. Civ. P. 33. *See also Clark Equip. Co. v. Keller*, 570 F.2d 778 (8th Cir.), *cert. denied*, 439 U.S. 825 (1978); *Troutman v. S. Ry Co.*, 441 F.2d 586 (5th Cir.), *cert. denied*, 404 U.S. 871

(1971); *United States Lines Co. v. King*, 363 F.2d 658 (4th Cir. 1966). *But see DeBenedetto v. Goodyear Tire & Rubber Co.*, 754 F.2d 512 (4th Cir. 1985) (refusal to allow jury to consider interrogatories for purposes of impeaching opposing party not in error where interrogatories and requests for admissions are considered irrelevant in light of the party's admissions at trial); *Dairyland Power Co-op v. United States*, 79 Fed. Cl. 722, 727 (Fed. Cl. 2007) (acknowledging the need for accurate interrogatory statements because interrogatory answers "provide a basis for further discovery, requests for stipulation, and impeachment at trial"); *Weiss v. Nat'l Westminster Bank, PLC*, 242 F.R.D. 33, 65 (E.D.N.Y. 2007) (interrogatories may be used as "affirmative evidence at trial and for impeachment and cross-examination purposes.").

# *Redirect* 11

## A. REHABILITATION, USE OF PRIOR CONSISTENT STATEMENT

During the course of a personal injury trial, defense counsel impeaches a witness for the plaintiff on the basis of fabricated testimony due to improper motive. The witness testified that he had been standing at the intersection and observed the defendant's motor vehicle strike the plaintiff. The thrust of defense counsel's attack is that the witness fabricated his testimony to aid the plaintiff, because the owner of the motor vehicle operated by the defendant was the C&P Telephone Company, where the witness is employed and against whom the witness has a grudge. The plaintiff's counsel rehabilitates the witness on redirect examination as follows:

### Plaintiff's Counsel:

Q. Mr. Valentine, prior to this trial, have you ever given a statement concerning the accident?

A. Yes, sir, I have.

Q. When was that statement made?

A. On January 3, approximately 20 minutes after the accident.

Q. In what form was your statement given?

A. It was given to Officer James P. Senior, a police officer who investigated the accident.

Q. Can you identify this document?

A. Yes, this is the statement that I gave to the police officer.

**Plaintiff's Counsel:** I now offer in evidence Plaintiff's Exhibit No. 32. If the court please, may I read pertinent portions of this statement to the jury?

**The Court:** Yes, you may. (Counsel reads to jury.)

Q. Mr. Valentine, when did you first learn that the owner of defendant's car was the C&P Telephone Company?

A. Today, during the course of my testimony.

### *Comment*

Rehabilitative evidence consisting of prior consistent testimony is admissible in federal court pursuant to Federal Rule of Evidence 801(d)(1) (B), when the testimony sought to be bolstered has first been impeached for truth and veracity. Mere contradiction of testimony is not enough. The federal rules limit the use of prior consistent testimony to rebuttal of an express or implied charge of recent fabrication or improper influence or motive. *See United States v. Caracappa*, 614 F.3d 20 (2nd Cir. 2010) (consistent statement, made before any motive to falsify existed, properly admitted for its truth under Rule 801(d)(1)(B)); *United States v. Alviar*, 573 F.3d 526 (7th Cir. 2009) (prior consistent statement made by cooperating witness was admissible under Rule 801(d)(1)(B) because defendant implied the witness had recently fabricated his testimony); *United States v. Chang Da Liu*, 538 F.3d 1078, 1086 (9th Cir. 2008) (for prior-consistent-statement exception to apply, it is imperative that the consistent statement be admitted to rebut the charge of improper motive); *United States v. Vance*, 494 F.3d 985, 993 (11th Cir. 2007), *superseded by statute on other grounds, United States v. Jerchower*, 631 F.3d 1181 (11th Cir. 2011) ("[P]rior consistent statements are treated as admissible non-hearsay *only* if they are offered to rebut a specific allegation of recent fabrication, not to rehabilitate credibility that has been generally called into question.") (quoting *United States v. Drury*, 396 F.3d 1303 (11th Cir. 2005)). *See also United States v. Williams*, 264 F.3d 561, 575 (5th Cir. 2001).

The Supreme Court "has imputed a 'premotive' requirement into Rule 801(d)(1)(B), so that statements are only admissible under the rule 'when those statements were made before the charged recent fabrication or improper influence or motive.'" *United States v. Frazier*, 469 F.3d 85, 92 (3d Cir. 2006) (quoting *Tome v. United States*, 513 U.S. 150, 167 (1995)). The purpose of this requirement "is that, in most instances, a consistent statement that predates the motive is more likely to be truthful than a prior consistent statement made after the motive to fabricate arose." *Frazier*, 469 F.3d at 92.

Federal Rule of Evidence 801 permits the prior consistent statement to be admitted as substantive evidence. *See Phoenix Assocs. III v. Stone*, 60 F.3d 95 (2d Cir. 1995); *Engebretsen v. Fairchild Aircraft Corp.*, 21 F.3d 721 (6th Cir. 1994); *United States v. White*, 11 F.3d 1446 (8th Cir. 1993); *United States v. Cherry*, 938 F.2d 748 (7th Cir. 1991); *United States v. Parry*, 649 F.2d 292 (5th Cir. 1981); *United States v. Dominguez*, 604 F.2d 304 (4th Cir. 1979), *cert. denied*, 444 U.S. 1014 (1980); *Grisanti v. Cioffi*, 2001 U.S. Dist. LEXIS 14358, at *22 (D. Conn. June 14, 2001); *United States v. Ealy*, 2002 U.S. Dist. LEXIS 3255, at *15 (W.D. Va. Feb. 26,

2002). *See also United States v. Simonelli*, 237 F.3d 19, 26–29 (1st Cir.) (discusses and distinguishes Tome and addresses a question of first impression in the First Circuit; states that just because Rule 801 does not preclude admissibility does not establish that there is a basis for admissibility and "join[s] the majority view, well expressed by the Fourth Circuit . . . that 'where prior consistent statements are not offered for their truth but for the limited purpose of rehabilitation, . . . Rule 801(d)(1)(B) and its concomitant restrictions do not apply' . . . [but w]hen the prior statements are offered for credibility, the question is not governed by Rule 801"), *cert. denied*, 122 S. Ct. 54 (2001); *Pursell v. Horn*, 187 F. Supp. 2d 260, 344 (W.D. Pa. 2002) ("In Pennsylvania, prior consistent statements of a witness are not admissible as either substantive evidence or as corroborative evidence . . . [with] certain well-recognized exceptions . . . : prior declarations of a witness, which are consistent with his present testimony, may be admissible to corroborate his present testimony if it be alleged that the witness' present testimony is recently fabricated, or if it be claimed that the witness is testifying from corrupt motives[; and e]vidence of consonant statements, if admissible, are admissible only for the purpose of showing that that which the witness now testifies to has not been recently fabricated and not for the purpose of proving the truth of the present testimony.").

# Part 3

## Use of Discovery Devices in Trial

# Depositions 12

## A. ADVERSE PARTY

Jones institutes suit against Weeks Exterminator Company on grounds of negligent entrustment of a company vehicle. Jones takes the deposition of the driver, Hannibal Smith, an employee of Weeks and also a defendant in the case. Smith was off on a frolic and not acting in the scope of his employment at the time of the accident. During the deposition, the driver testifies that his employer was aware of his poor driving record prior to entrusting him with the vehicle. The plaintiff does not wish to call the driver as a witness at trial, because the driver may attempt to change his testimony or explain it away. However, the plaintiff wishes to get the driver's clear admission into evidence and let defense counsel, if he wishes, call the driver as a defense witness. The following procedure is adopted by plaintiff's counsel:

> **The Court:** Mr. Darrow, call your next witness, please.
>
> **Mr. Darrow:** Your Honor, before we call our next witness, we would request permission to read in evidence a portion of the deposition of defendant Smith.
>
> **Weeks' Counsel:** We would object because Hannibal Smith is present in court and available to testify, and also because Smith is adverse to my client on the issue of negligent entrustment, and his deposition testimony on that issue cannot be admitted against my client.
>
> **The Court:** The rules of procedure are clear. Plaintiff's counsel has the right to use the deposition of a party for any purpose. He can therefore read in evidence portions or all of the deposition of the driver, and this evidence can be considered as part of the plaintiff's case against both defendants. You, on the other hand, have the right to introduce any other part of the deposition that ought, in fairness, to be considered with those portions introduced by plaintiff's counsel. *See* Fed. R. Civ. P. 32 (a)(4).
>
> **Mr. Darrow:** If the court please, I should read for the jury from page 38 of the defendant driver's deposition, line 3, which states as follows: "Mr. Weeks, president of the tire company, told me that I had too many accidents, and if I had another automobile accident, I would have to find another job, because he couldn't take the chance of being sued on my account."

## Comment

Plaintiff's counsel used the deposition testimony of the driver as substantive evidence, rather than merely for impeachment. In this way, he put the burden, tactically, onto the defense attorney to clarify this point. If plaintiff's counsel questioned the president of the exterminating company, after the president testified and denied making the statement testified to by Mr. Smith, the deposition testimony could have been used for impeachment by prior inconsistent statement. *See* Fed. R. Civ. P. 32; *Santos v. Murdock*, 243 F.3d 681, 684 (2d Cir. 2001); *Fey v. Walston & Co., Inc.*, 493 F.2d 1036 (7th Cir. 1974). Another alternative available to plaintiff's counsel would be to call the president of the exterminating company or the driver as an adverse party. *See* Fed. R. Evid. 801(d)(2), which provides for the admission of a party opponent as non-hearsay. Alternatively, counsel can treat the admission as an exception to the hearsay rule. *See* Fed. R. Evid. 607. This rule provides that the credibility of a witness may be attacked by any party, including the party calling the witness.

If the person who made the damaging statement read from the driver's deposition is available for trial and was a lower-level supervisor who on deposition admitted making the same statement, that person's deposition also could be used as substantive evidence in the case if the deposition testimony was inconsistent with the supervisor's trial testimony. Federal Rule of Evidence 801(d)(2) (admissions of party opponent) provides for the admissibility against a party of statements by the party's agent or employee. However, before the court can find that a statement is admissible as a statement made by the agent of a party-opponent, the court must determine that the declarant was in fact an agent of the party at the time the statement was made. *Bourjaily v. United States*, 483 U.S. 171 (1987). This case reflects the federal view of "bootstrapping" the statement itself in making the determination of whether the statement was made within the scope of employment. The federal view is that the statement is considered in determining the issue of scope of employment. *See also, e.g., Sea-Land Serv. v. Lozen Int'l*, 285 F.3d 808 (9th Cir. 2002); *Weston-Smith v. Cooley Dickinson Hosp., Inc.*, 282 F.3d 60, 66 (1st Cir. 2002); *Albright v. Virtue*, 273 F.3d 564, 569 (3d Cir. 2001); *Yates v. Rexton, Inc.*, 267 F.3d 793, 802 (8th Cir. 2001); *Fischer v. Forestwood Co., Inc.*, 525 F.3d 972, 984 (10th Cir. 2008) (finding that company president's conversations were admissible even though they were between a father and son); *Metro-Goldwyn-Mayer Studios v. Grokster, Ltd.*, 454 F. Supp. 2d 966, 973 (C.D. Cal. 2006)

("The rule 'requires the proffering party to lay a foundation to show that an otherwise excludable statement relates to a matter within the scope of the agent's employment.' *Breneman v. Kennecott Corp.*, 799 F.2d 470, 473 (9th Cir. 1986.") Further, though the statement itself may be considered in this determination, the contents of the statement alone may not be enough to establish an agency relationship existed.). *See also Morisseau v. DLA Piper*, 532 F. Supp. 2d 595, 621 n.164 (S.D.N.Y. 2008) ("[T]he proponent of an admission by a party opponent must establish the declarant's competence; office or plant gossip does not become admissible simply because it is put into the mouth of someone whose statements are not subject to hearsay objection.") (citing *Thomas v. Stone Container Corp.*, 922 F. Supp. 950, 957 (S.D.N.Y. 1996)).

## B.  WITNESS NOT AVAILABLE

**Defense Counsel:** Your Honor, at this point defendants would like to read in evidence the deposition of James McCullough. Mr. McCullough, whose deposition was taken last April, is now in Lewiston, Maine, a distance greater than 100 miles from this courthouse. We are prepared to present evidence to this effect, if that is necessary.

**The Court:** Is there any dispute as to the location of the witness?

**Plaintiff's Counsel:** No, Your Honor.

**The Court:** Very well, proceed.

**Defense Counsel:** Your Honor, I would ask that my co-counsel, Mr. Ames, take the witness stand. I will read the questions asked of Mr. McCullough during his deposition, and Mr. Ames will read Mr. McCullough's answers. Your Honor, will you explain to the jury the nature and effect of a deposition?

**The Court:** Very well. (Court explains nature and effect of a deposition, how it is taken, the fact that it is evidence, the same as if McCullough were personally on the witness stand.)

(Counsel then reads the questions and co-counsel reads the answers.)

## *Comment*

Federal Rule of Civil Procedure 32(a)(4)(B) provides that the witness is unavailable if he or she is more than 100 miles from the place of trial. The reading or showing the video of a deposition of a witness, if that witness is unavailable, is permitted under Federal Rule of Civil Procedure 32(a)(4).

*Griffin v. Foley*, 542 F.3d 209, 213 & n.8 (7th Cir. 2008); *Bouygues Telecom, S.A. v. Tekelec, Inc.*, 238 F.R.D. 413, 414 (E.D.N.C. 2006); *Tatman v. Collins*, 938 F.2d 509 (4th Cir. 1991). *Cf. Battle v. Mem'l Hosp.*, 228 F.3d 544, 551 (5th Cir. 2000) (nothing prevents the use of a discovery [as opposed to a trial] deposition at trial, particularly against the party who conducted it); *Rosebud Sioux Tribe v. A & P Steel, Inc.*, 733 F.2d 509 (8th Cir.) (reading of deposition into evidence constituted an unfair manipulation of the rules of evidence when unavailability of witness was due to invocation of Fifth Amendment), *cert. denied*, 469 U.S. 1072 (1984).

Defendant's attorney calls his co-counsel to read the answers for the testimonial effect of having a live witness clearly and articulately respond in order to maintain the jury's interest.

When a deposition of an unavailable witness is introduced in evidence and read to the jury, it is customary for counsel to request, and for the court to give, an explanatory comment to the jury.

## C. IMPEACHMENT WITH PRIOR DEPOSITION TESTIMONY

*See* Chapter 10, *supra*, pp. 271–276, "Impeachment with Prior Deposition Testimony."

# *Interrogatories* 13

## A. USE IN COURT

Plaintiff sues defendant for damages resulting from an automobile collision. Plaintiff claims $50,000 special damages. Before resting his case, defendant's counsel proceeds as follows:

> **Defendant's Counsel**: Your Honor, before defendants close their case, we would like to read in evidence No. 27 of defendant's interrogatories or questions to plaintiff and the answer to that question, which plaintiff gave under oath.
>
> **Plaintiff's Counsel:** We object. The plaintiff is available in court, and if defense counsel wishes to question or cross-examine plaintiff, he has the opportunity to do so.
>
> **The Court:** Federal Rule of Civil Procedure 33(c) provides that the answers to interrogatories may be used for any purpose, to the extent permitted by the rules of evidence. Unless there is some relevancy objection, I am going to allow defendant's counsel to proceed.
>
> **Defendant's Counsel**: Thank you, Your Honor. Interrogatory, or Question 27: "Itemize the expenses paid or incurred by you as a result of the occurrence." The answer to that question was filed on April 23, 1978, and reads as follows: "1. Property damage—$5,000. 2. Medical bills—$6,000."

### *Comment*

The use of interrogatories during trial follows a pattern similar to the use of depositions. *See* Fed. R. Civ. P. 33. *See also Exum v. General Elec. Co.*, 819 F.2d 1158 (D.C. Cir. 1987). *But see Frankel v. Burke's Excavating, Inc.*, 397 F.2d 167 (3d Cir. 1968) (refusal to allow party to read into evidence opposing party's answers to interrogatories not erroneous due to binding instructions given to jury).

## B. IMPEACHMENT USING INTERROGATORIES

*See* Chapter 10, *supra*, pp. 276–277, "Impeachment Using Interrogatories."

# *Index*